Shojo Beat

Demon Love Spell

5

STORY AND
ART BY
MAYU
SHINJO

Contents

Story Thus Far

Miko Tsubaki is the daughter of the head priest of the
Otsubaki Shrine, and she is destined to follow in his footsteps.
She works hard day and night to become a great priestess,
but it seems she inherited none of her father's powers...

One day Miko seals the powers of the incubus Kagura—the
strongest demon—by accident, and the two start living together.
After defeating various demons they fall in love, though Miko
is having trouble accepting her feelings for a demon.

After surviving a fire, Miko finds herself having to face another
crisis: protecting her chastity! After various troubles, Kagura makes
a proposal of marriage to Miko. ♥ Miko accepts and the two head
to the demon realm to obtain the blessing of Kagura's family. But as
soon as they return, Miko's soul is trapped inside her father's body.
It seems Miko and Kagura's relationship has a long way to go.

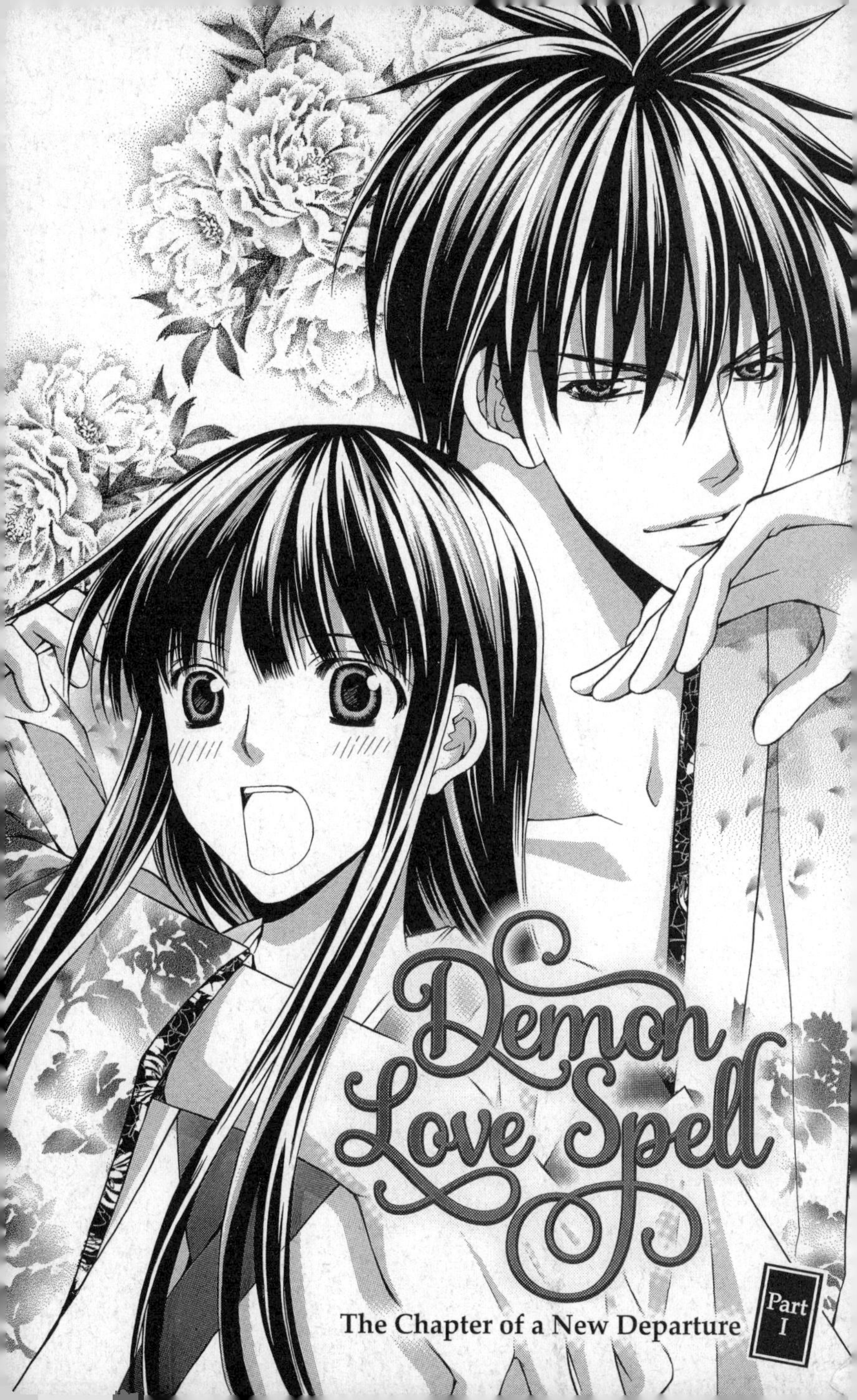
Demon Love Spell
The Chapter of a New Departure
Part I

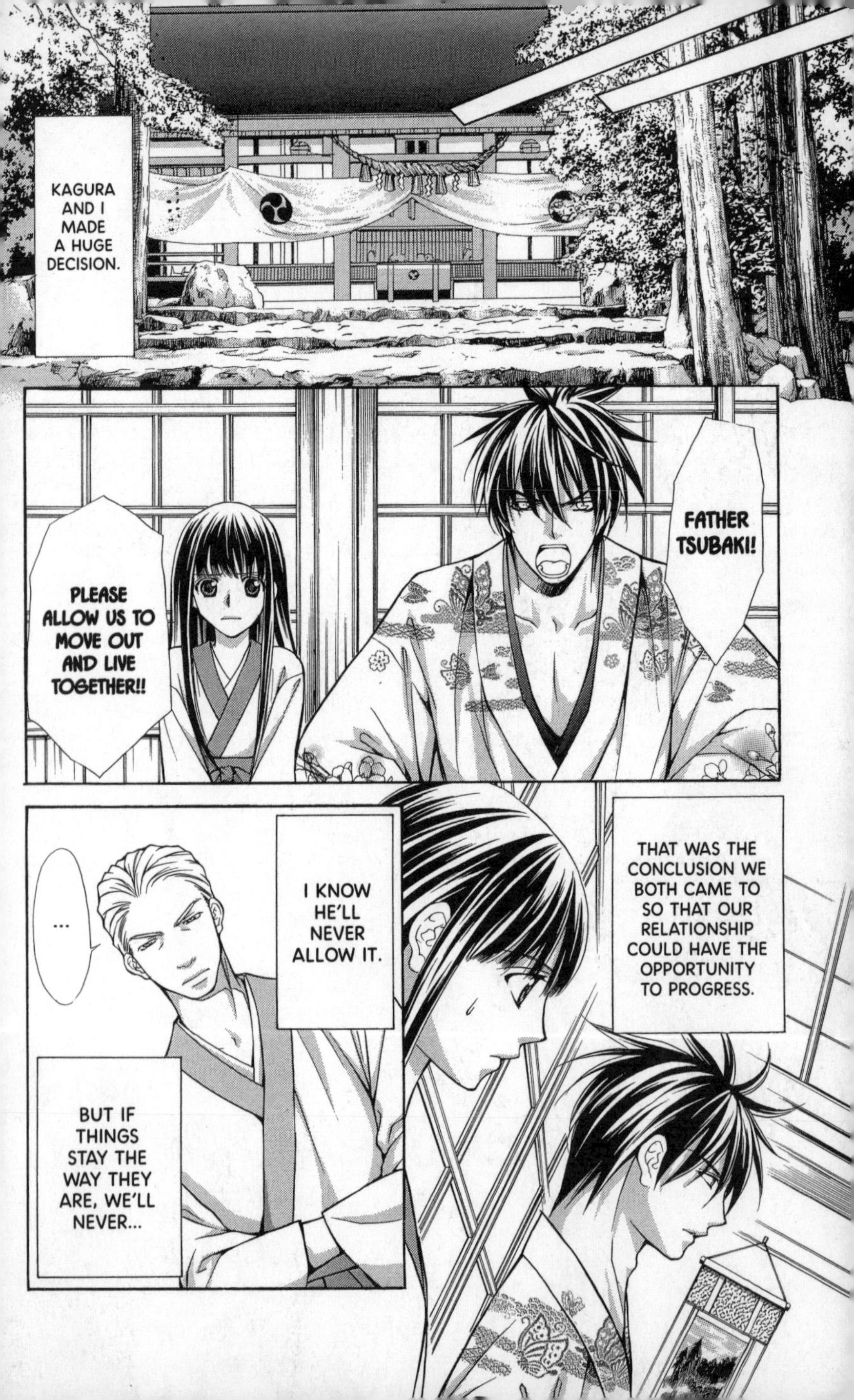
KAGURA AND I MADE A HUGE DECISION.
FATHER TSUBAKI!
PLEASE ALLOW US TO MOVE OUT AND LIVE TOGETHER!!
THAT WAS THE CONCLUSION WE BOTH CAME TO SO THAT OUR RELATIONSHIP COULD HAVE THE OPPORTUNITY TO PROGRESS.
I KNOW HE'LL NEVER ALLOW IT.
...
BUT IF THINGS STAY THE WAY THEY ARE, WE'LL NEVER...

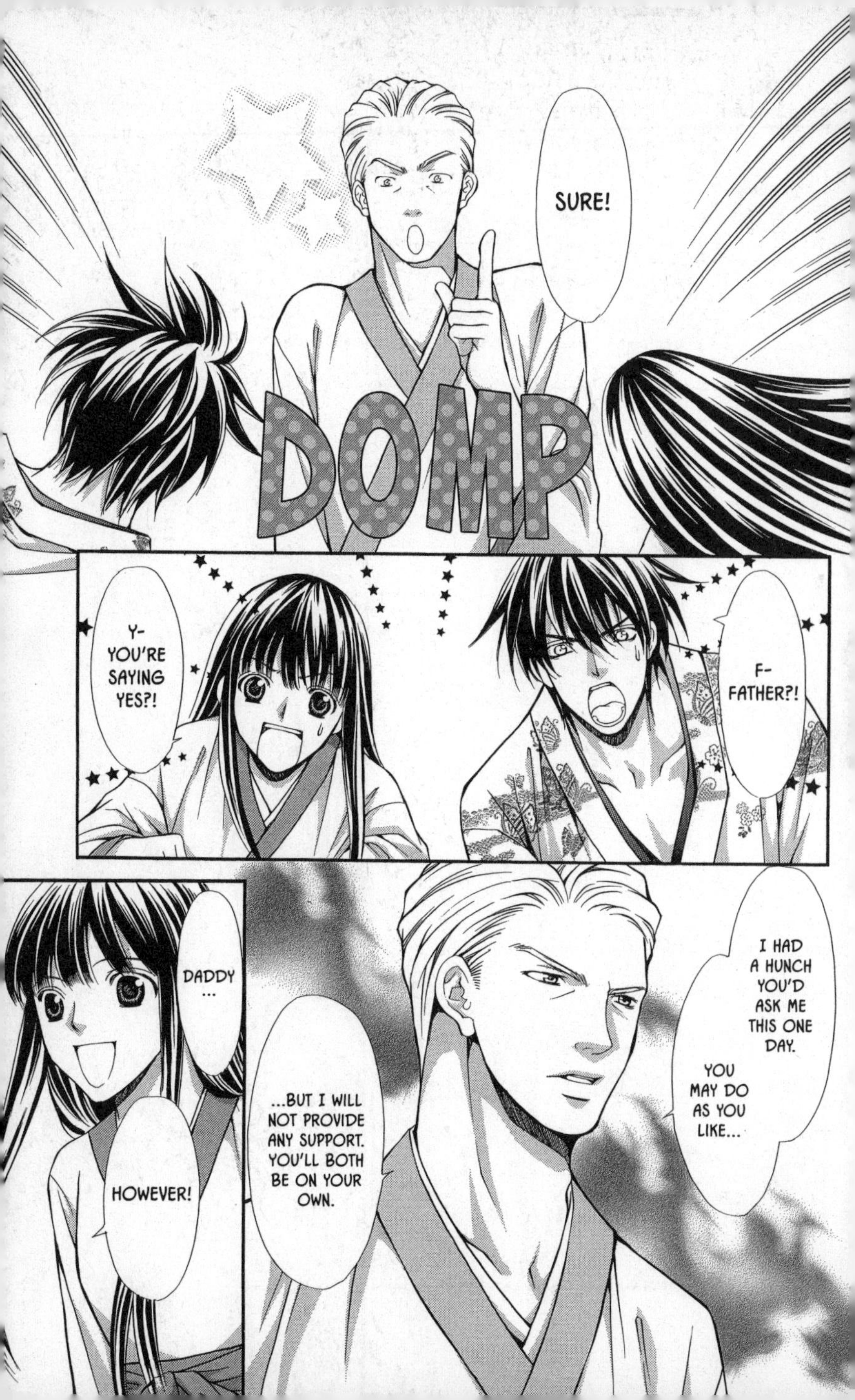
SURE!
DOMP
F-
FATHER?!
Y-
YOU'RE
SAYING
YES?!
I HAD A HUNCH YOU'D ASK ME THIS ONE DAY.
YOU MAY DO AS YOU LIKE...
DADDY ...
HOWEVER!
...BUT I WILL NOT PROVIDE ANY SUPPORT. YOU'LL BOTH BE ON YOUR OWN.

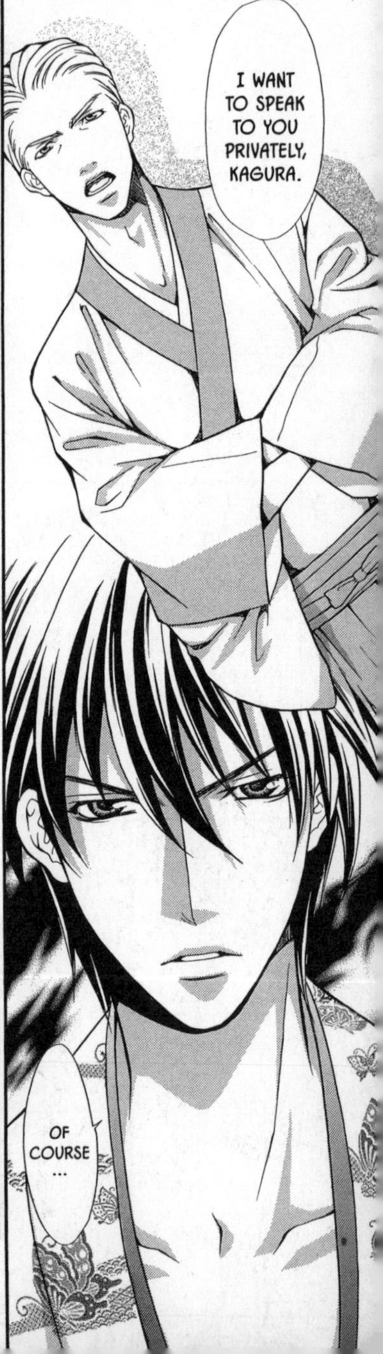
I WANT TO SPEAK TO YOU PRIVATELY, KAGURA.
OF COURSE...

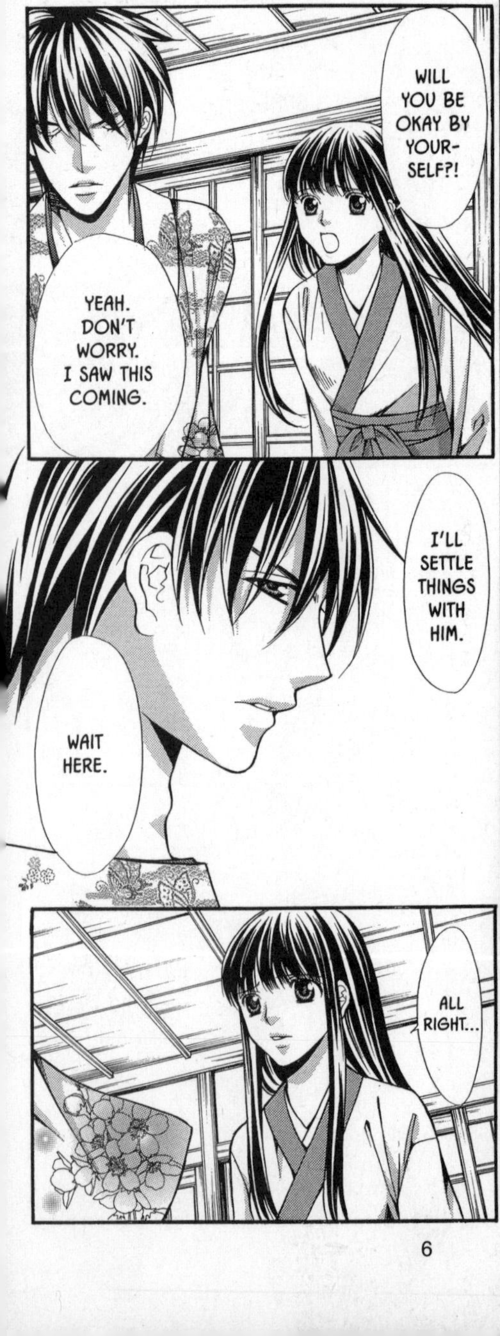
WILL YOU BE OKAY BY YOUR-SELF?!
YEAH. DON'T WORRY. I SAW THIS COMING.
I'LL SETTLE THINGS WITH HIM.
WAIT HERE.
ALL RIGHT...

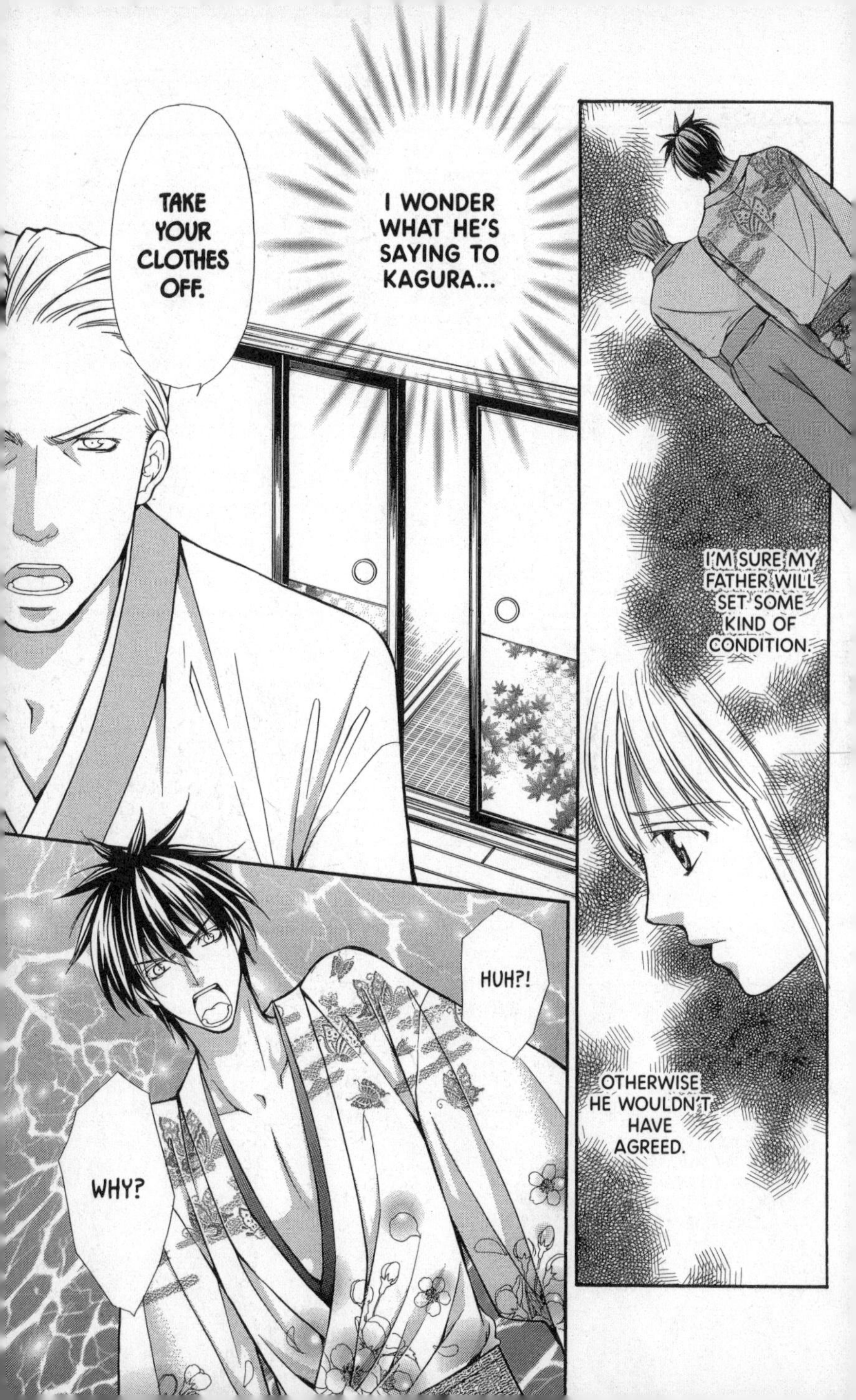
I'M SURE MY FATHER WILL SET SOME KIND OF CONDITION.
OTHERWISE HE WOULDN'T HAVE AGREED.
I WONDER WHAT HE'S SAYING TO KAGURA...
TAKE YOUR CLOTHES OFF.
HUH?!
WHY?

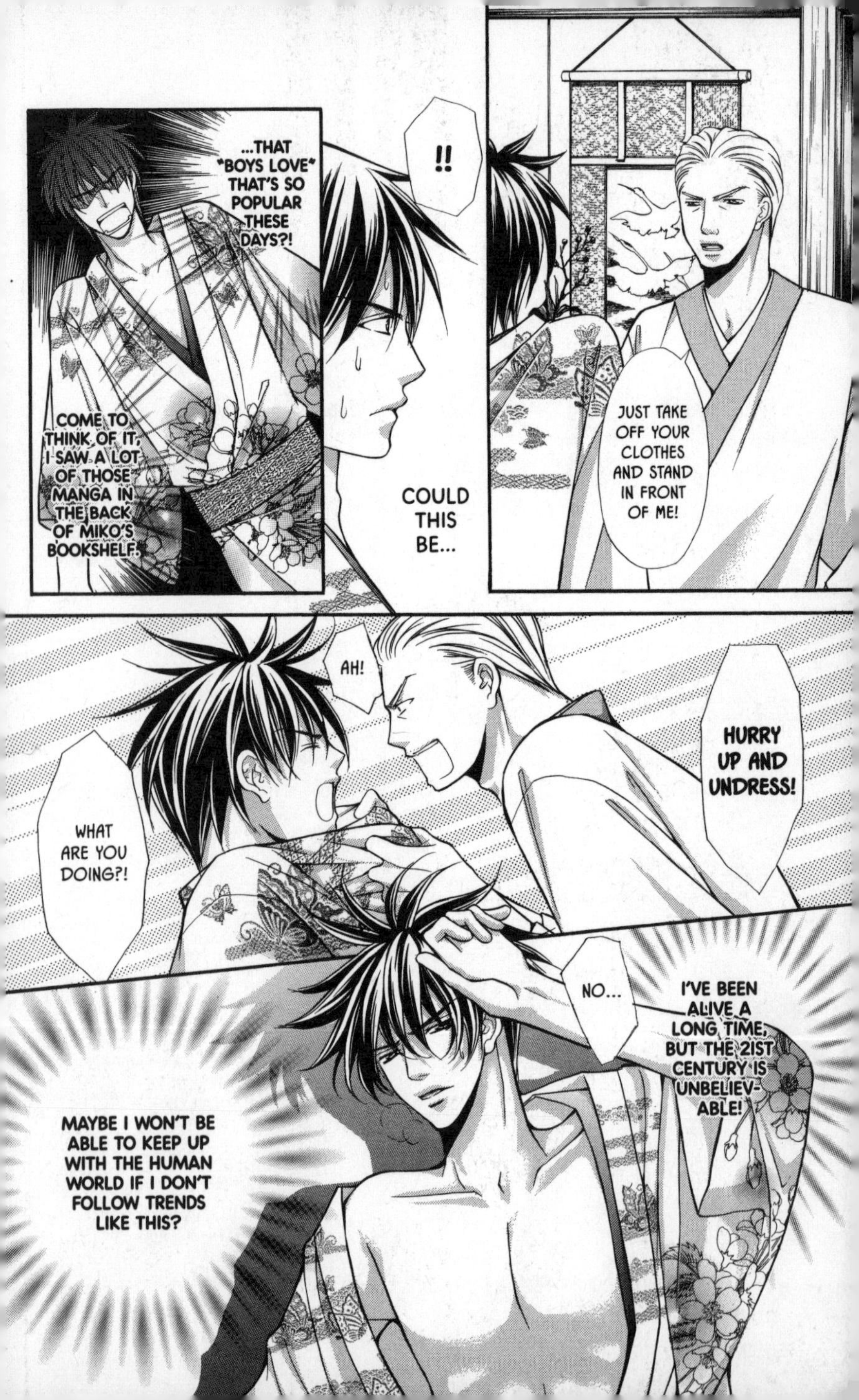
JUST TAKE OFF YOUR CLOTHES AND STAND IN FRONT OF ME!
!!
COULD THIS BE...
...THAT "BOYS LOVE" THAT'S SO POPULAR THESE DAYS?!
COME TO THINK OF IT, I SAW A LOT OF THOSE MANGA IN THE BACK OF MIKO'S BOOKSHELF.
HURRY UP AND UNDRESS!
AH!
WHAT ARE YOU DOING?!
NO...
I'VE BEEN ALIVE A LONG TIME, BUT THE 21ST CENTURY IS UNBELIEV-ABLE!
MAYBE I WON'T BE ABLE TO KEEP UP WITH THE HUMAN WORLD IF I DON'T FOLLOW TRENDS LIKE THIS?

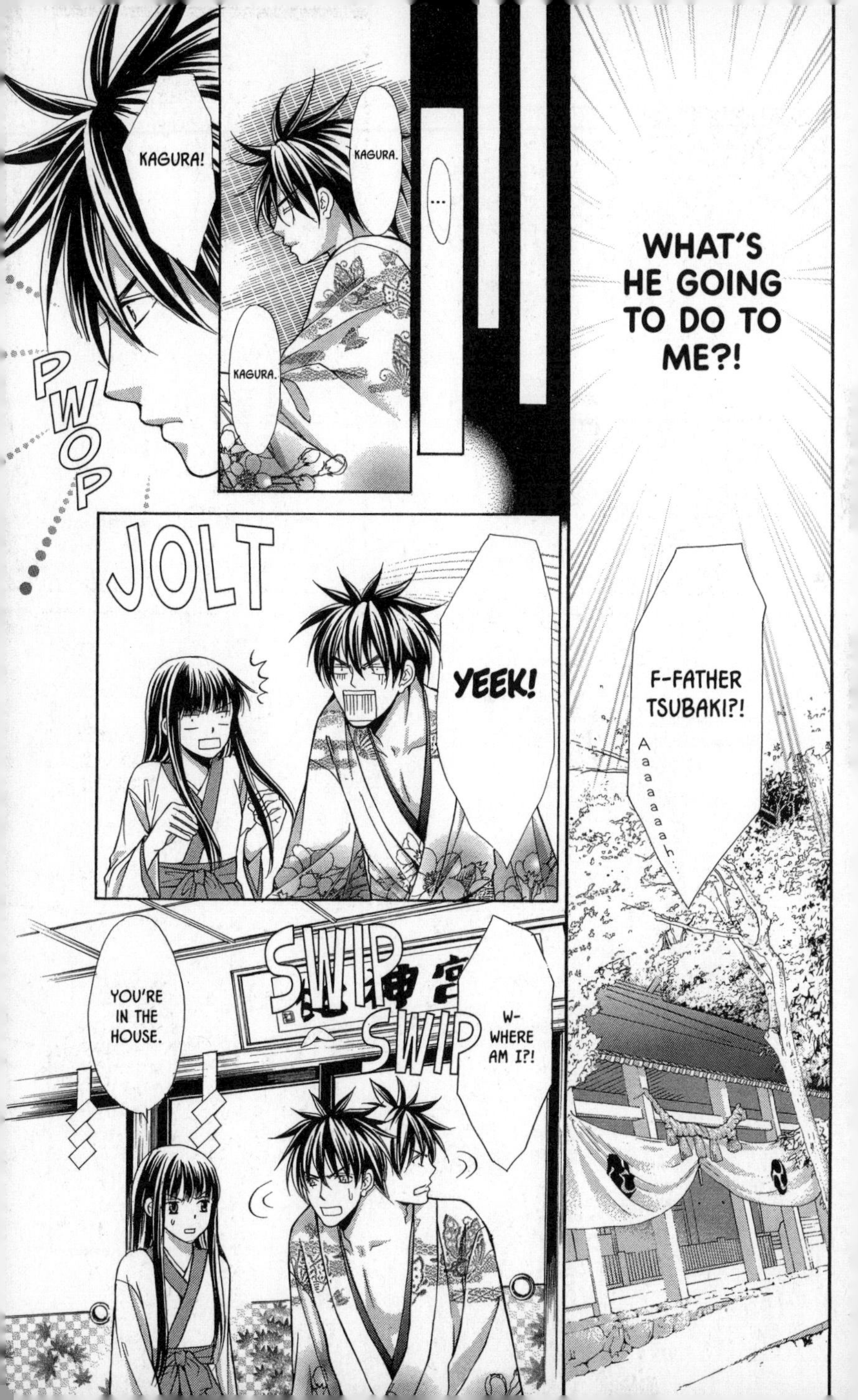
WHAT'S HE GOING TO DO TO ME?!
F-FATHER TSUBAKI?!
Aaaaaaah...
...
KAGURA.
KAGURA.
KAGURA!
PWOP
YEEK!
JOLT
W-WHERE AM I?!
SWIP SWIP
YOU'RE IN THE HOUSE.

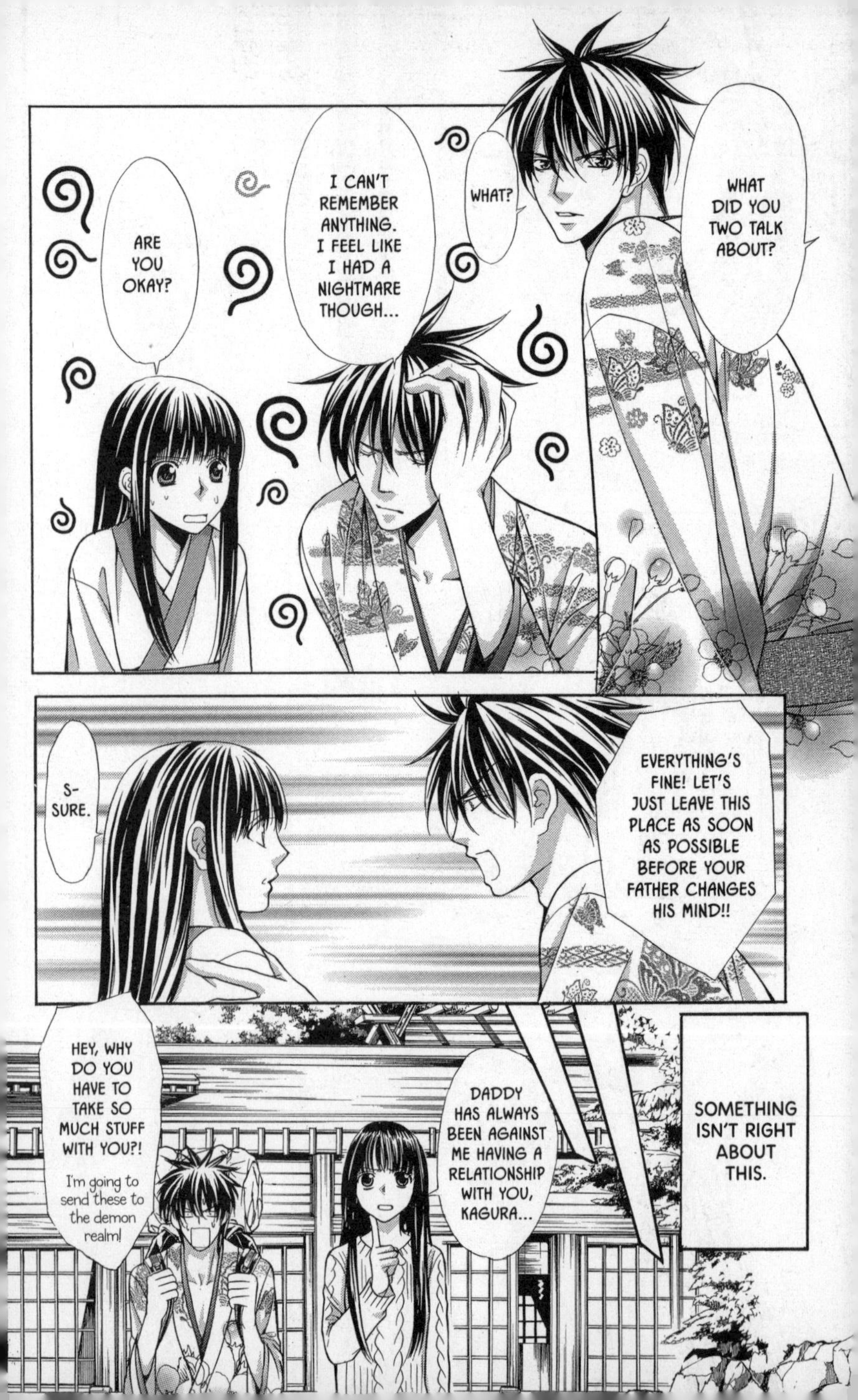
WHAT DID YOU TWO TALK ABOUT?
WHAT?
I CAN'T REMEMBER ANYTHING. I FEEL LIKE I HAD A NIGHTMARE THOUGH...
ARE YOU OKAY?
EVERYTHING'S FINE! LET'S JUST LEAVE THIS PLACE AS SOON AS POSSIBLE BEFORE YOUR FATHER CHANGES HIS MIND!!
S-SURE.
SOMETHING ISN'T RIGHT ABOUT THIS.
DADDY HAS ALWAYS BEEN AGAINST ME HAVING A RELATIONSHIP WITH YOU, KAGURA...
HEY, WHY DO YOU HAVE TO TAKE SO MUCH STUFF WITH YOU?!
I'm going to send these to the demon realm!

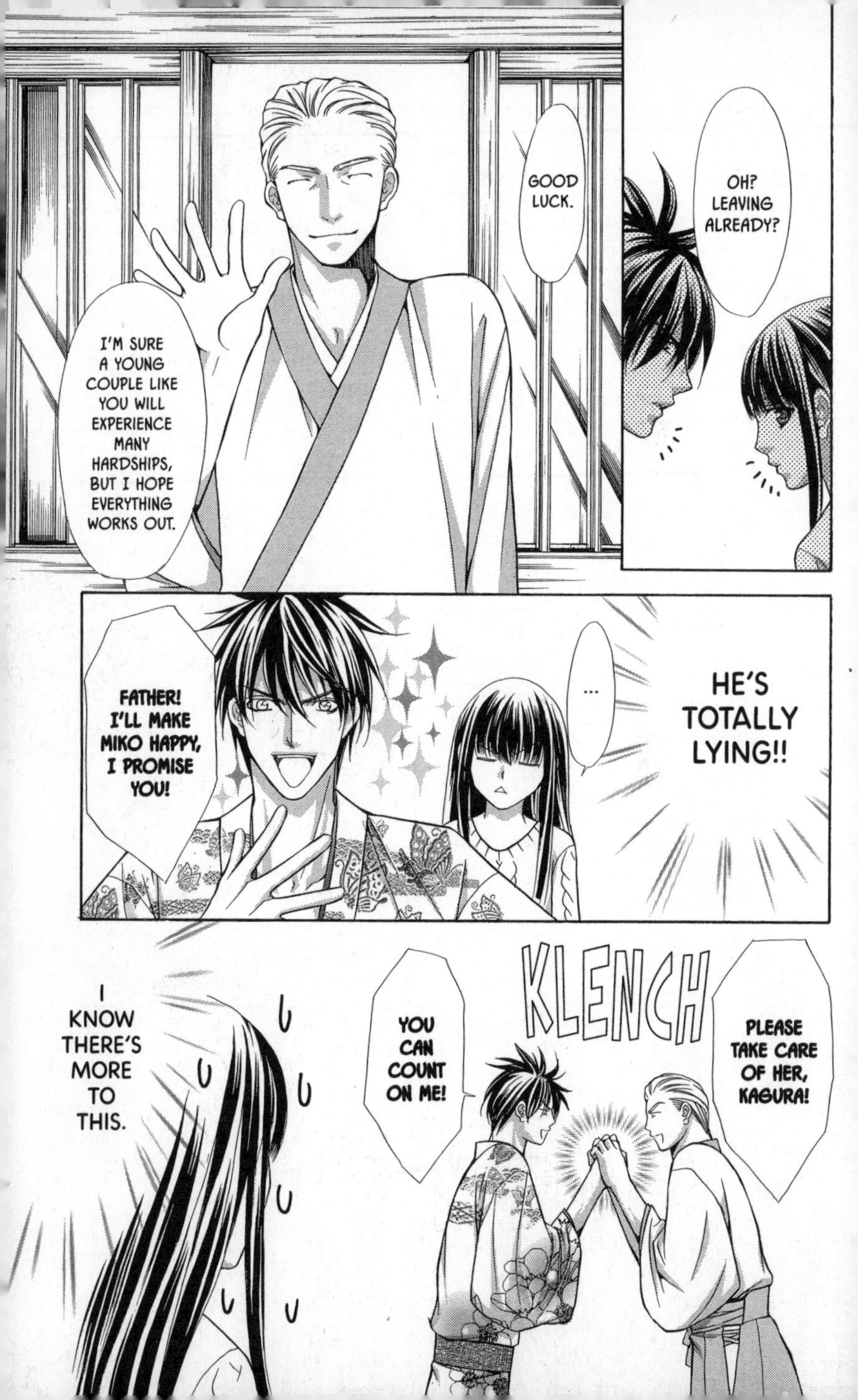
OH? LEAVING ALREADY?
GOOD LUCK.
I'M SURE A YOUNG COUPLE LIKE YOU WILL EXPERIENCE MANY HARDSHIPS, BUT I HOPE EVERYTHING WORKS OUT.
HE'S TOTALLY LYING!!
...
FATHER! I'LL MAKE MIKO HAPPY, I PROMISE YOU!
PLEASE TAKE CARE OF HER, KAGURA!
KLENCH
YOU CAN COUNT ON ME!
I KNOW THERE'S MORE TO THIS.

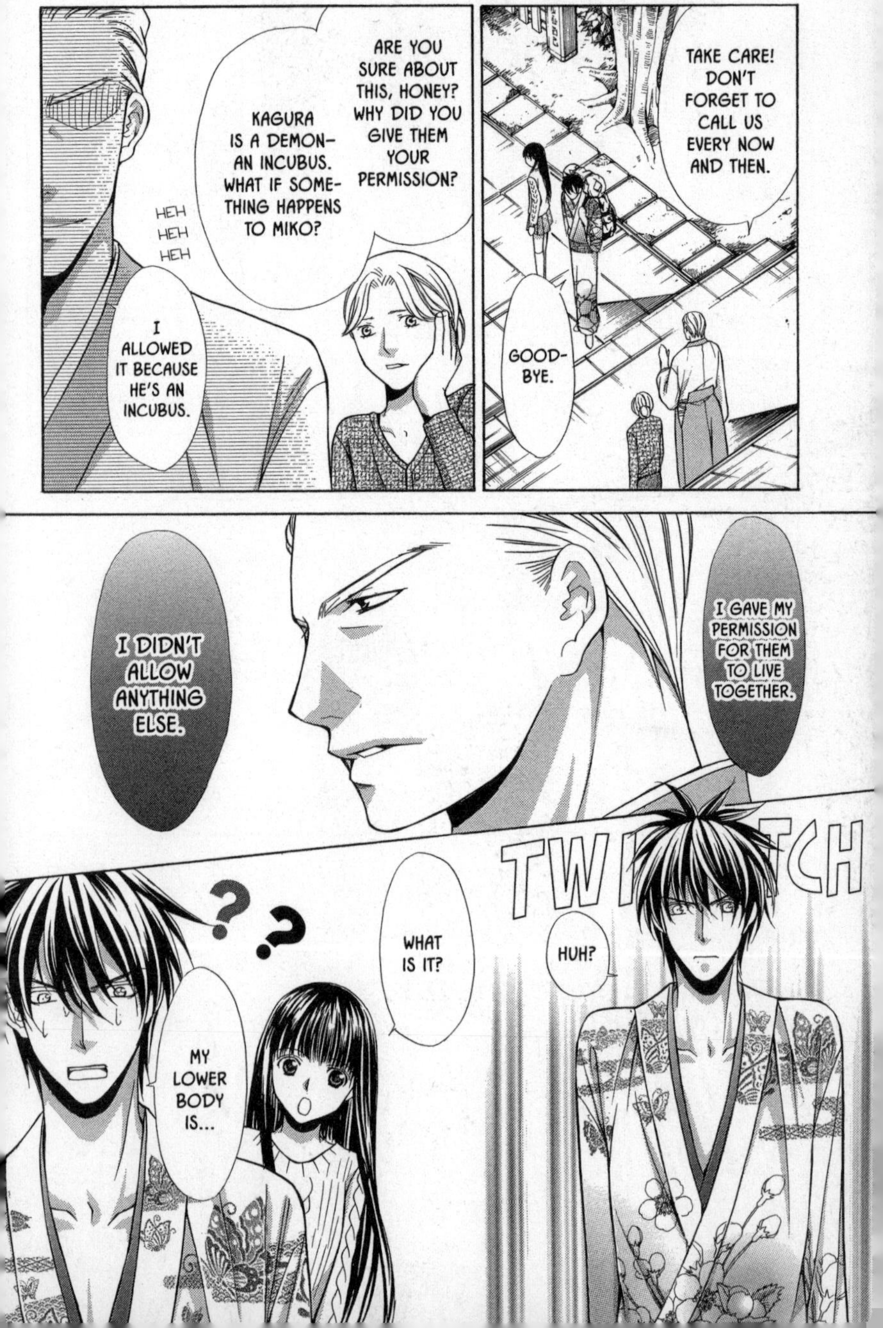
TAKE CARE! DON'T FORGET TO CALL US EVERY NOW AND THEN.
GOOD-BYE.
ARE YOU SURE ABOUT THIS, HONEY? WHY DID YOU GIVE THEM YOUR PERMISSION?
KAGURA IS A DEMON— AN INCUBUS. WHAT IF SOMETHING HAPPENS TO MIKO?
HEH HEH HEH
I ALLOWED IT BECAUSE HE'S AN INCUBUS.
I GAVE MY PERMISSION FOR THEM TO LIVE TOGETHER.
I DIDN'T ALLOW ANYTHING ELSE.
HUH?
WHAT IS IT?
MY LOWER BODY IS...

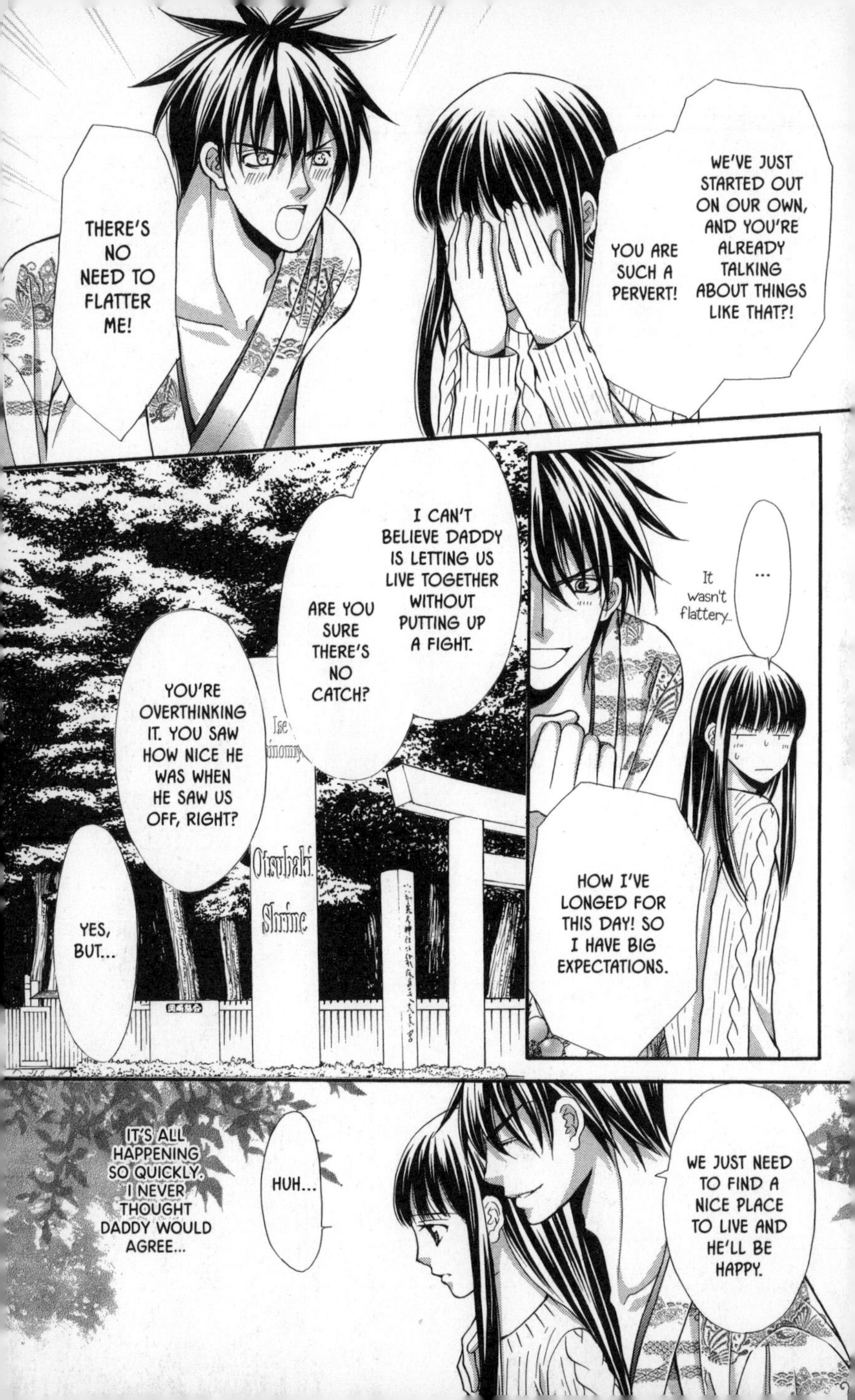
WE'VE JUST STARTED OUT ON OUR OWN, AND YOU'RE ALREADY TALKING ABOUT THINGS LIKE THAT?!
YOU ARE SUCH A PERVERT!
THERE'S NO NEED TO FLATTER ME!
...
It wasn't flattery...
HOW I'VE LONGED FOR THIS DAY! SO I HAVE BIG EXPECTATIONS.
I CAN'T BELIEVE DADDY IS LETTING US LIVE TOGETHER WITHOUT PUTTING UP A FIGHT.
ARE YOU SURE THERE'S NO CATCH?
Otsubaki Shrine
YOU'RE OVERTHINKING IT. YOU SAW HOW NICE HE WAS WHEN HE SAW US OFF, RIGHT?
YES, BUT...
WE JUST NEED TO FIND A NICE PLACE TO LIVE AND HE'LL BE HAPPY.
HUH...
IT'S ALL HAPPENING SO QUICKLY. I NEVER THOUGHT DADDY WOULD AGREE...

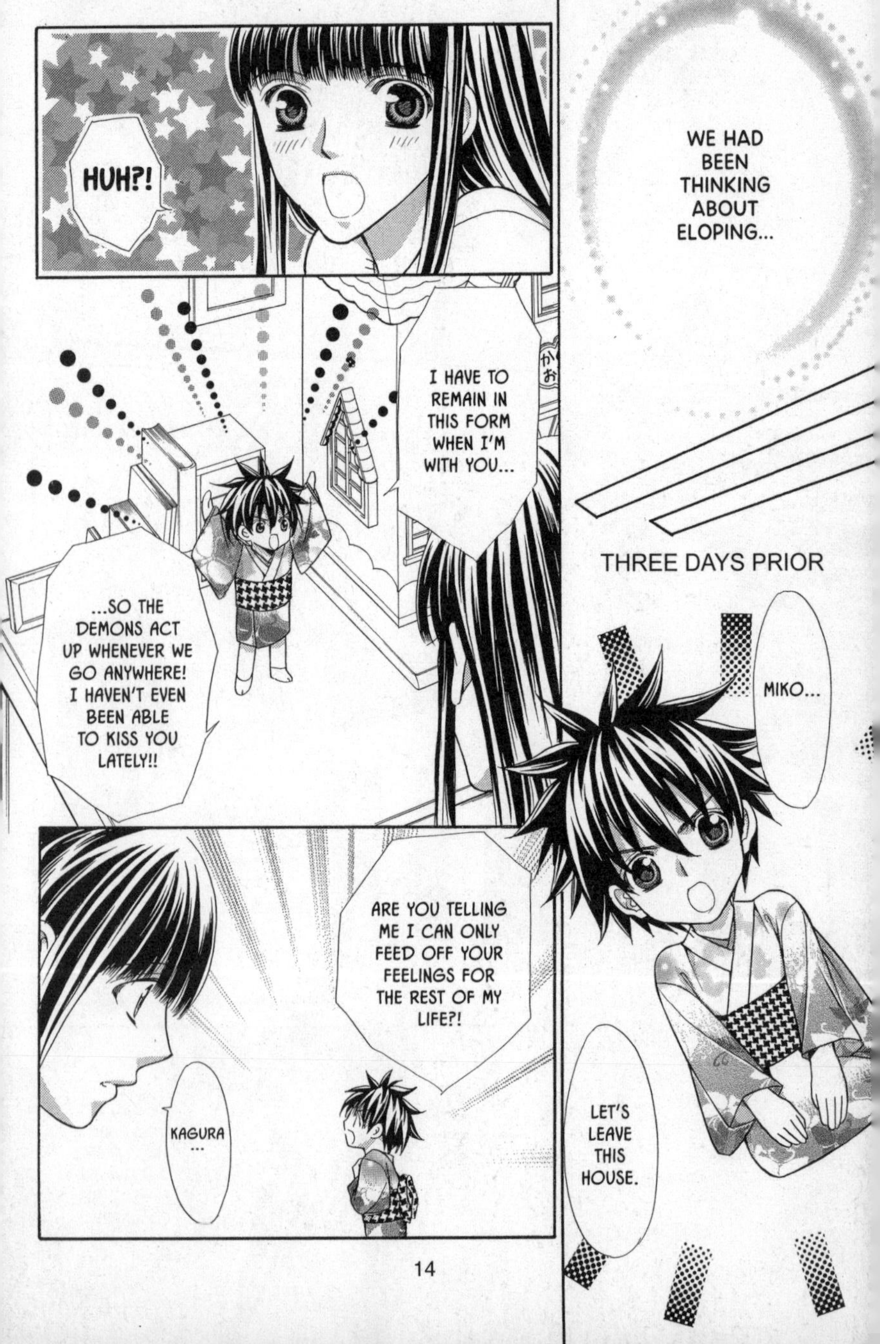
WE HAD BEEN THINKING ABOUT ELOPING...
THREE DAYS PRIOR
MIKO...
LET'S LEAVE THIS HOUSE.
HUH?!
I HAVE TO REMAIN IN THIS FORM WHEN I'M WITH YOU...
...SO THE DEMONS ACT UP WHENEVER WE GO ANYWHERE! I HAVEN'T EVEN BEEN ABLE TO KISS YOU LATELY!!
ARE YOU TELLING ME I CAN ONLY FEED OFF YOUR FEELINGS FOR THE REST OF MY LIFE?!
KAGURA...

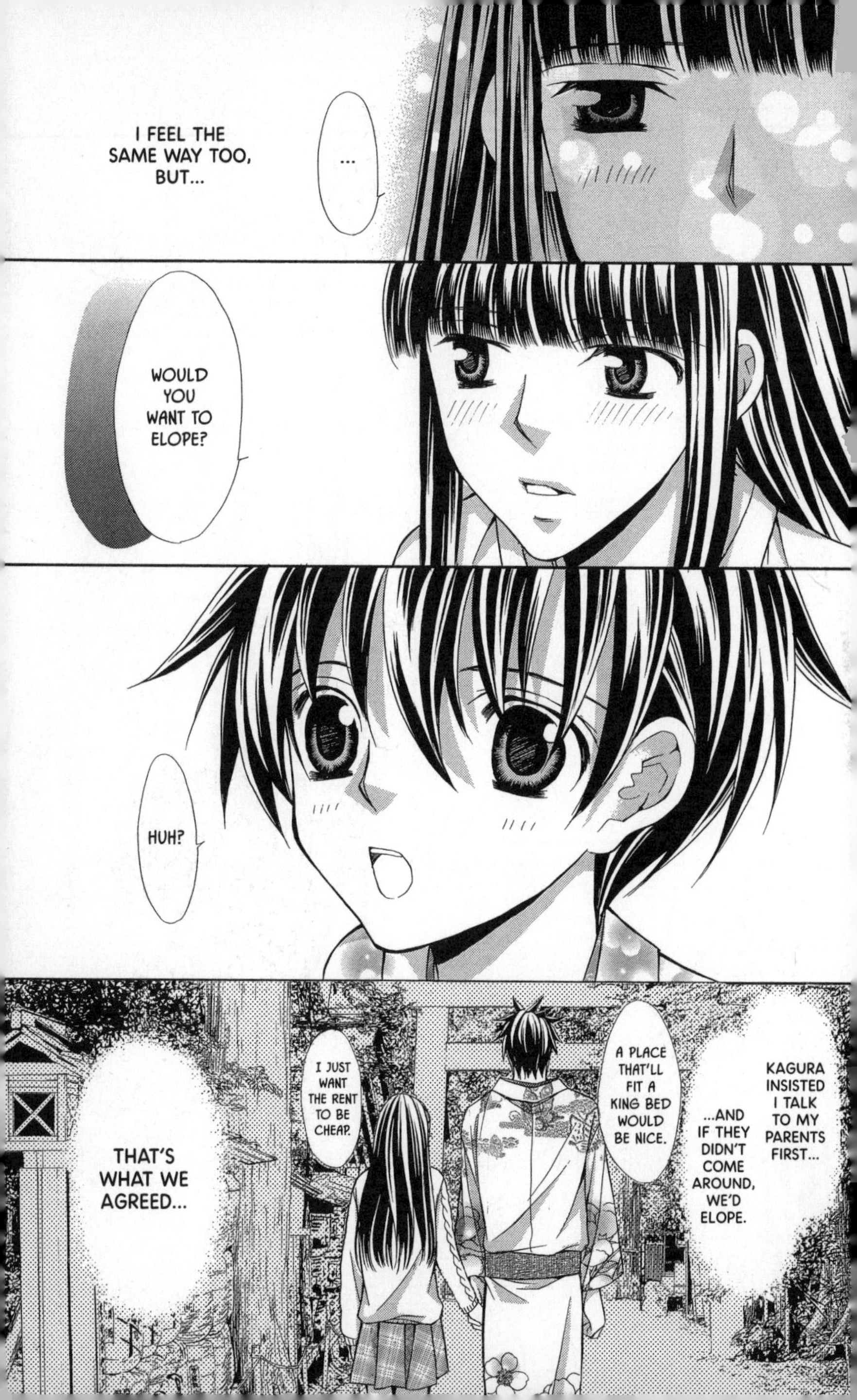
...
I FEEL THE SAME WAY TOO, BUT...
WOULD YOU WANT TO ELOPE?
HUH?
KAGURA INSISTED I TALK TO MY PARENTS FIRST...
...AND IF THEY DIDN'T COME AROUND, WE'D ELOPE.
A PLACE THAT'LL FIT A KING BED WOULD BE NICE.
I JUST WANT THE RENT TO BE CHEAP.
THAT'S WHAT WE AGREED...

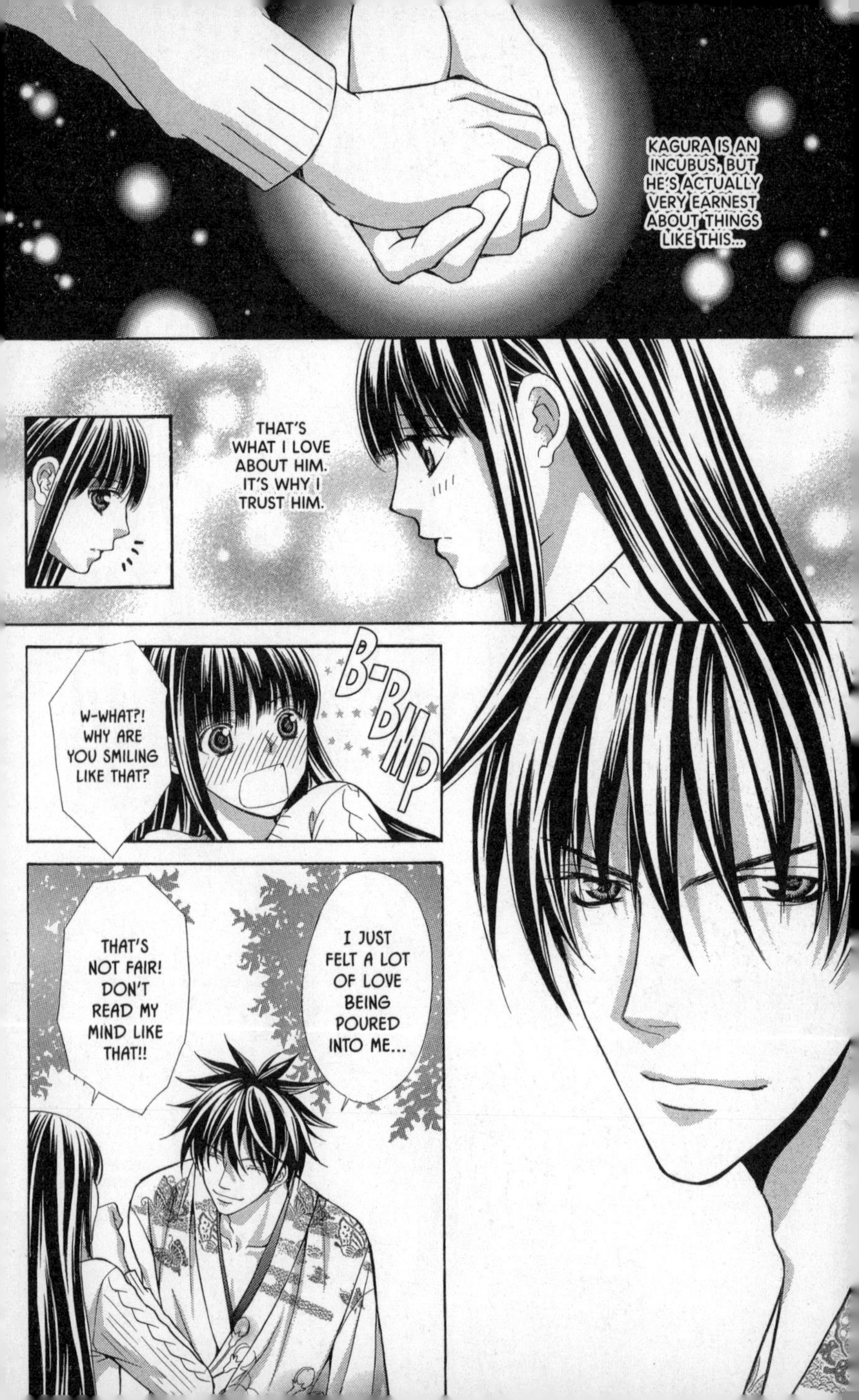
KAGURA IS AN INCUBUS, BUT HE'S ACTUALLY VERY EARNEST ABOUT THINGS LIKE THIS...
THAT'S WHAT I LOVE ABOUT HIM. IT'S WHY I TRUST HIM.
B-BMP
W-WHAT?! WHY ARE YOU SMILING LIKE THAT?
I JUST FELT A LOT OF LOVE BEING POURED INTO ME...
THAT'S NOT FAIR! DON'T READ MY MIND LIKE THAT!!

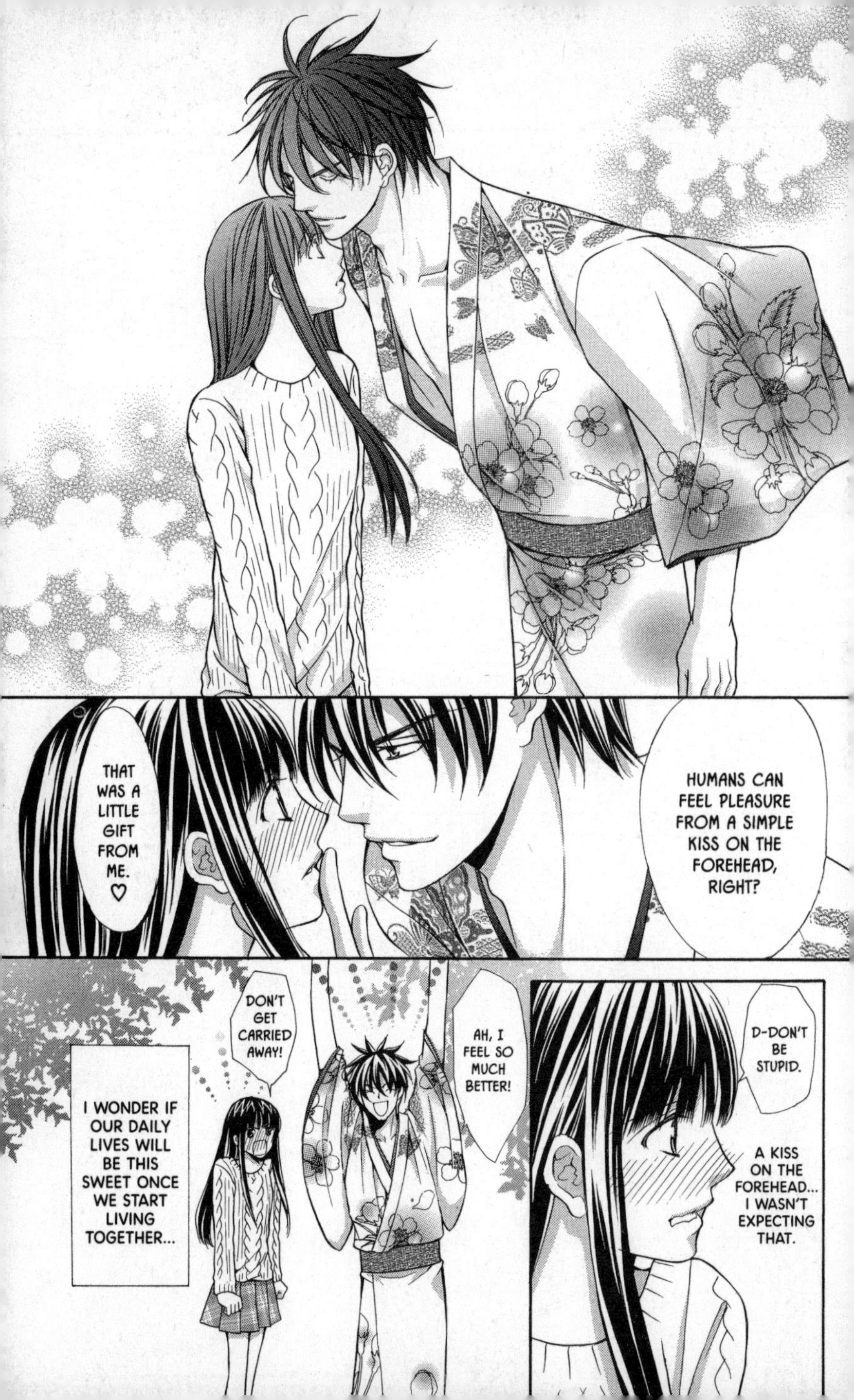
HUMANS CAN FEEL PLEASURE FROM A SIMPLE KISS ON THE FOREHEAD, RIGHT?
THAT WAS A LITTLE GIFT FROM ME. ♡
D-DON'T BE STUPID.
A KISS ON THE FOREHEAD... I WASN'T EXPECTING THAT.
AH, I FEEL SO MUCH BETTER!
DON'T GET CARRIED AWAY!
I WONDER IF OUR DAILY LIVES WILL BE THIS SWEET ONCE WE START LIVING TOGETHER...

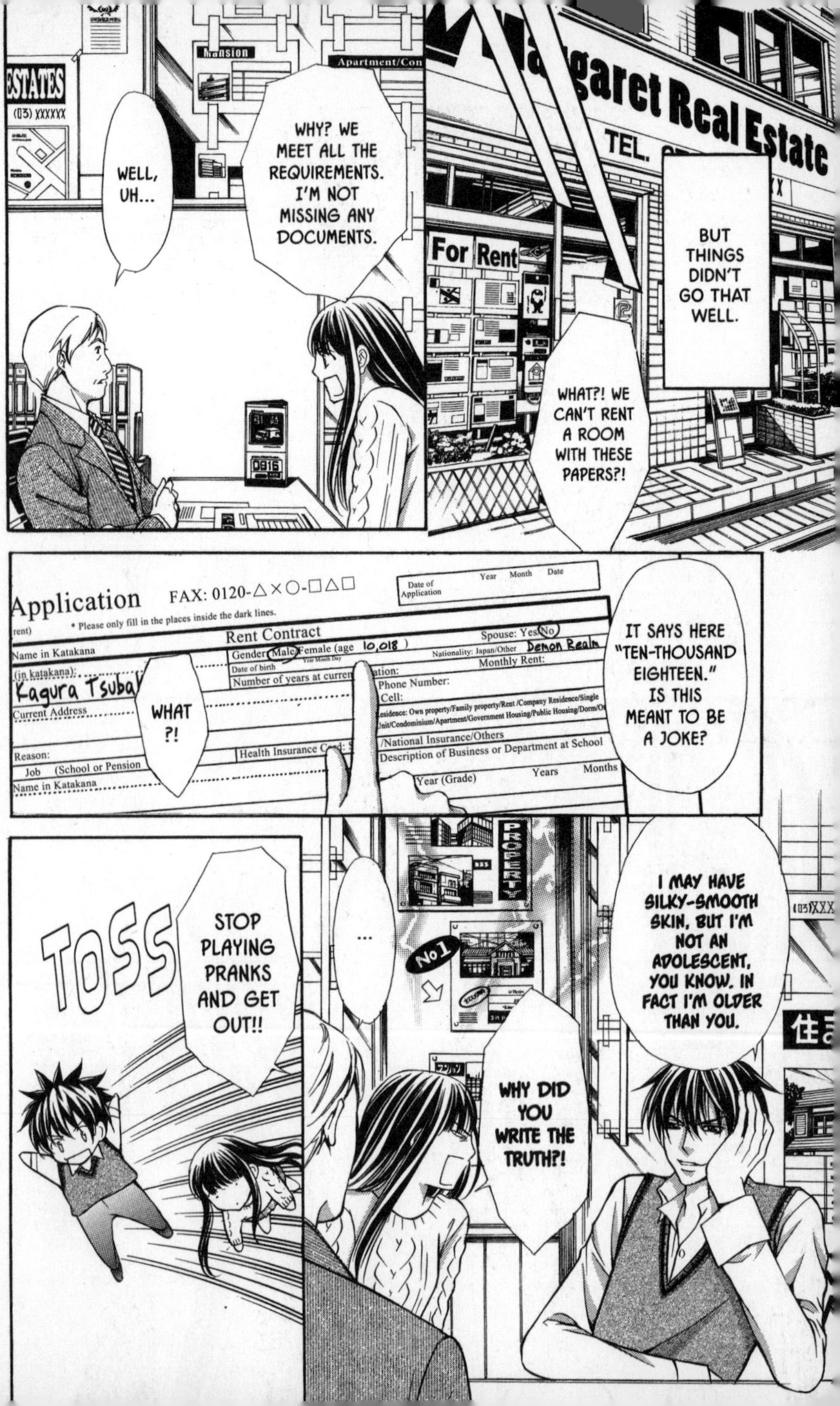

Margaret Real Estate
TEL.
For Rent
BUT THINGS DIDN'T GO THAT WELL.
WHAT?! WE CAN'T RENT A ROOM WITH THESE PAPERS?!
Apartment/Con
Mansion
ESTATES
(03) XXXXXX
WHY? WE MEET ALL THE REQUIREMENTS. I'M NOT MISSING ANY DOCUMENTS.
WELL, UH...
IT SAYS HERE "TEN-THOUSAND EIGHTEEN." IS THIS MEANT TO BE A JOKE?
Application FAX: 0120-△×○-□△□
Date of Application Year Month Date
• Please only fill in the places inside the dark lines.
Rent Contract
Spouse: Yes/No
Name in Katakana
Gender: Male/Female (age 10,018)
Nationality: Japan/Other Demon Realm
Date of birth
Monthly Rent:
(in katakana):
Number of years at curren
Phone Number:
Kagura Tsuba
Cell:
Current Address
Residence: Own property/Family property/Rent/Company Residence/Single
Unit/Condominium/Apartment/Government Housing/Public Housing/Dorm/O
/National Insurance/Others
Reason:
Health Insurance Card:
Description of Business or Department at School
Job (School or Pension
Name in Katakana
Year (Grade) Years Months
WHAT?!
I MAY HAVE SILKY-SMOOTH SKIN, BUT I'M NOT AN ADOLESCENT, YOU KNOW. IN FACT I'M OLDER THAN YOU.
WHY DID YOU WRITE THE TRUTH?!
PROPERTY
No 1
...
STOP PLAYING PRANKS AND GET OUT!!
TOSS

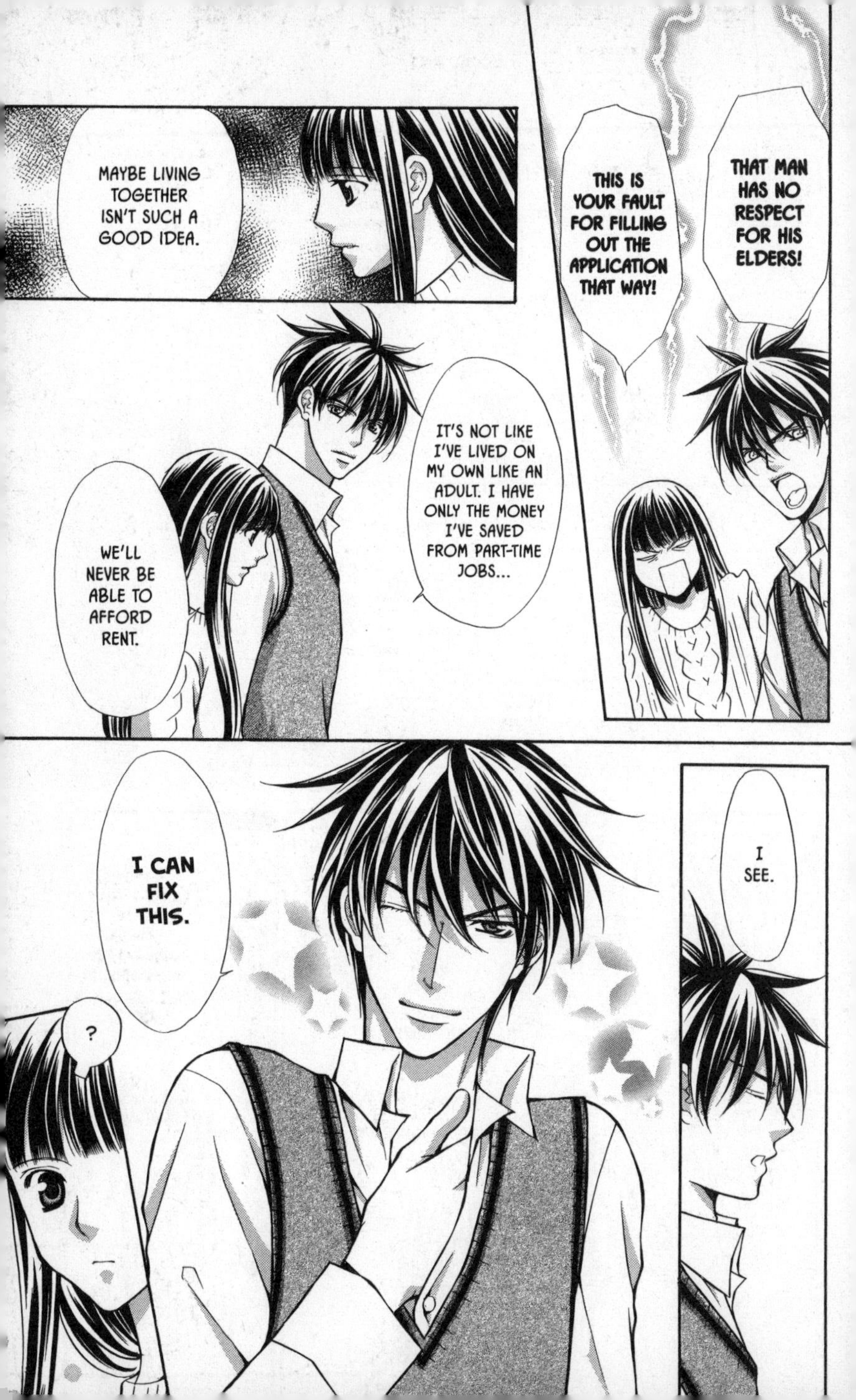
THAT MAN HAS NO RESPECT FOR HIS ELDERS!
THIS IS YOUR FAULT FOR FILLING OUT THE APPLICATION THAT WAY!
MAYBE LIVING TOGETHER ISN'T SUCH A GOOD IDEA.
IT'S NOT LIKE I'VE LIVED ON MY OWN LIKE AN ADULT. I HAVE ONLY THE MONEY I'VE SAVED FROM PART-TIME JOBS...
WE'LL NEVER BE ABLE TO AFFORD RENT.
I SEE.
I CAN FIX THIS.
?

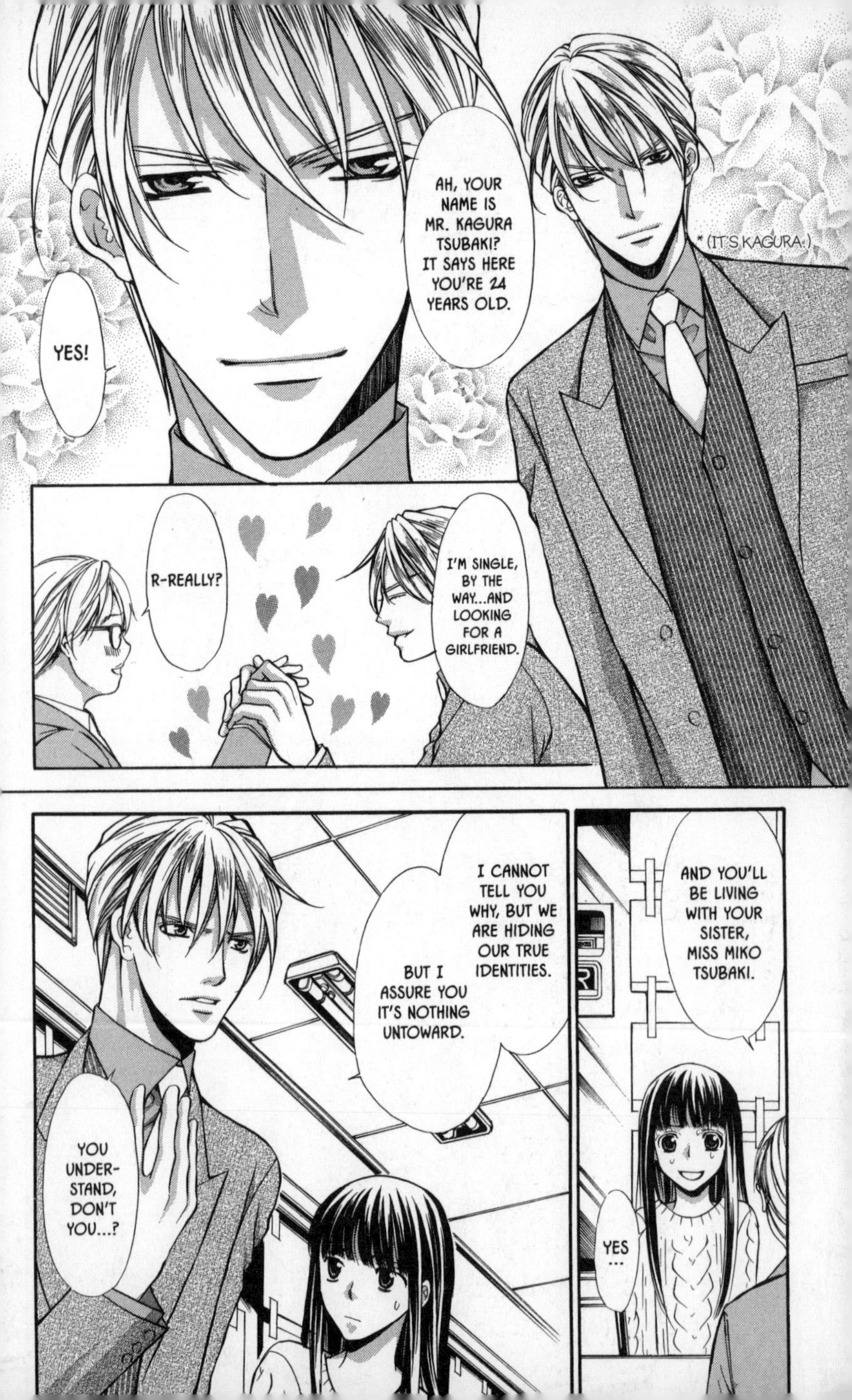
AH, YOUR NAME IS MR. KAGURA TSUBAKI? IT SAYS HERE YOU'RE 24 YEARS OLD.
* (IT'S KAGURA.)
YES!
I'M SINGLE, BY THE WAY...AND LOOKING FOR A GIRLFRIEND.
R-REALLY?
AND YOU'LL BE LIVING WITH YOUR SISTER, MISS MIKO TSUBAKI.
YES...
I CANNOT TELL YOU WHY, BUT WE ARE HIDING OUR TRUE IDENTITIES.
BUT I ASSURE YOU IT'S NOTHING UNTOWARD.
YOU UNDERSTAND, DON'T YOU...?

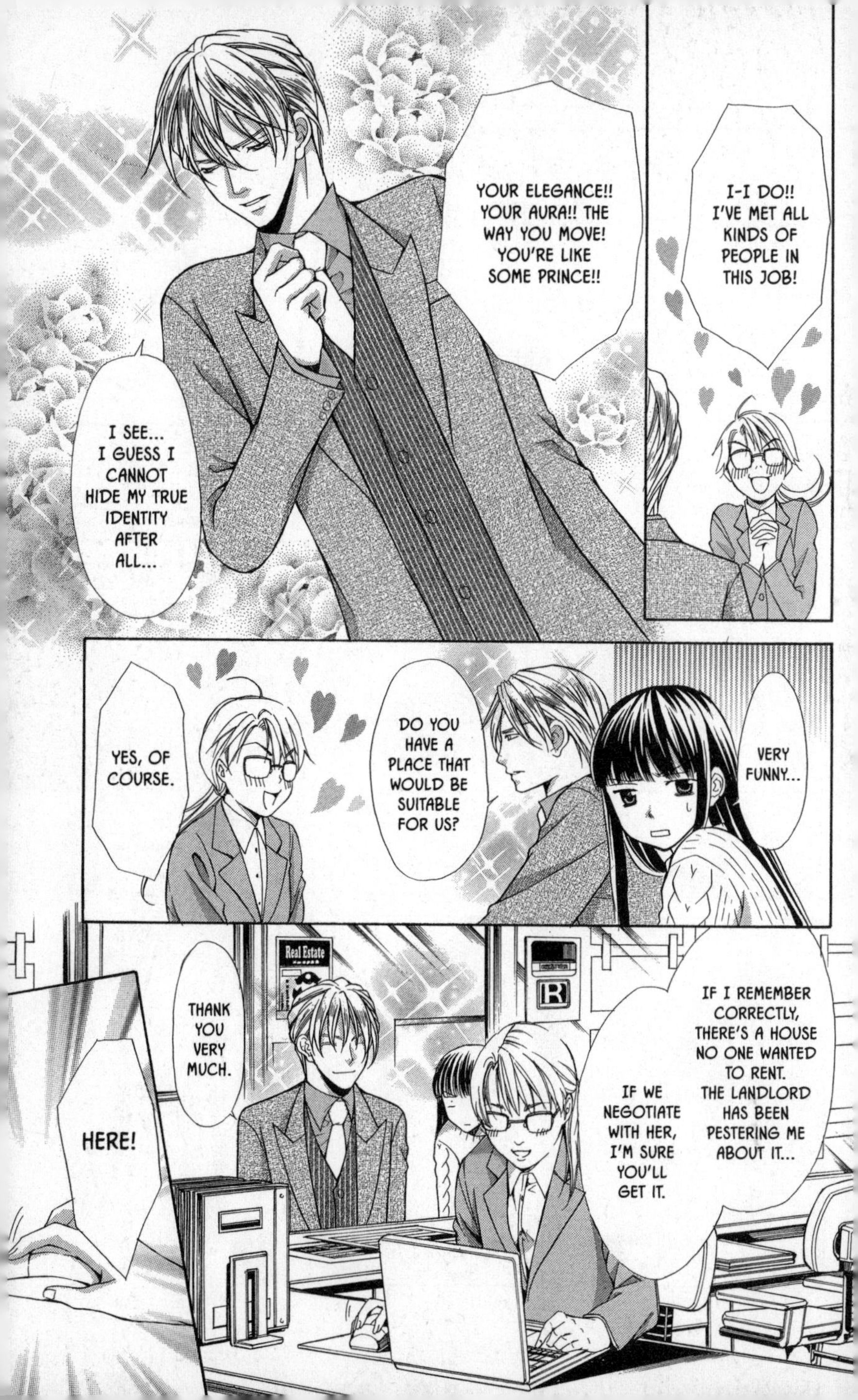
I-I DO!! I'VE MET ALL KINDS OF PEOPLE IN THIS JOB!
YOUR ELEGANCE!! YOUR AURA!! THE WAY YOU MOVE! YOU'RE LIKE SOME PRINCE!!
I SEE... I GUESS I CANNOT HIDE MY TRUE IDENTITY AFTER ALL...
VERY FUNNY...
DO YOU HAVE A PLACE THAT WOULD BE SUITABLE FOR US?
YES, OF COURSE.
IF I REMEMBER CORRECTLY, THERE'S A HOUSE NO ONE WANTED TO RENT. THE LANDLORD HAS BEEN PESTERING ME ABOUT IT...
IF WE NEGOTIATE WITH HER, I'M SURE YOU'LL GET IT.
Real Estate
THANK YOU VERY MUCH.
HERE!

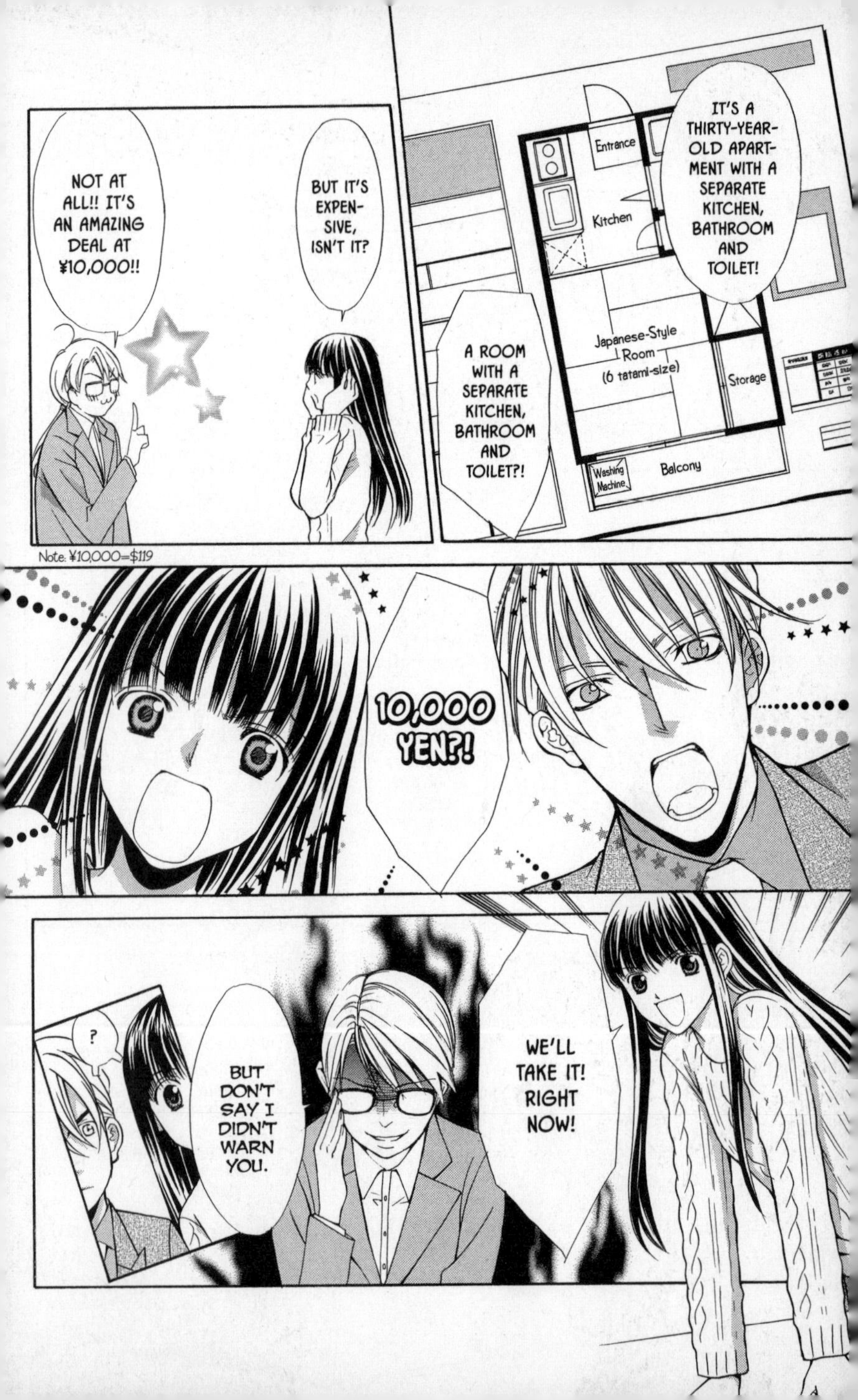
IT'S A THIRTY-YEAR-OLD APARTMENT WITH A SEPARATE KITCHEN, BATHROOM AND TOILET!
Entrance
Kitchen
Japanese-Style Room (6 tatami-size)
Storage
Washing Machine
Balcony
A ROOM WITH A SEPARATE KITCHEN, BATHROOM AND TOILET?!
BUT IT'S EXPENSIVE, ISN'T IT?
NOT AT ALL!! IT'S AN AMAZING DEAL AT ¥10,000!!
10,000 YEN?!
WE'LL TAKE IT! RIGHT NOW!
BUT DON'T SAY I DIDN'T WARN YOU.
?
Note: ¥10,000=$119

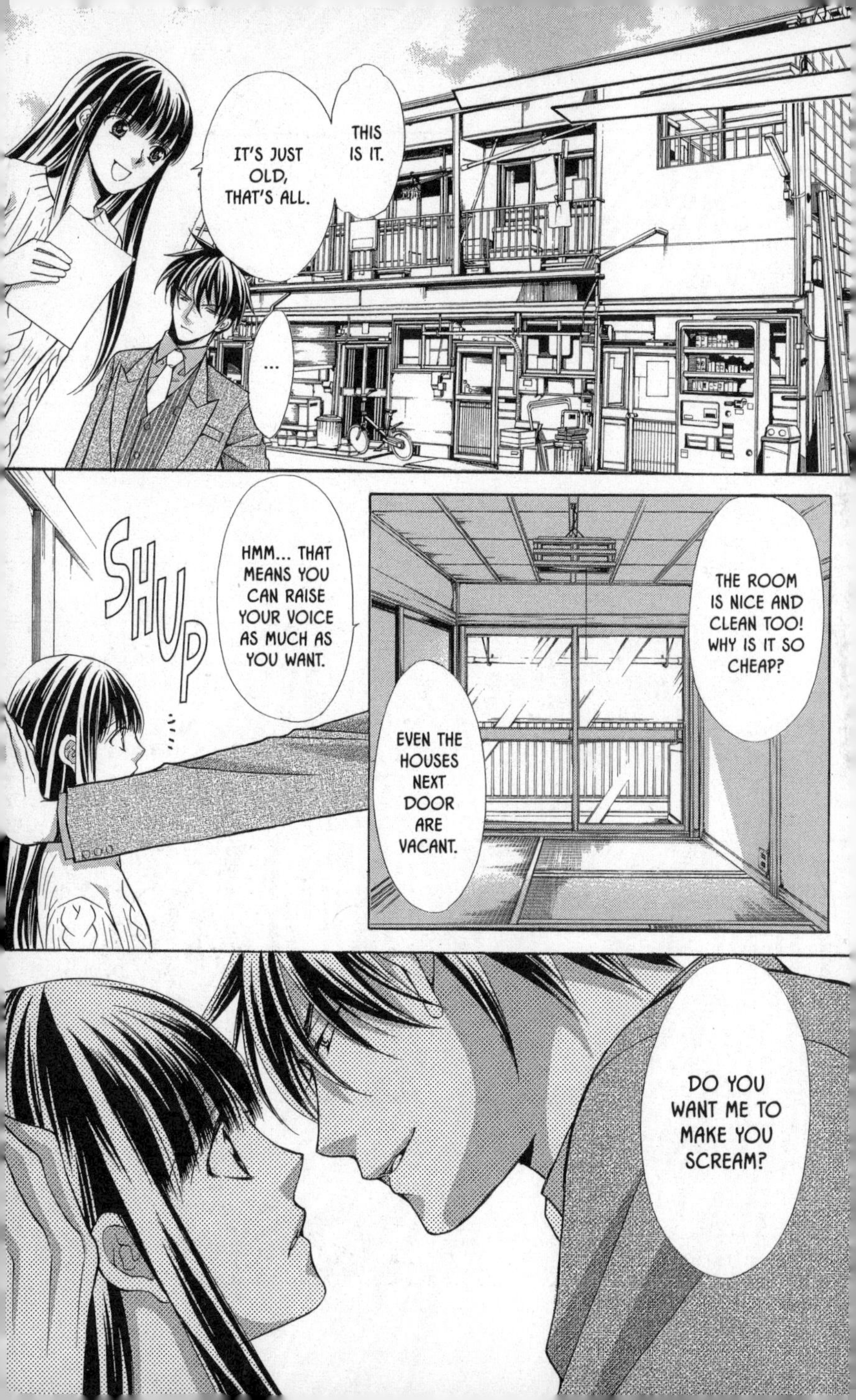
THIS IS IT.
IT'S JUST OLD, THAT'S ALL.
...
THE ROOM IS NICE AND CLEAN TOO! WHY IS IT SO CHEAP?
EVEN THE HOUSES NEXT DOOR ARE VACANT.
HMM... THAT MEANS YOU CAN RAISE YOUR VOICE AS MUCH AS YOU WANT.
SHUP
DO YOU WANT ME TO MAKE YOU SCREAM?

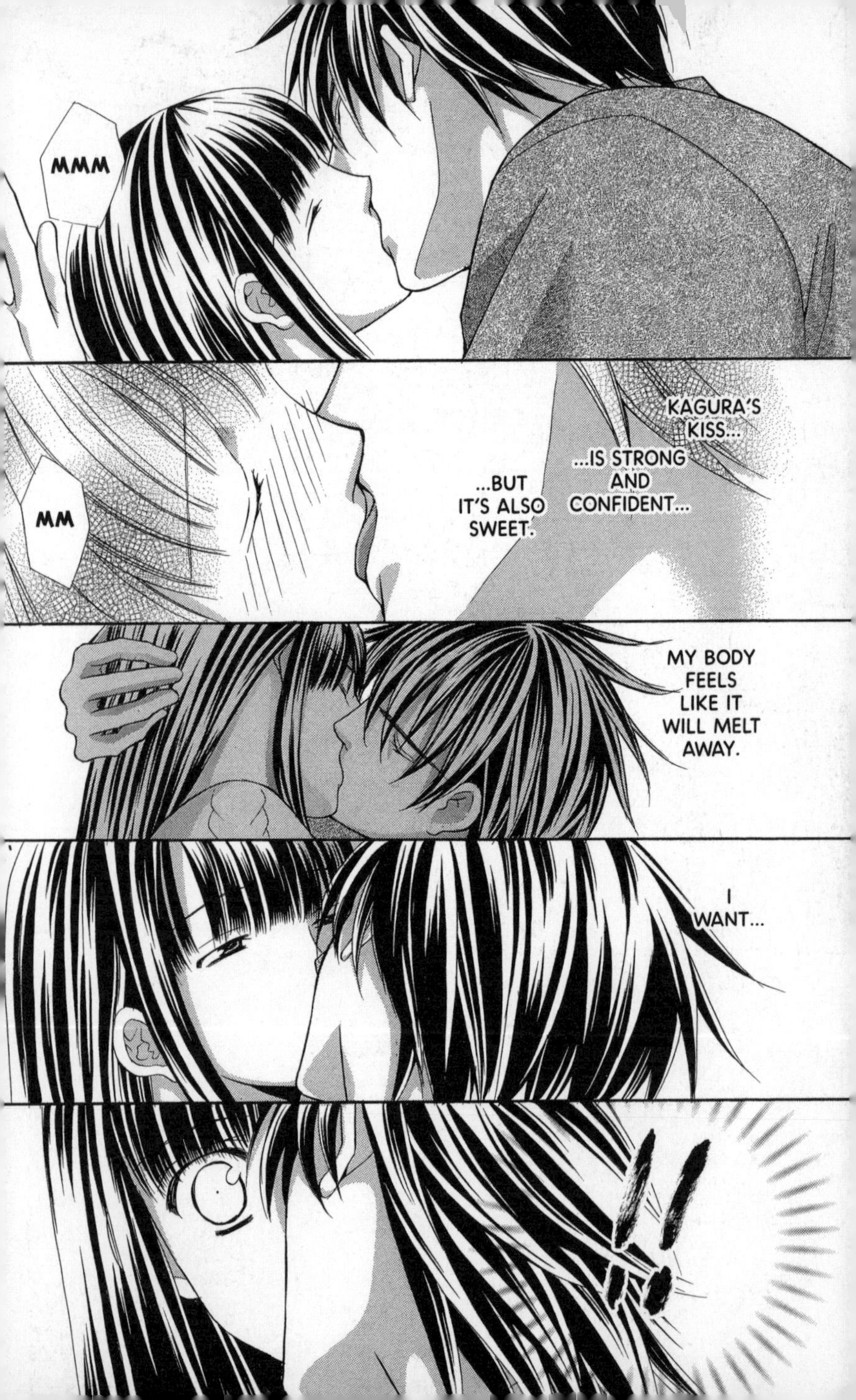
MMM
KAGURA'S KISS...
...IS STRONG AND CONFIDENT...
...BUT IT'S ALSO SWEET.
MM
MY BODY FEELS LIKE IT WILL MELT AWAY.
I WANT...
!!

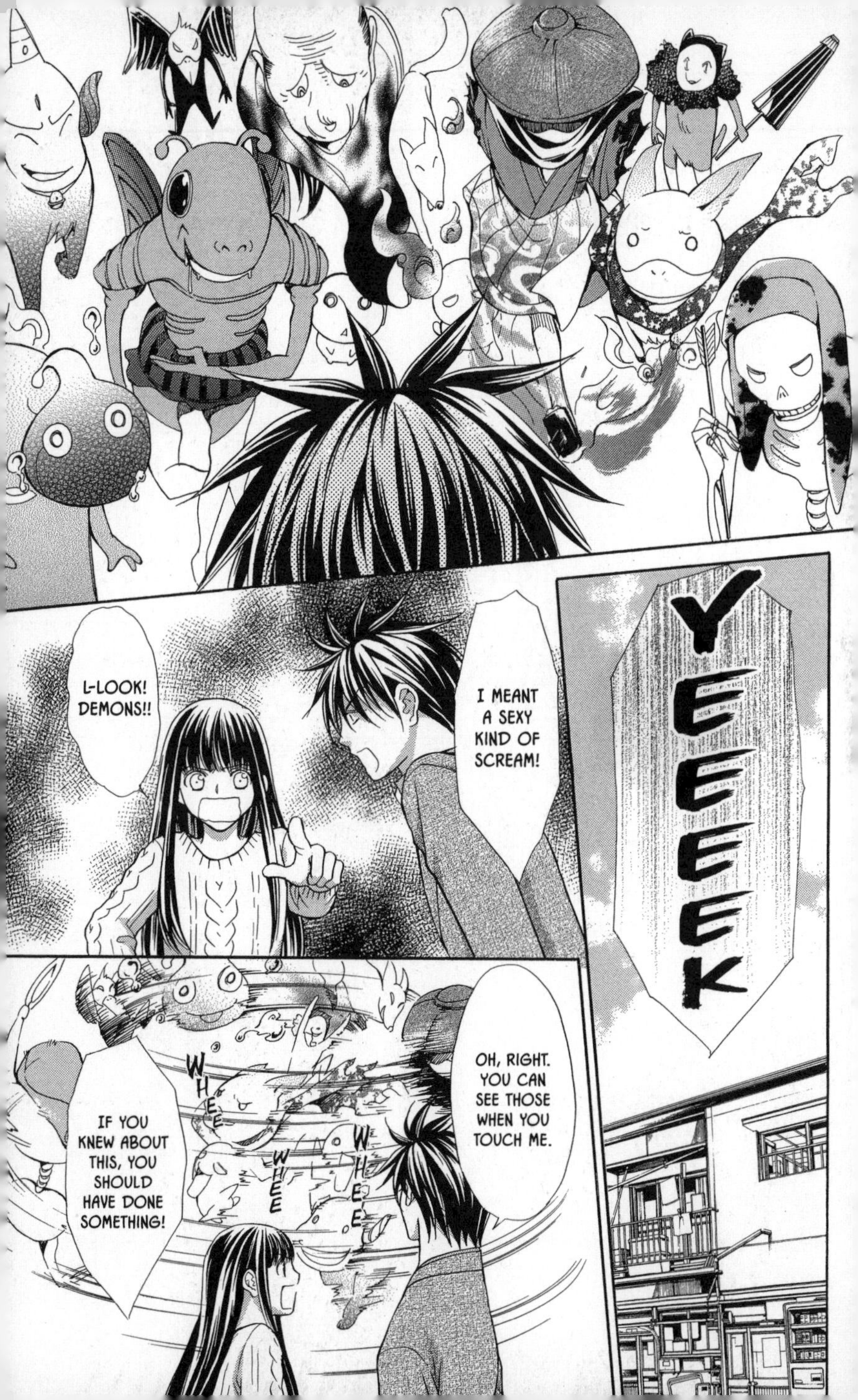
YEEEEK
I MEANT A SEXY KIND OF SCREAM!
L-LOOK! DEMONS!!
OH, RIGHT. YOU CAN SEE THOSE WHEN YOU TOUCH ME.
WHEE
WHEE
WHEE
IF YOU KNEW ABOUT THIS, YOU SHOULD HAVE DONE SOMETHING!

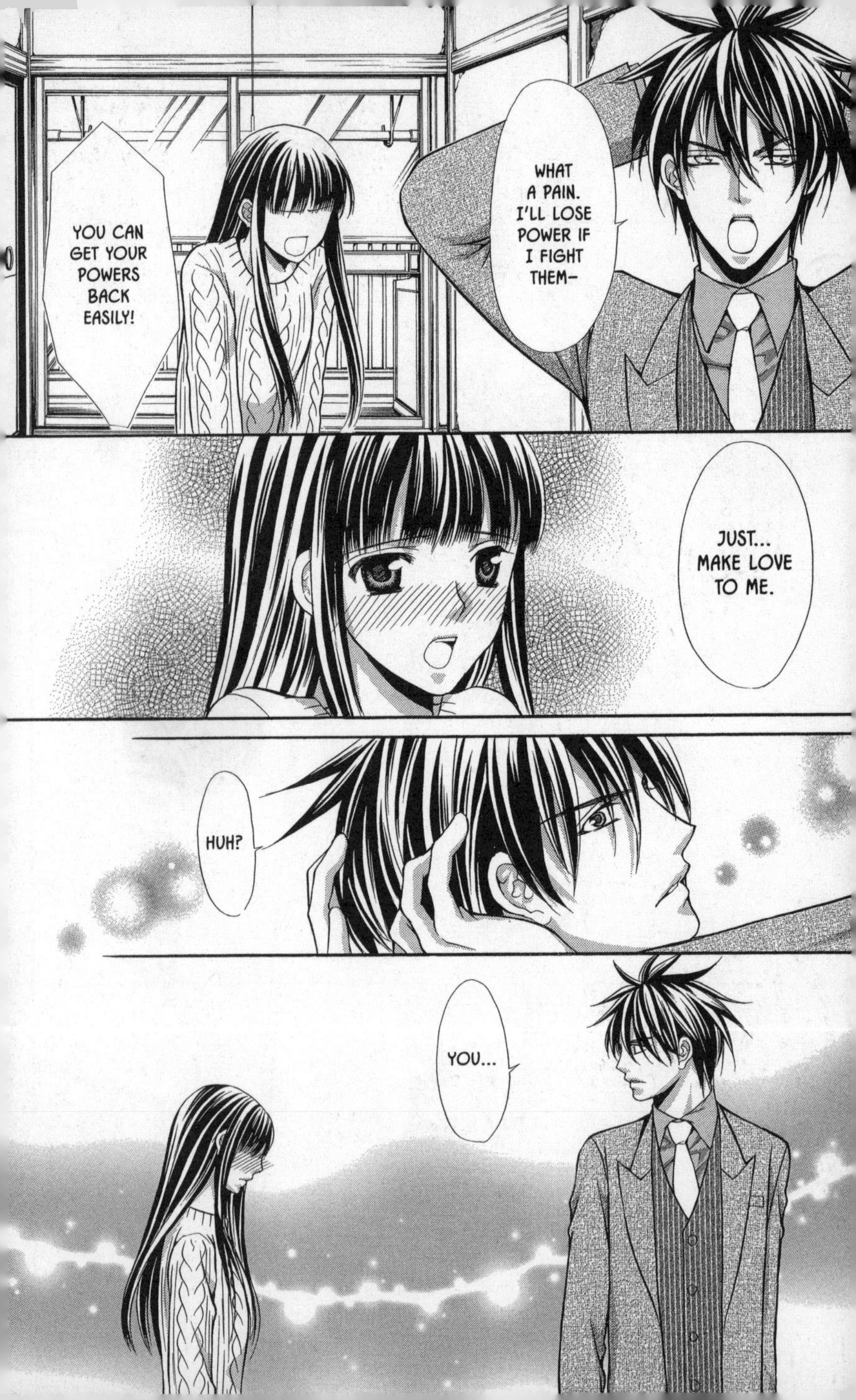
WHAT A PAIN. I'LL LOSE POWER IF I FIGHT THEM—
YOU CAN GET YOUR POWERS BACK EASILY!
JUST... MAKE LOVE TO ME.
HUH?
YOU...

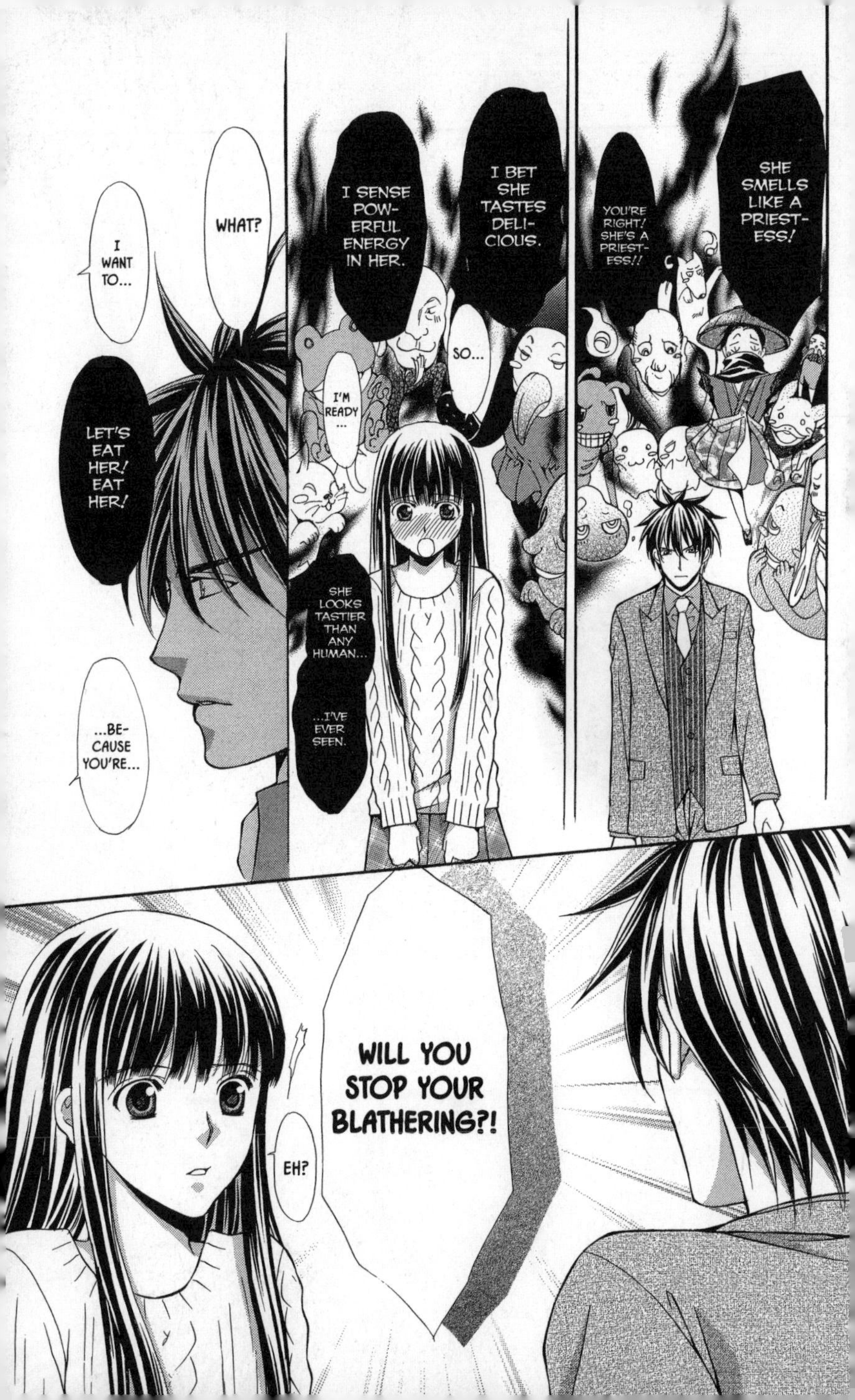
SHE SMELLS LIKE A PRIEST-ESS!
YOU'RE RIGHT! SHE'S A PRIEST-ESS!!
I BET SHE TASTES DELI-CIOUS.
I SENSE POW-ERFUL ENERGY IN HER.
SO...
I'M READY ...
SHE LOOKS TASTIER THAN ANY HUMAN...
...I'VE EVER SEEN.
WHAT?
I WANT TO...
LET'S EAT HER! EAT HER!
...BE-CAUSE YOU'RE...
WILL YOU STOP YOUR BLATHERING?!
EH?

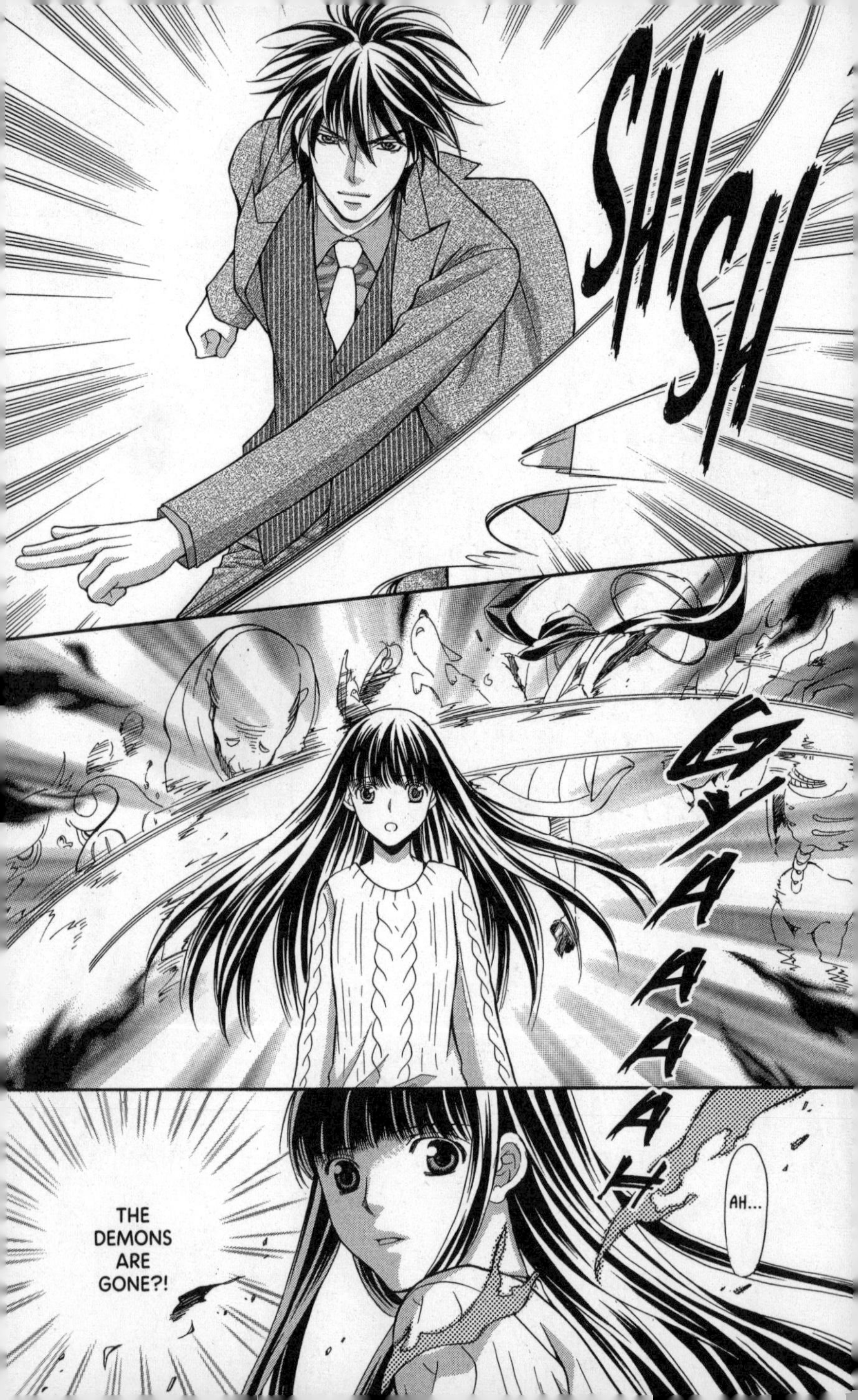
SHISH
GYAAAAAH
AH...
THE DEMONS ARE GONE?!

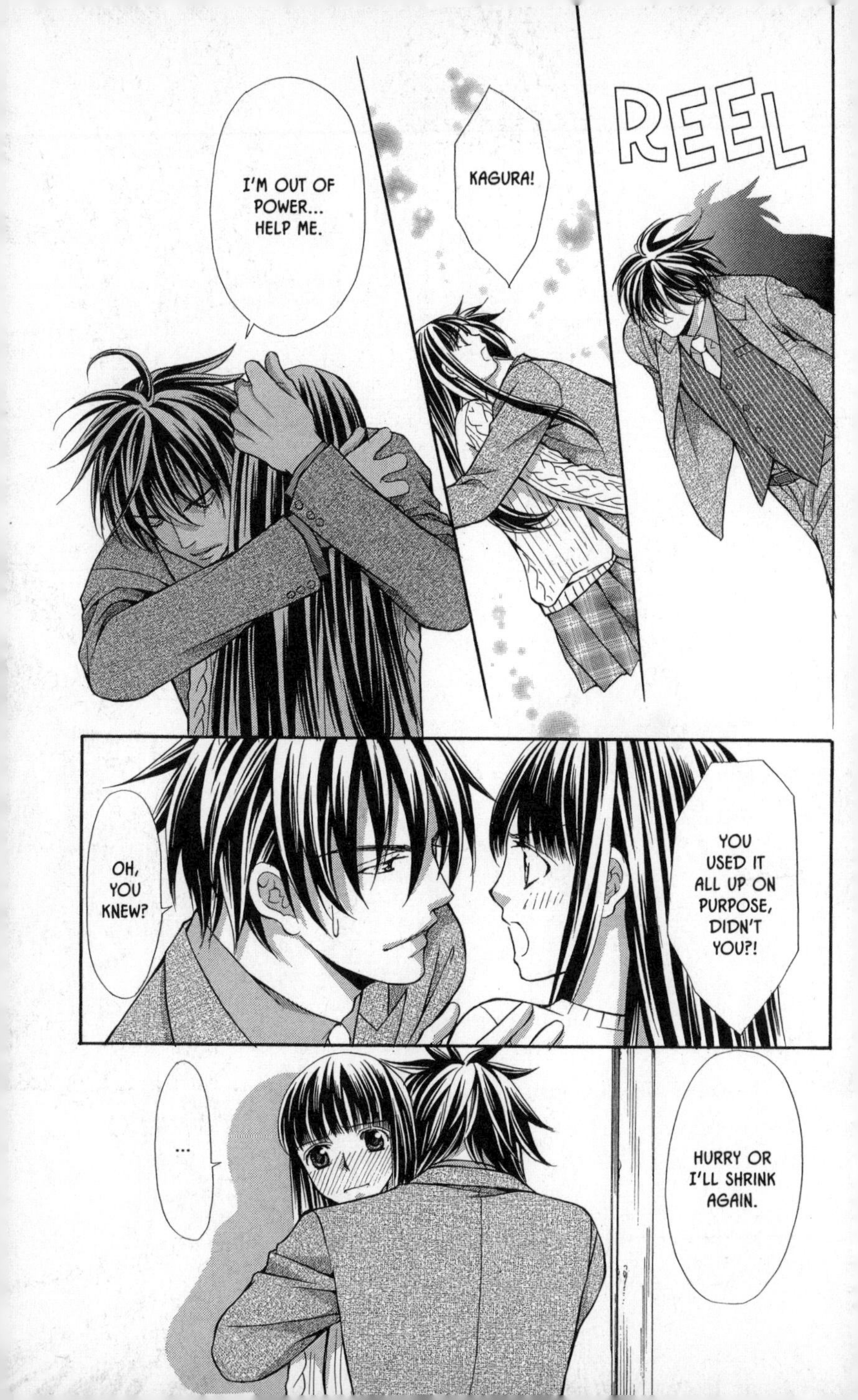
REEL
KAGURA!
I'M OUT OF POWER... HELP ME.
YOU USED IT ALL UP ON PURPOSE, DIDN'T YOU?!
OH, YOU KNEW?
HURRY OR I'LL SHRINK AGAIN.
...

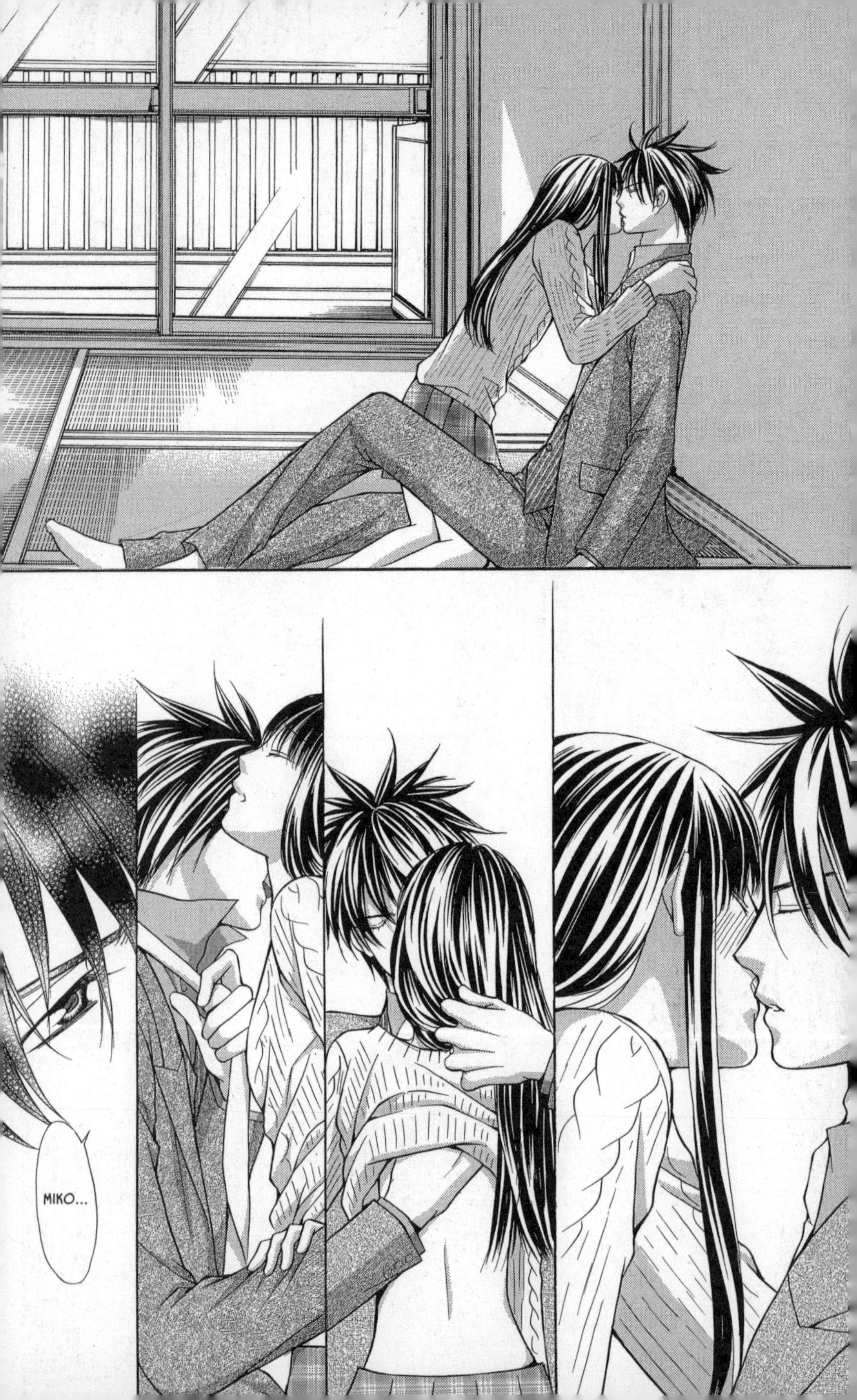
MIKO...

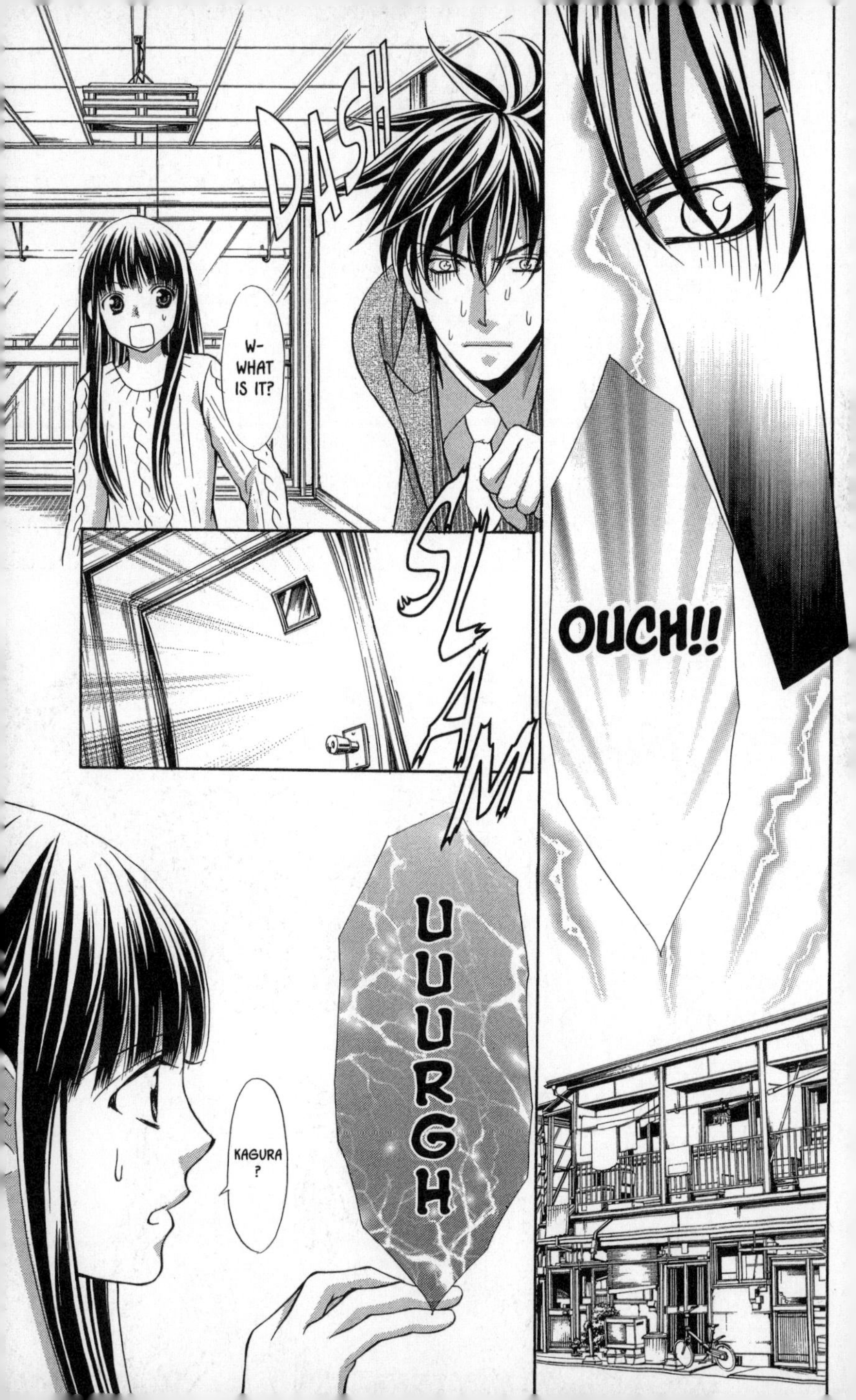
OUCH!!
DASH
W-WHAT IS IT?
SLAM
UUURGH
KAGURA?

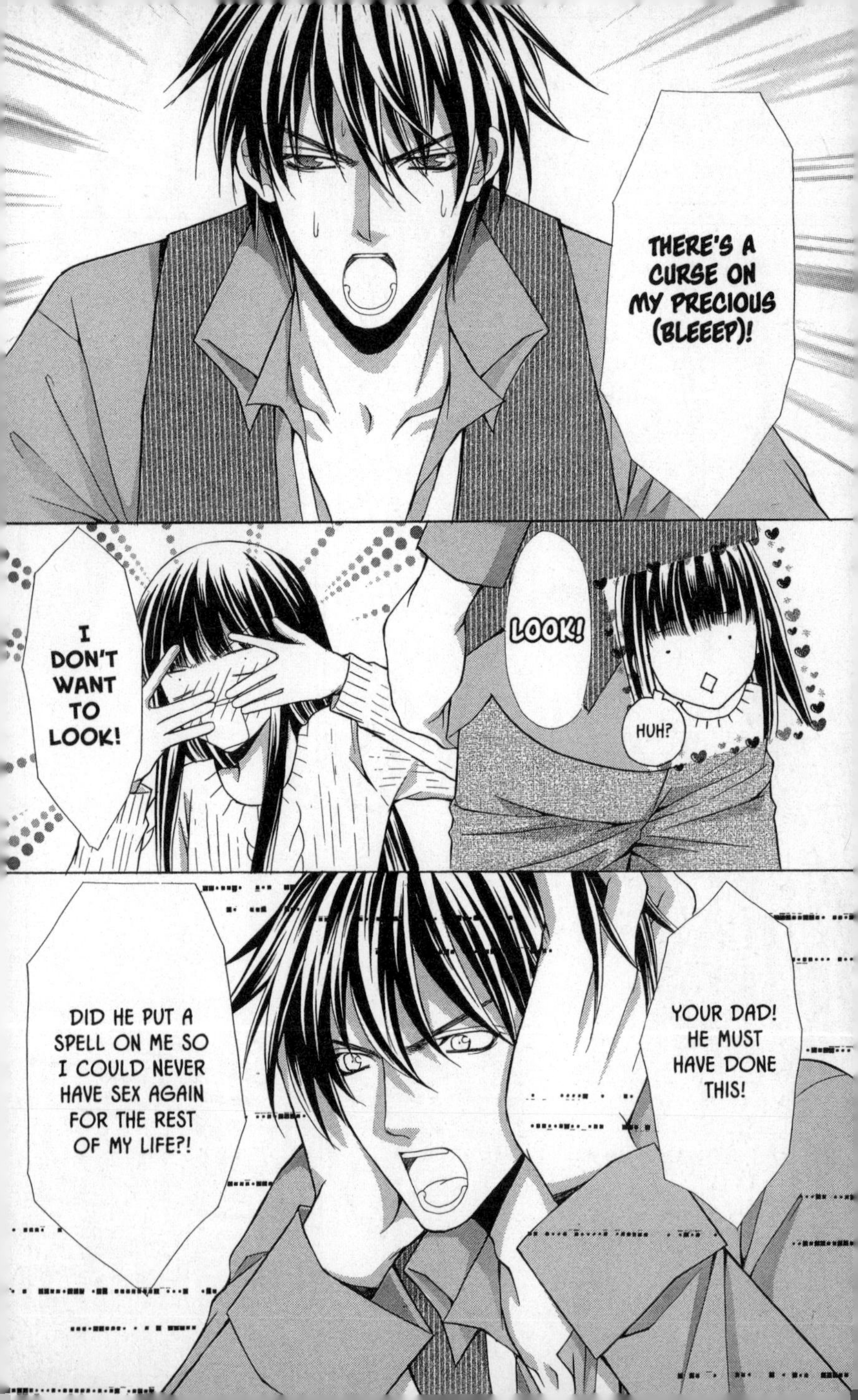
THERE'S A CURSE ON MY PRECIOUS (BLEEEP)!
LOOK!
HUH?
I DON'T WANT TO LOOK!
YOUR DAD! HE MUST HAVE DONE THIS!
DID HE PUT A SPELL ON ME SO I COULD NEVER HAVE SEX AGAIN FOR THE REST OF MY LIFE?!

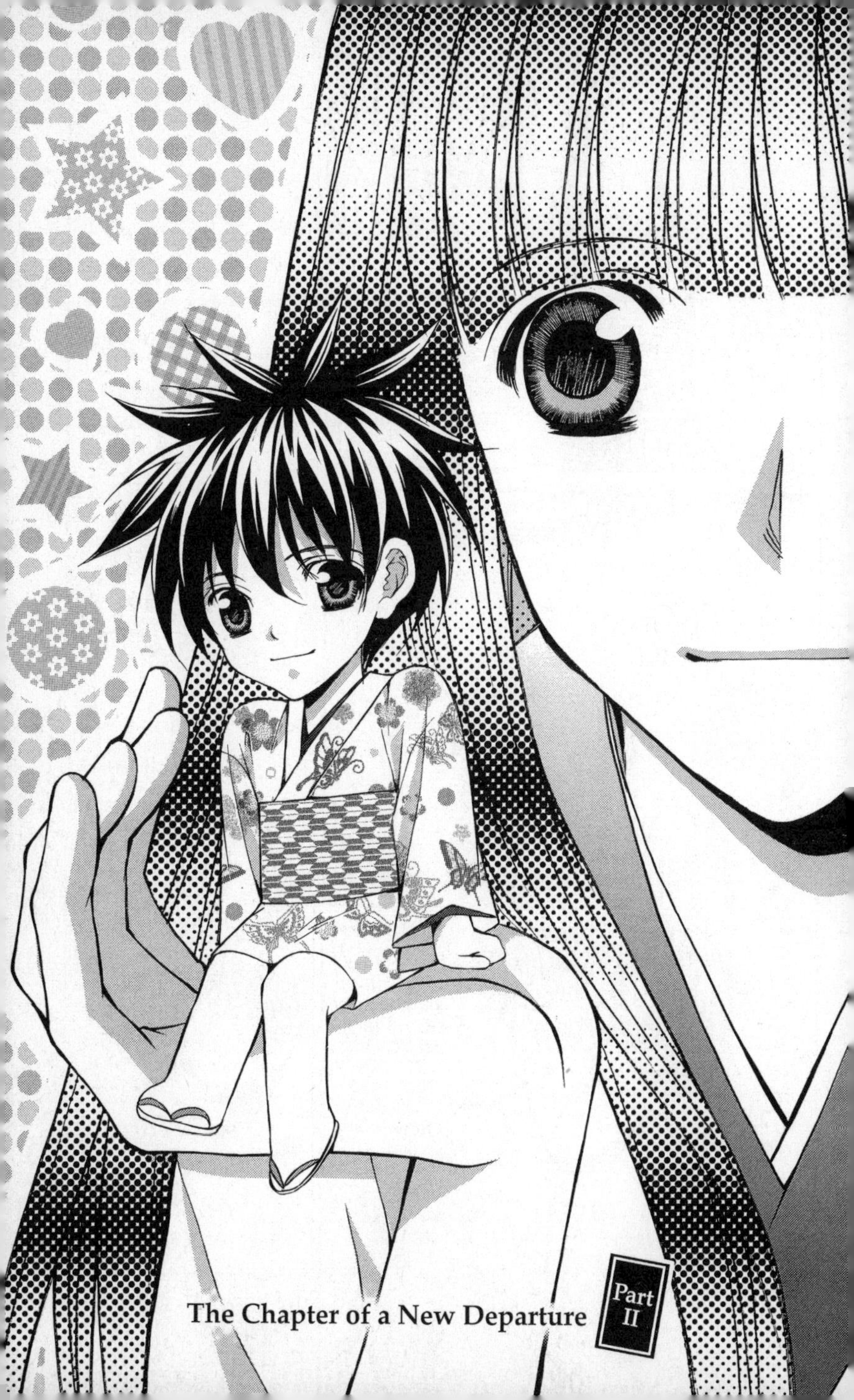

The Chapter of a New Departure

Part II

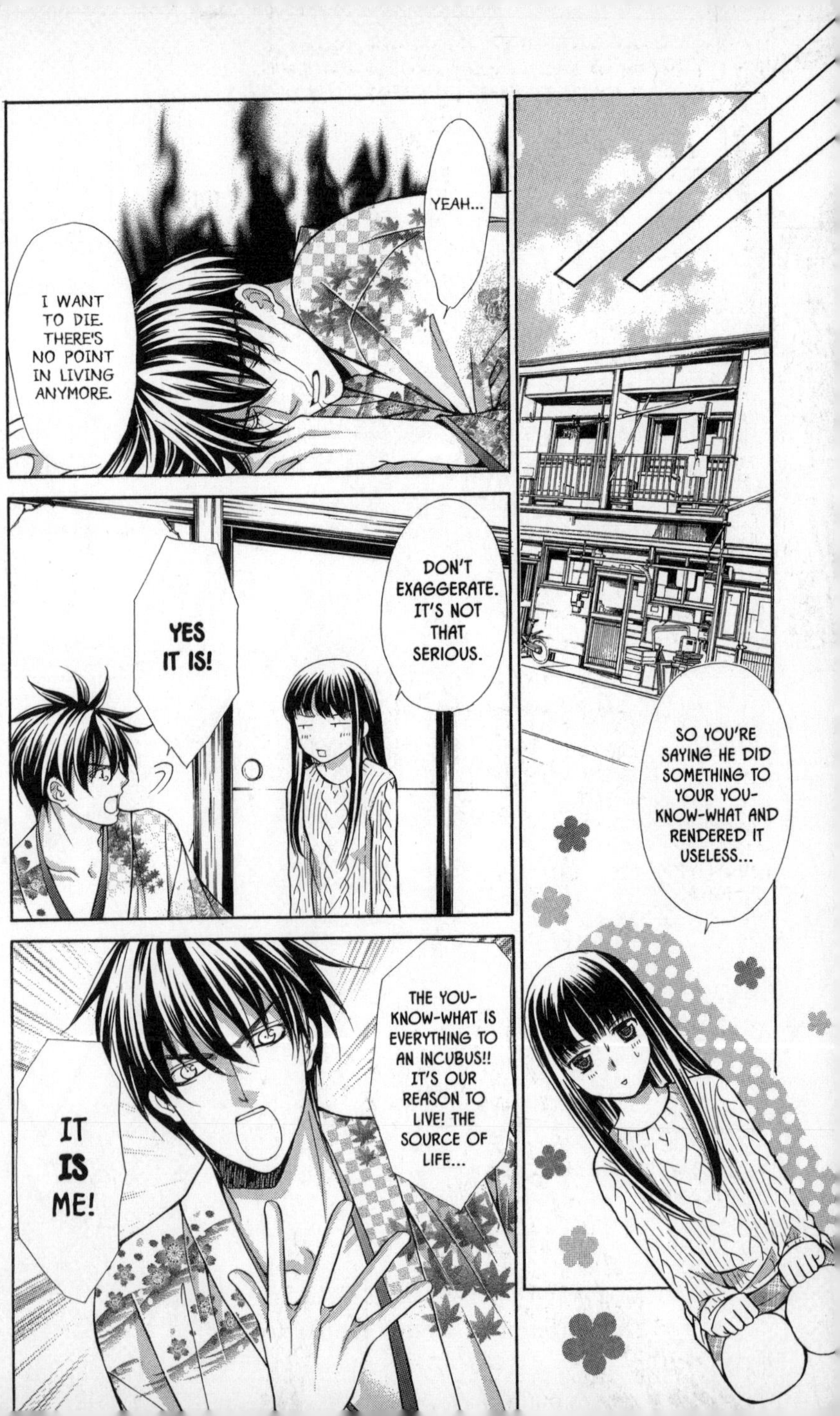
SO YOU'RE SAYING HE DID SOMETHING TO YOUR YOU-KNOW-WHAT AND RENDERED IT USELESS...
YEAH...
I WANT TO DIE. THERE'S NO POINT IN LIVING ANYMORE.
DON'T EXAGGERATE. IT'S NOT THAT SERIOUS.
YES IT IS!
THE YOU-KNOW-WHAT IS EVERYTHING TO AN INCUBUS!! IT'S OUR REASON TO LIVE! THE SOURCE OF LIFE...
IT IS ME!

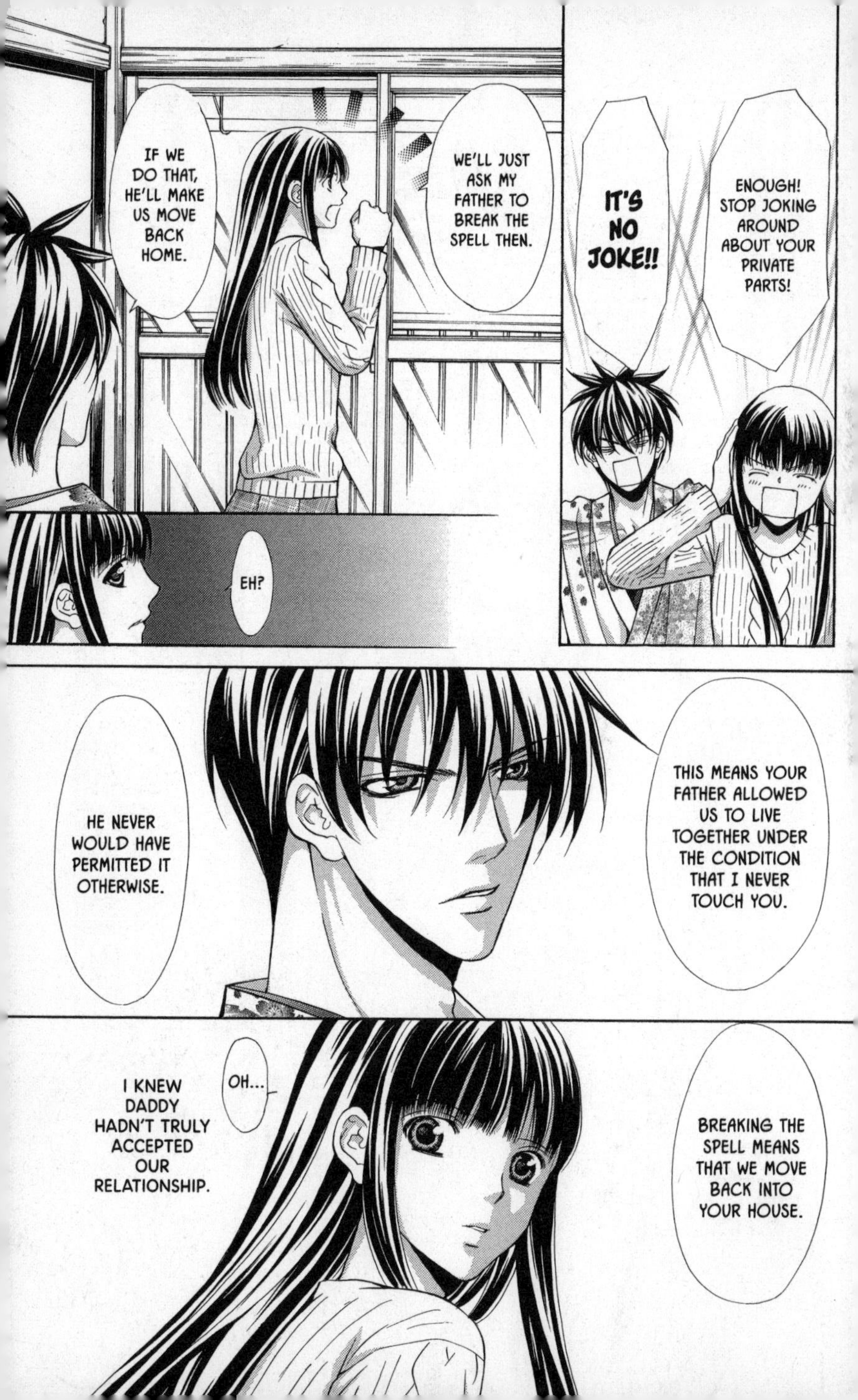
ENOUGH! STOP JOKING AROUND ABOUT YOUR PRIVATE PARTS!
IT'S NO JOKE!!
WE'LL JUST ASK MY FATHER TO BREAK THE SPELL THEN.
IF WE DO THAT, HE'LL MAKE US MOVE BACK HOME.
EH?
THIS MEANS YOUR FATHER ALLOWED US TO LIVE TOGETHER UNDER THE CONDITION THAT I NEVER TOUCH YOU.
HE NEVER WOULD HAVE PERMITTED IT OTHERWISE.
BREAKING THE SPELL MEANS THAT WE MOVE BACK INTO YOUR HOUSE.
OH...
I KNEW DADDY HADN'T TRULY ACCEPTED OUR RELATIONSHIP.

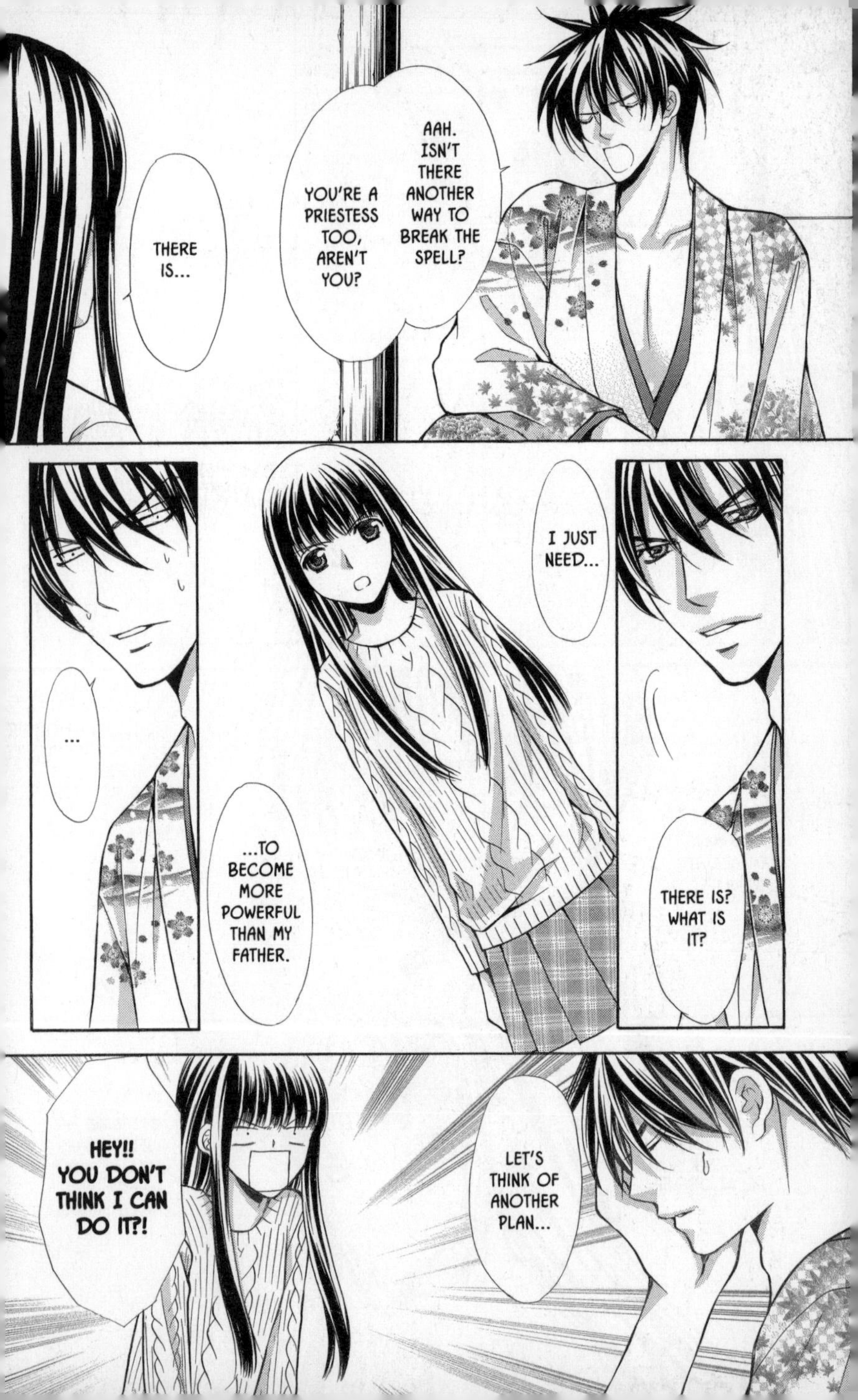
AAH. ISN'T THERE ANOTHER WAY TO BREAK THE SPELL?
YOU'RE A PRIESTESS TOO, AREN'T YOU?
THERE IS...
THERE IS? WHAT IS IT?
I JUST NEED...
...TO BECOME MORE POWERFUL THAN MY FATHER.
...
LET'S THINK OF ANOTHER PLAN...
HEY!! YOU DON'T THINK I CAN DO IT?!

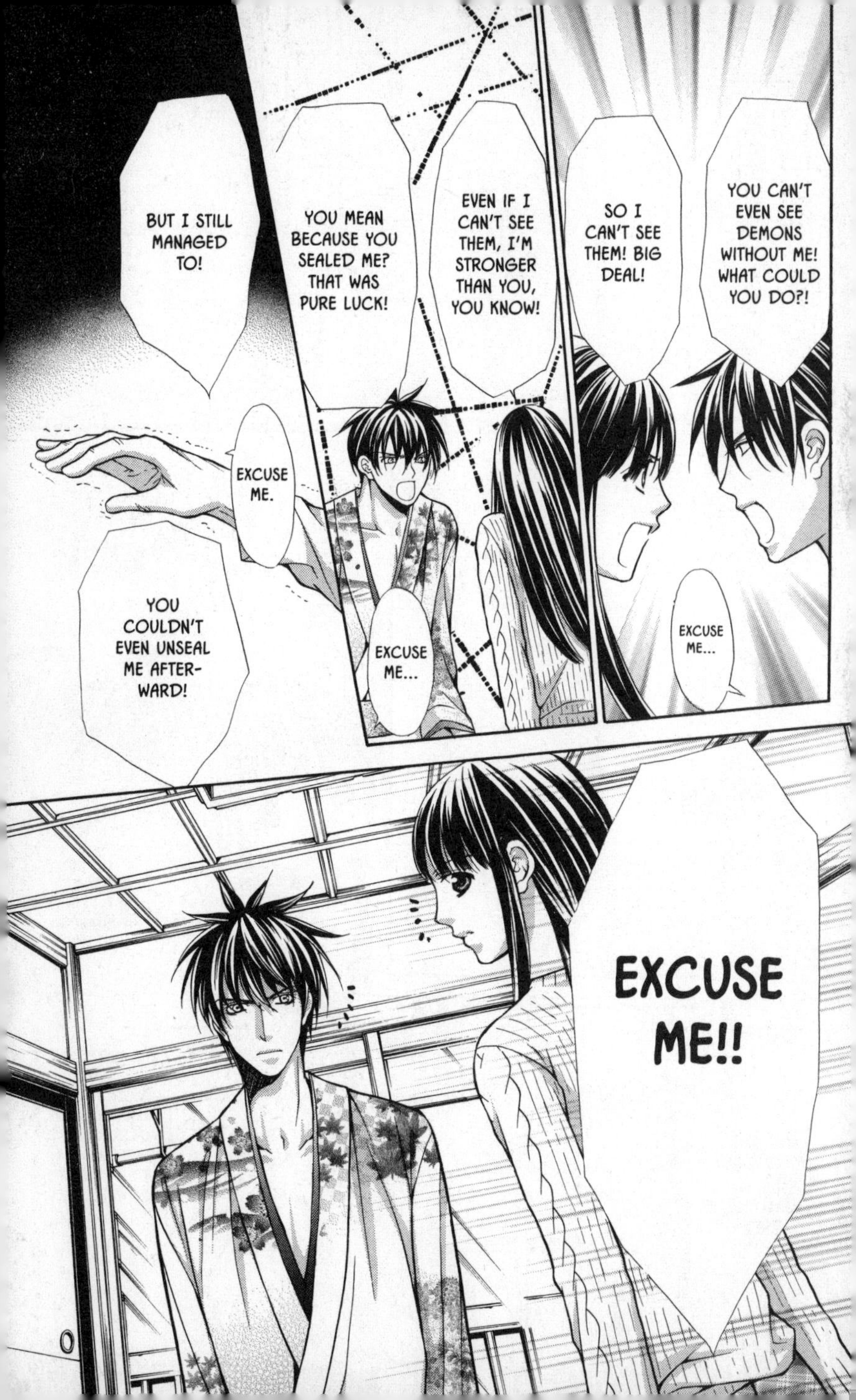
YOU CAN'T EVEN SEE DEMONS WITHOUT ME! WHAT COULD YOU DO?!
SO I CAN'T SEE THEM! BIG DEAL!
EXCUSE ME...
EVEN IF I CAN'T SEE THEM, I'M STRONGER THAN YOU, YOU KNOW!
YOU MEAN BECAUSE YOU SEALED ME? THAT WAS PURE LUCK!
EXCUSE ME...
BUT I STILL MANAGED TO!
EXCUSE ME.
YOU COULDN'T EVEN UNSEAL ME AFTER-WARD!
EXCUSE ME!!

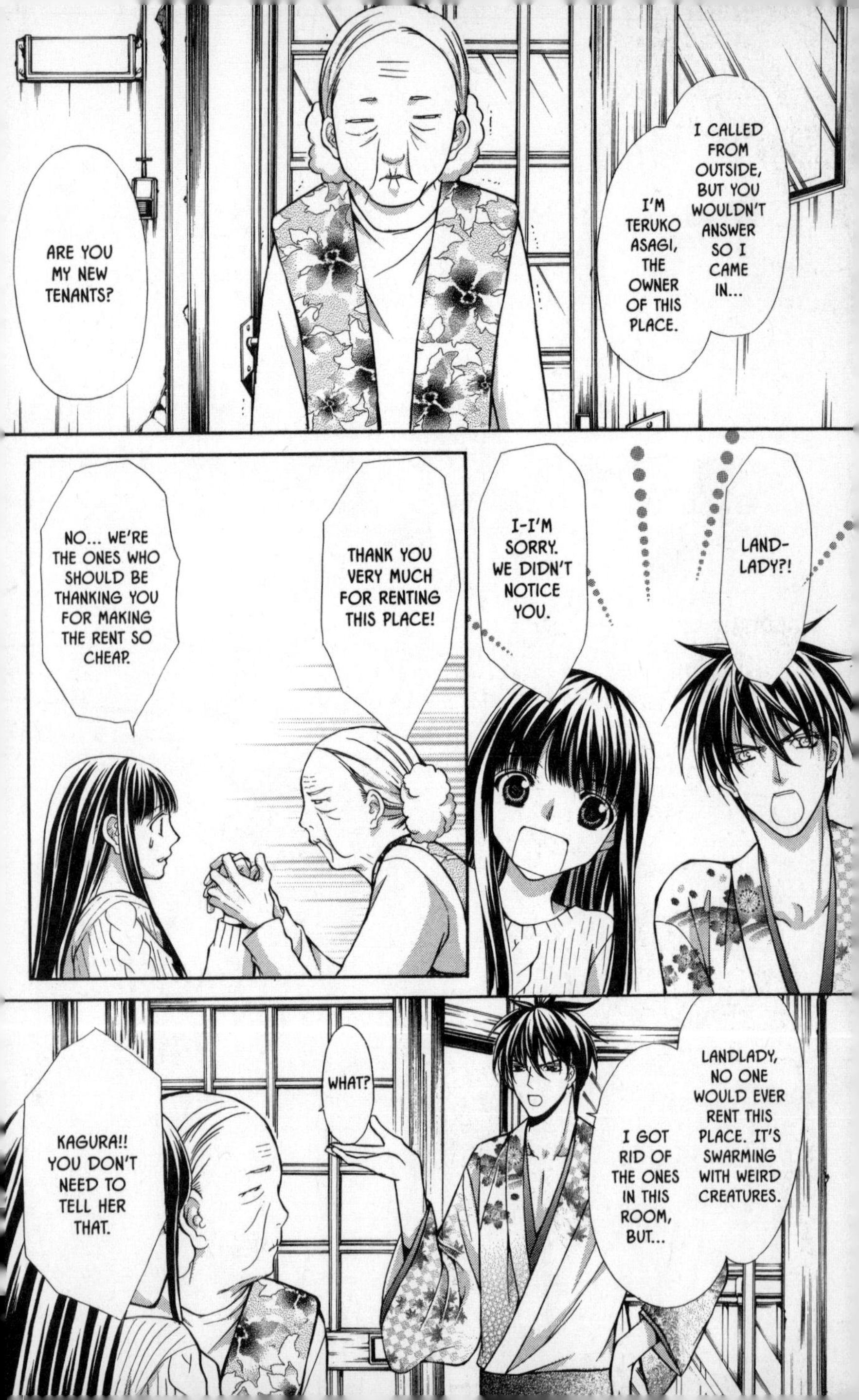
I CALLED FROM OUTSIDE, BUT YOU WOULDN'T ANSWER SO I CAME IN...
I'M TERUKO ASAGI, THE OWNER OF THIS PLACE.
ARE YOU MY NEW TENANTS?
LAND-LADY?!
I-I'M SORRY. WE DIDN'T NOTICE YOU.
THANK YOU VERY MUCH FOR RENTING THIS PLACE!
NO... WE'RE THE ONES WHO SHOULD BE THANKING YOU FOR MAKING THE RENT SO CHEAP.
LANDLADY, NO ONE WOULD EVER RENT THIS PLACE. IT'S SWARMING WITH WEIRD CREATURES.
I GOT RID OF THE ONES IN THIS ROOM, BUT...
WHAT?
KAGURA!! YOU DON'T NEED TO TELL HER THAT.

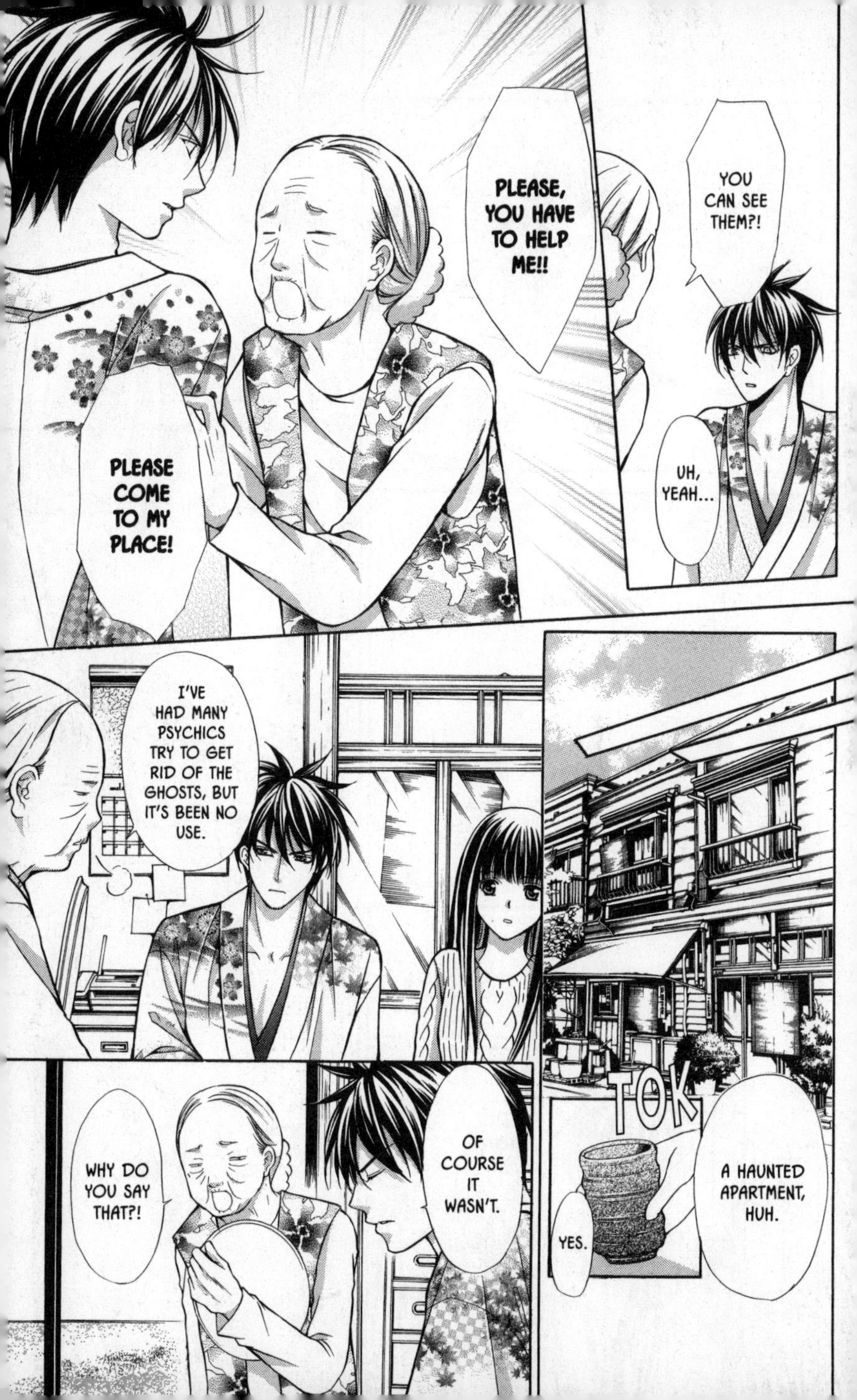
YOU CAN SEE THEM?!
UH, YEAH...
PLEASE, YOU HAVE TO HELP ME!!
PLEASE COME TO MY PLACE!
TOK
A HAUNTED APARTMENT, HUH.
YES.
I'VE HAD MANY PSYCHICS TRY TO GET RID OF THE GHOSTS, BUT IT'S BEEN NO USE.
OF COURSE IT WASN'T.
WHY DO YOU SAY THAT?!

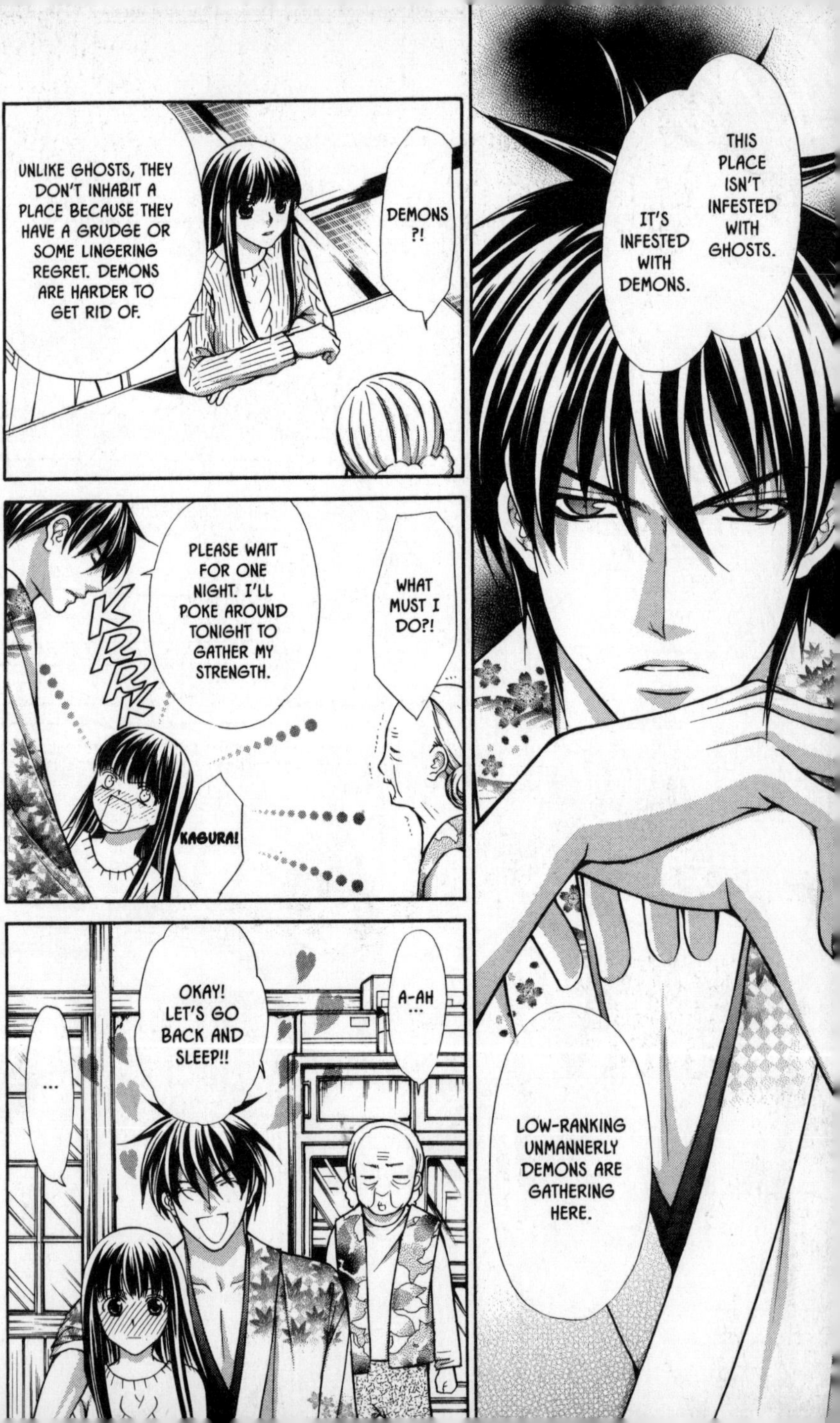
THIS PLACE ISN'T INFESTED WITH GHOSTS.
IT'S INFESTED WITH DEMONS.
LOW-RANKING UNMANNERLY DEMONS ARE GATHERING HERE.
DEMONS?!
UNLIKE GHOSTS, THEY DON'T INHABIT A PLACE BECAUSE THEY HAVE A GRUDGE OR SOME LINGERING REGRET. DEMONS ARE HARDER TO GET RID OF.
WHAT MUST I DO?!
PLEASE WAIT FOR ONE NIGHT. I'LL POKE AROUND TONIGHT TO GATHER MY STRENGTH.
KRRRK
KAGURA!
A-AH...
OKAY! LET'S GO BACK AND SLEEP!!
...

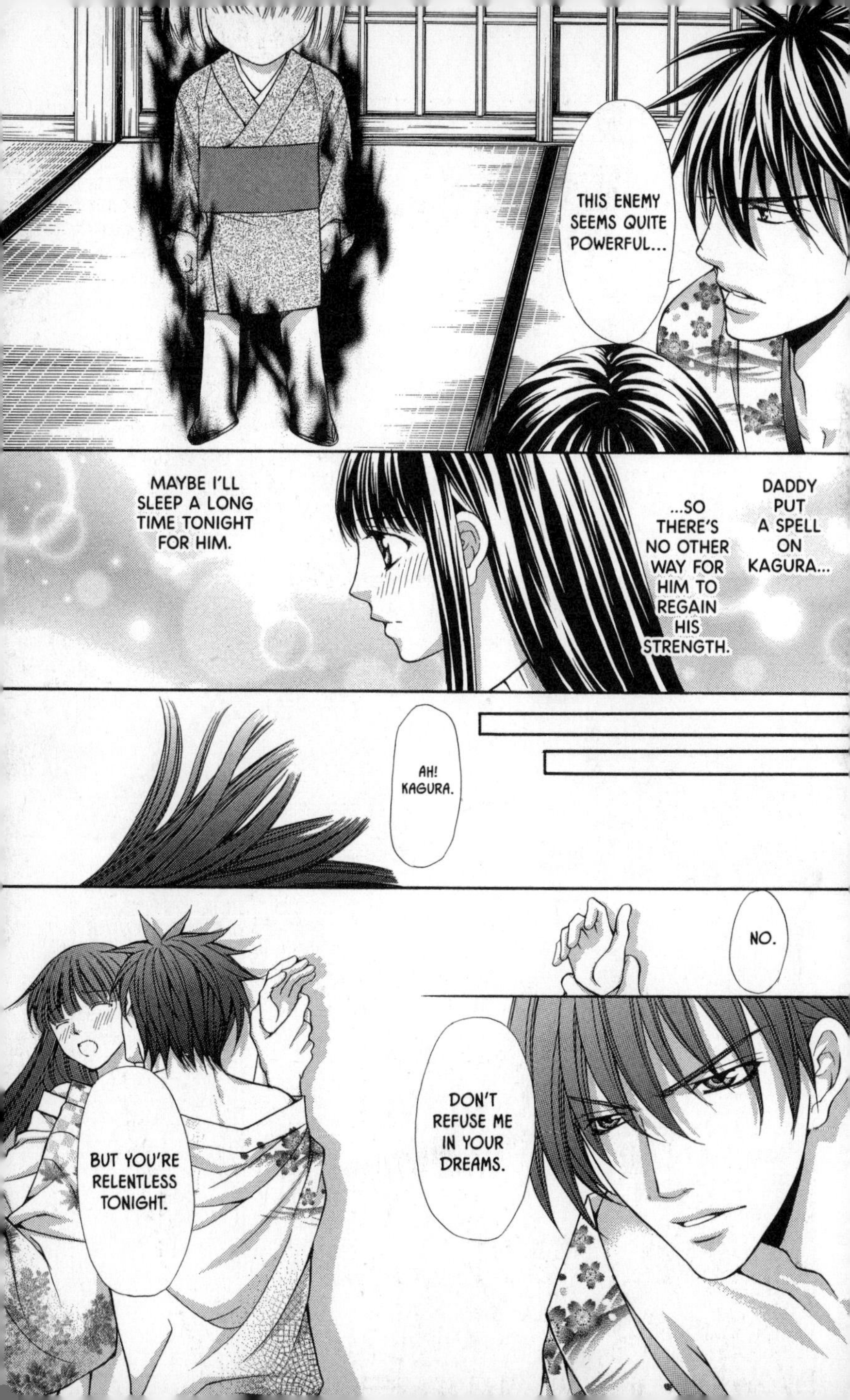
THIS ENEMY SEEMS QUITE POWERFUL...
DADDY PUT A SPELL ON KAGURA...
...SO THERE'S NO OTHER WAY FOR HIM TO REGAIN HIS STRENGTH.
MAYBE I'LL SLEEP A LONG TIME TONIGHT FOR HIM.
AH! KAGURA.
NO.
DON'T REFUSE ME IN YOUR DREAMS.
BUT YOU'RE RELENTLESS TONIGHT.

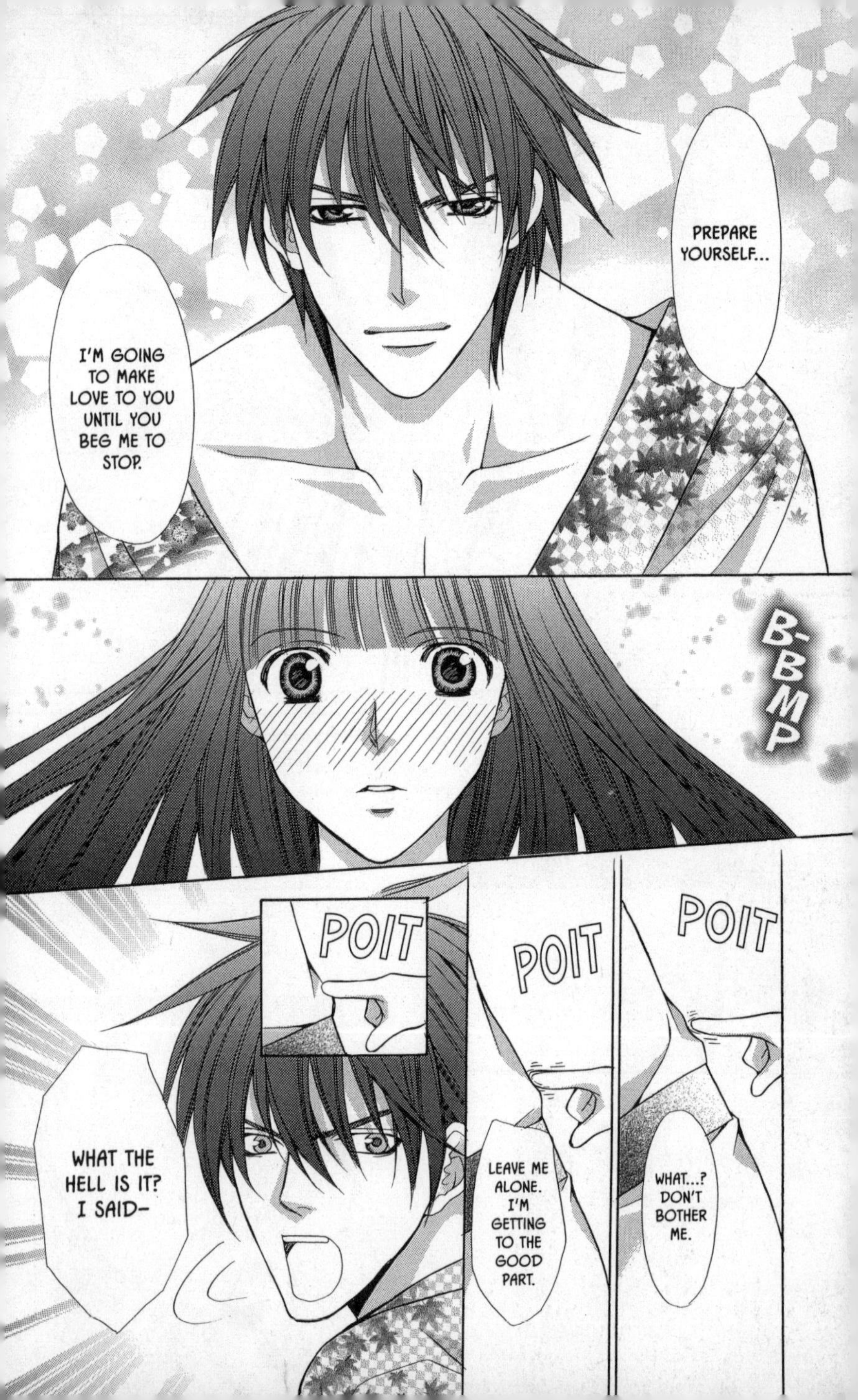
PREPARE YOURSELF...
I'M GOING TO MAKE LOVE TO YOU UNTIL YOU BEG ME TO STOP.
B-BMP
POIT
WHAT...? DON'T BOTHER ME.
POIT
LEAVE ME ALONE. I'M GETTING TO THE GOOD PART.
POIT
WHAT THE HELL IS IT? I SAID–

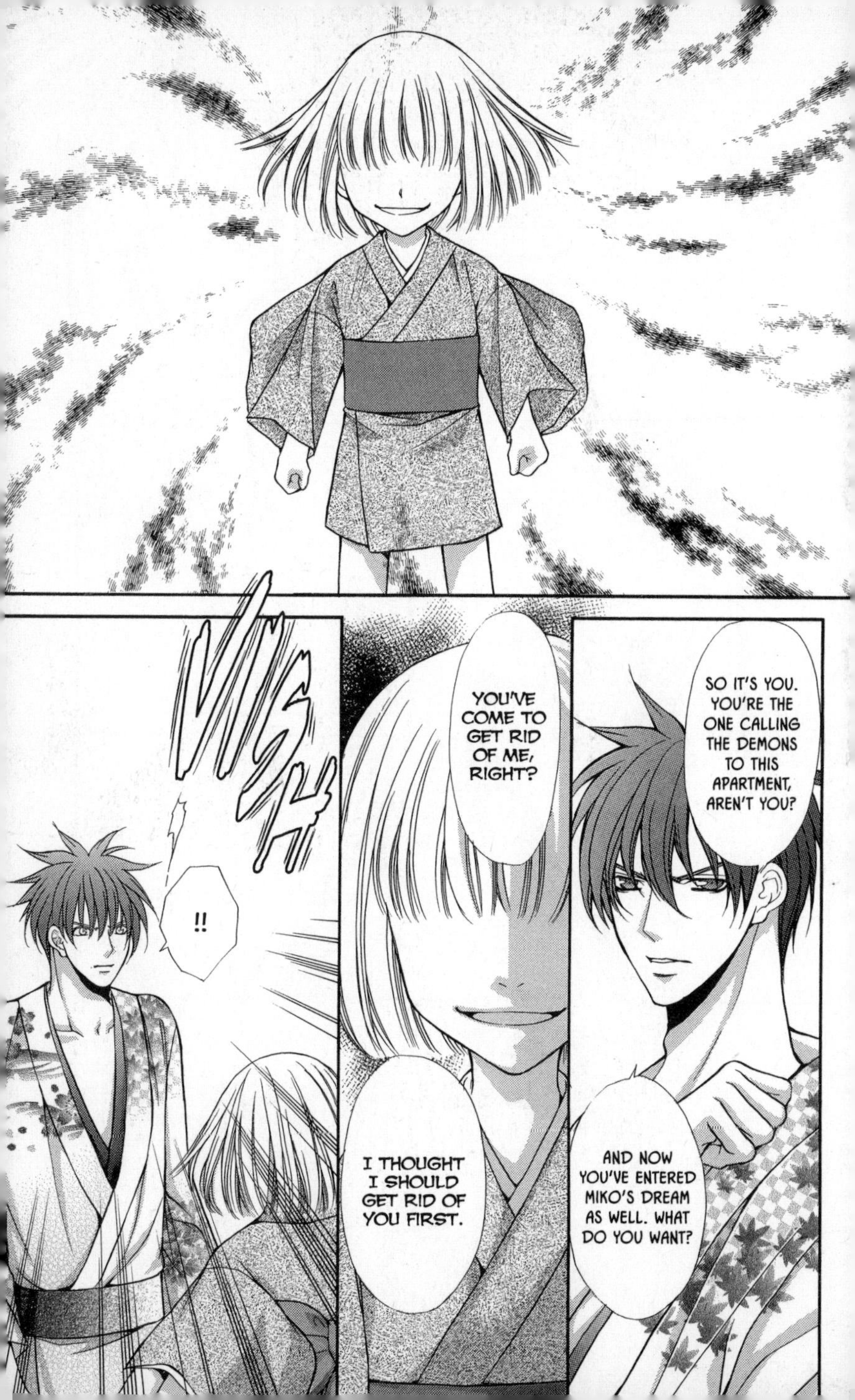

SO IT'S YOU. YOU'RE THE ONE CALLING THE DEMONS TO THIS APARTMENT, AREN'T YOU?
AND NOW YOU'VE ENTERED MIKO'S DREAM AS WELL. WHAT DO YOU WANT?
YOU'VE COME TO GET RID OF ME, RIGHT?
I THOUGHT I SHOULD GET RID OF YOU FIRST.
VISH
!!

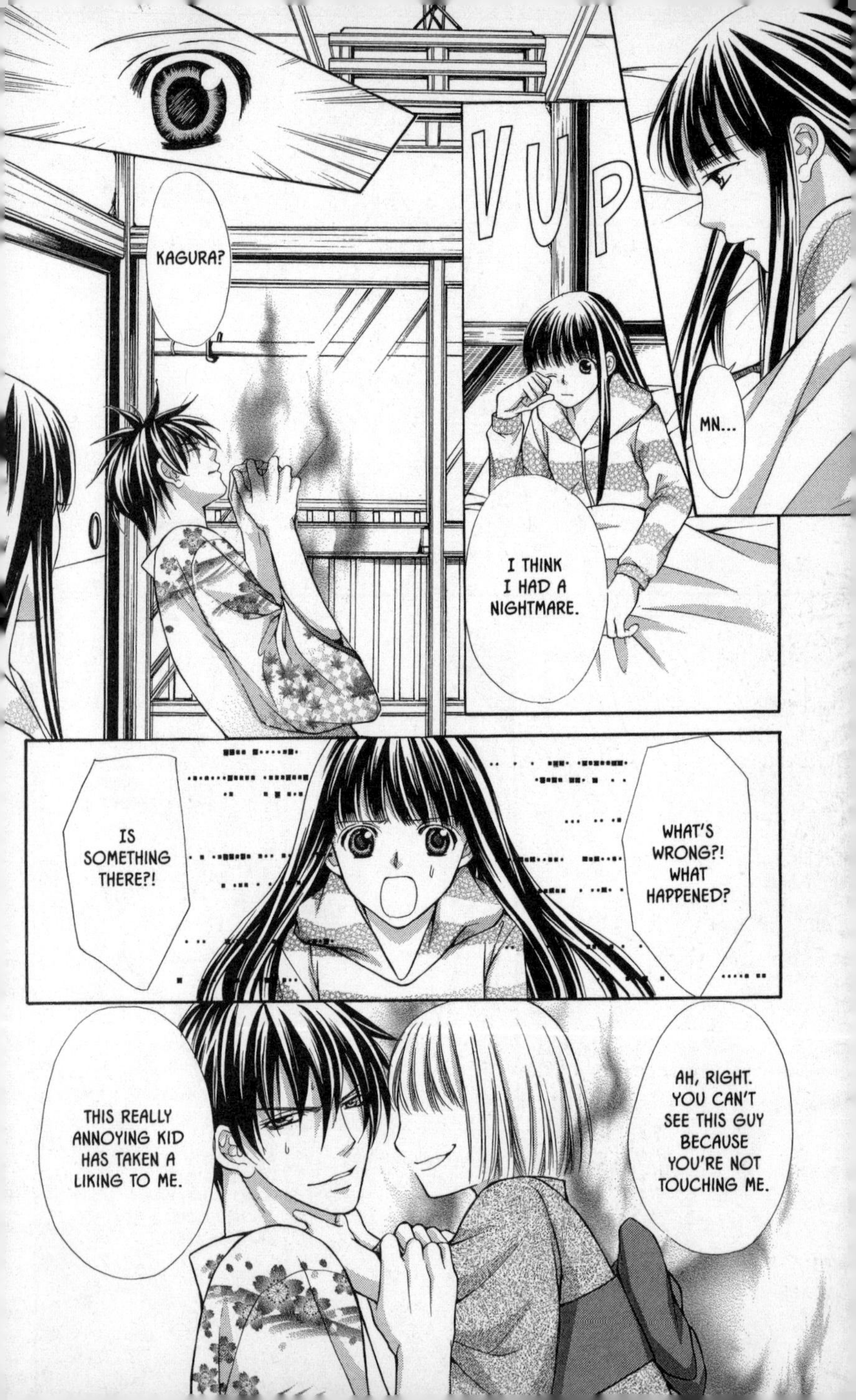
MN...
VUP
I THINK I HAD A NIGHTMARE.
KAGURA?
WHAT'S WRONG?! WHAT HAPPENED?
IS SOMETHING THERE?!
AH, RIGHT. YOU CAN'T SEE THIS GUY BECAUSE YOU'RE NOT TOUCHING ME.
THIS REALLY ANNOYING KID HAS TAKEN A LIKING TO ME.

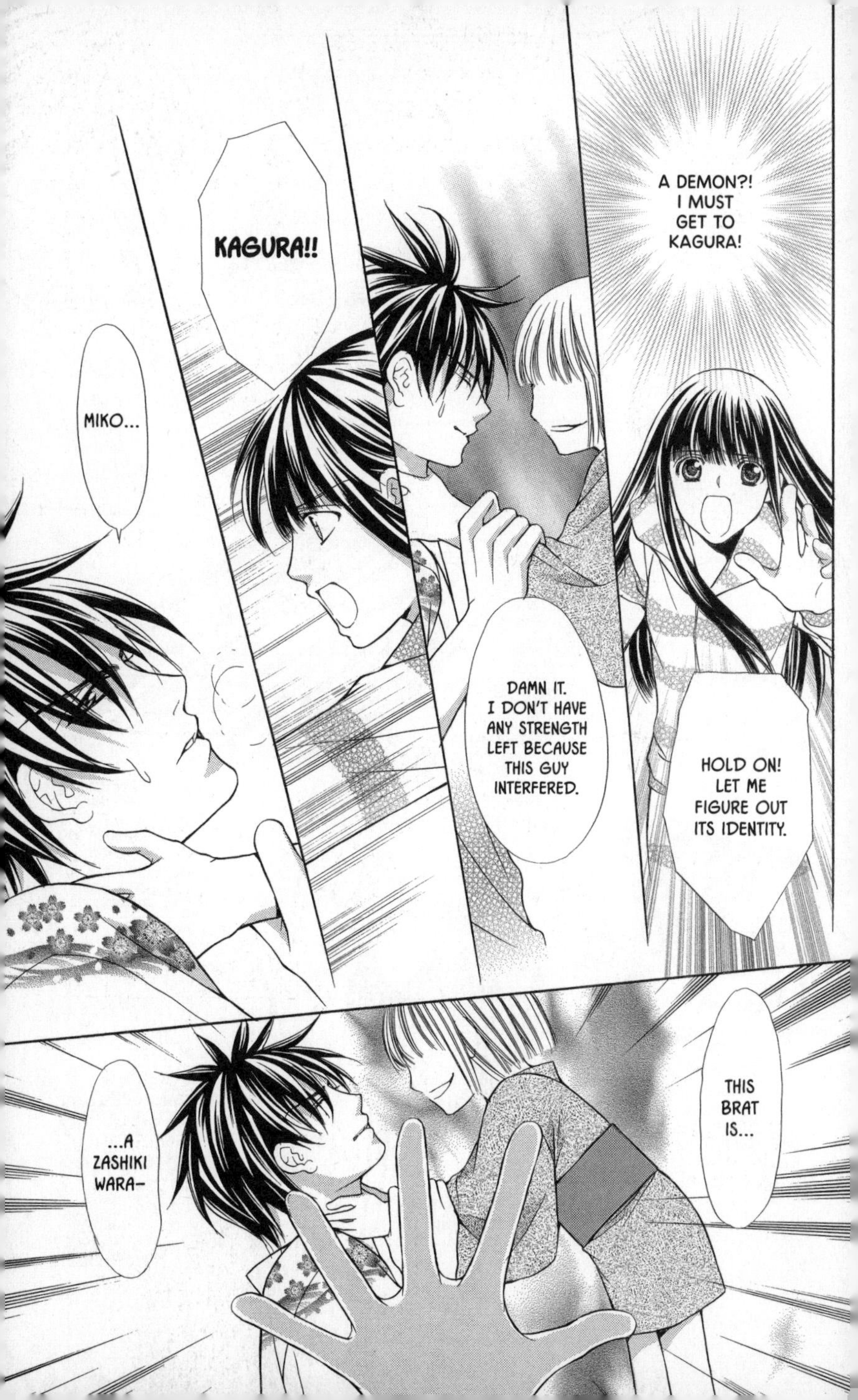
A DEMON?! I MUST GET TO KAGURA!
HOLD ON! LET ME FIGURE OUT ITS IDENTITY.
DAMN IT. I DON'T HAVE ANY STRENGTH LEFT BECAUSE THIS GUY INTERFERED.
KAGURA!!
MIKO...
THIS BRAT IS...
...A ZASHIKI WARA-

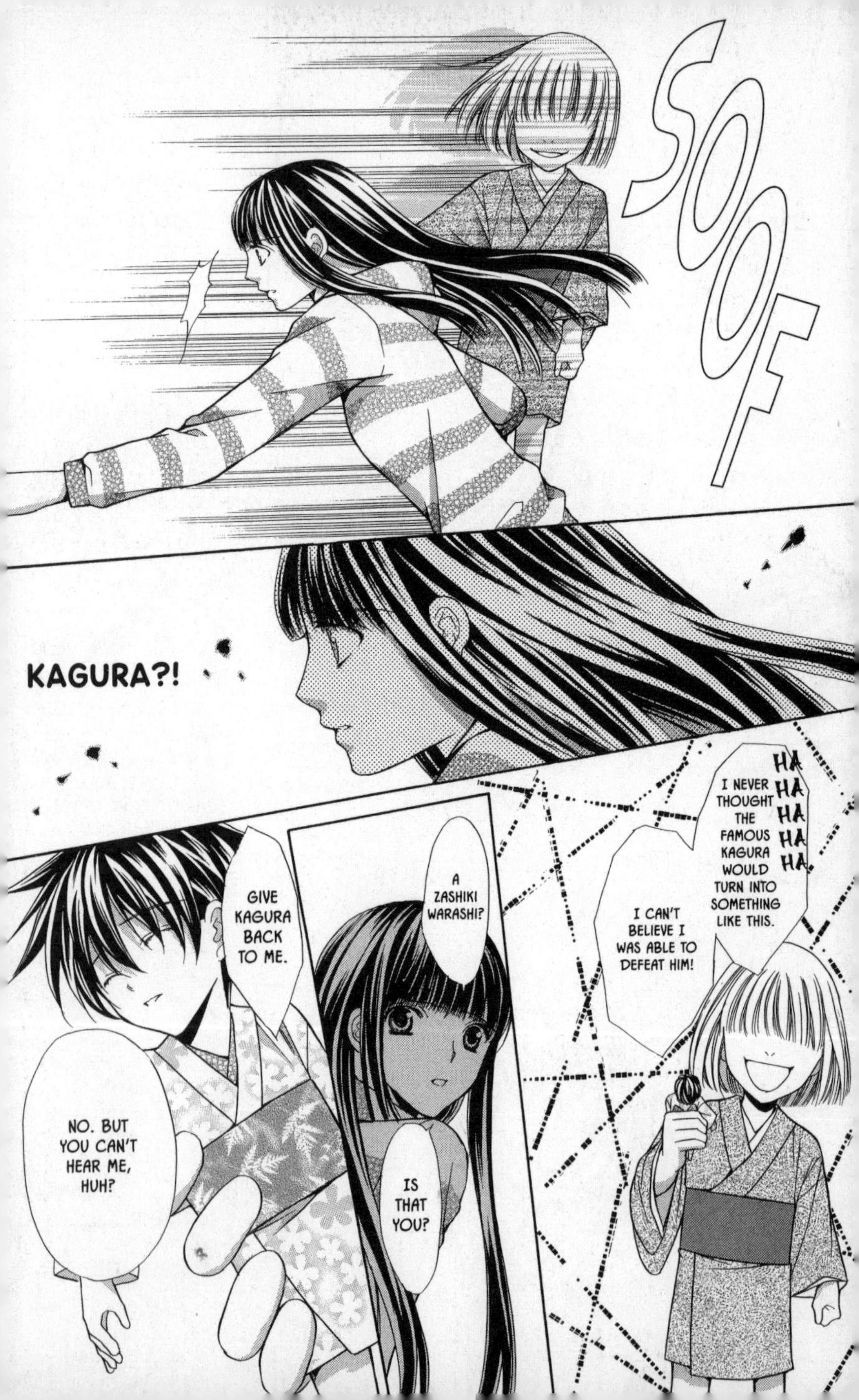
SOOF
KAGURA?!
HA HA HA HA HA
I NEVER THOUGHT THE FAMOUS KAGURA WOULD TURN INTO SOMETHING LIKE THIS.
I CAN'T BELIEVE I WAS ABLE TO DEFEAT HIM!
A ZASHIKI WARASHI?
IS THAT YOU?
GIVE KAGURA BACK TO ME.
NO. BUT YOU CAN'T HEAR ME, HUH?

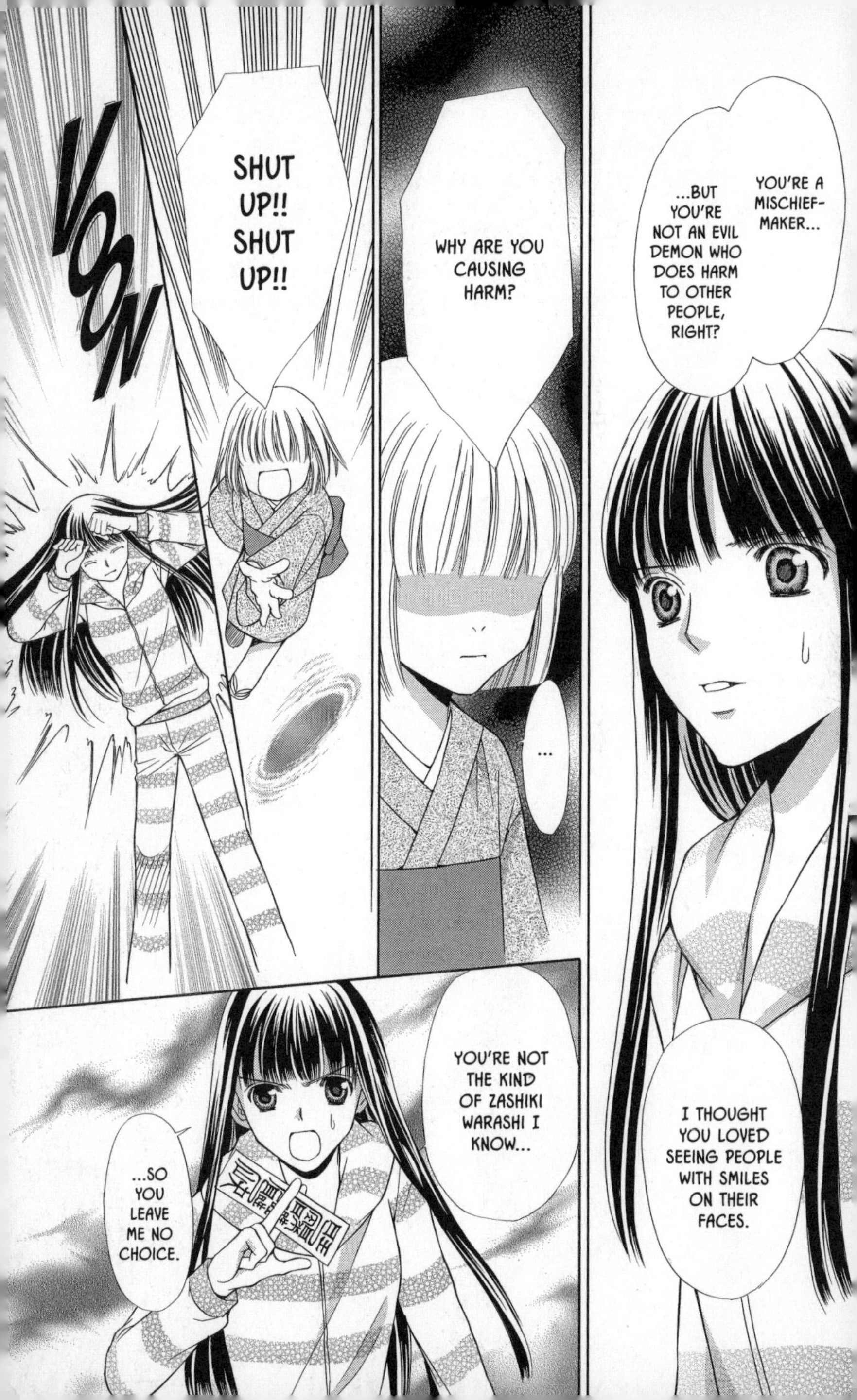
YOU'RE A MISCHIEF-MAKER...
...BUT YOU'RE NOT AN EVIL DEMON WHO DOES HARM TO OTHER PEOPLE, RIGHT?
I THOUGHT YOU LOVED SEEING PEOPLE WITH SMILES ON THEIR FACES.
WHY ARE YOU CAUSING HARM?
...
SHUT UP!! SHUT UP!!
VOON
YOU'RE NOT THE KIND OF ZASHIKI WARASHI I KNOW...
...SO YOU LEAVE ME NO CHOICE.

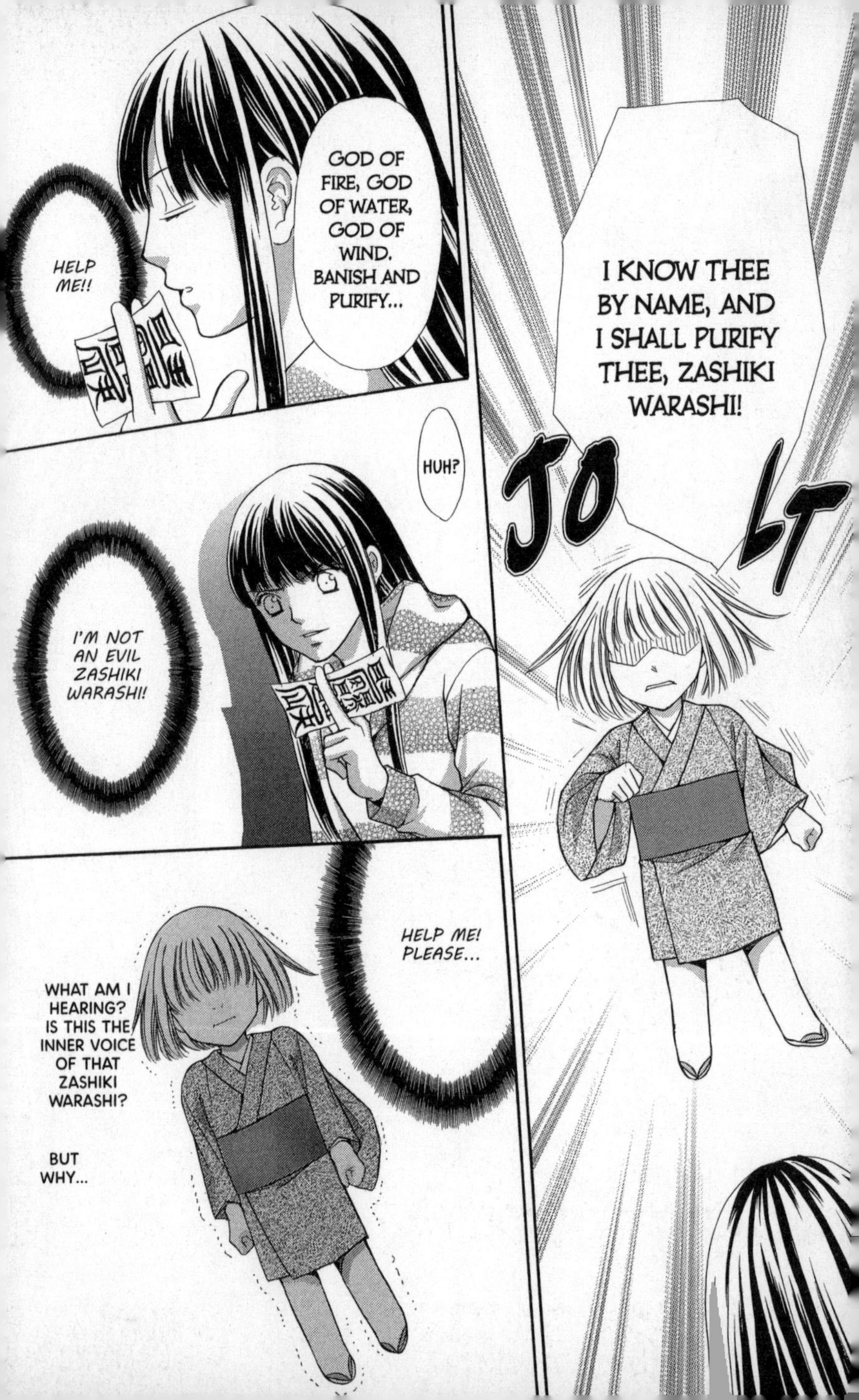
I KNOW THEE BY NAME, AND I SHALL PURIFY THEE, ZASHIKI WARASHI!
JOLT
GOD OF FIRE, GOD OF WATER, GOD OF WIND. BANISH AND PURIFY...
HELP ME!!
HUH?
I'M NOT AN EVIL ZASHIKI WARASHI!
HELP ME! PLEASE...
WHAT AM I HEARING? IS THIS THE INNER VOICE OF THAT ZASHIKI WARASHI?
BUT WHY...

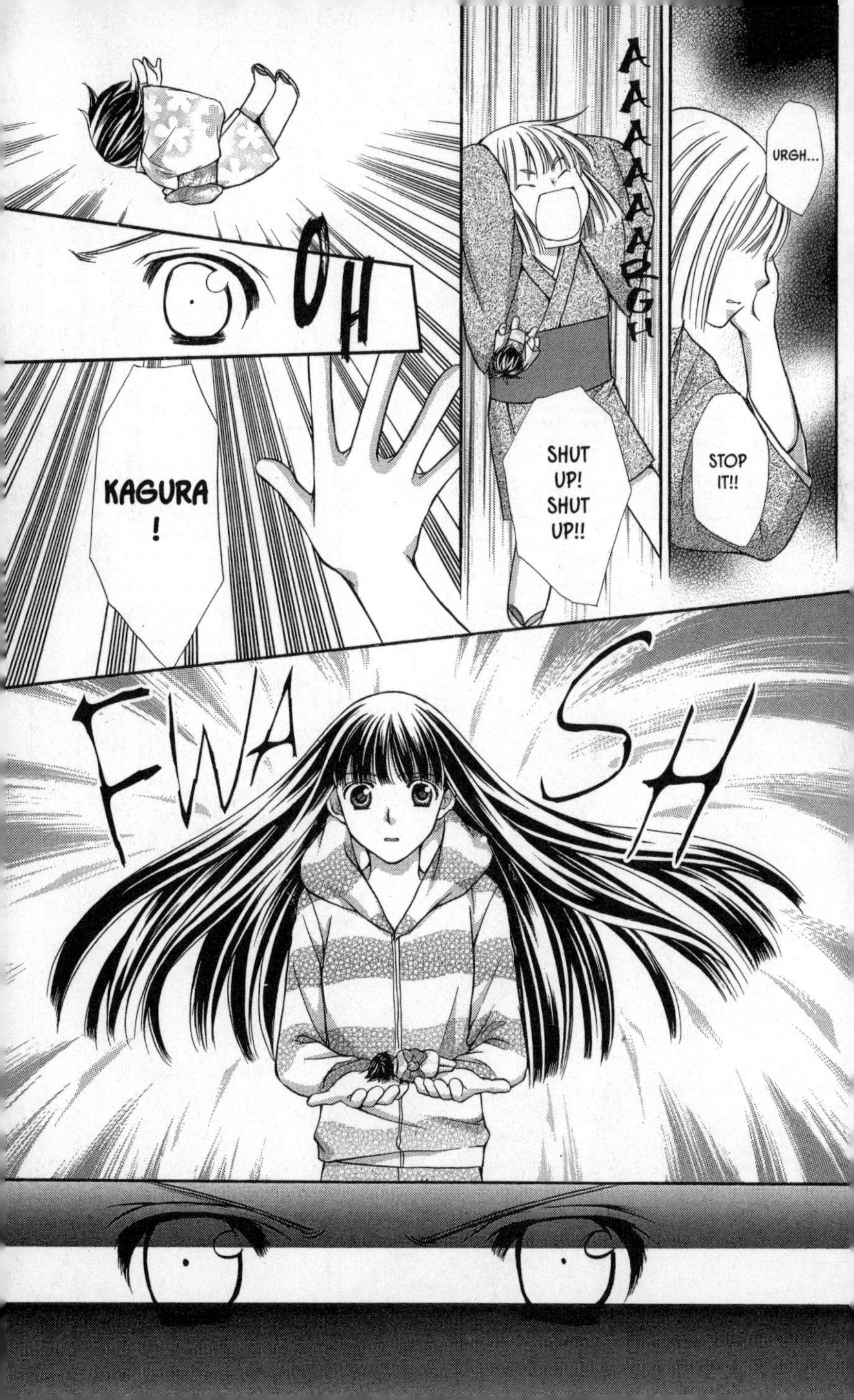
URGH...
STOP IT!!
AAAAAARGH
SHUT UP! SHUT UP!!
OH
KAGURA!
FWASH

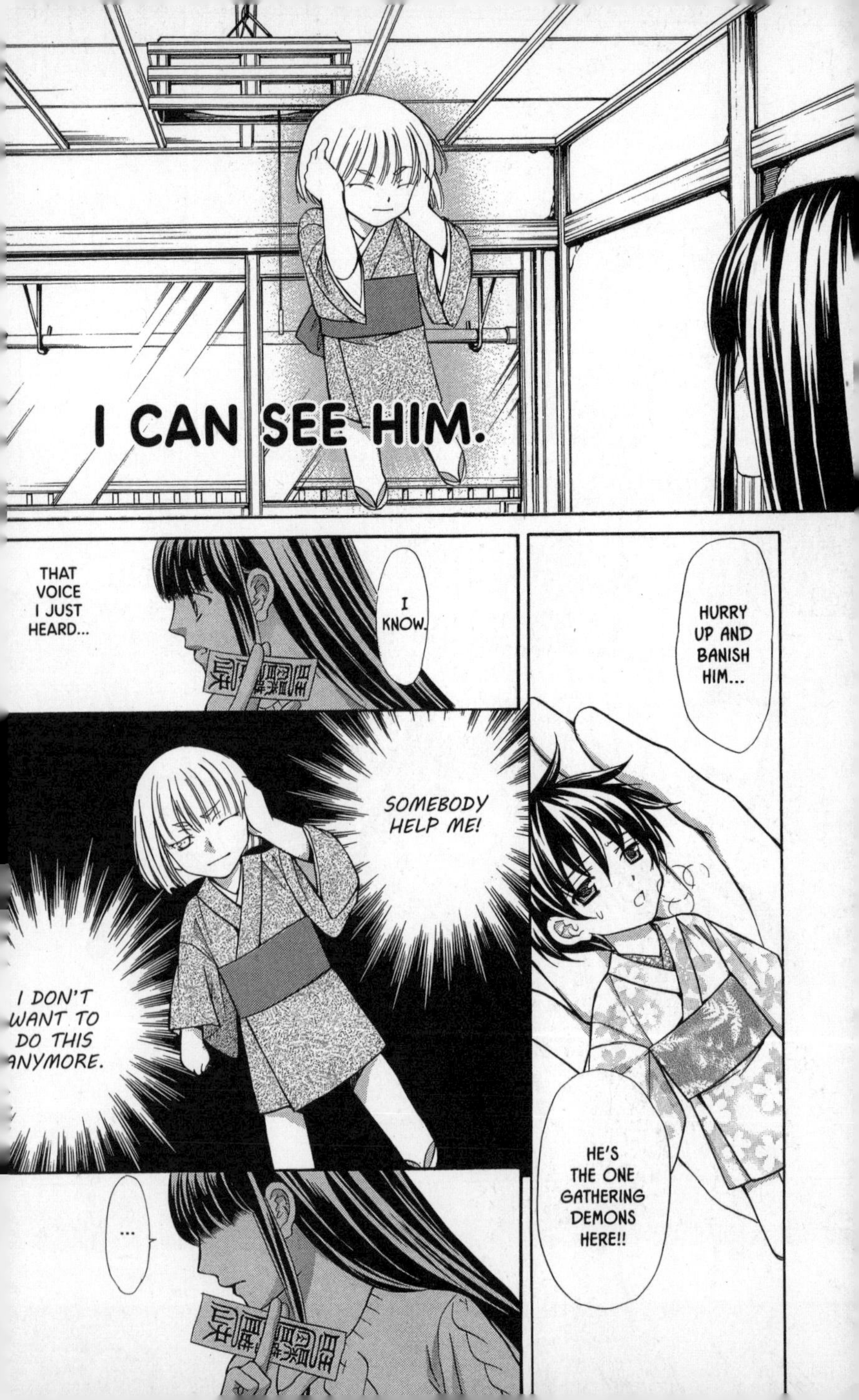
I CAN SEE HIM.
HURRY UP AND BANISH HIM...
HE'S THE ONE GATHERING DEMONS HERE!!
I KNOW.
THAT VOICE I JUST HEARD...
SOMEBODY HELP ME!
I DON'T WANT TO DO THIS ANYMORE.
...

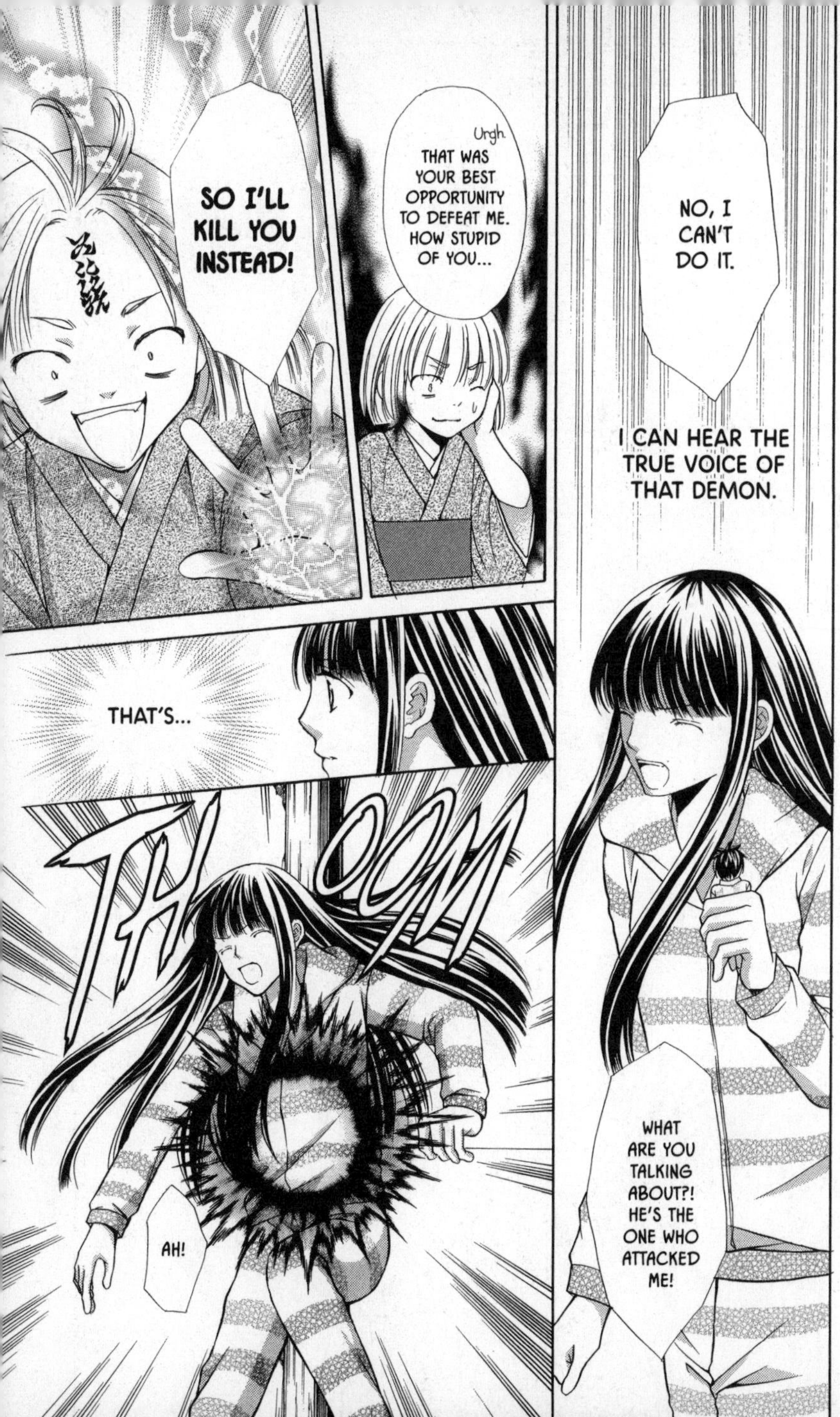
NO, I CAN'T DO IT.
I CAN HEAR THE TRUE VOICE OF THAT DEMON.
WHAT ARE YOU TALKING ABOUT?! HE'S THE ONE WHO ATTACKED ME!
Urgh.
THAT WAS YOUR BEST OPPORTUNITY TO DEFEAT ME. HOW STUPID OF YOU...
SO I'LL KILL YOU INSTEAD!
THAT'S...
THOOM
AH!

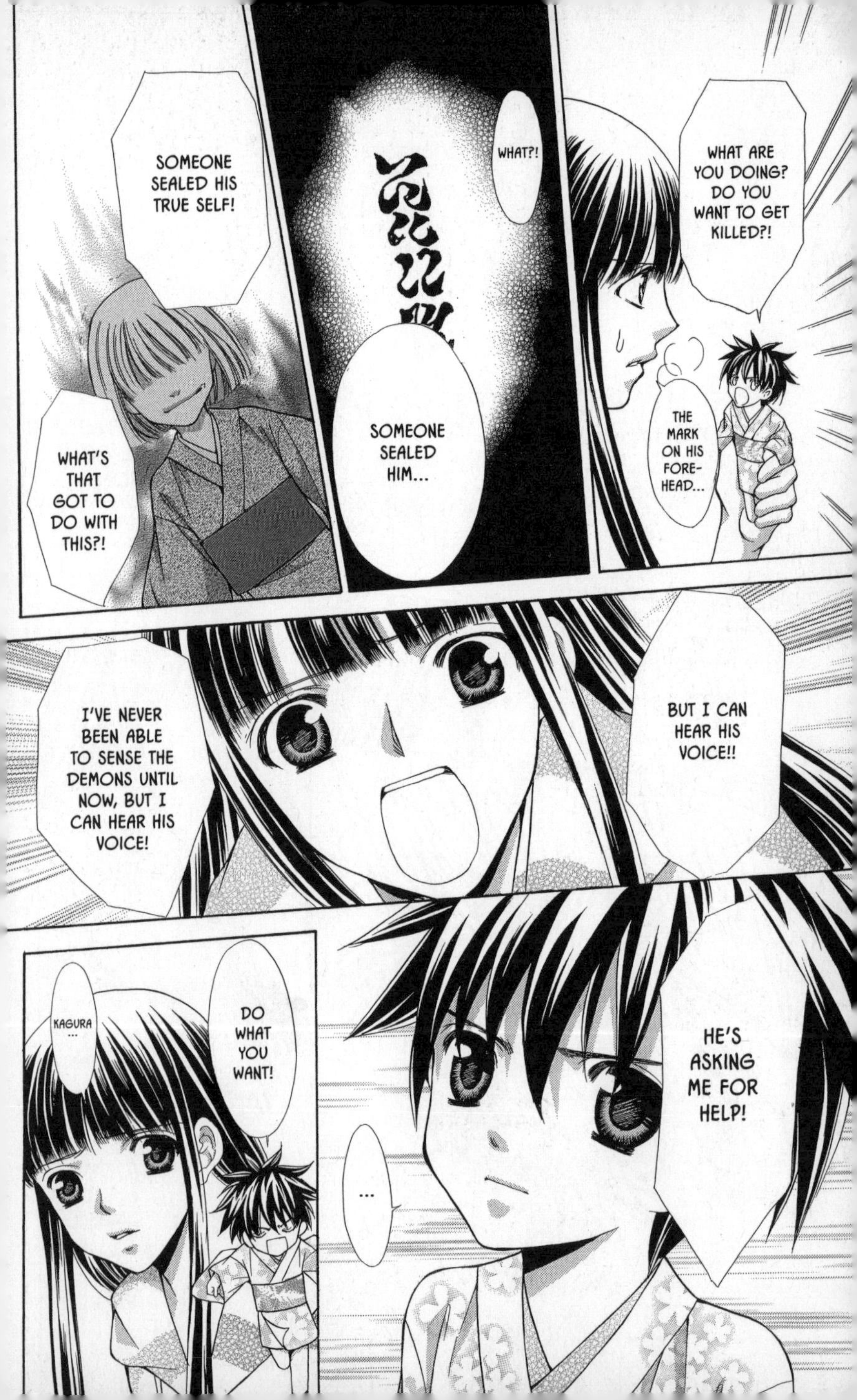
WHAT ARE YOU DOING? DO YOU WANT TO GET KILLED?!
WHAT?!
THE MARK ON HIS FORE-HEAD...
SOMEONE SEALED HIM...
SOMEONE SEALED HIS TRUE SELF!
WHAT'S THAT GOT TO DO WITH THIS?!
BUT I CAN HEAR HIS VOICE!!
I'VE NEVER BEEN ABLE TO SENSE THE DEMONS UNTIL NOW, BUT I CAN HEAR HIS VOICE!
HE'S ASKING ME FOR HELP!
...
DO WHAT YOU WANT!
KAGURA...

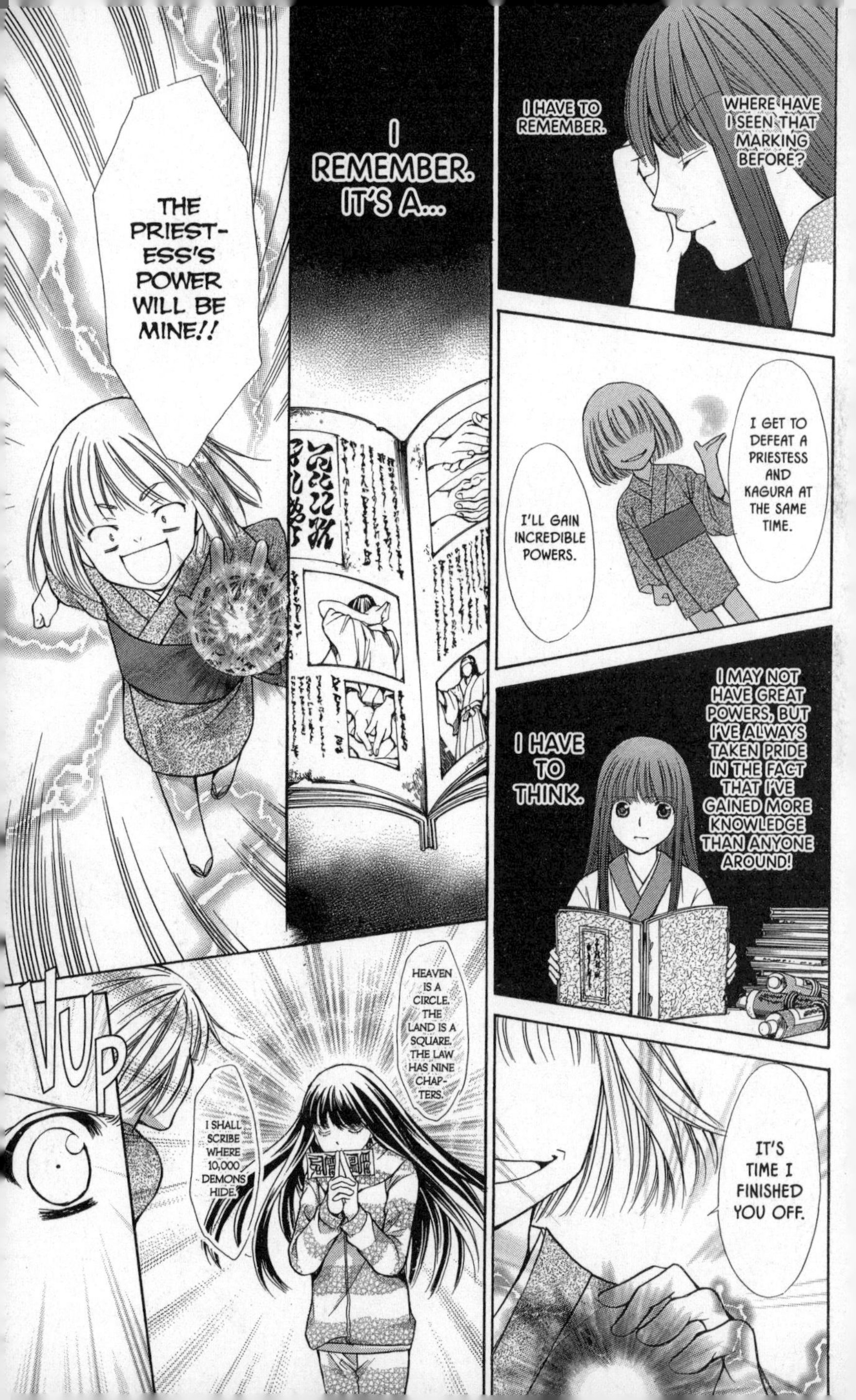
WHERE HAVE I SEEN THAT MARKING BEFORE?
I HAVE TO REMEMBER.
I GET TO DEFEAT A PRIESTESS AND KAGURA AT THE SAME TIME.
I'LL GAIN INCREDIBLE POWERS.
I MAY NOT HAVE GREAT POWERS, BUT I'VE ALWAYS TAKEN PRIDE IN THE FACT THAT I'VE GAINED MORE KNOWLEDGE THAN ANYONE AROUND!
I HAVE TO THINK.
I REMEMBER. IT'S A...
THE PRIEST-ESS'S POWER WILL BE MINE!!
IT'S TIME I FINISHED YOU OFF.
HEAVEN IS A CIRCLE. THE LAND IS A SQUARE. THE LAW HAS NINE CHAP-TERS.
I SHALL SCRIBE WHERE 10,000 DEMONS HIDE.
VUP

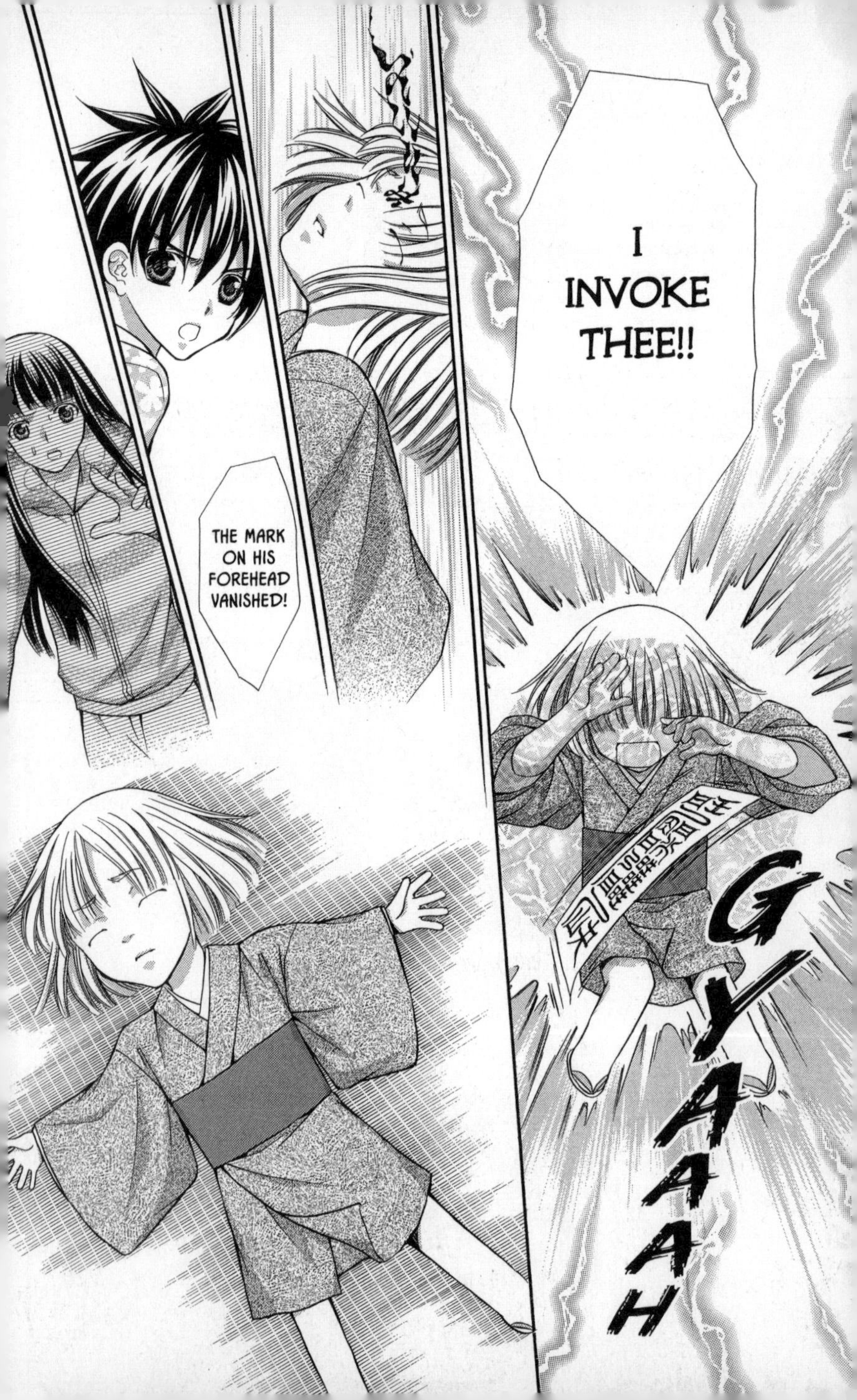
I INVOKE THEE!!
GYAAAAH
THE MARK ON HIS FOREHEAD VANISHED!

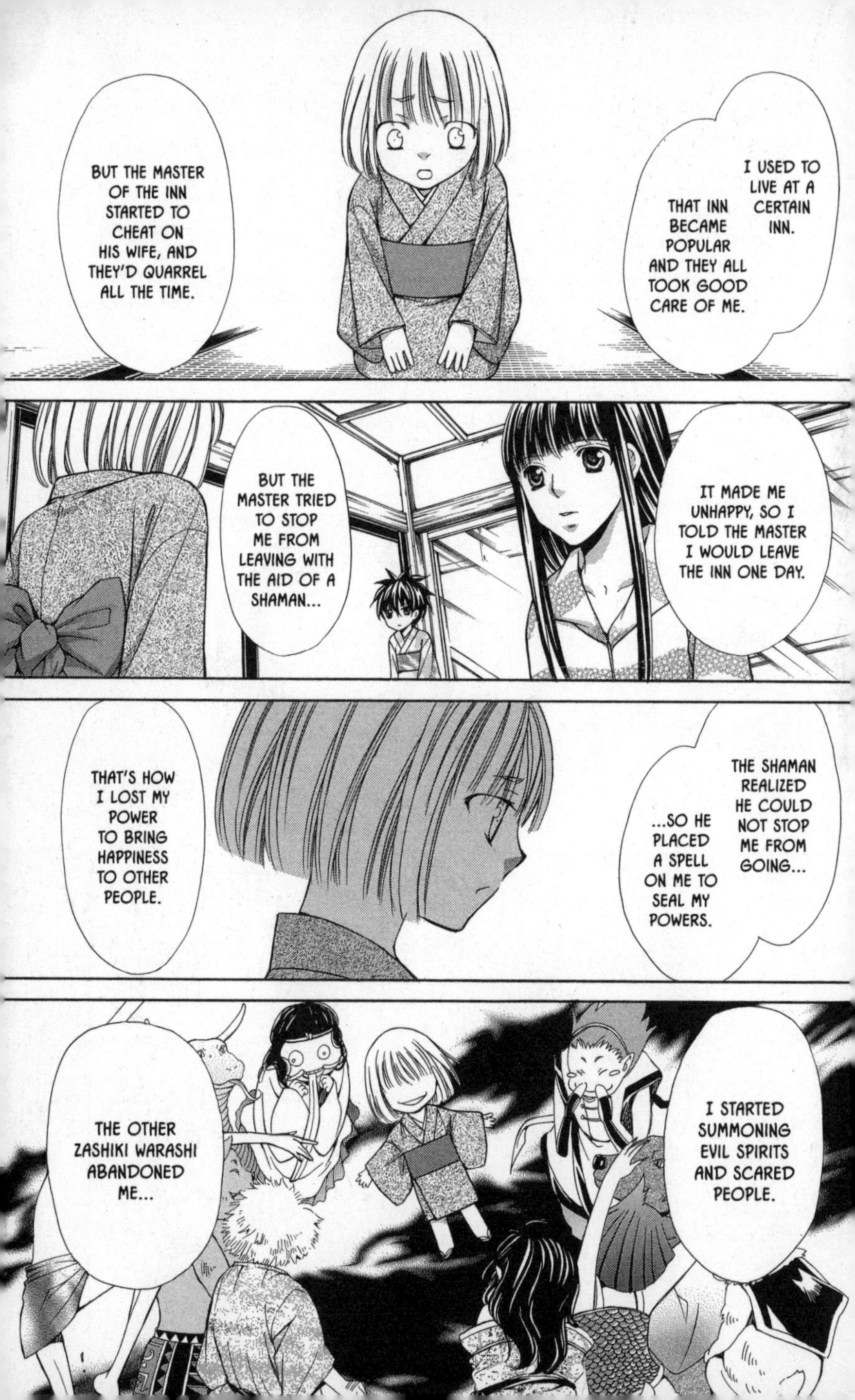
I USED TO LIVE AT A CERTAIN INN.
THAT INN BECAME POPULAR AND THEY ALL TOOK GOOD CARE OF ME.
BUT THE MASTER OF THE INN STARTED TO CHEAT ON HIS WIFE, AND THEY'D QUARREL ALL THE TIME.
IT MADE ME UNHAPPY, SO I TOLD THE MASTER I WOULD LEAVE THE INN ONE DAY.
BUT THE MASTER TRIED TO STOP ME FROM LEAVING WITH THE AID OF A SHAMAN...
THE SHAMAN REALIZED HE COULD NOT STOP ME FROM GOING...
...SO HE PLACED A SPELL ON ME TO SEAL MY POWERS.
THAT'S HOW I LOST MY POWER TO BRING HAPPINESS TO OTHER PEOPLE.
I STARTED SUMMONING EVIL SPIRITS AND SCARED PEOPLE.
THE OTHER ZASHIKI WARASHI ABANDONED ME...

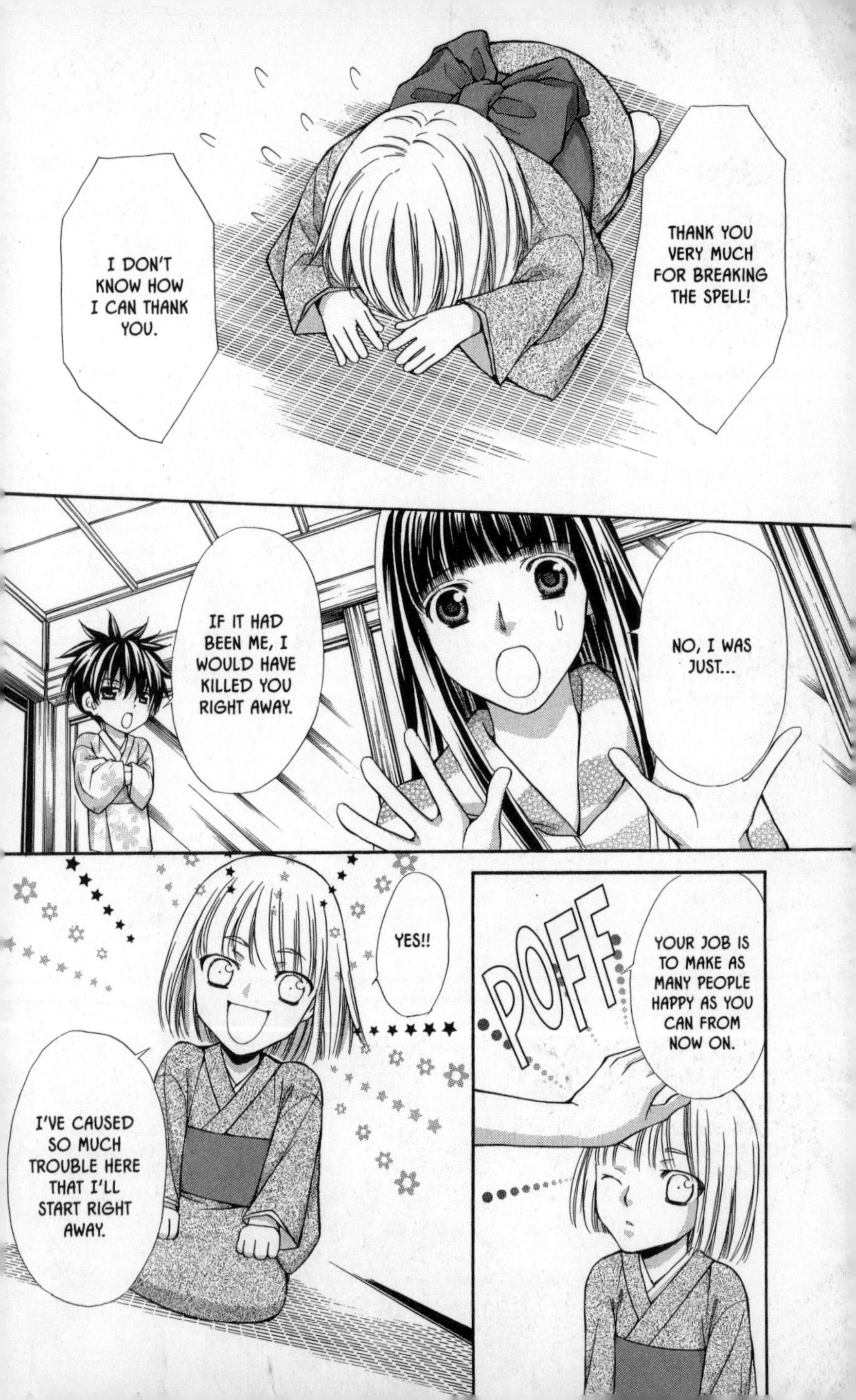
THANK YOU VERY MUCH FOR BREAKING THE SPELL!
I DON'T KNOW HOW I CAN THANK YOU.
NO, I WAS JUST...
IF IT HAD BEEN ME, I WOULD HAVE KILLED YOU RIGHT AWAY.
POFF
YOUR JOB IS TO MAKE AS MANY PEOPLE HAPPY AS YOU CAN FROM NOW ON.
YES!!
I'VE CAUSED SO MUCH TROUBLE HERE THAT I'LL START RIGHT AWAY.

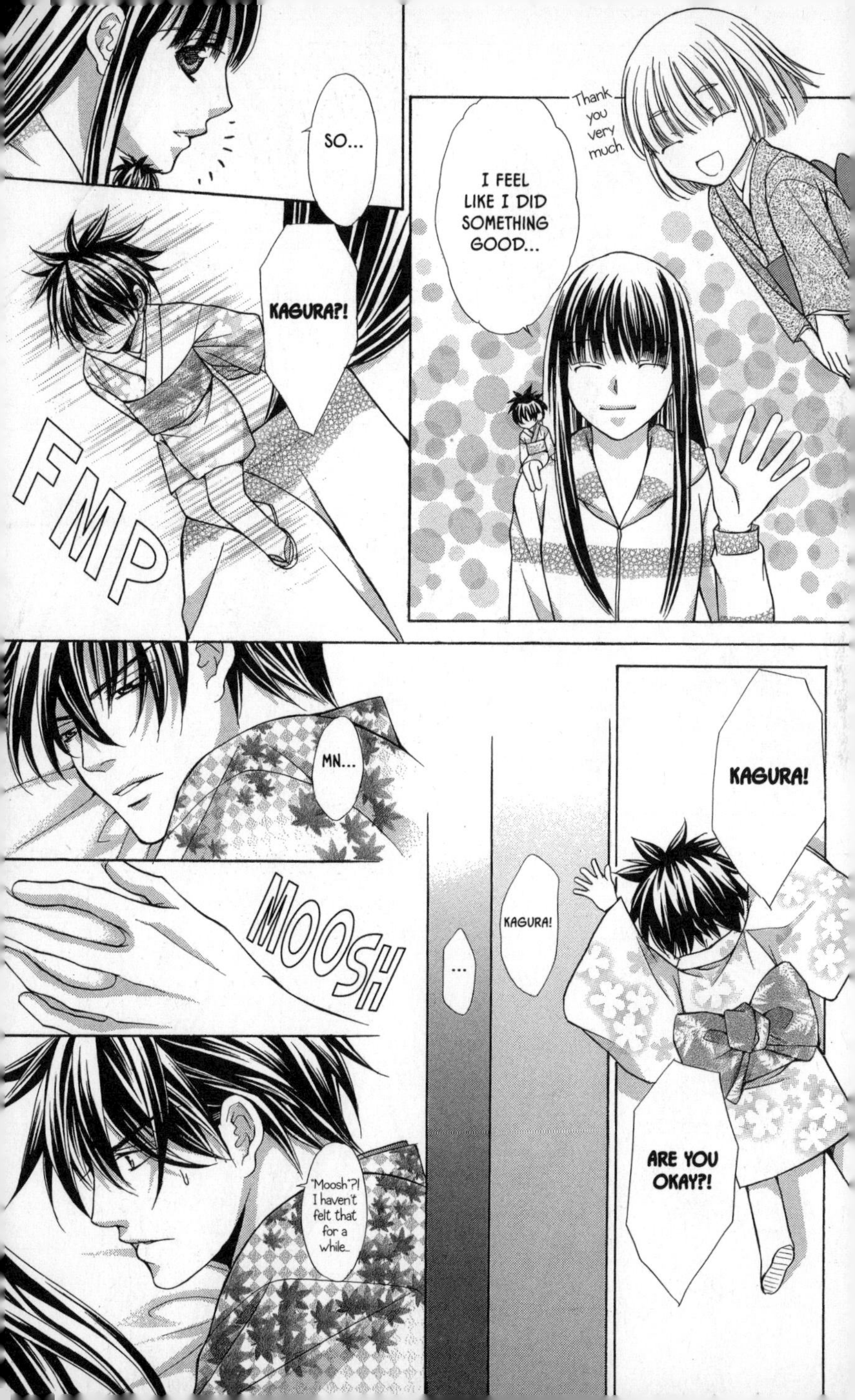
Thank you very much.
I FEEL LIKE I DID SOMETHING GOOD...
SO...
KAGURA?!
FMP
KAGURA!
ARE YOU OKAY?!
KAGURA!
...
MN...
MOOSH
"Moosh"?! I haven't felt that for a while...

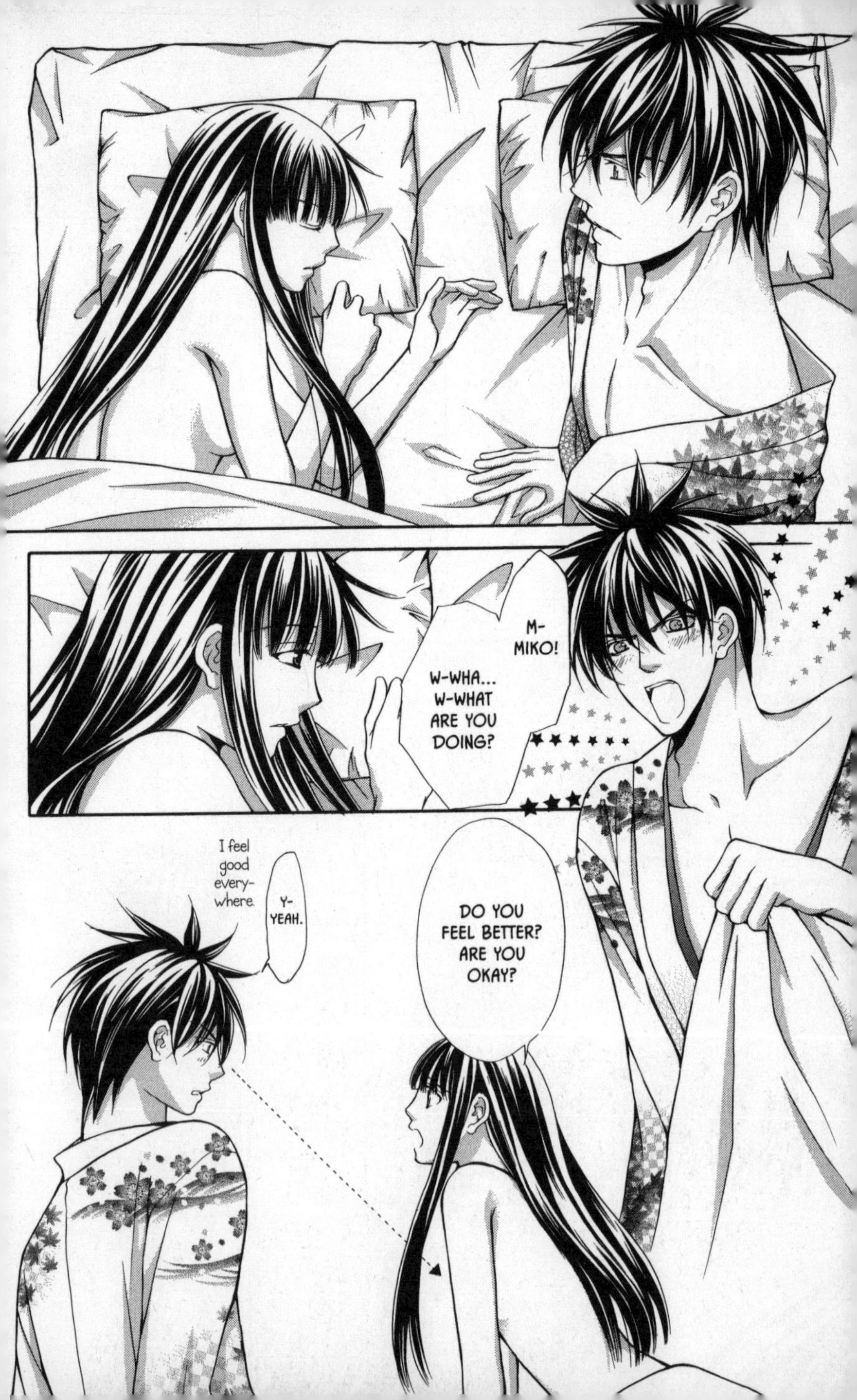
M-MIKO!
W-WHA... W-WHAT ARE YOU DOING?
DO YOU FEEL BETTER? ARE YOU OKAY?
Y-YEAH.
I feel good every-where.

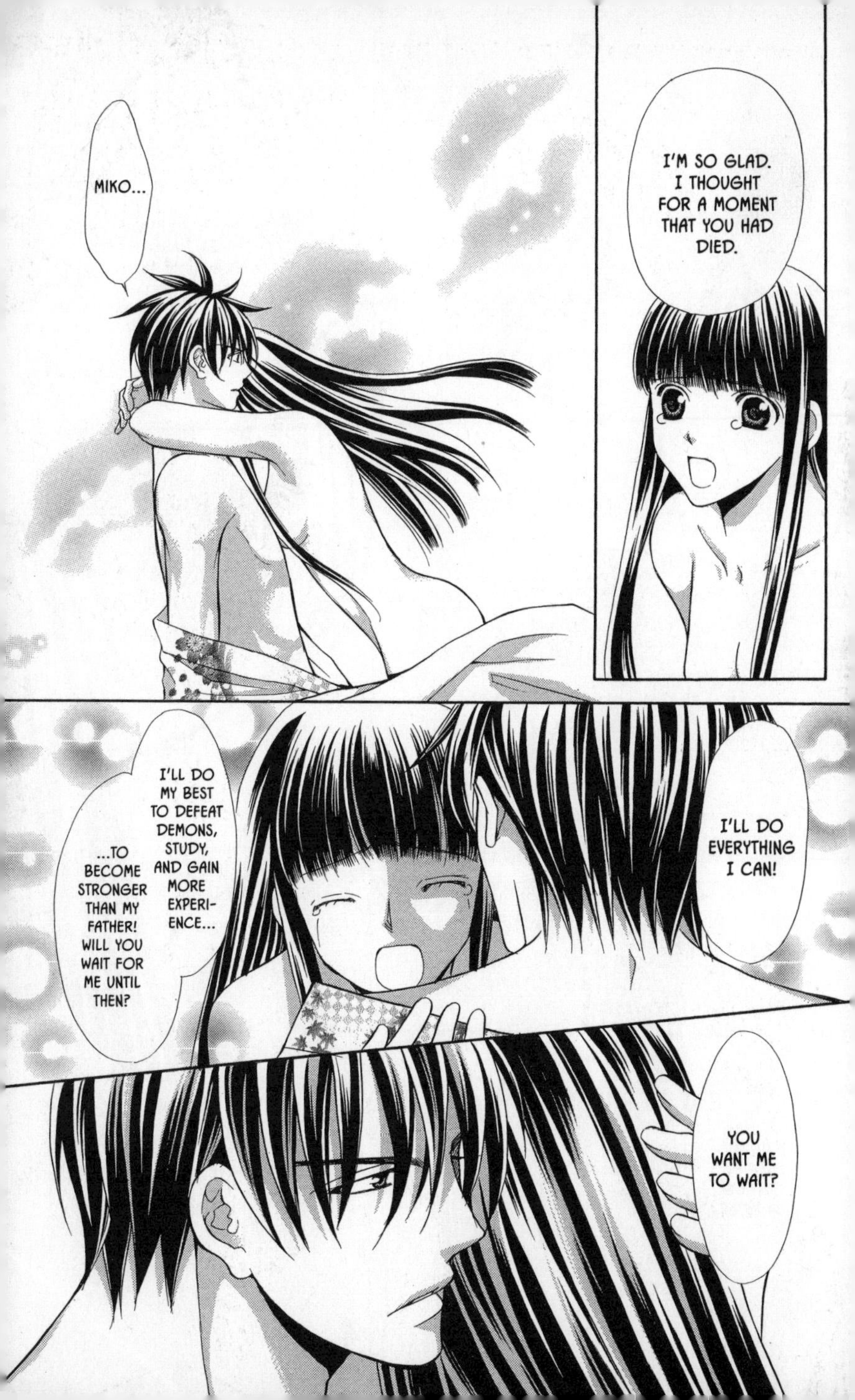
I'M SO GLAD. I THOUGHT FOR A MOMENT THAT YOU HAD DIED.
MIKO...
I'LL DO EVERYTHING I CAN!
I'LL DO MY BEST TO DEFEAT DEMONS, STUDY, AND GAIN MORE EXPERI-ENCE...
...TO BECOME STRONGER THAN MY FATHER! WILL YOU WAIT FOR ME UNTIL THEN?
YOU WANT ME TO WAIT?

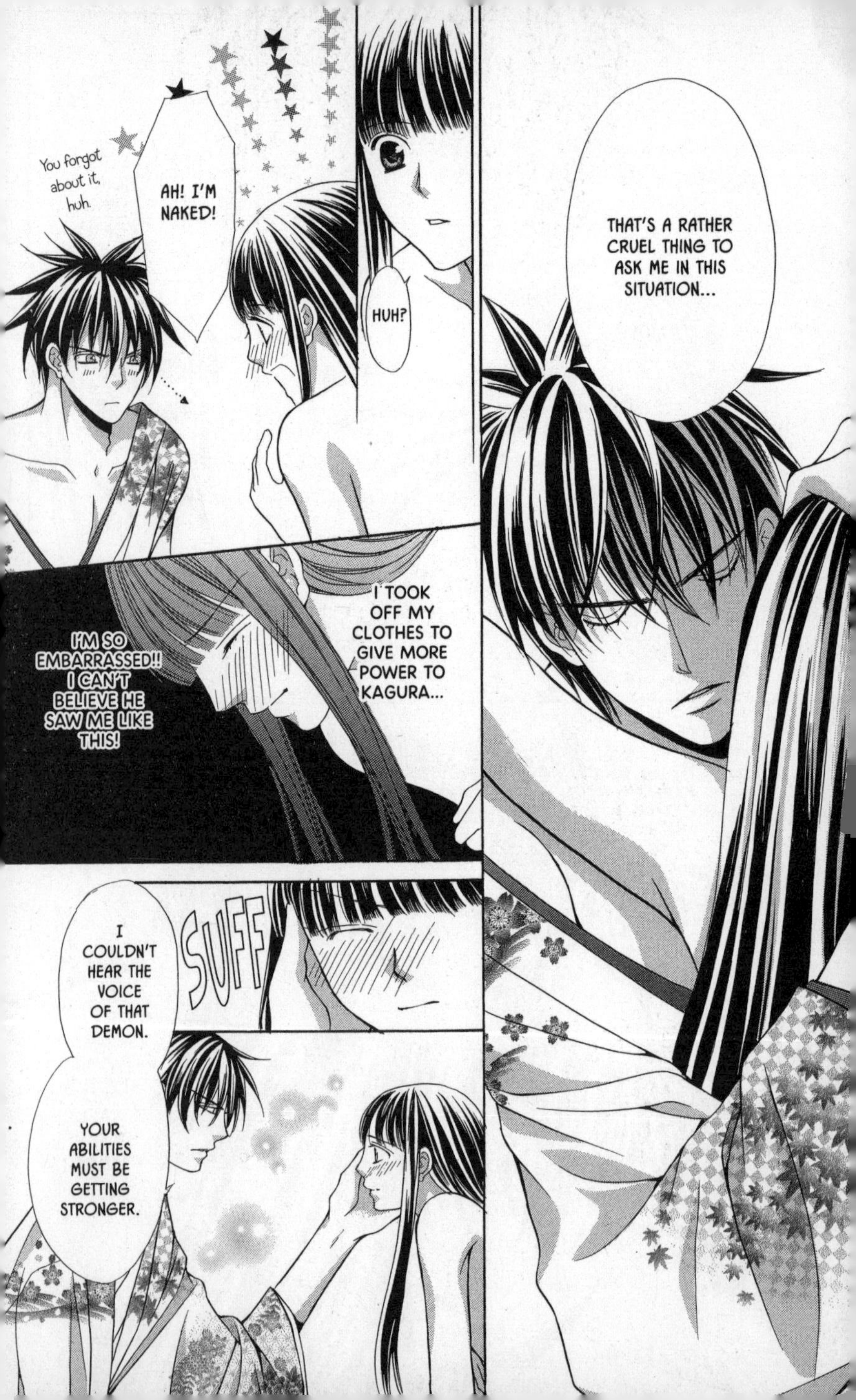
THAT'S A RATHER CRUEL THING TO ASK ME IN THIS SITUATION...
HUH?
AH! I'M NAKED!
You forgot about it, huh.
I TOOK OFF MY CLOTHES TO GIVE MORE POWER TO KAGURA...
I'M SO EMBARRASSED!! I CAN'T BELIEVE HE SAW ME LIKE THIS!
SUFF
I COULDN'T HEAR THE VOICE OF THAT DEMON.
YOUR ABILITIES MUST BE GETTING STRONGER.

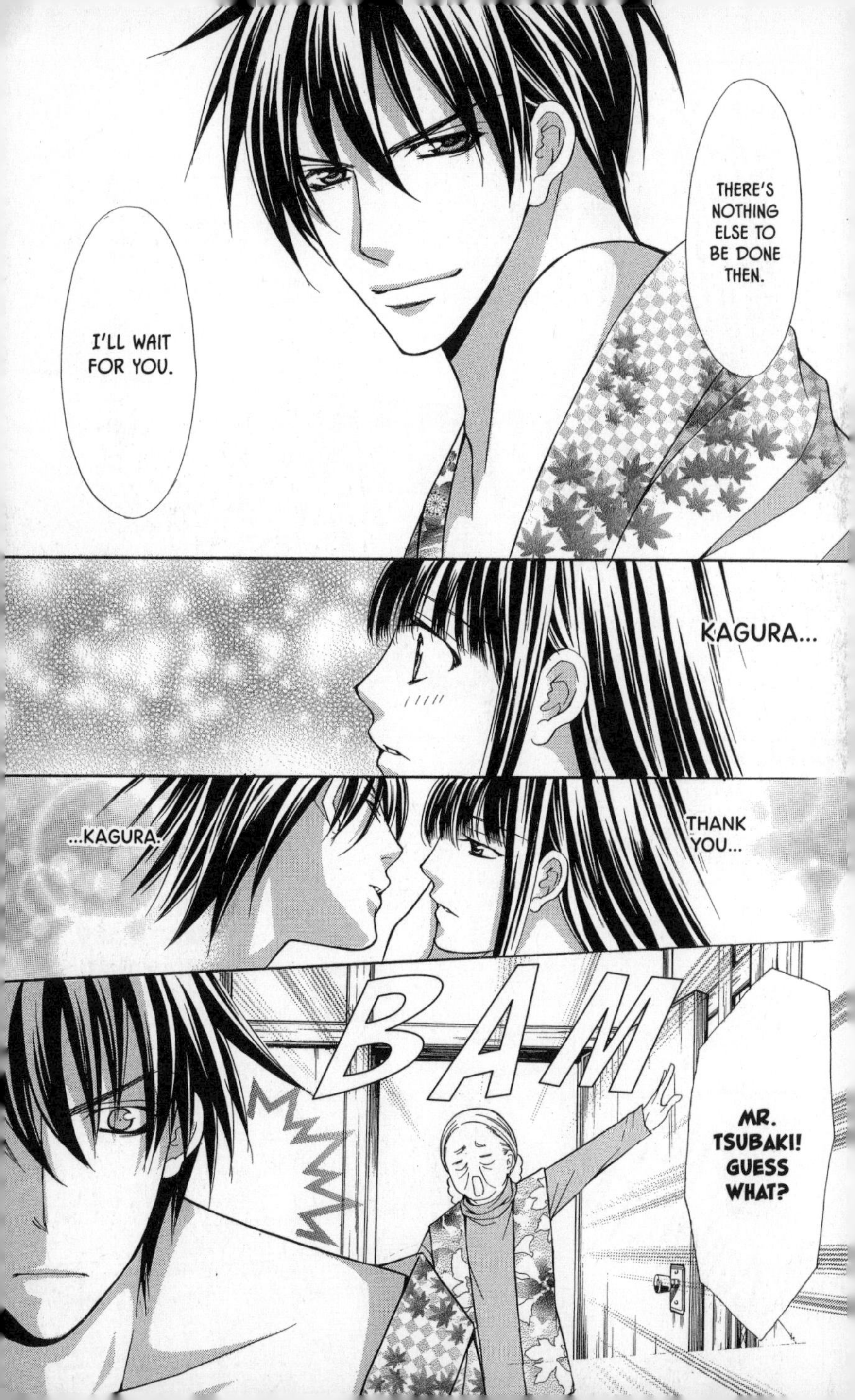
THERE'S NOTHING ELSE TO BE DONE THEN.
I'LL WAIT FOR YOU.
KAGURA...
THANK YOU...
...KAGURA.
BAM
MR. TSUBAKI! GUESS WHAT?

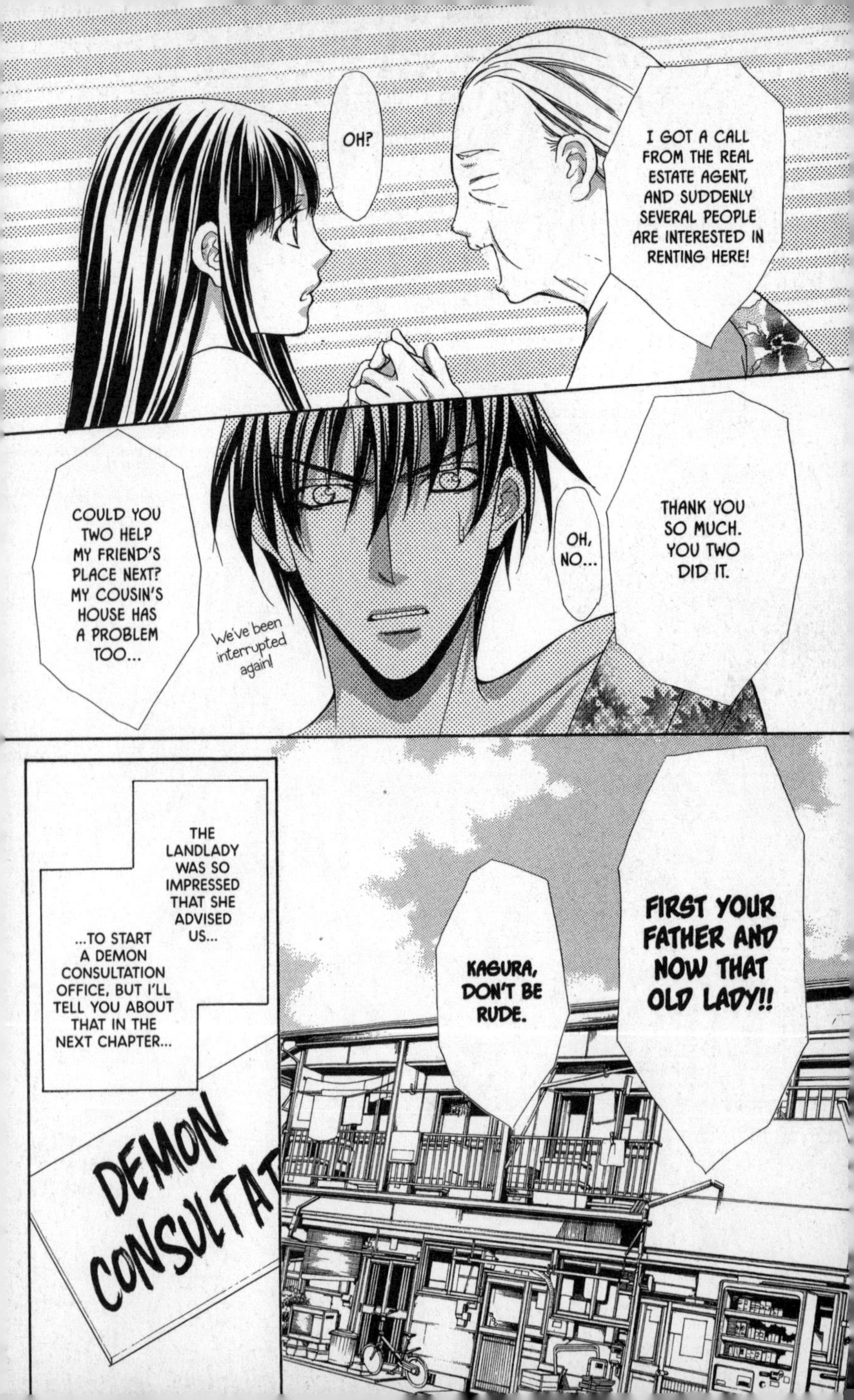
I GOT A CALL FROM THE REAL ESTATE AGENT, AND SUDDENLY SEVERAL PEOPLE ARE INTERESTED IN RENTING HERE!
OH?
THANK YOU SO MUCH. YOU TWO DID IT.
OH, NO...
We've been interrupted again!
COULD YOU TWO HELP MY FRIEND'S PLACE NEXT? MY COUSIN'S HOUSE HAS A PROBLEM TOO...
FIRST YOUR FATHER AND NOW THAT OLD LADY!!
KAGURA, DON'T BE RUDE.
THE LANDLADY WAS SO IMPRESSED THAT SHE ADVISED US...
...TO START A DEMON CONSULTATION OFFICE, BUT I'LL TELL YOU ABOUT THAT IN THE NEXT CHAPTER...
DEMON CONSULTAT

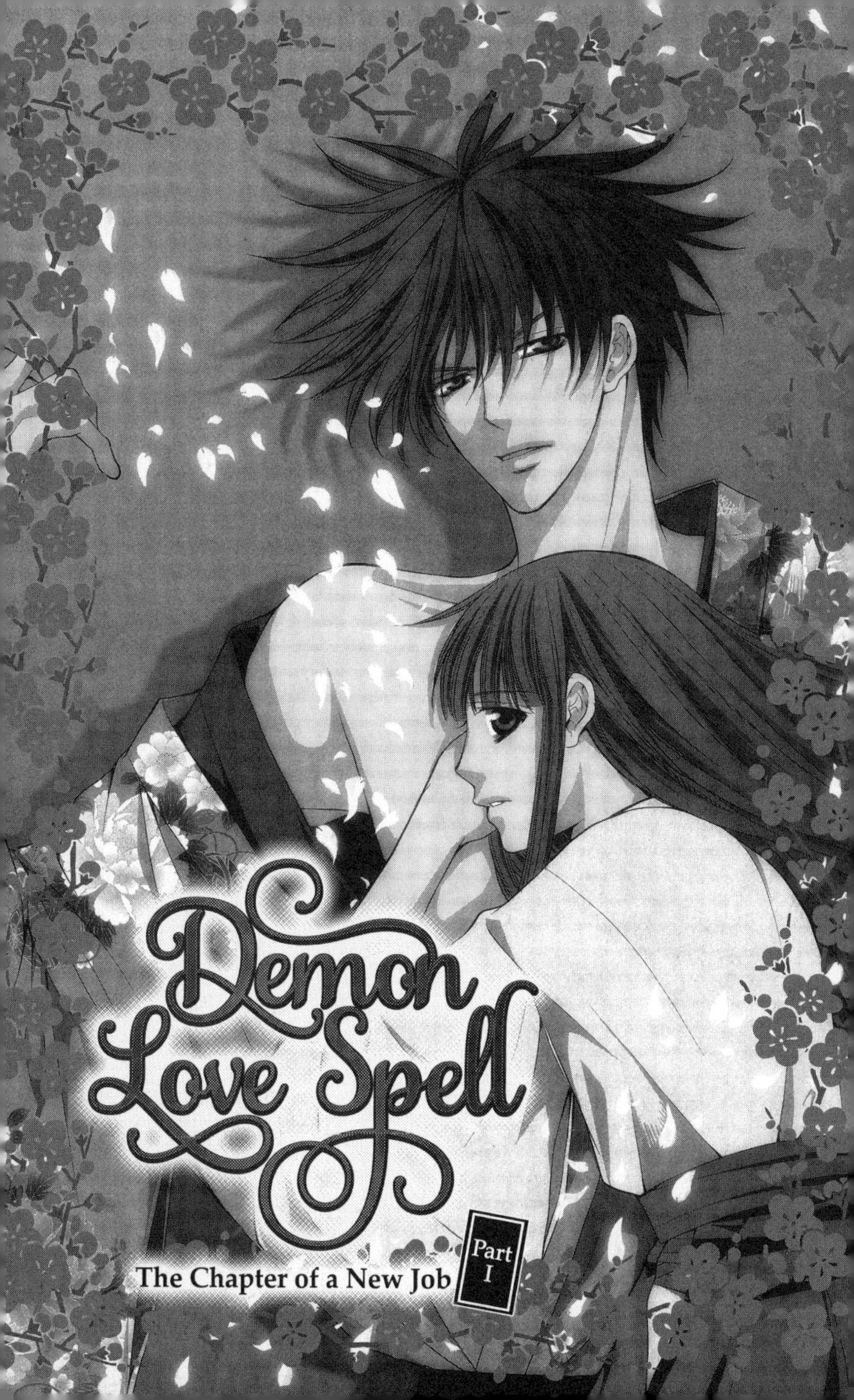
Demon Love Spell
Part I
The Chapter of a New Job

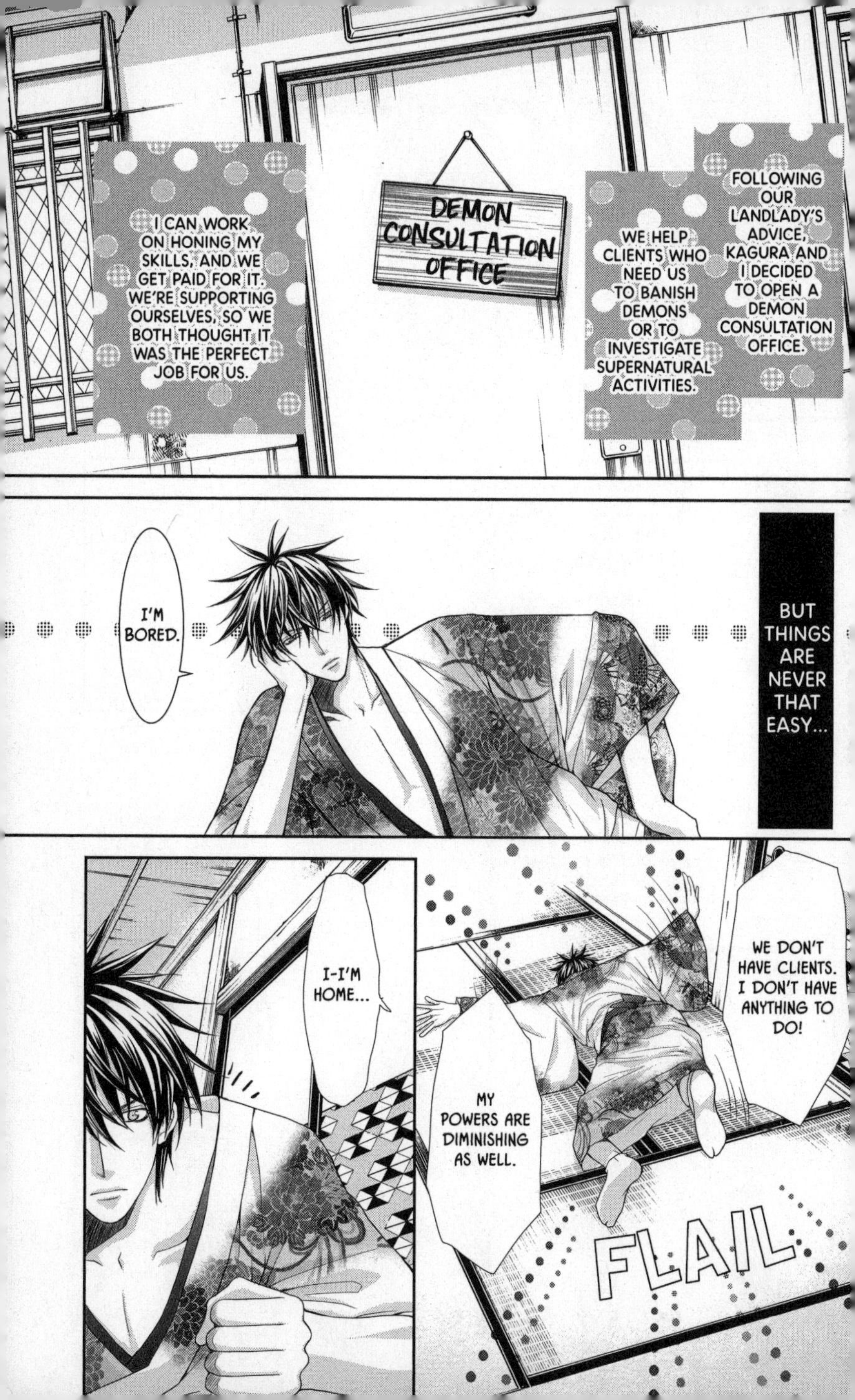
FOLLOWING OUR LANDLADY'S ADVICE, KAGURA AND I DECIDED TO OPEN A DEMON CONSULTATION OFFICE.
WE HELP CLIENTS WHO NEED US TO BANISH DEMONS OR TO INVESTIGATE SUPERNATURAL ACTIVITIES.
DEMON CONSULTATION OFFICE
I CAN WORK ON HONING MY SKILLS, AND WE GET PAID FOR IT. WE'RE SUPPORTING OURSELVES, SO WE BOTH THOUGHT IT WAS THE PERFECT JOB FOR US.
BUT THINGS ARE NEVER THAT EASY...
I'M BORED.
WE DON'T HAVE CLIENTS. I DON'T HAVE ANYTHING TO DO!
MY POWERS ARE DIMINISHING AS WELL.
FLAIL
I-I'M HOME...

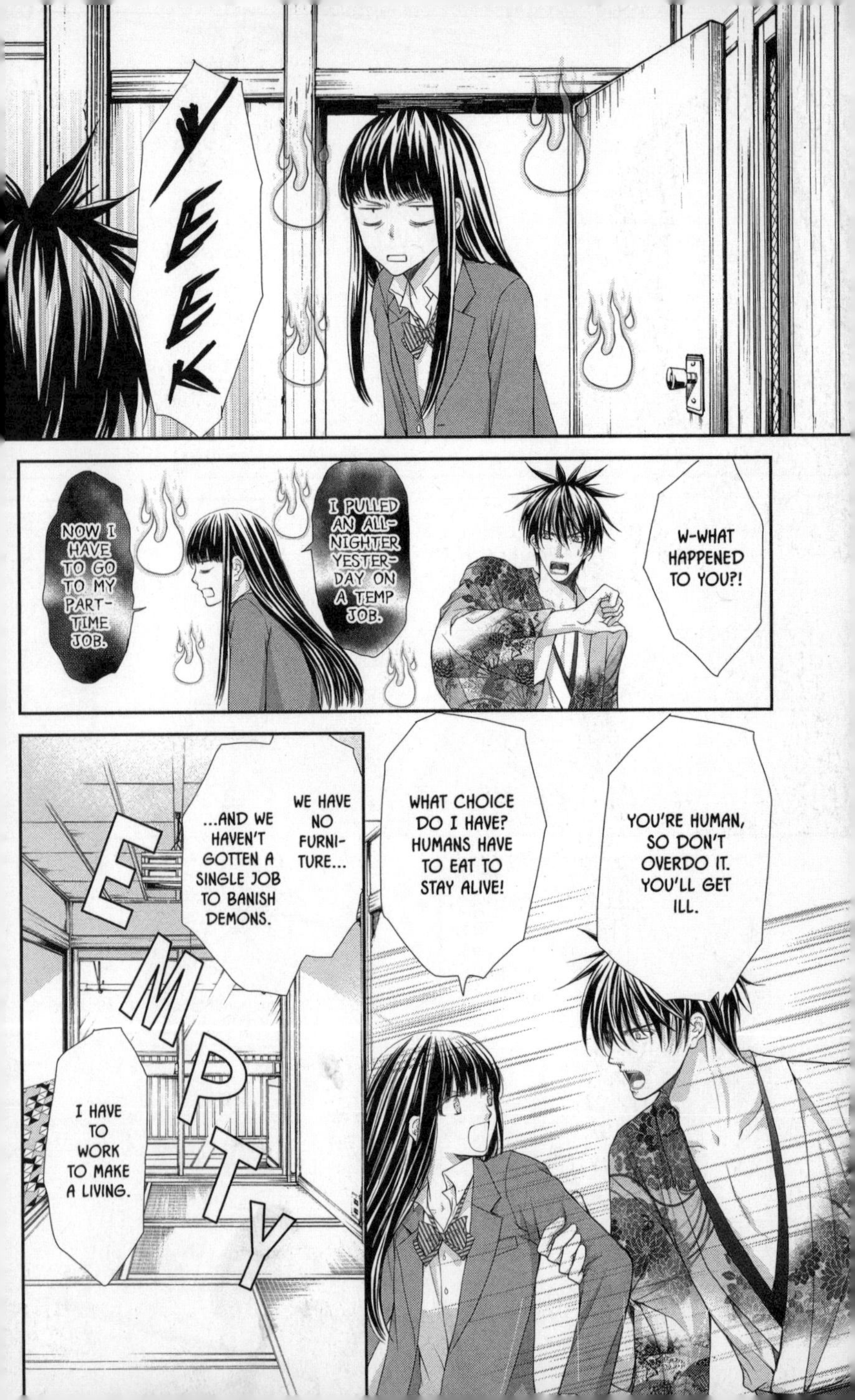
YEEEK
W-WHAT HAPPENED TO YOU?!
I PULLED AN ALL-NIGHTER YESTERDAY ON A TEMP JOB.
NOW I HAVE TO GO TO MY PART-TIME JOB.
YOU'RE HUMAN, SO DON'T OVERDO IT. YOU'LL GET ILL.
WHAT CHOICE DO I HAVE? HUMANS HAVE TO EAT TO STAY ALIVE!
WE HAVE NO FURNITURE...
...AND WE HAVEN'T GOTTEN A SINGLE JOB TO BANISH DEMONS.
EMPTY
I HAVE TO WORK TO MAKE A LIVING.

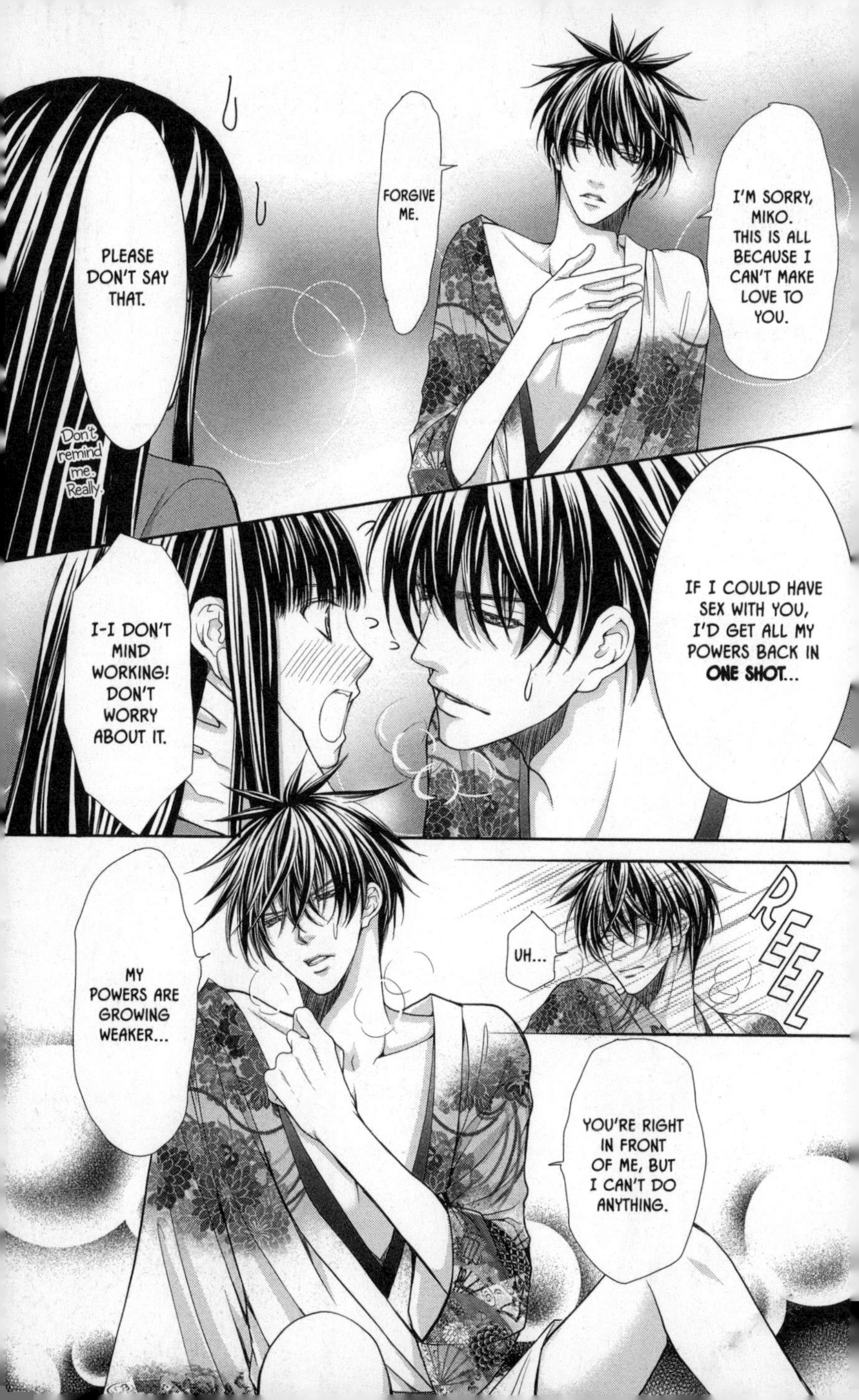
I'M SORRY, MIKO. THIS IS ALL BECAUSE I CAN'T MAKE LOVE TO YOU.
FORGIVE ME.
PLEASE DON'T SAY THAT.
Don't remind me. Really.
IF I COULD HAVE SEX WITH YOU, I'D GET ALL MY POWERS BACK IN **ONE SHOT**...
I-I DON'T MIND WORKING! DON'T WORRY ABOUT IT.
REEL
UH...
MY POWERS ARE GROWING WEAKER...
YOU'RE RIGHT IN FRONT OF ME, BUT I CAN'T DO ANYTHING.

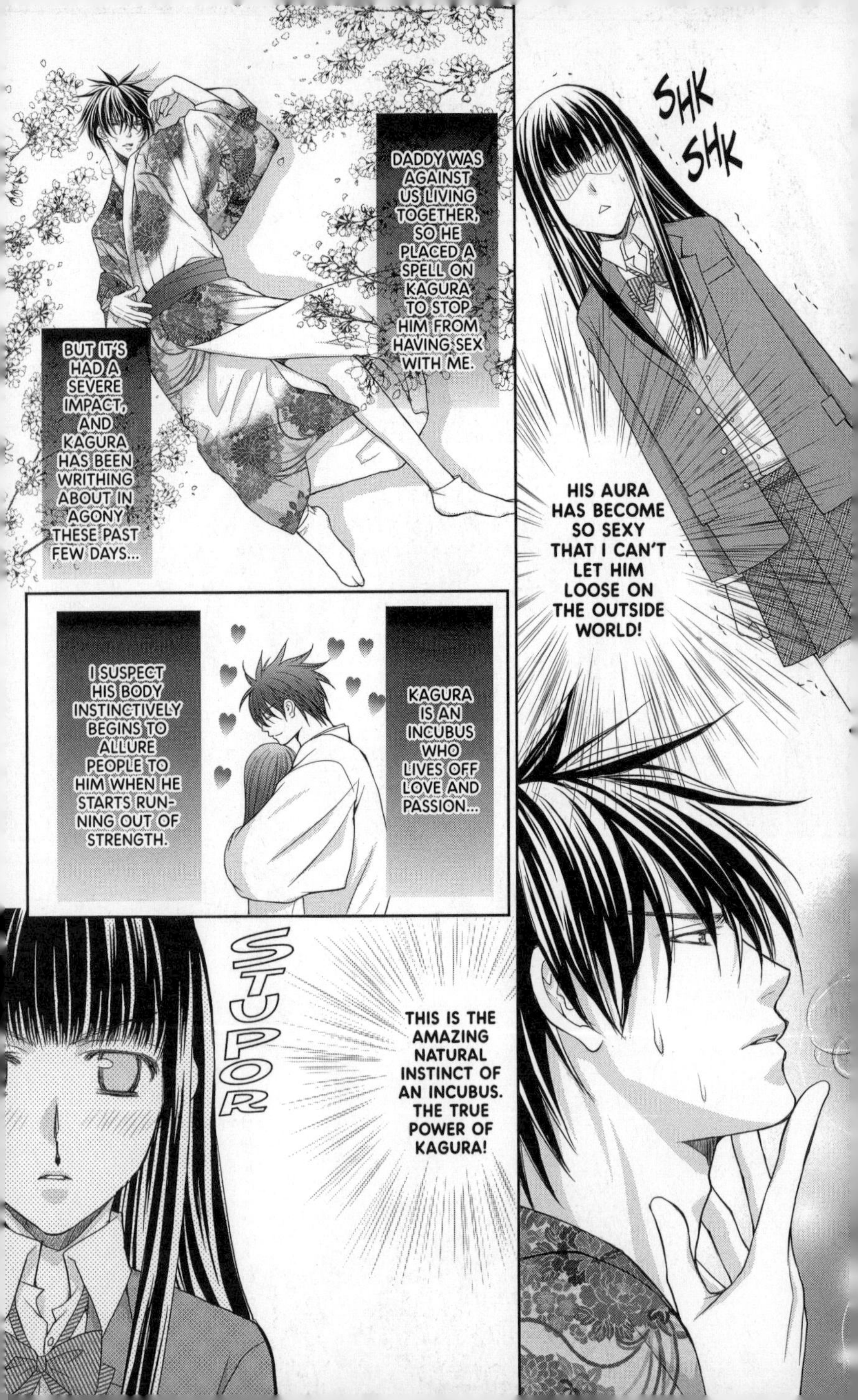
DADDY WAS AGAINST US LIVING TOGETHER, SO HE PLACED A SPELL ON KAGURA TO STOP HIM FROM HAVING SEX WITH ME.
BUT IT'S HAD A SEVERE IMPACT, AND KAGURA HAS BEEN WRITHING ABOUT IN AGONY THESE PAST FEW DAYS...
KAGURA IS AN INCUBUS WHO LIVES OFF LOVE AND PASSION...
I SUSPECT HIS BODY INSTINCTIVELY BEGINS TO ALLURE PEOPLE TO HIM WHEN HE STARTS RUN-NING OUT OF STRENGTH.
SHK SHK
HIS AURA HAS BECOME SO SEXY THAT I CAN'T LET HIM LOOSE ON THE OUTSIDE WORLD!
STUPOR
THIS IS THE AMAZING NATURAL INSTINCT OF AN INCUBUS. THE TRUE POWER OF KAGURA!

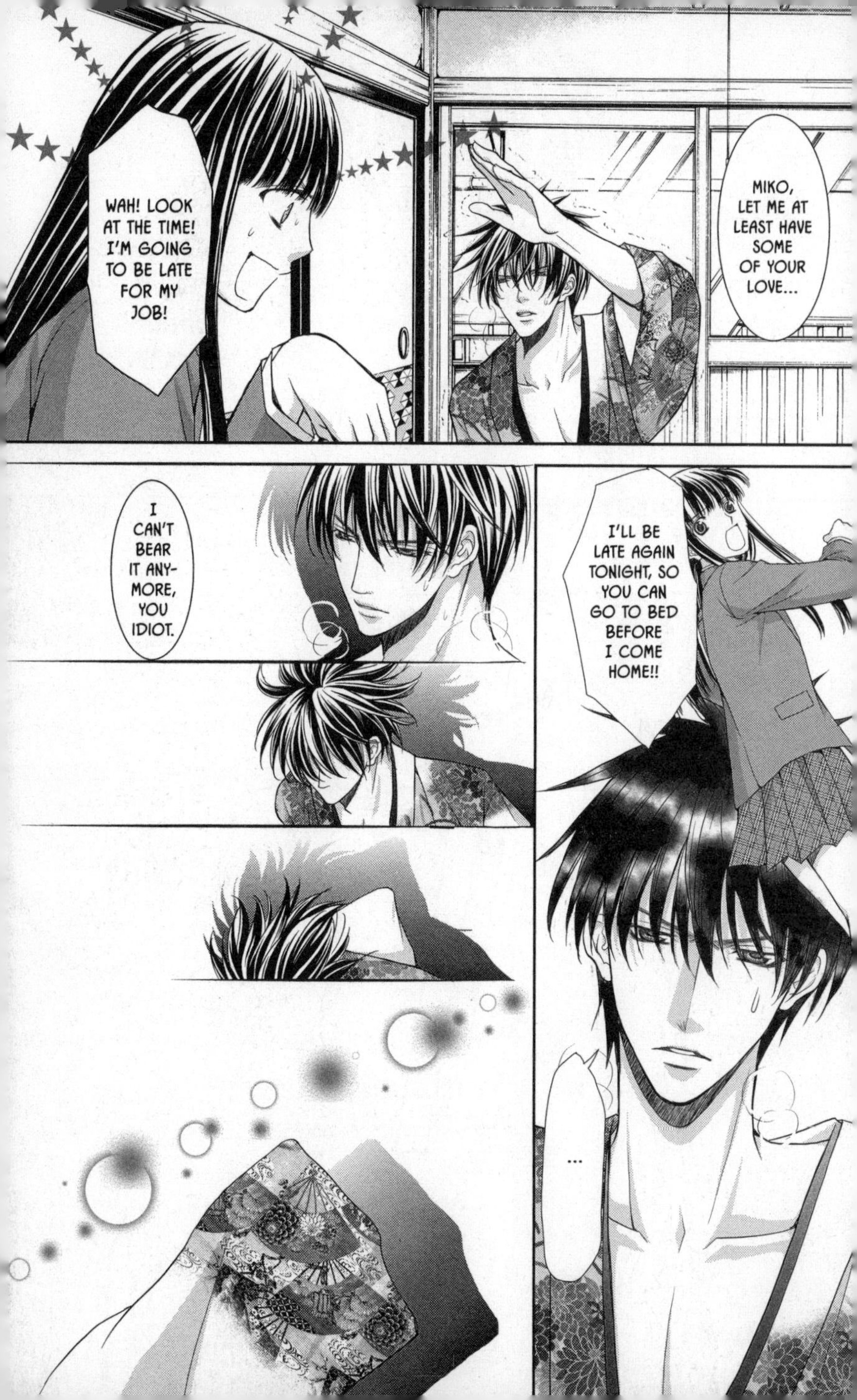
MIKO, LET ME AT LEAST HAVE SOME OF YOUR LOVE...
WAH! LOOK AT THE TIME! I'M GOING TO BE LATE FOR MY JOB!
I'LL BE LATE AGAIN TONIGHT, SO YOU CAN GO TO BED BEFORE I COME HOME!!
...
I CAN'T BEAR IT ANY-MORE, YOU IDIOT.

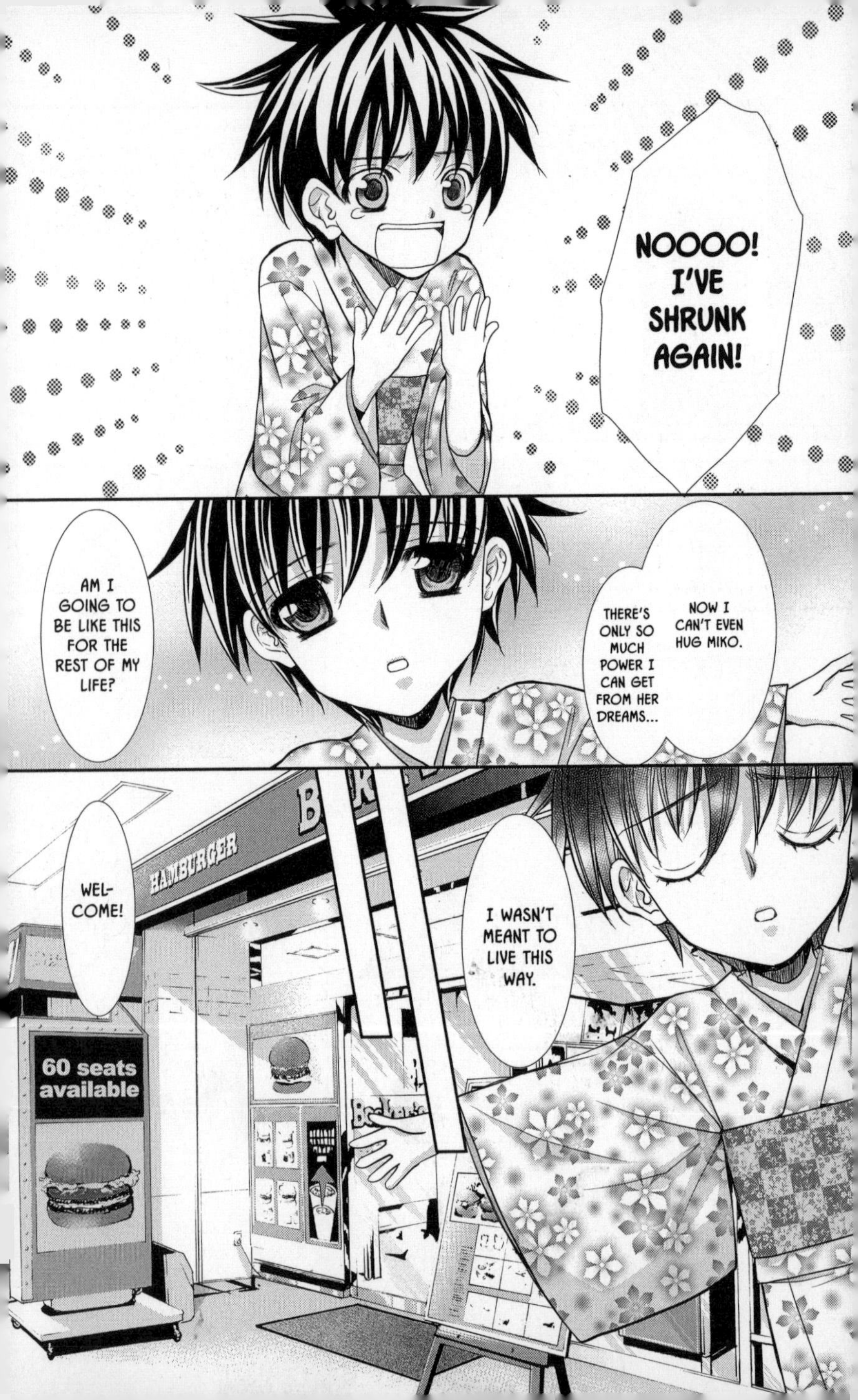
NOOOO! I'VE SHRUNK AGAIN!
NOW I CAN'T EVEN HUG MIKO.
THERE'S ONLY SO MUCH POWER I CAN GET FROM HER DREAMS...
AM I GOING TO BE LIKE THIS FOR THE REST OF MY LIFE?
I WASN'T MEANT TO LIVE THIS WAY.
WEL-COME!
HAMBURGER
60 seats available

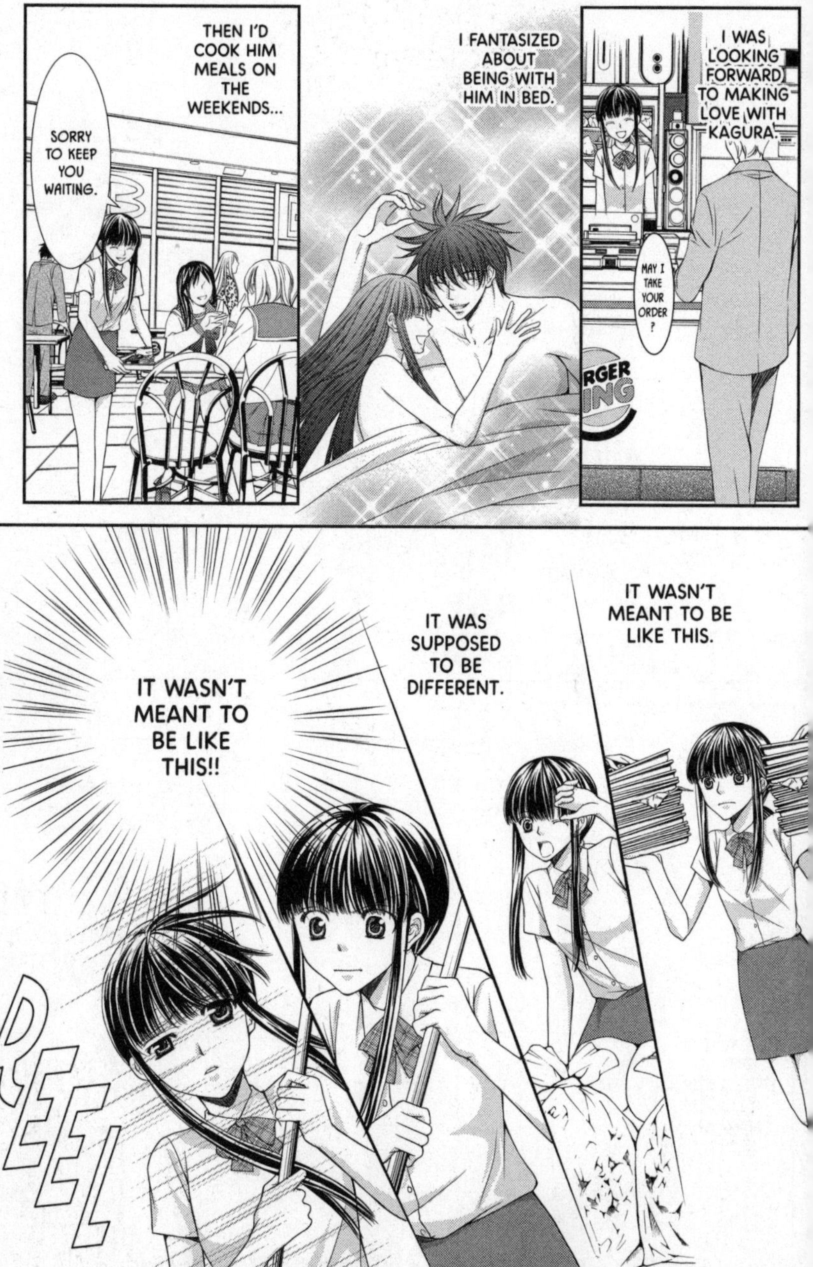
I WAS LOOKING FORWARD TO MAKING LOVE WITH KAGURA.
MAY I TAKE YOUR ORDER?
I FANTASIZED ABOUT BEING WITH HIM IN BED.
THEN I'D COOK HIM MEALS ON THE WEEKENDS...
SORRY TO KEEP YOU WAITING.
IT WASN'T MEANT TO BE LIKE THIS.
IT WAS SUPPOSED TO BE DIFFERENT.
IT WASN'T MEANT TO BE LIKE THIS!!
REEL

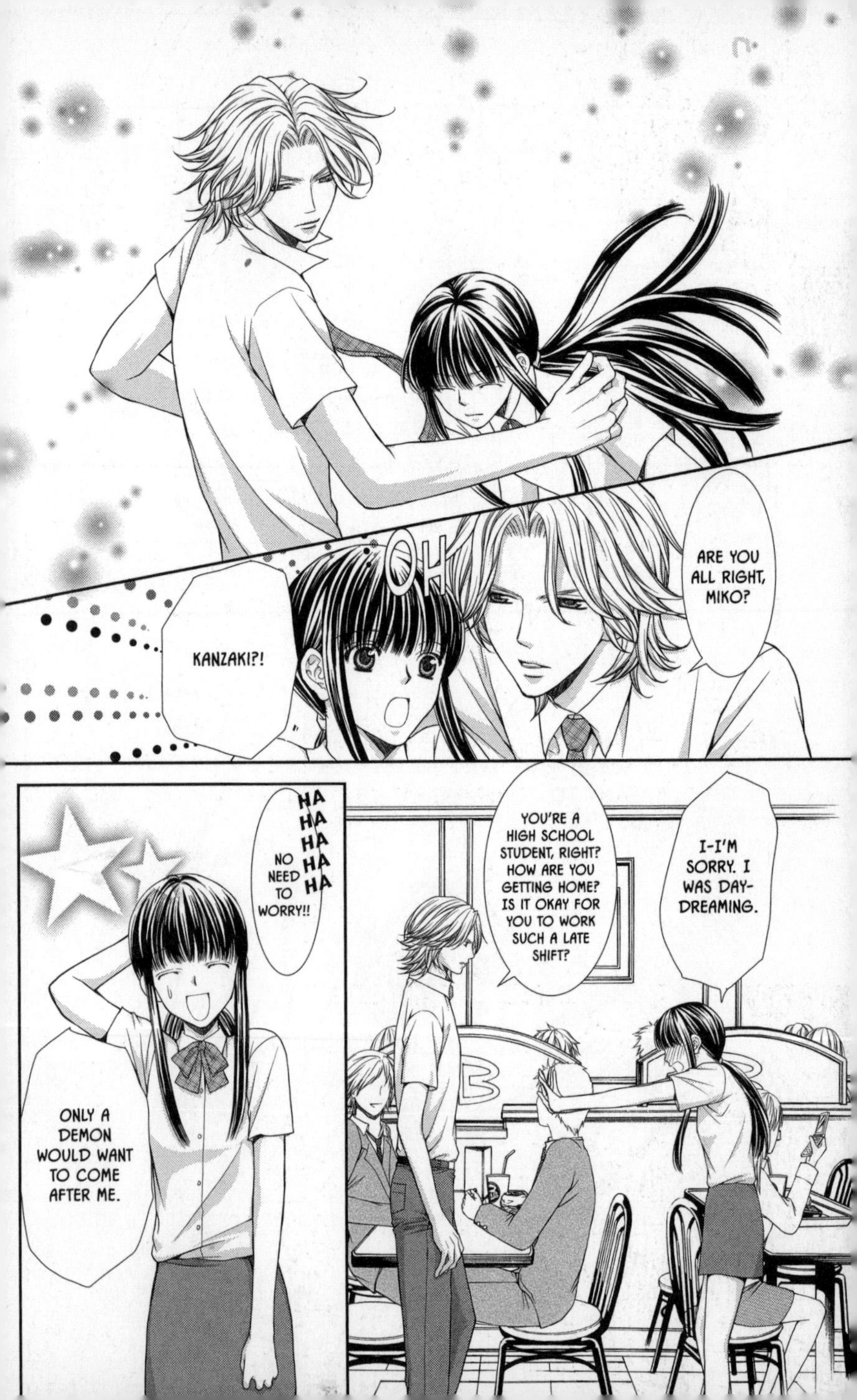
OH
ARE YOU ALL RIGHT, MIKO?
KANZAKI?!
I-I'M SORRY. I WAS DAY-DREAMING.
YOU'RE A HIGH SCHOOL STUDENT, RIGHT? HOW ARE YOU GETTING HOME? IS IT OKAY FOR YOU TO WORK SUCH A LATE SHIFT?
HA HA HA HA HA
NO NEED TO WORRY!!
ONLY A DEMON WOULD WANT TO COME AFTER ME.

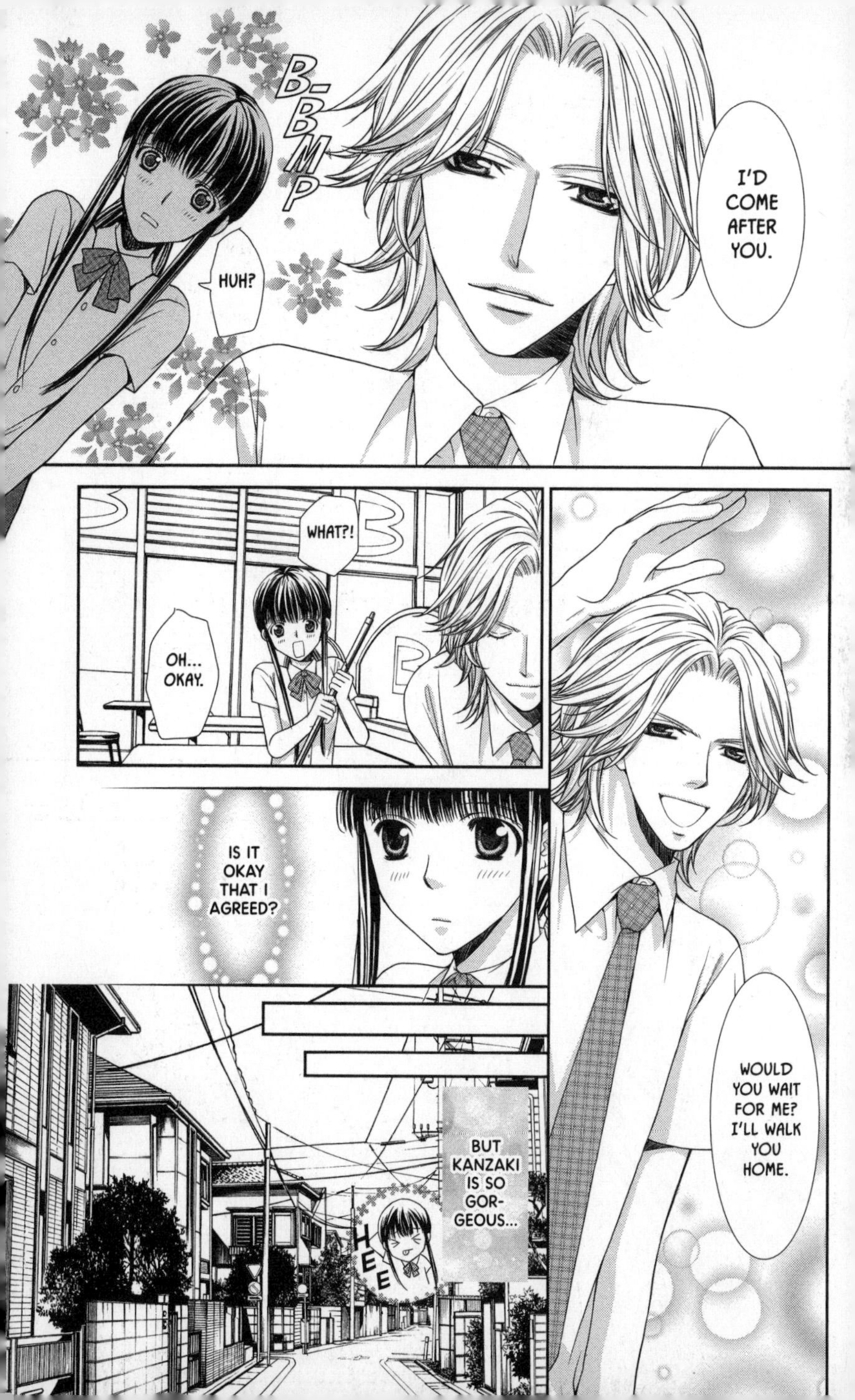
I'D COME AFTER YOU.
B-BMP
HUH?
WOULD YOU WAIT FOR ME? I'LL WALK YOU HOME.
WHAT?!
OH... OKAY.
IS IT OKAY THAT I AGREED?
BUT KANZAKI IS SO GOR-GEOUS...
HEE

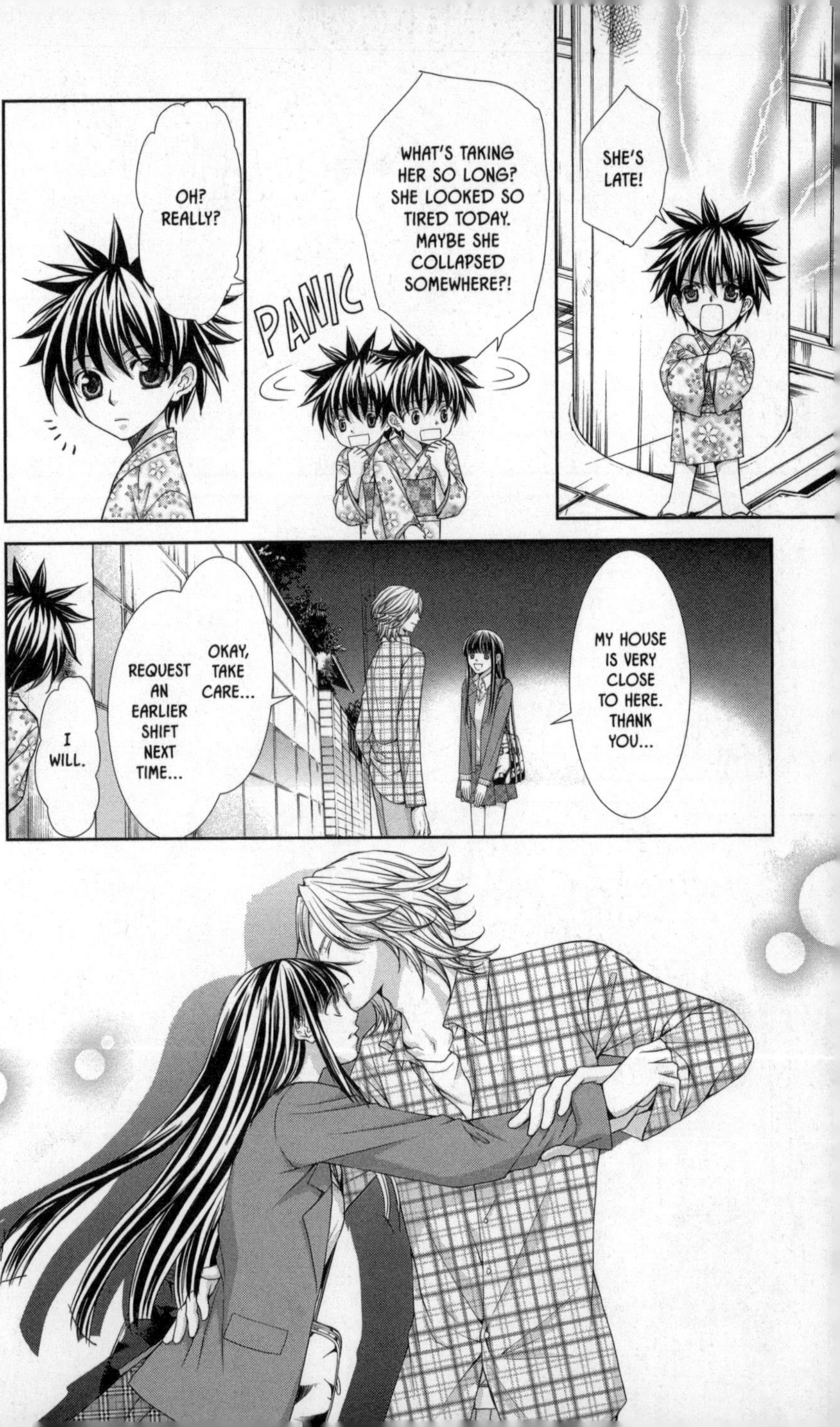
SHE'S LATE!
PANIC
WHAT'S TAKING HER SO LONG? SHE LOOKED SO TIRED TODAY. MAYBE SHE COLLAPSED SOMEWHERE?!
OH? REALLY?
MY HOUSE IS VERY CLOSE TO HERE. THANK YOU...
OKAY, TAKE CARE...
REQUEST AN EARLIER SHIFT NEXT TIME...
I WILL.

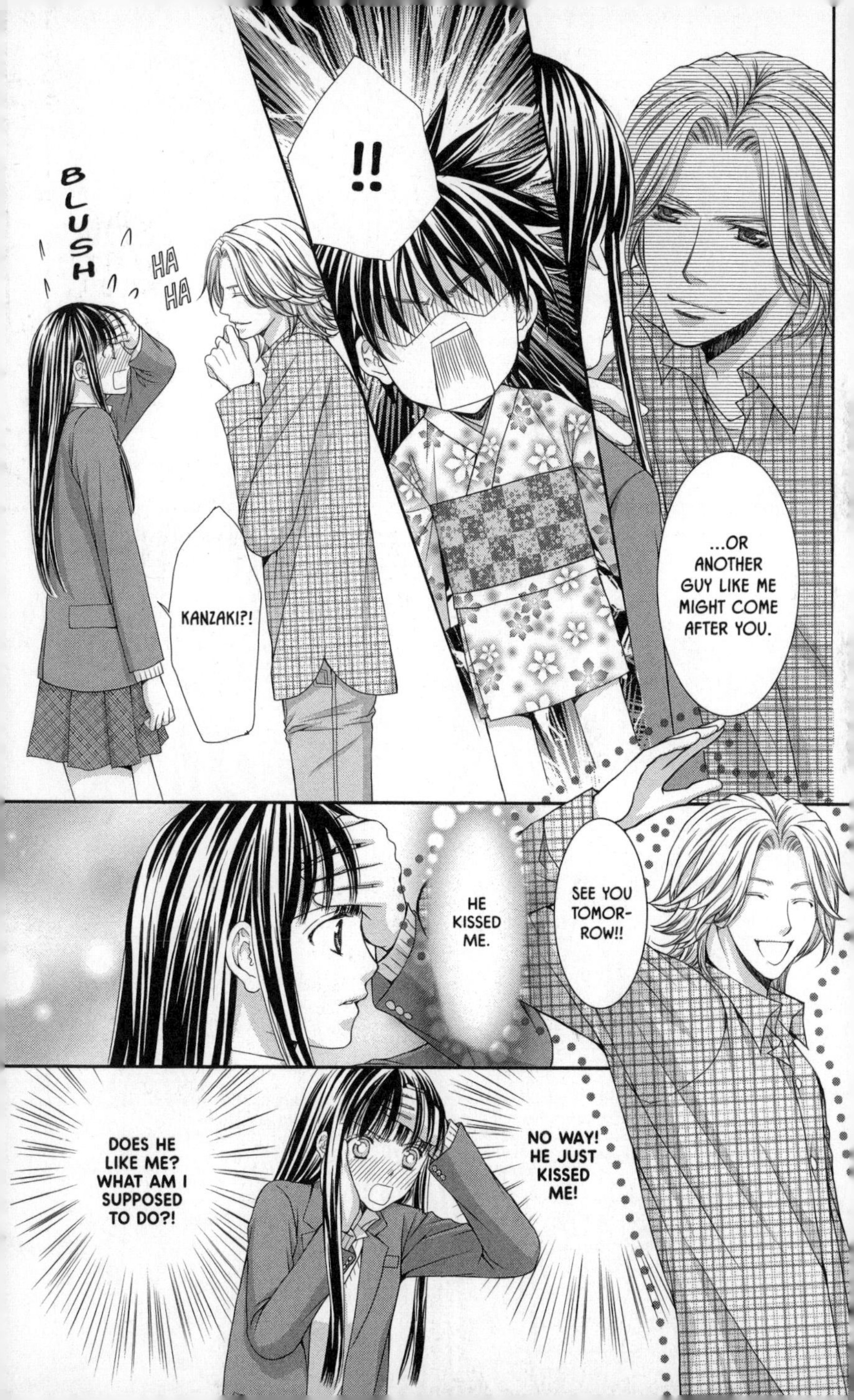
...OR ANOTHER GUY LIKE ME MIGHT COME AFTER YOU.
!!
BLUSH
HA HA
KANZAKI?!
SEE YOU TOMOR-ROW!!
HE KISSED ME.
NO WAY! HE JUST KISSED ME!
DOES HE LIKE ME? WHAT AM I SUPPOSED TO DO?!

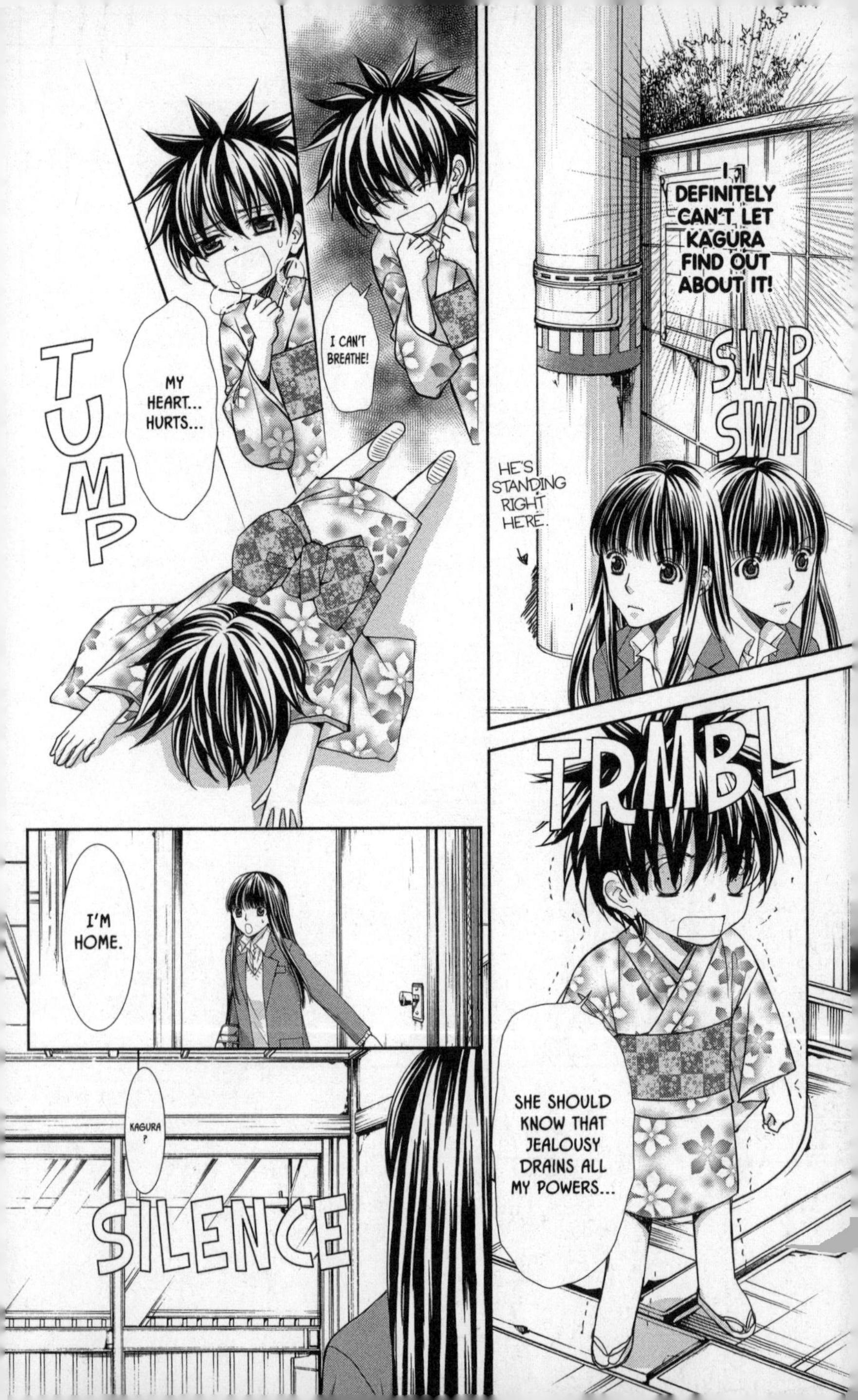
I DEFINITELY CAN'T LET KAGURA FIND OUT ABOUT IT!
SWIP SWIP
HE'S STANDING RIGHT HERE.
TRMBL
SHE SHOULD KNOW THAT JEALOUSY DRAINS ALL MY POWERS...
I CAN'T BREATHE!
MY HEART... HURTS...
TUMP
I'M HOME.
KAGURA?
SILENCE

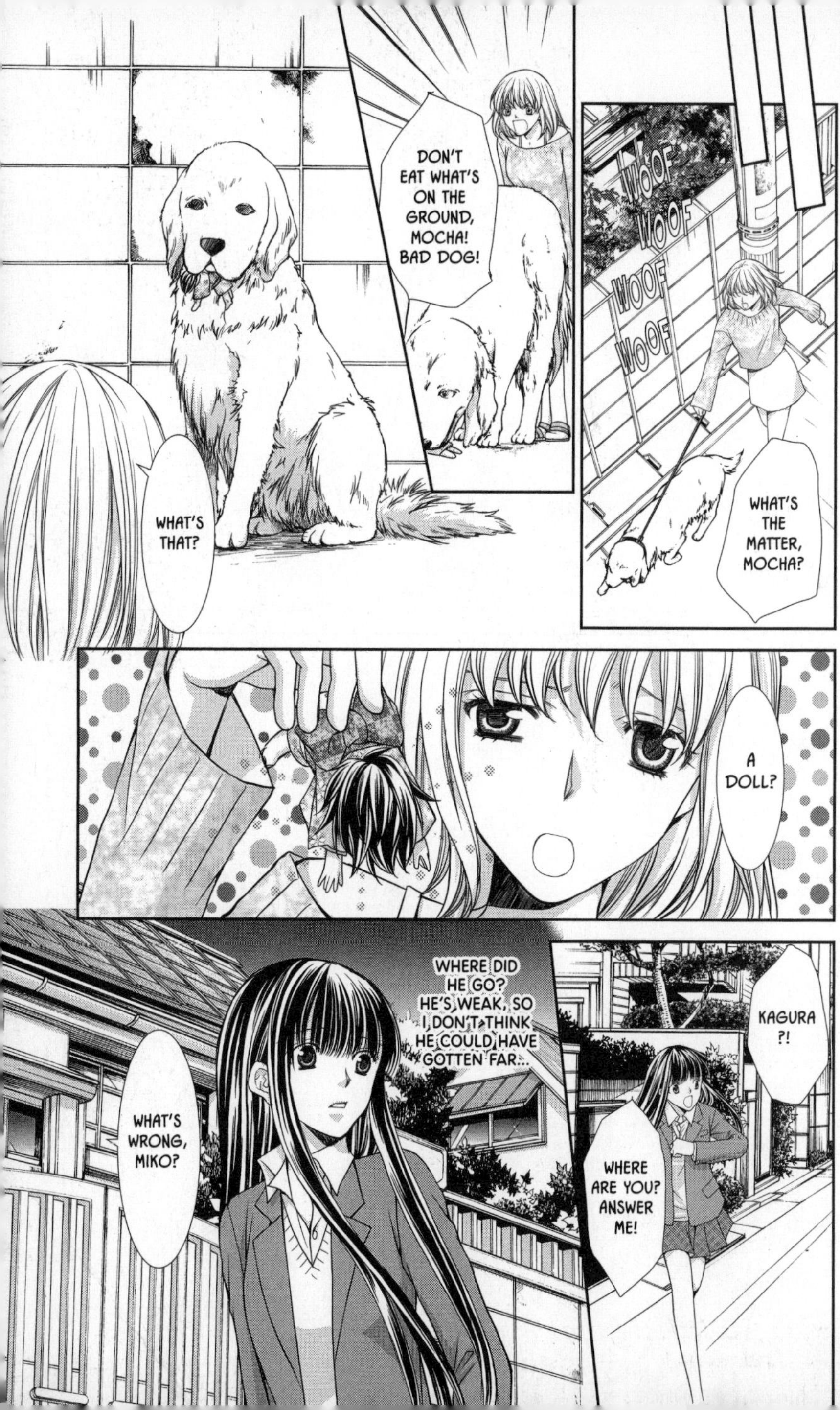
WOOF
WOOF
WOOF
WOOF
WHAT'S THE MATTER, MOCHA?
DON'T EAT WHAT'S ON THE GROUND, MOCHA! BAD DOG!
WHAT'S THAT?
A DOLL?
KAGURA?!
WHERE ARE YOU? ANSWER ME!
WHERE DID HE GO? HE'S WEAK, SO I DON'T THINK HE COULD HAVE GOTTEN FAR...
WHAT'S WRONG, MIKO?

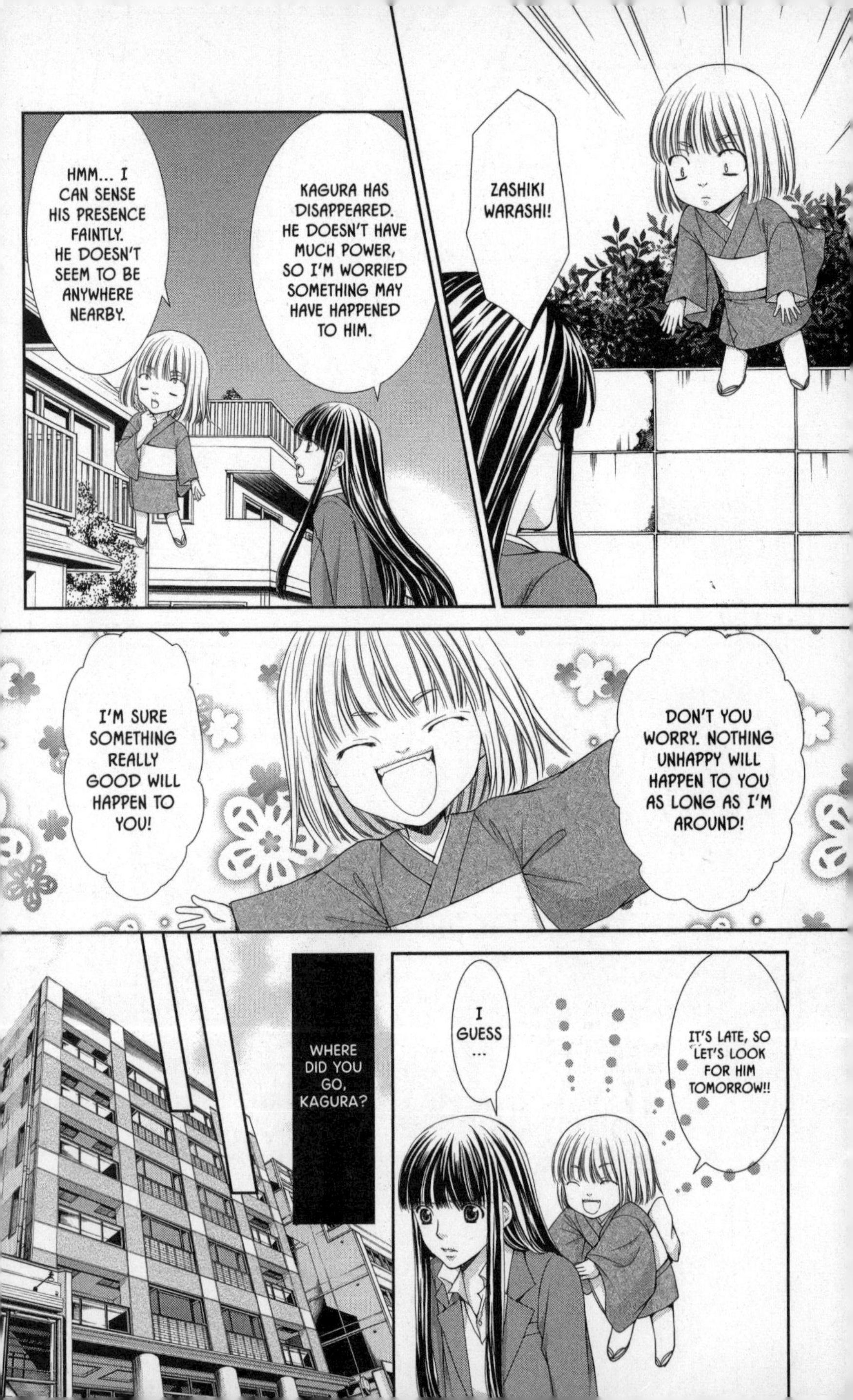
ZASHIKI WARASHI!
KAGURA HAS DISAPPEARED. HE DOESN'T HAVE MUCH POWER, SO I'M WORRIED SOMETHING MAY HAVE HAPPENED TO HIM.
HMM... I CAN SENSE HIS PRESENCE FAINTLY. HE DOESN'T SEEM TO BE ANYWHERE NEARBY.
DON'T YOU WORRY. NOTHING UNHAPPY WILL HAPPEN TO YOU AS LONG AS I'M AROUND!
I'M SURE SOMETHING REALLY GOOD WILL HAPPEN TO YOU!
IT'S LATE, SO LET'S LOOK FOR HIM TOMORROW!!
I GUESS...
WHERE DID YOU GO, KAGURA?

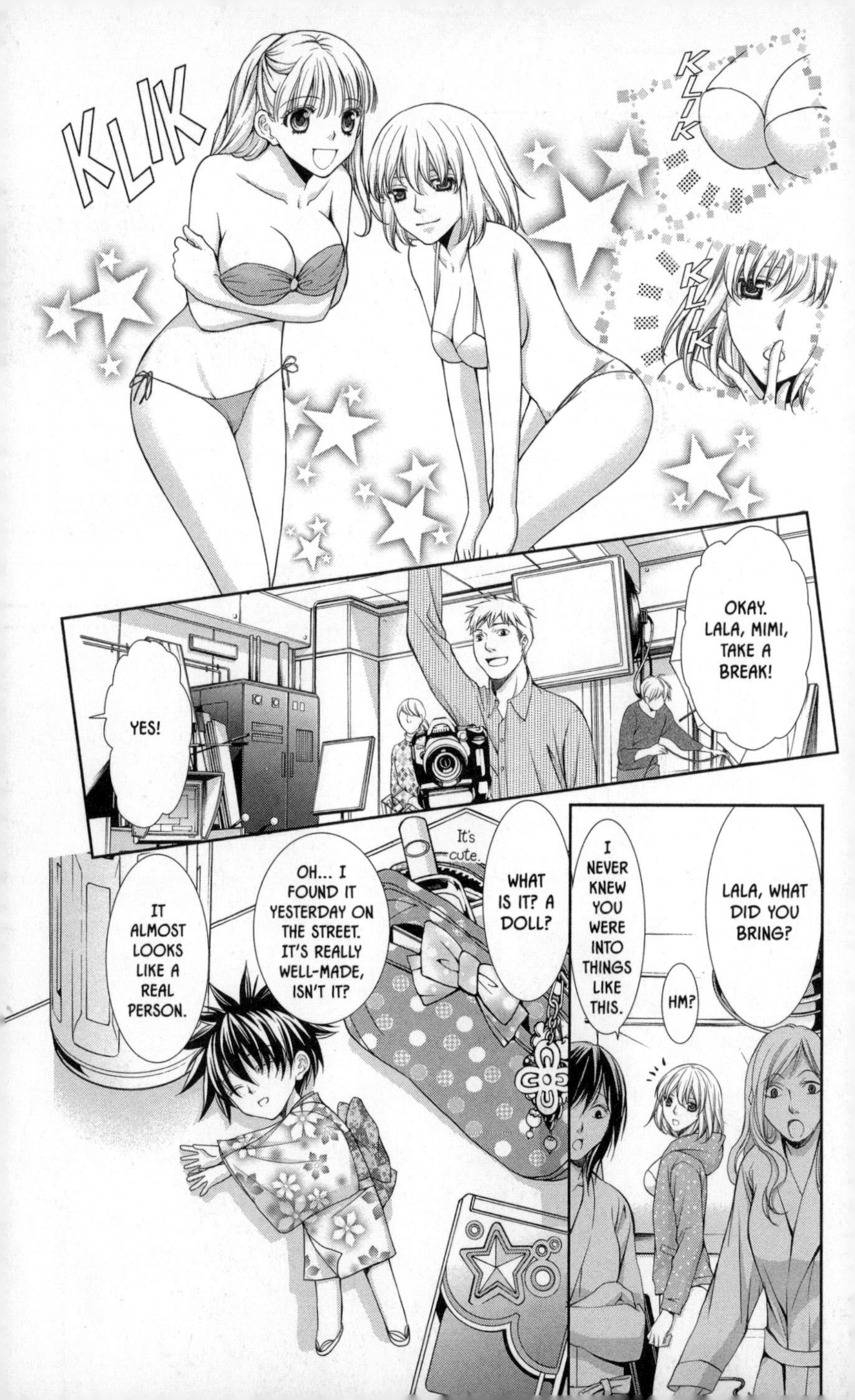
KLIK
KLIK
KLIK
OKAY. LALA, MIMI, TAKE A BREAK!
YES!
LALA, WHAT DID YOU BRING?
HM?
I NEVER KNEW YOU WERE INTO THINGS LIKE THIS.
WHAT IS IT? A DOLL?
It's cute.
OH... I FOUND IT YESTERDAY ON THE STREET. IT'S REALLY WELL-MADE, ISN'T IT?
IT ALMOST LOOKS LIKE A REAL PERSON.

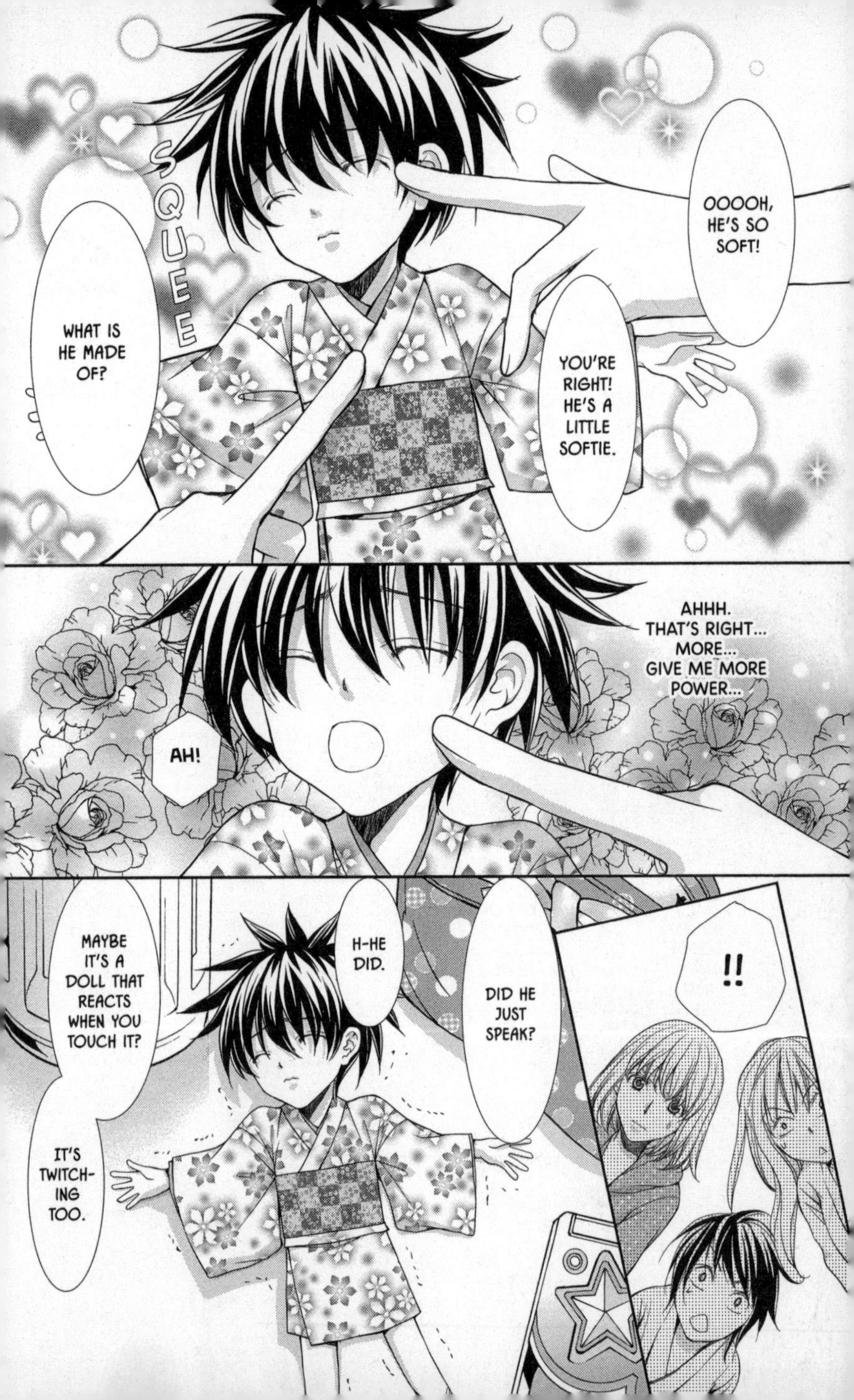
OOOOH, HE'S SO SOFT!
YOU'RE RIGHT! HE'S A LITTLE SOFTIE.
SQUEE
WHAT IS HE MADE OF?
AHHH. THAT'S RIGHT... MORE... GIVE ME MORE POWER...
AH!
!!
DID HE JUST SPEAK?
H-HE DID.
MAYBE IT'S A DOLL THAT REACTS WHEN YOU TOUCH IT?
IT'S TWITCHING TOO.

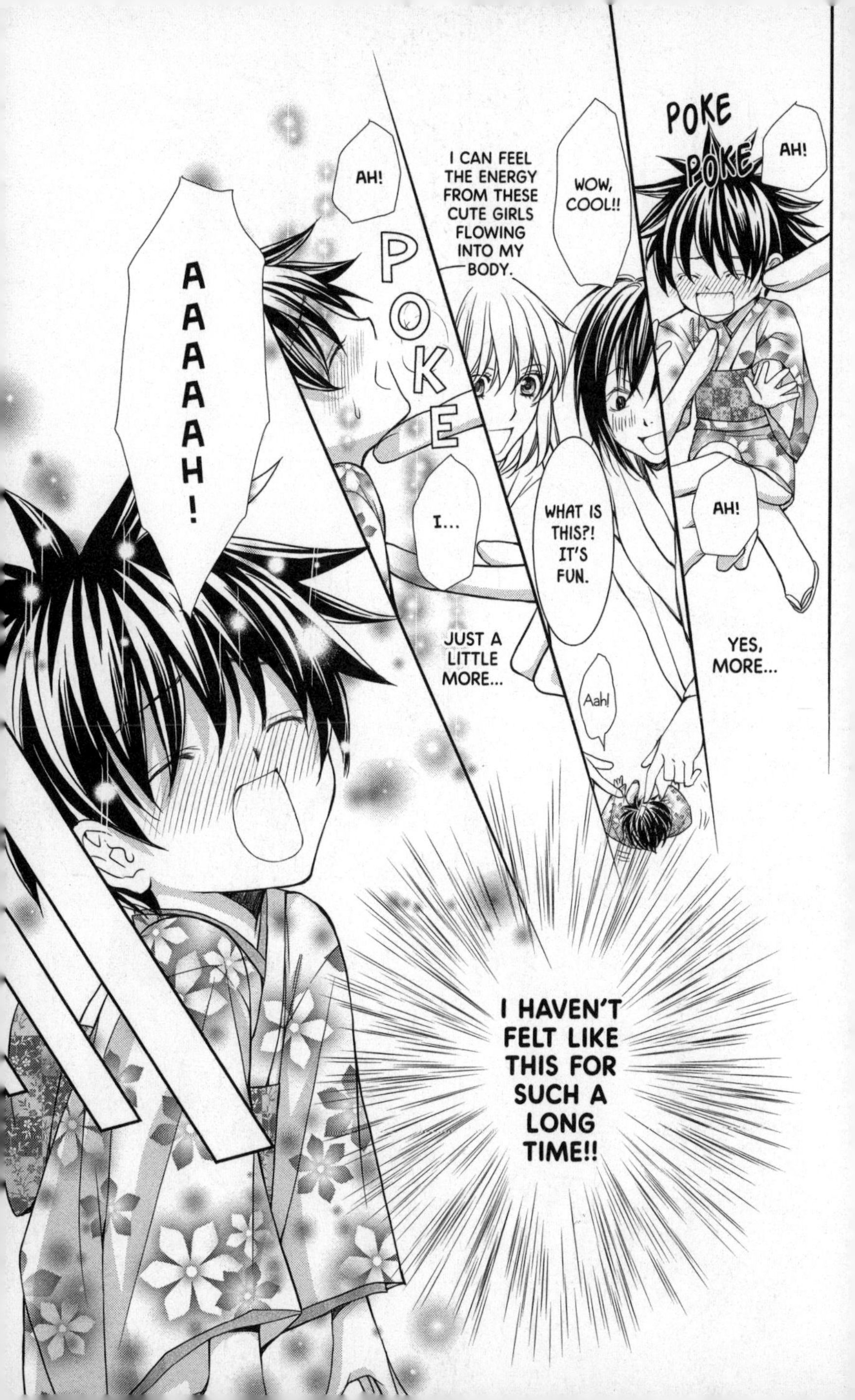
POKE
POKE
AH!
AH!
YES, MORE...
WOW, COOL!!
WHAT IS THIS?! IT'S FUN.
Aah!
I CAN FEEL THE ENERGY FROM THESE CUTE GIRLS FLOWING INTO MY BODY.
AH!
POKE
I...
JUST A LITTLE MORE...
AAAAAAH!
I HAVEN'T FELT LIKE THIS FOR SUCH A LONG TIME!!

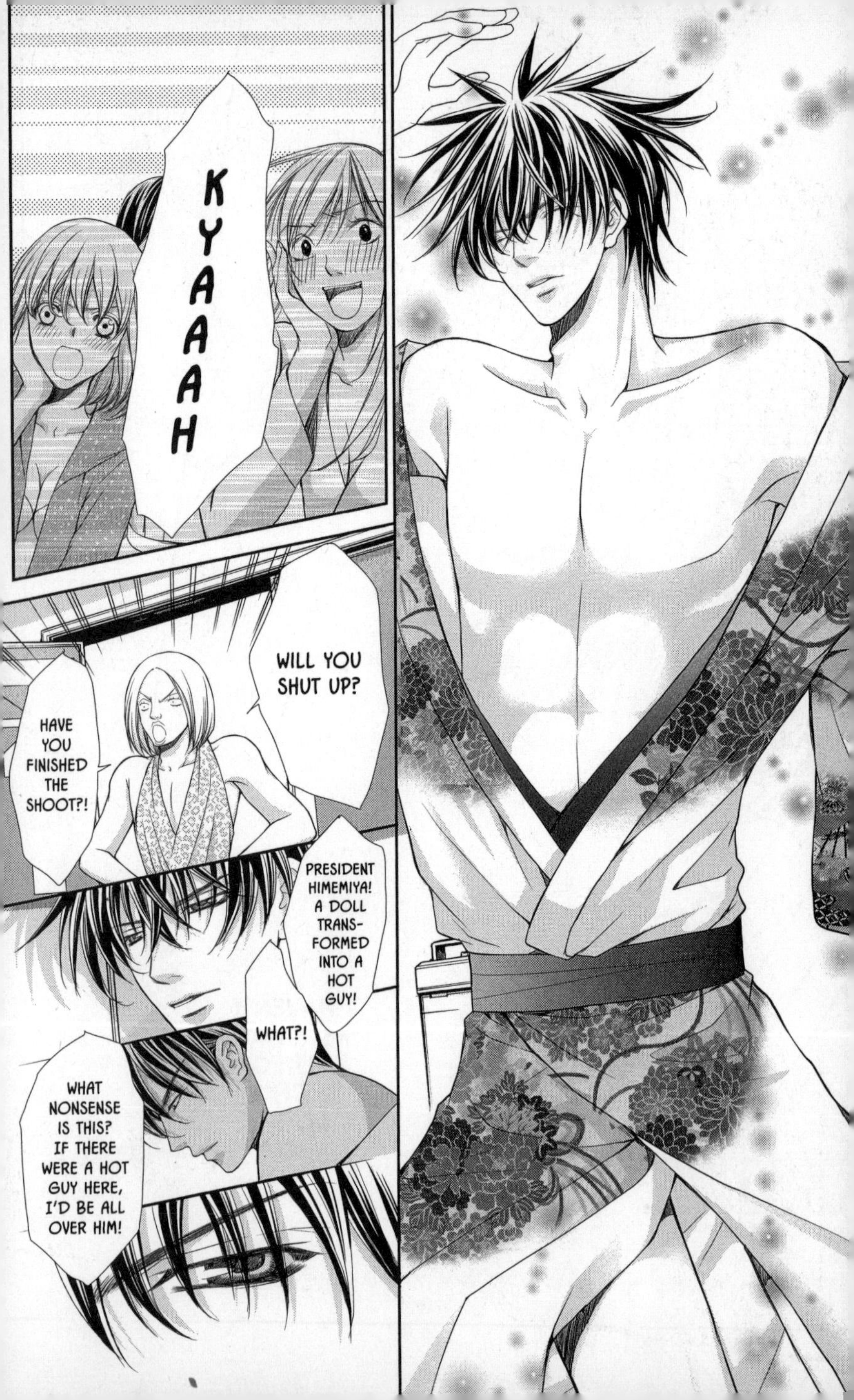
KYAAAH
WILL YOU SHUT UP?
HAVE YOU FINISHED THE SHOOT?!
PRESIDENT HIMEMIYA! A DOLL TRANSFORMED INTO A HOT GUY!
WHAT?!
WHAT NONSENSE IS THIS? IF THERE WERE A HOT GUY HERE, I'D BE ALL OVER HIM!

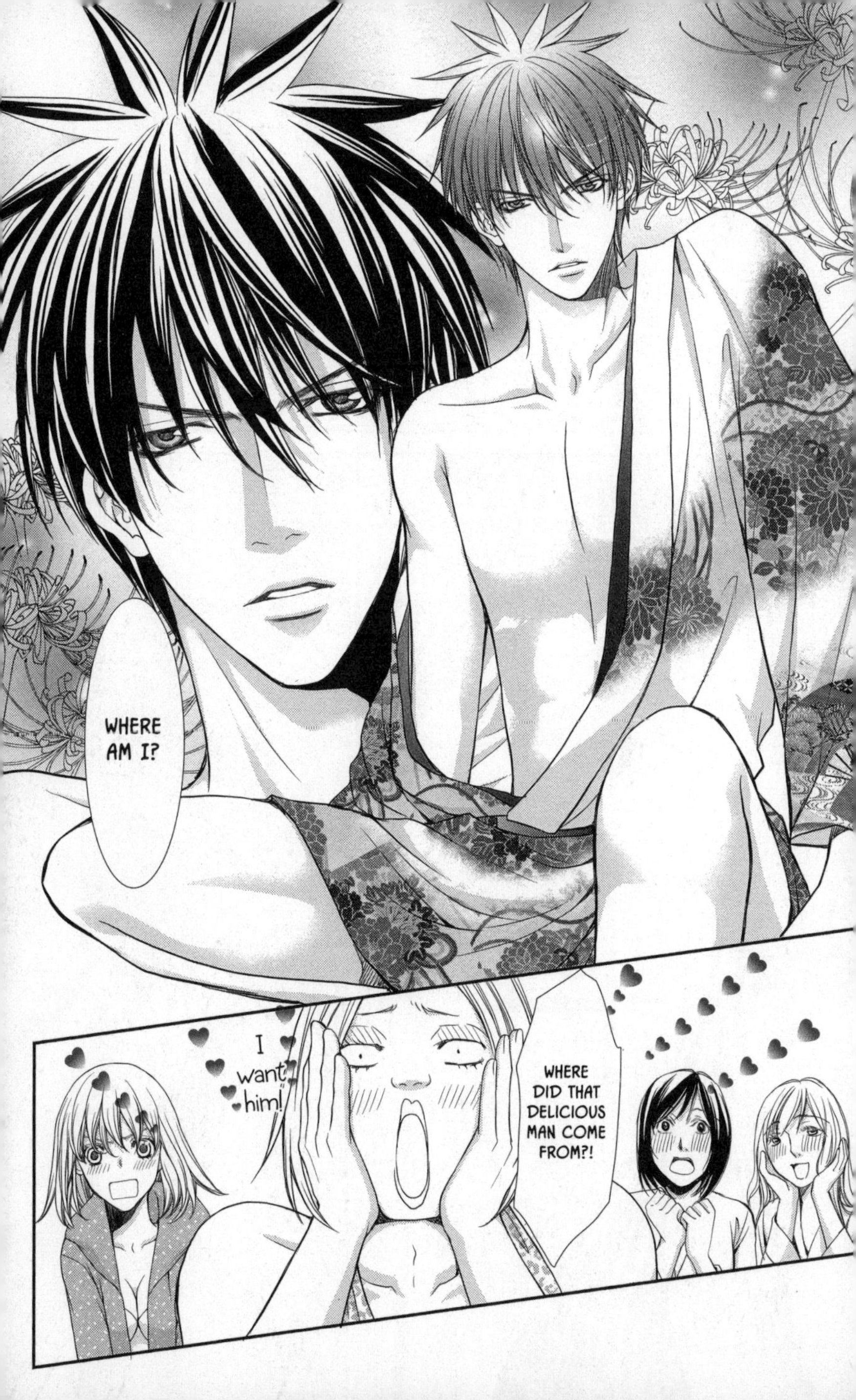
WHERE AM I?
WHERE DID THAT DELICIOUS MAN COME FROM?!
I want him!

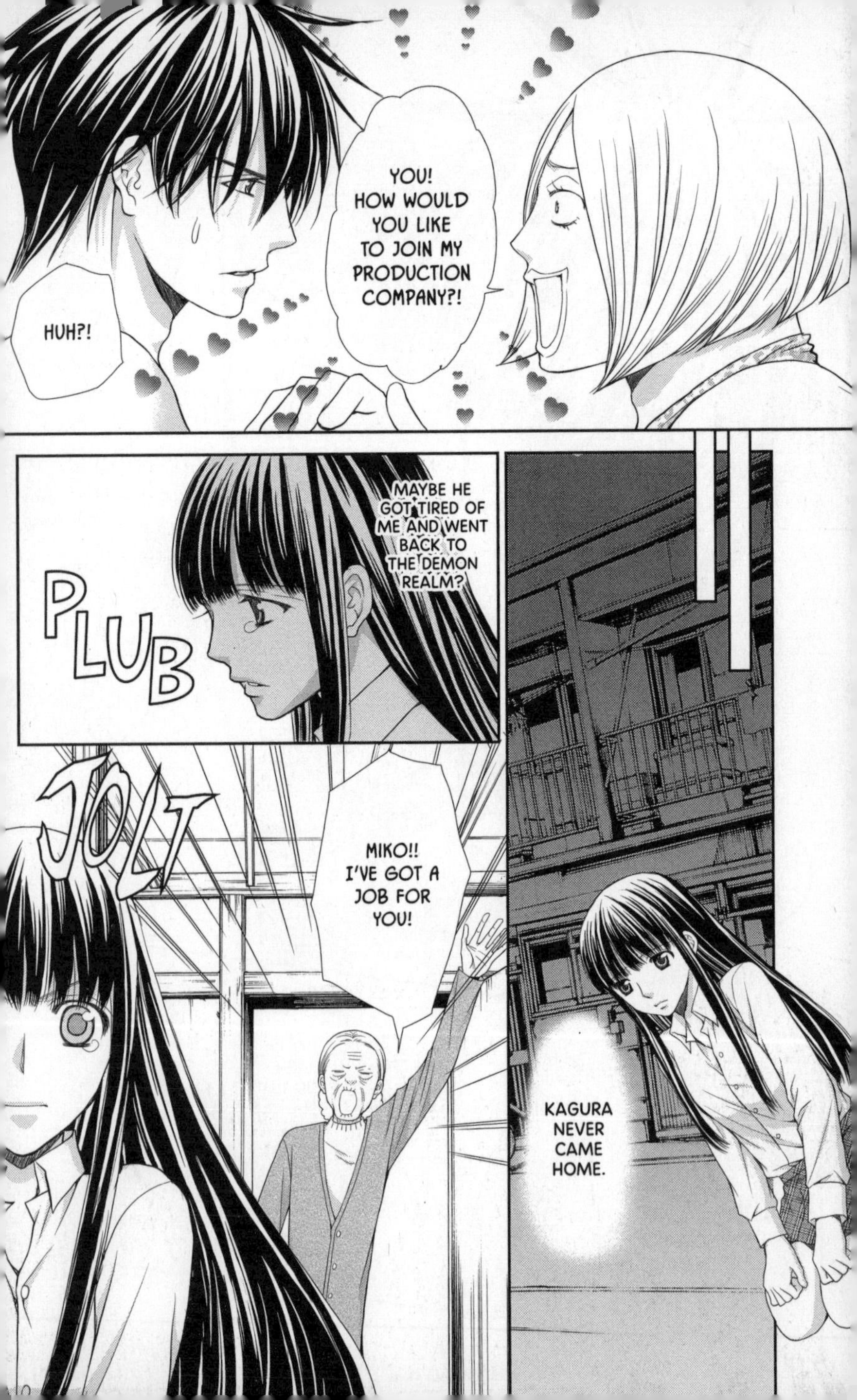
YOU! HOW WOULD YOU LIKE TO JOIN MY PRODUCTION COMPANY?!
HUH?!
KAGURA NEVER CAME HOME.
MAYBE HE GOT TIRED OF ME AND WENT BACK TO THE DEMON REALM?
PLUB
MIKO!! I'VE GOT A JOB FOR YOU!
JOLT

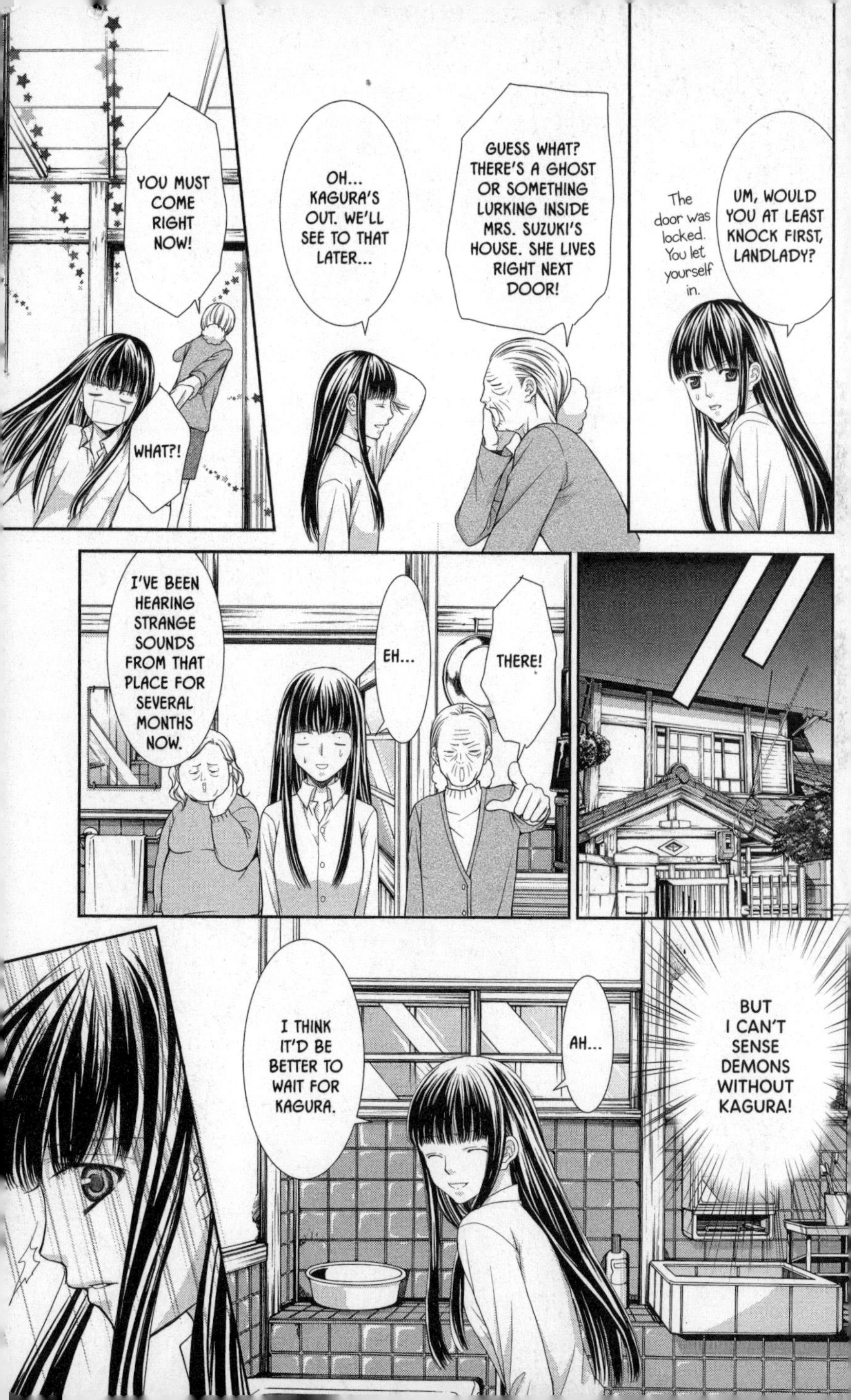
UM, WOULD YOU AT LEAST KNOCK FIRST, LANDLADY?
The door was locked. You let yourself in.
GUESS WHAT? THERE'S A GHOST OR SOMETHING LURKING INSIDE MRS. SUZUKI'S HOUSE. SHE LIVES RIGHT NEXT DOOR!
OH... KAGURA'S OUT. WE'LL SEE TO THAT LATER...
YOU MUST COME RIGHT NOW!
WHAT?!
THERE!
EH...
I'VE BEEN HEARING STRANGE SOUNDS FROM THAT PLACE FOR SEVERAL MONTHS NOW.
BUT I CAN'T SENSE DEMONS WITHOUT KAGURA!
AH...
I THINK IT'D BE BETTER TO WAIT FOR KAGURA.

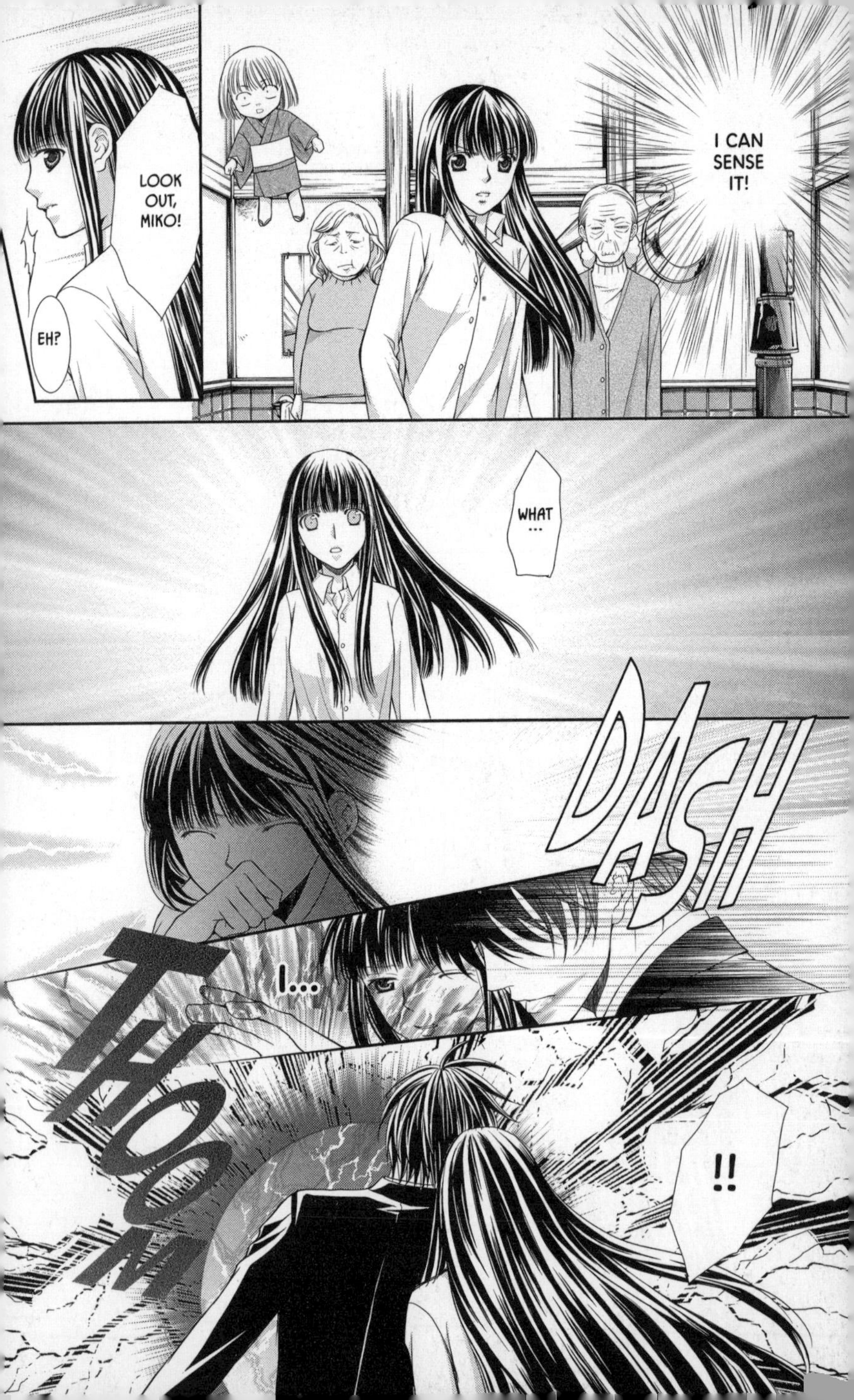
I CAN SENSE IT!
LOOK OUT, MIKO!
EH?
WHAT...
DASH
I...
THOOM
!!

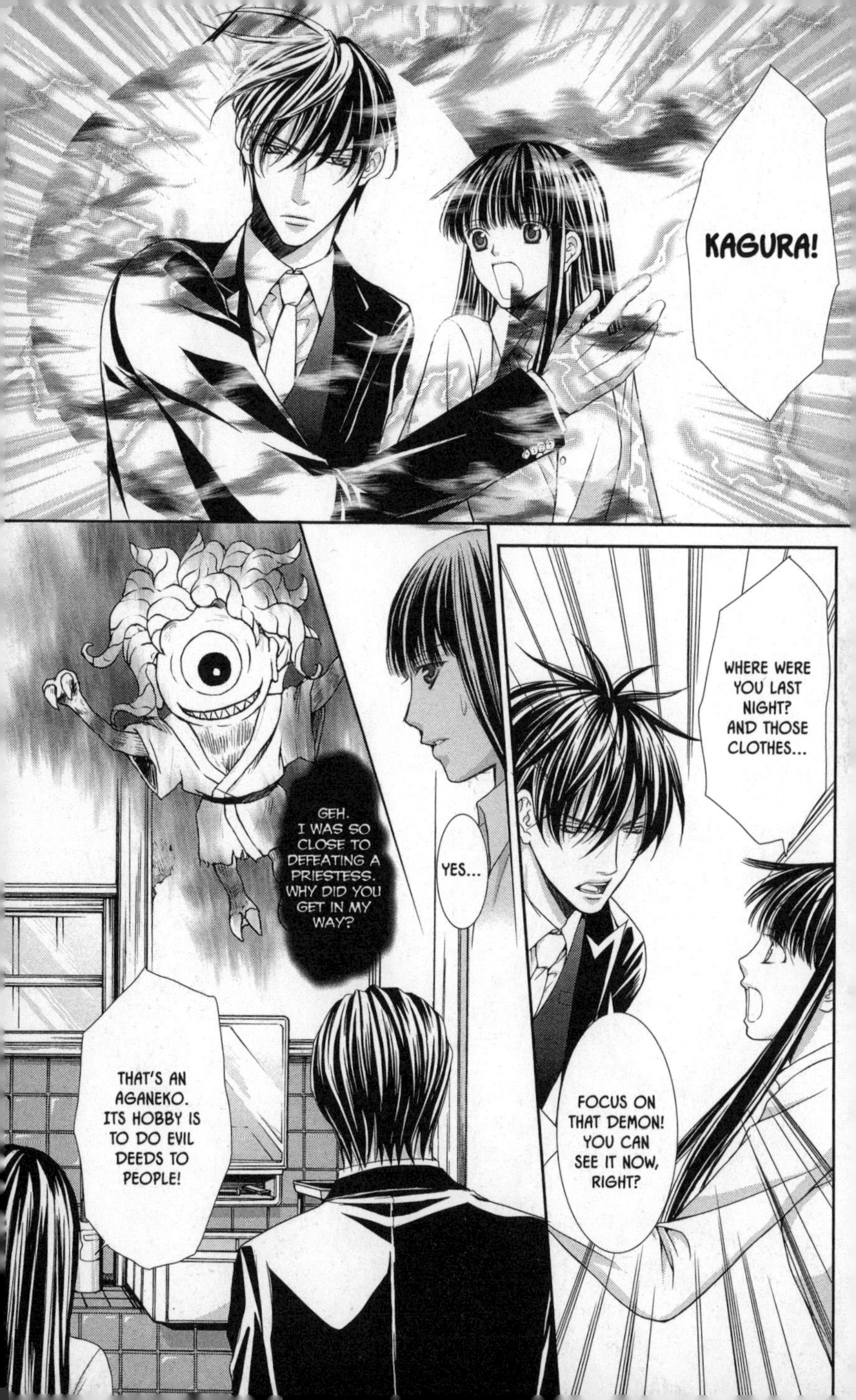
KAGURA!
WHERE WERE YOU LAST NIGHT? AND THOSE CLOTHES...
YES...
GEH. I WAS SO CLOSE TO DEFEATING A PRIESTESS. WHY DID YOU GET IN MY WAY?
FOCUS ON THAT DEMON! YOU CAN SEE IT NOW, RIGHT?
THAT'S AN AGANEKO. ITS HOBBY IS TO DO EVIL DEEDS TO PEOPLE!

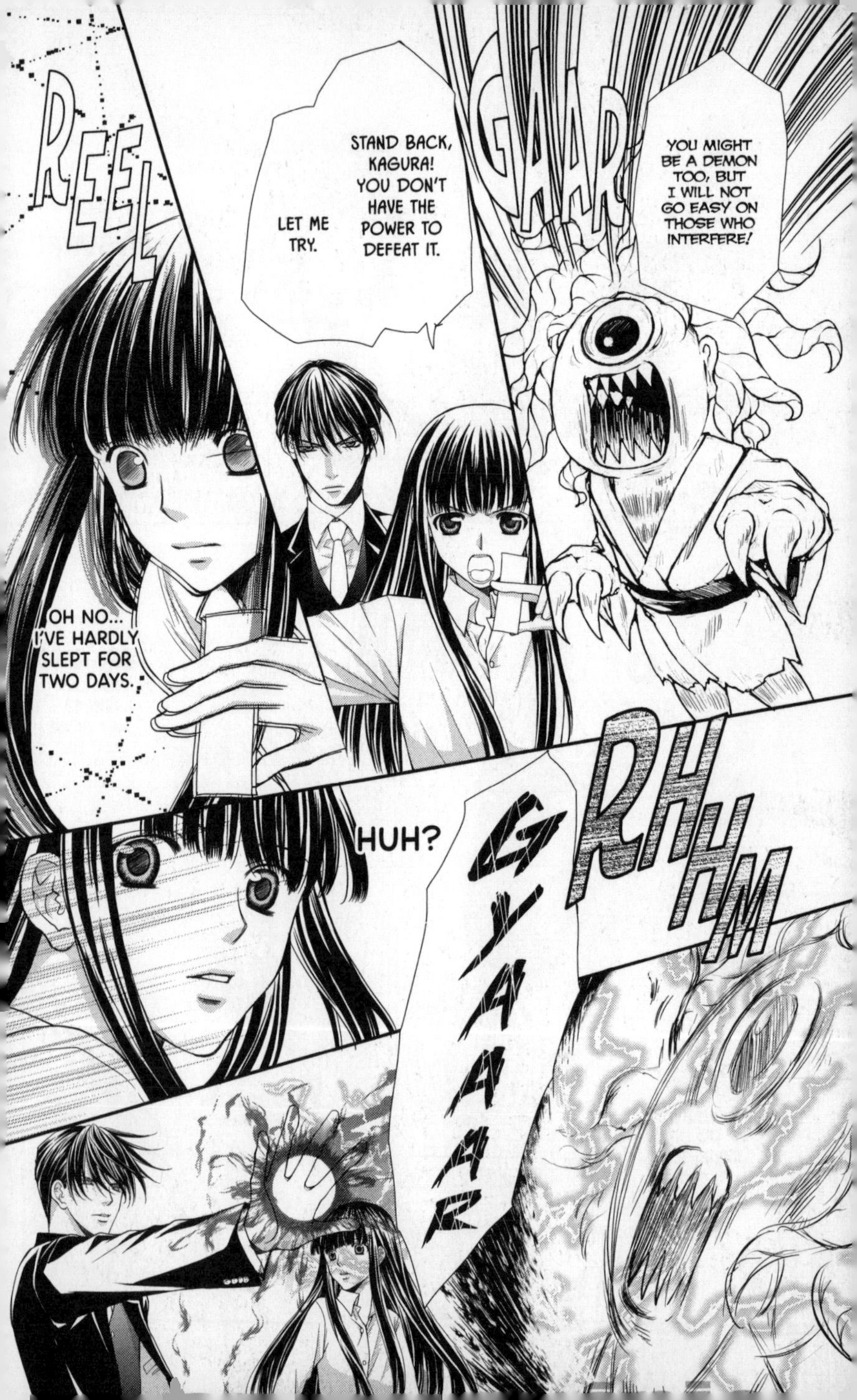
GAAR
YOU MIGHT BE A DEMON TOO, BUT I WILL NOT GO EASY ON THOSE WHO INTERFERE!
STAND BACK, KAGURA! YOU DON'T HAVE THE POWER TO DEFEAT IT.
LET ME TRY.
REEL
OH NO... I'VE HARDLY SLEPT FOR TWO DAYS.
RHHM
GYAAAAR
HUH?

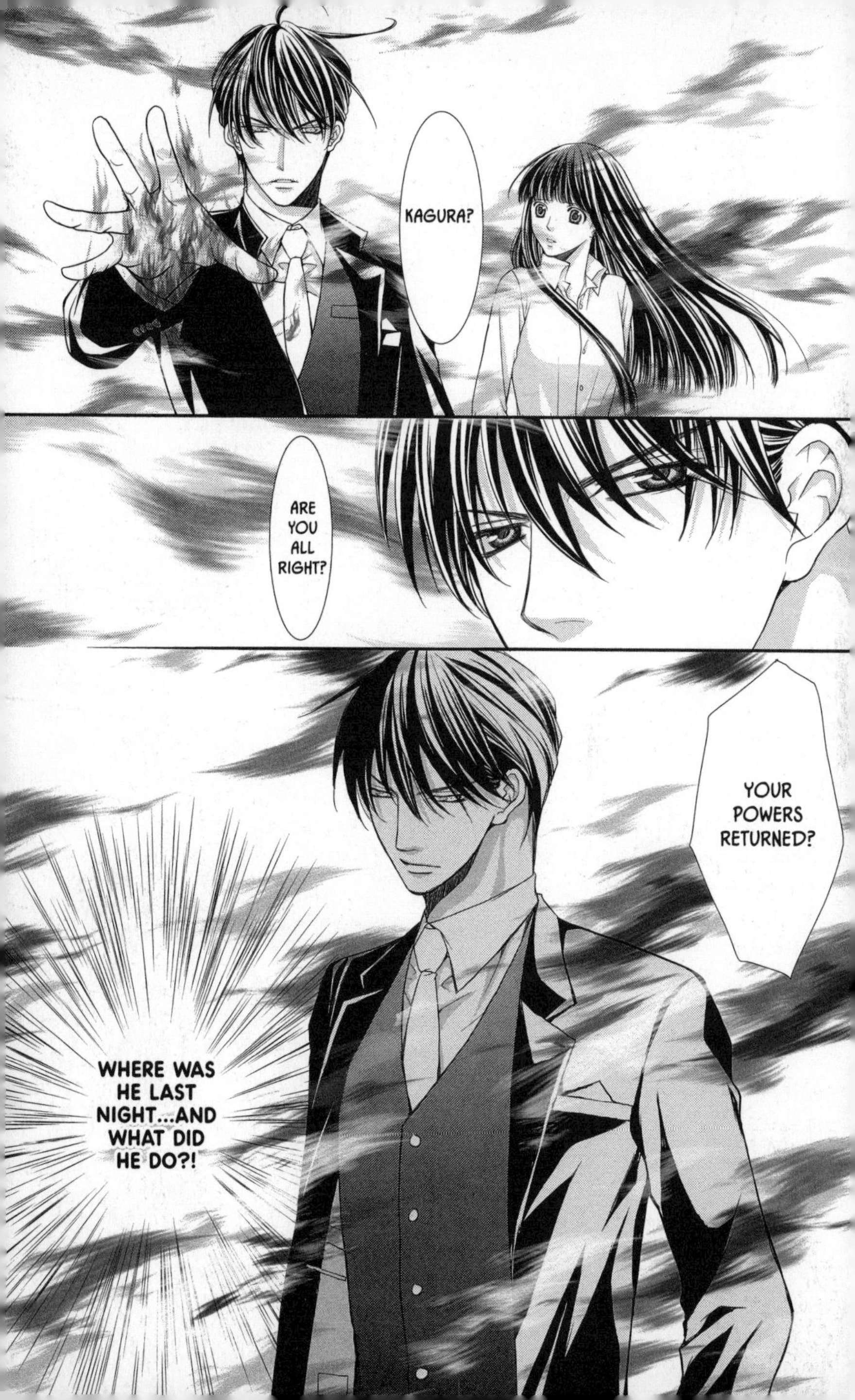
KAGURA?
ARE YOU ALL RIGHT?
YOUR POWERS RETURNED?
WHERE WAS HE LAST NIGHT...AND WHAT DID HE DO?!

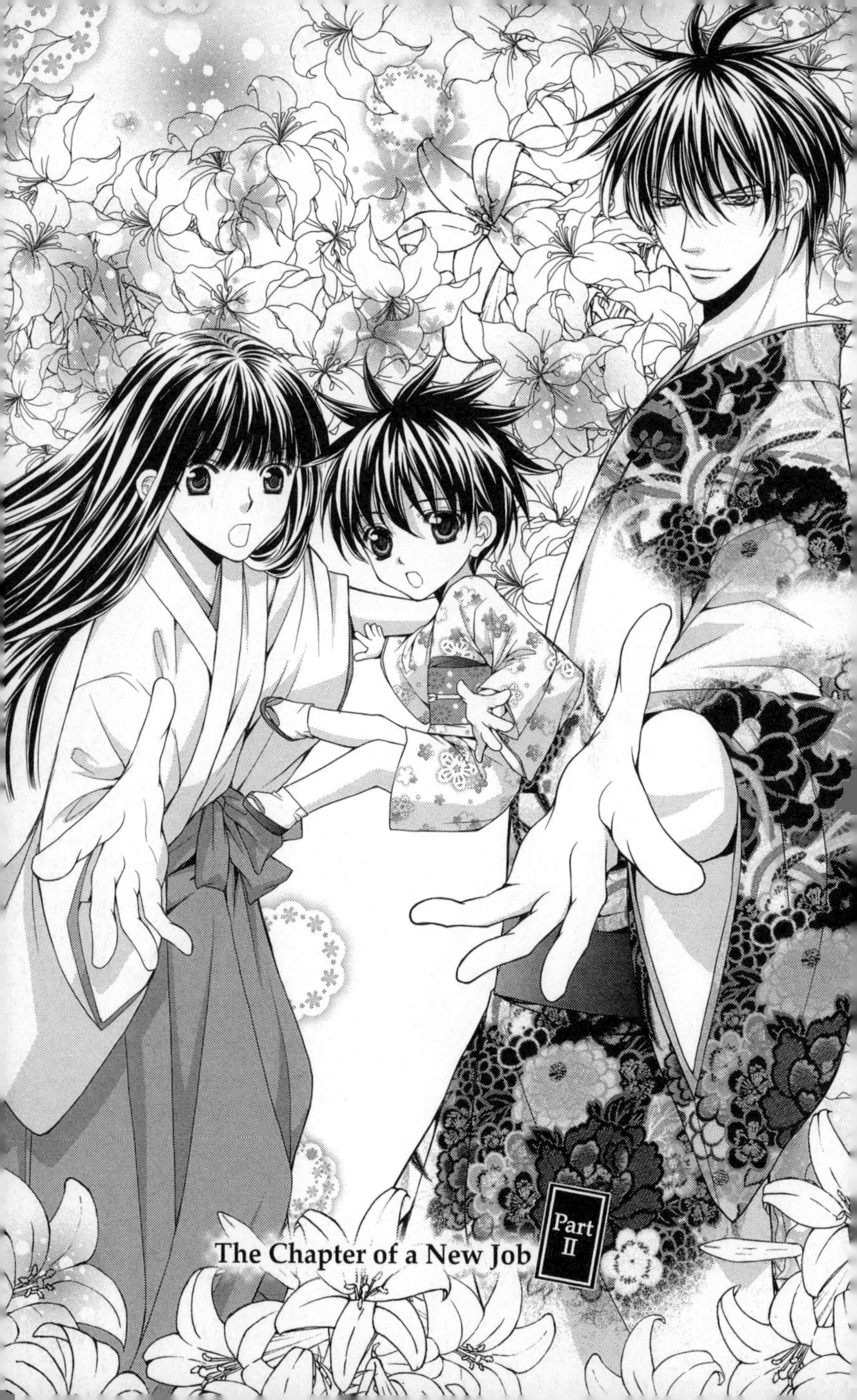
The Chapter of a New Job
Part II

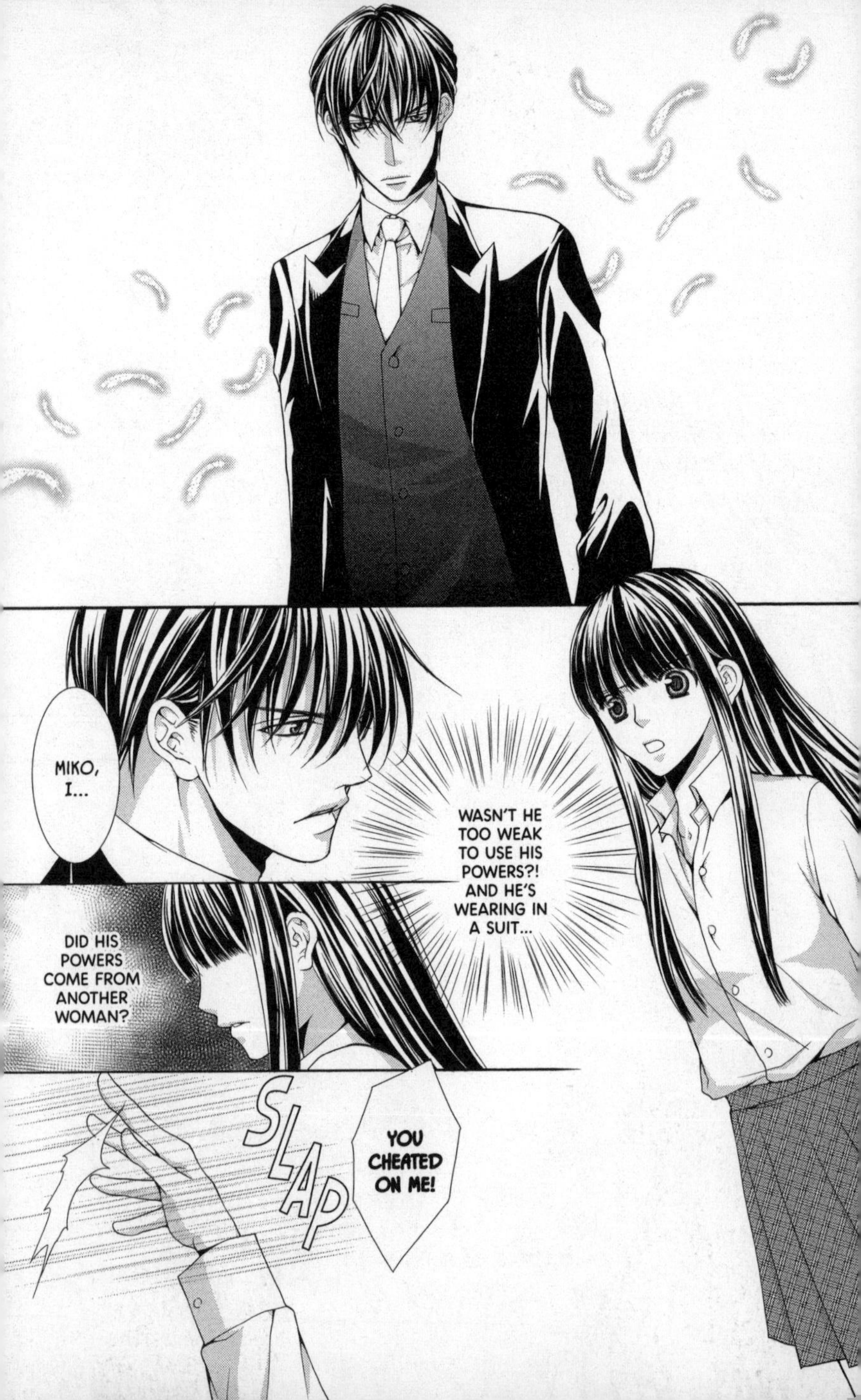
WASN'T HE TOO WEAK TO USE HIS POWERS?! AND HE'S WEARING IN A SUIT...
MIKO, I...
DID HIS POWERS COME FROM ANOTHER WOMAN?
YOU CHEATED ON ME!
SLAP

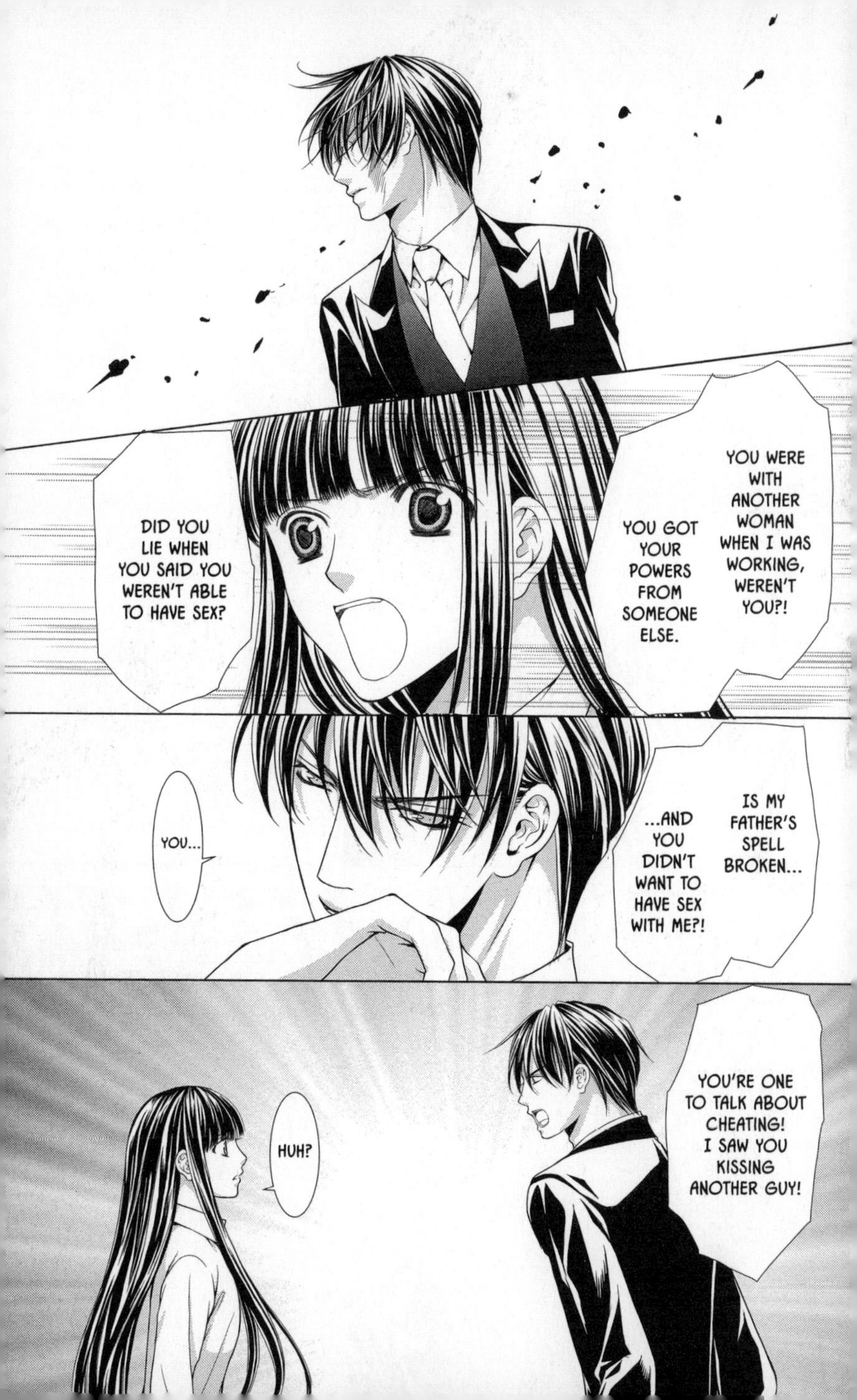
YOU WERE WITH ANOTHER WOMAN WHEN I WAS WORKING, WEREN'T YOU?!
YOU GOT YOUR POWERS FROM SOMEONE ELSE.
DID YOU LIE WHEN YOU SAID YOU WEREN'T ABLE TO HAVE SEX?
IS MY FATHER'S SPELL BROKEN...
...AND YOU DIDN'T WANT TO HAVE SEX WITH ME?!
YOU...
YOU'RE ONE TO TALK ABOUT CHEATING! I SAW YOU KISSING ANOTHER GUY!
HUH?

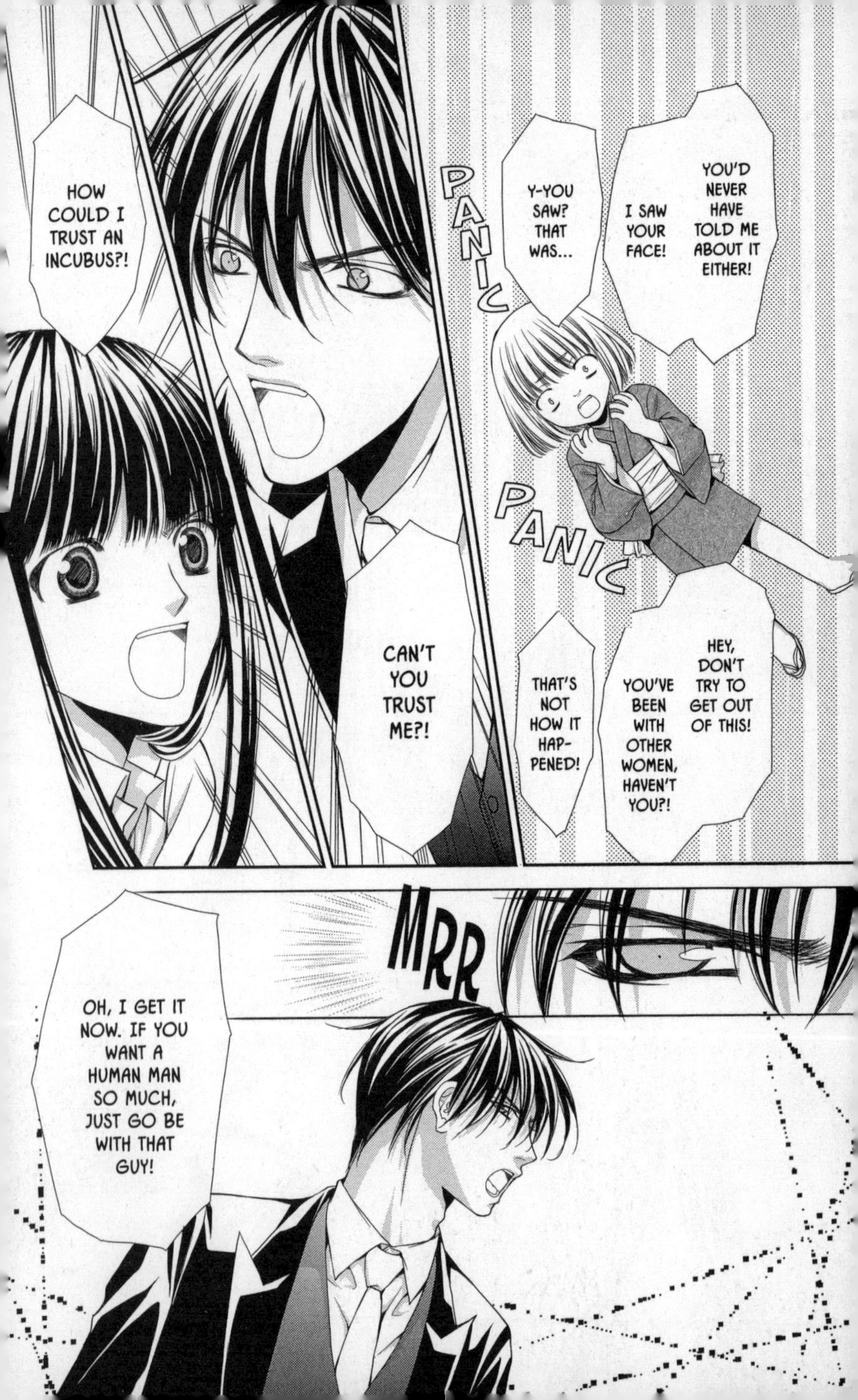
YOU'D NEVER HAVE TOLD ME ABOUT IT EITHER!
I SAW YOUR FACE!
Y-YOU SAW? THAT WAS...
PANIC
PANIC
HEY, DON'T TRY TO GET OUT OF THIS!
YOU'VE BEEN WITH OTHER WOMEN, HAVEN'T YOU?!
THAT'S NOT HOW IT HAP-PENED!
CAN'T YOU TRUST ME?!
HOW COULD I TRUST AN INCUBUS?!
MRR
OH, I GET IT NOW. IF YOU WANT A HUMAN MAN SO MUCH, JUST GO BE WITH THAT GUY!

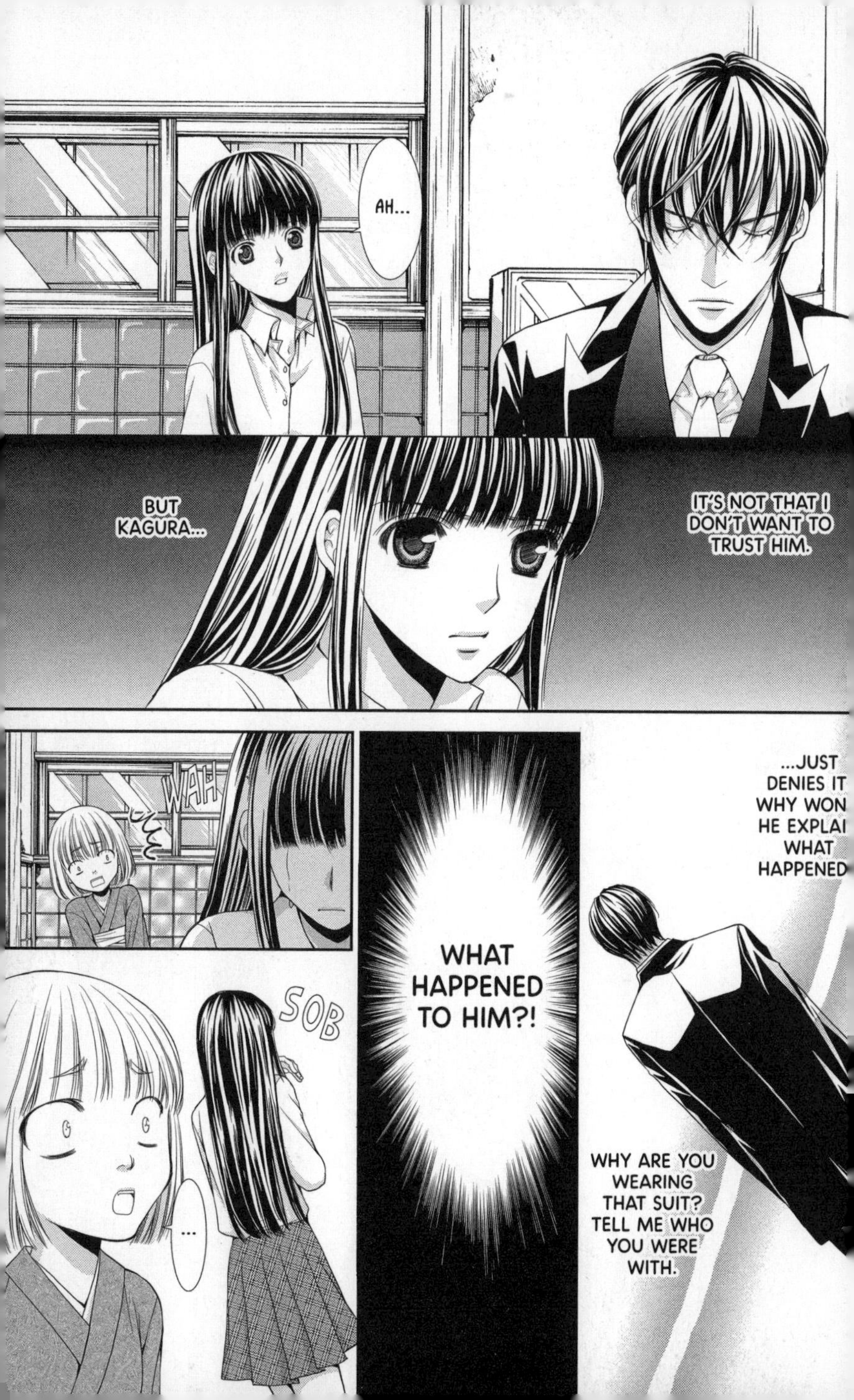
AH...
IT'S NOT THAT I DON'T WANT TO TRUST HIM.
BUT KAGURA...
...JUST DENIES IT WHY WON HE EXPLAI WHAT HAPPENED
WHY ARE YOU WEARING THAT SUIT? TELL ME WHO YOU WERE WITH.
WHAT HAPPENED TO HIM?!
WAH
SOB
...

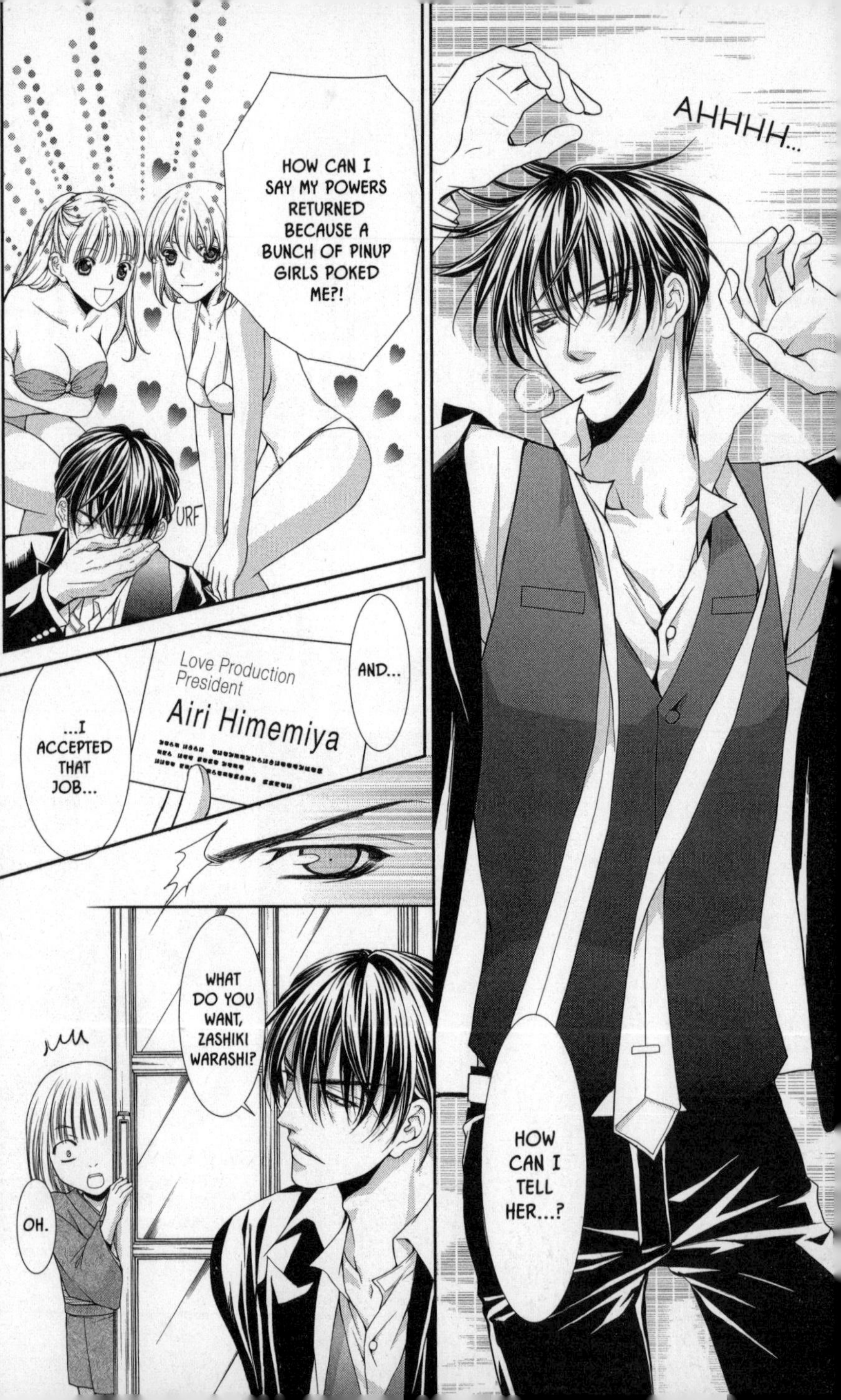
AHHHH...
HOW CAN I TELL HER...?
HOW CAN I SAY MY POWERS RETURNED BECAUSE A BUNCH OF PINUP GIRLS POKED ME?!
URF
AND...
...I ACCEPTED THAT JOB...
Love Production President
Airi Himemiya
WHAT DO YOU WANT, ZASHIKI WARASHI?
OH.

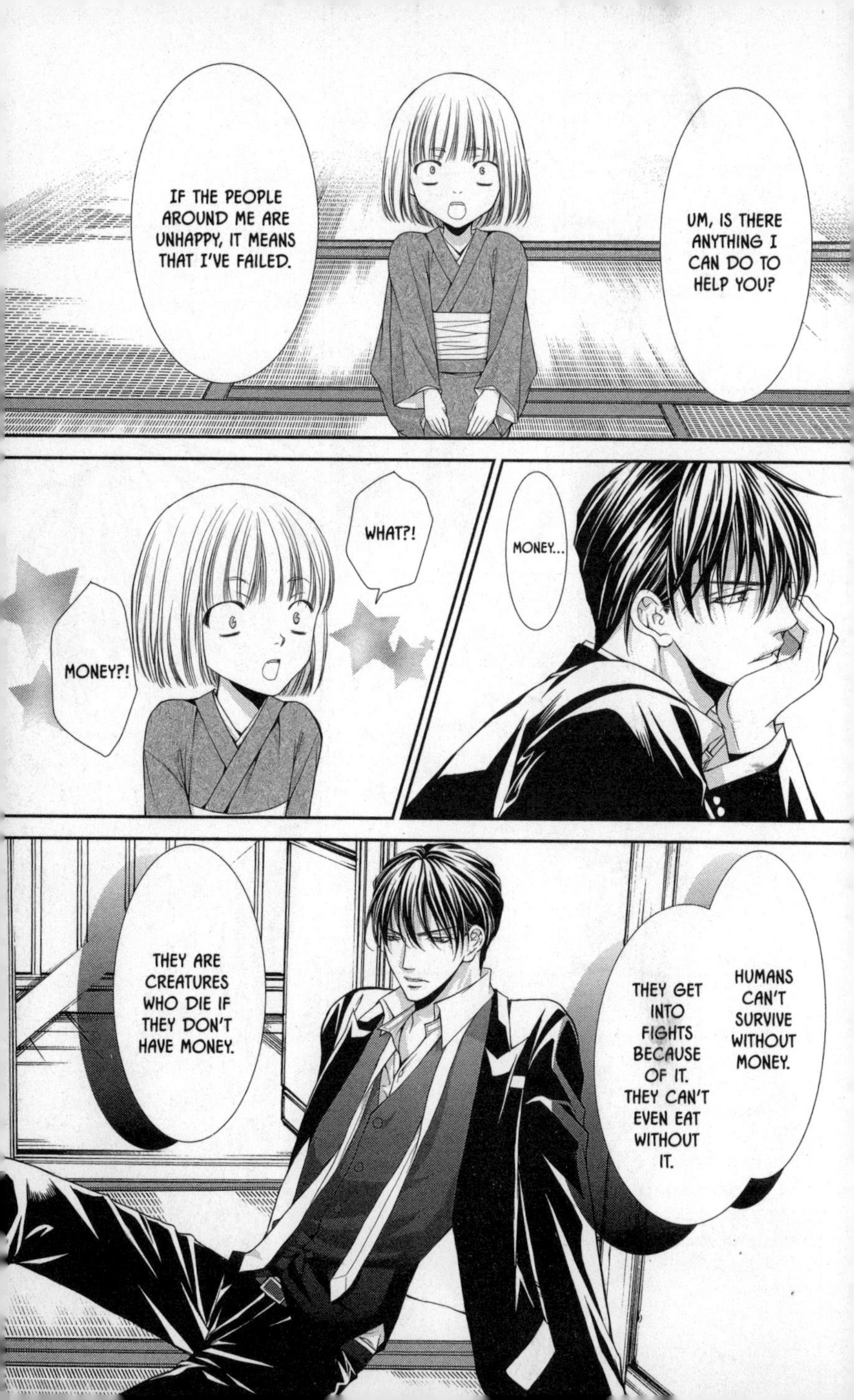
UM, IS THERE ANYTHING I CAN DO TO HELP YOU?
IF THE PEOPLE AROUND ME ARE UNHAPPY, IT MEANS THAT I'VE FAILED.
MONEY...
WHAT?!
MONEY?!
HUMANS CAN'T SURVIVE WITHOUT MONEY.
THEY GET INTO FIGHTS BECAUSE OF IT. THEY CAN'T EVEN EAT WITHOUT IT.
THEY ARE CREATURES WHO DIE IF THEY DON'T HAVE MONEY.

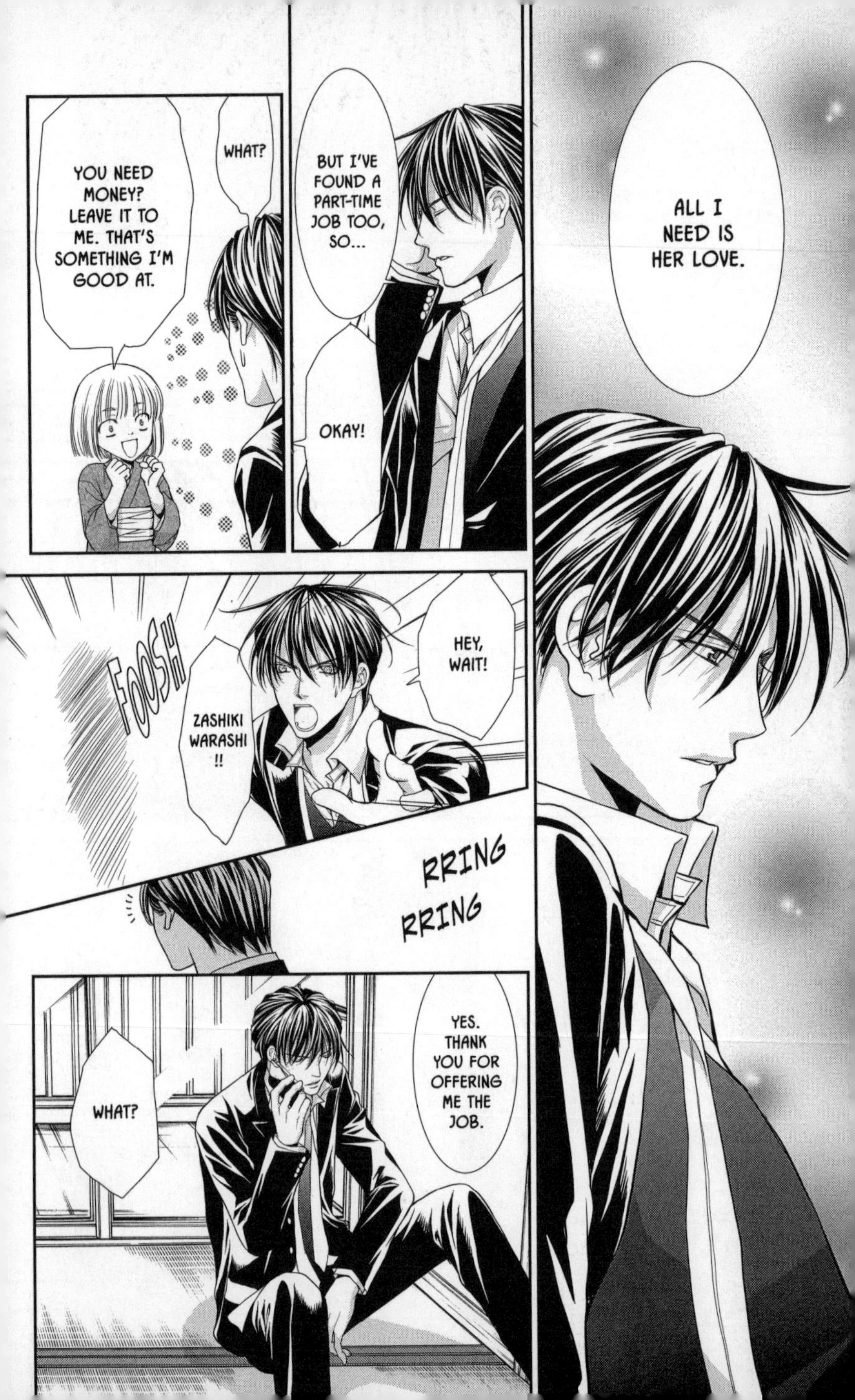
ALL I NEED IS HER LOVE.
BUT I'VE FOUND A PART-TIME JOB TOO, SO...
OKAY!
WHAT?
YOU NEED MONEY? LEAVE IT TO ME. THAT'S SOMETHING I'M GOOD AT.
HEY, WAIT!
ZASHIKI WARASHI !!
FOOSH
RRING RRING
YES. THANK YOU FOR OFFERING ME THE JOB.
WHAT?

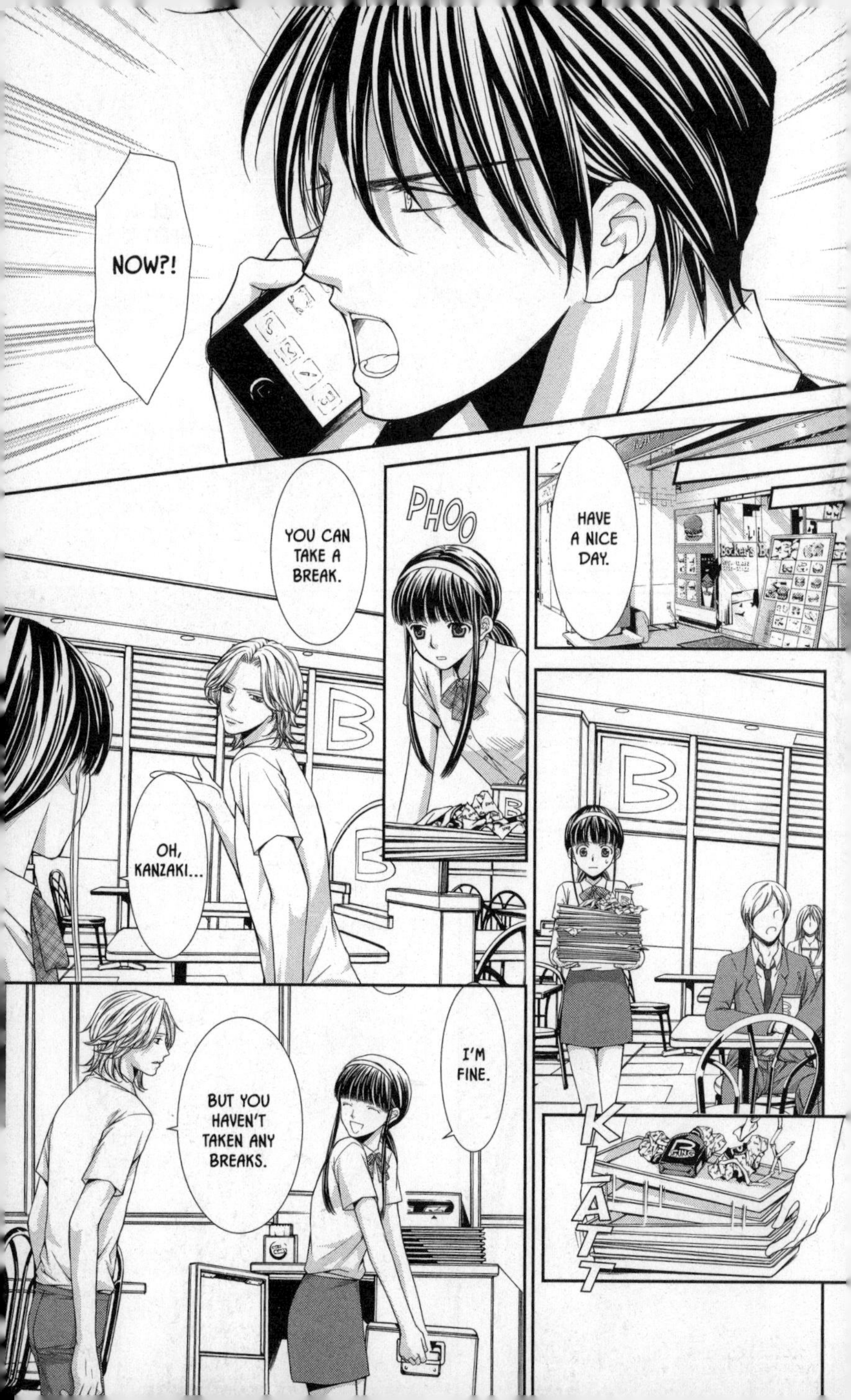
NOW?!
HAVE A NICE DAY.
KLATT
PHOO
YOU CAN TAKE A BREAK.
OH, KANZAKI...
I'M FINE.
BUT YOU HAVEN'T TAKEN ANY BREAKS.

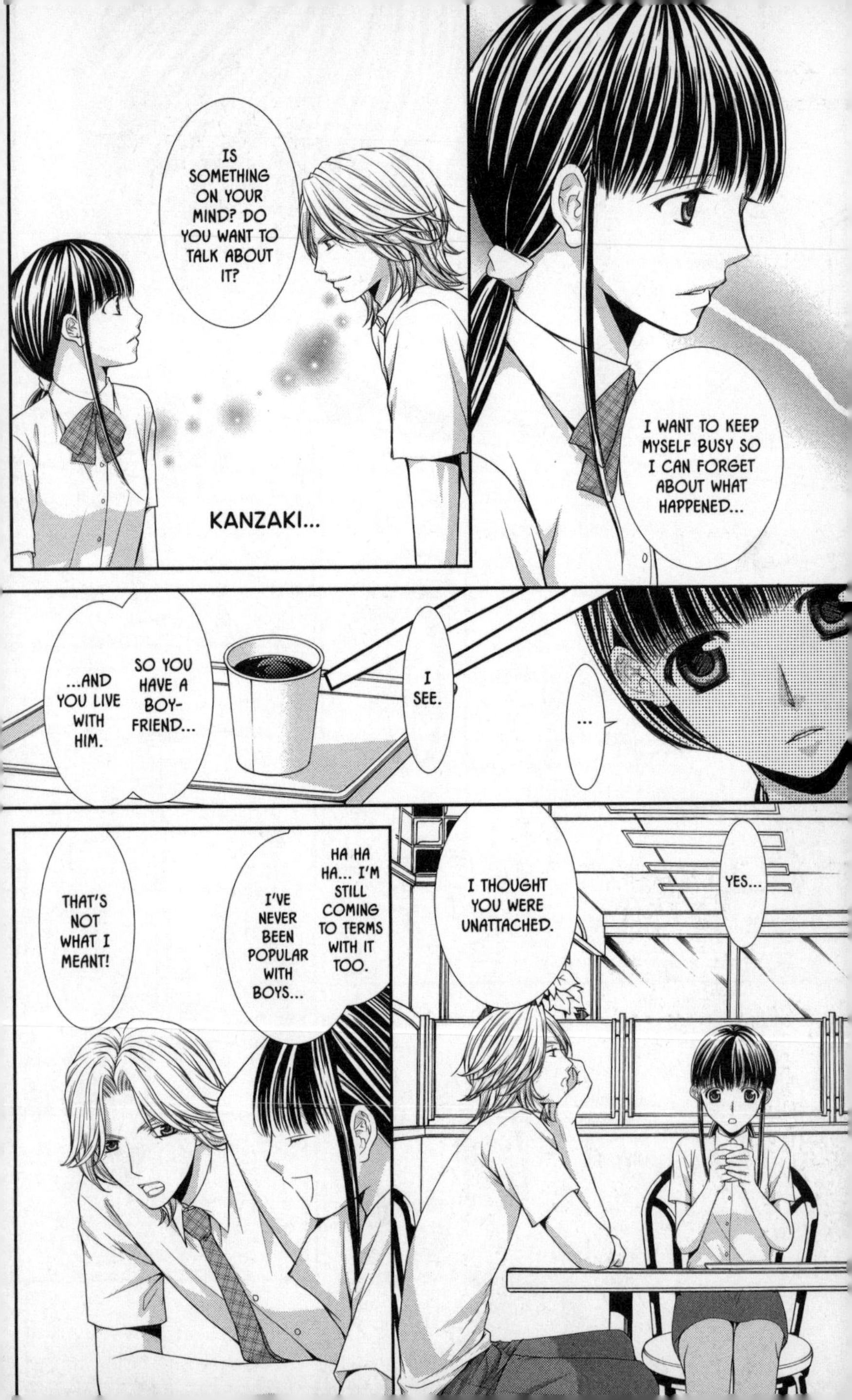
I WANT TO KEEP MYSELF BUSY SO I CAN FORGET ABOUT WHAT HAPPENED...
IS SOMETHING ON YOUR MIND? DO YOU WANT TO TALK ABOUT IT?
KANZAKI...
...
I SEE.
SO YOU HAVE A BOY-FRIEND...
...AND YOU LIVE WITH HIM.
YES...
I THOUGHT YOU WERE UNATTACHED.
HA HA HA... I'M STILL COMING TO TERMS WITH IT TOO.
I'VE NEVER BEEN POPULAR WITH BOYS...
THAT'S NOT WHAT I MEANT!

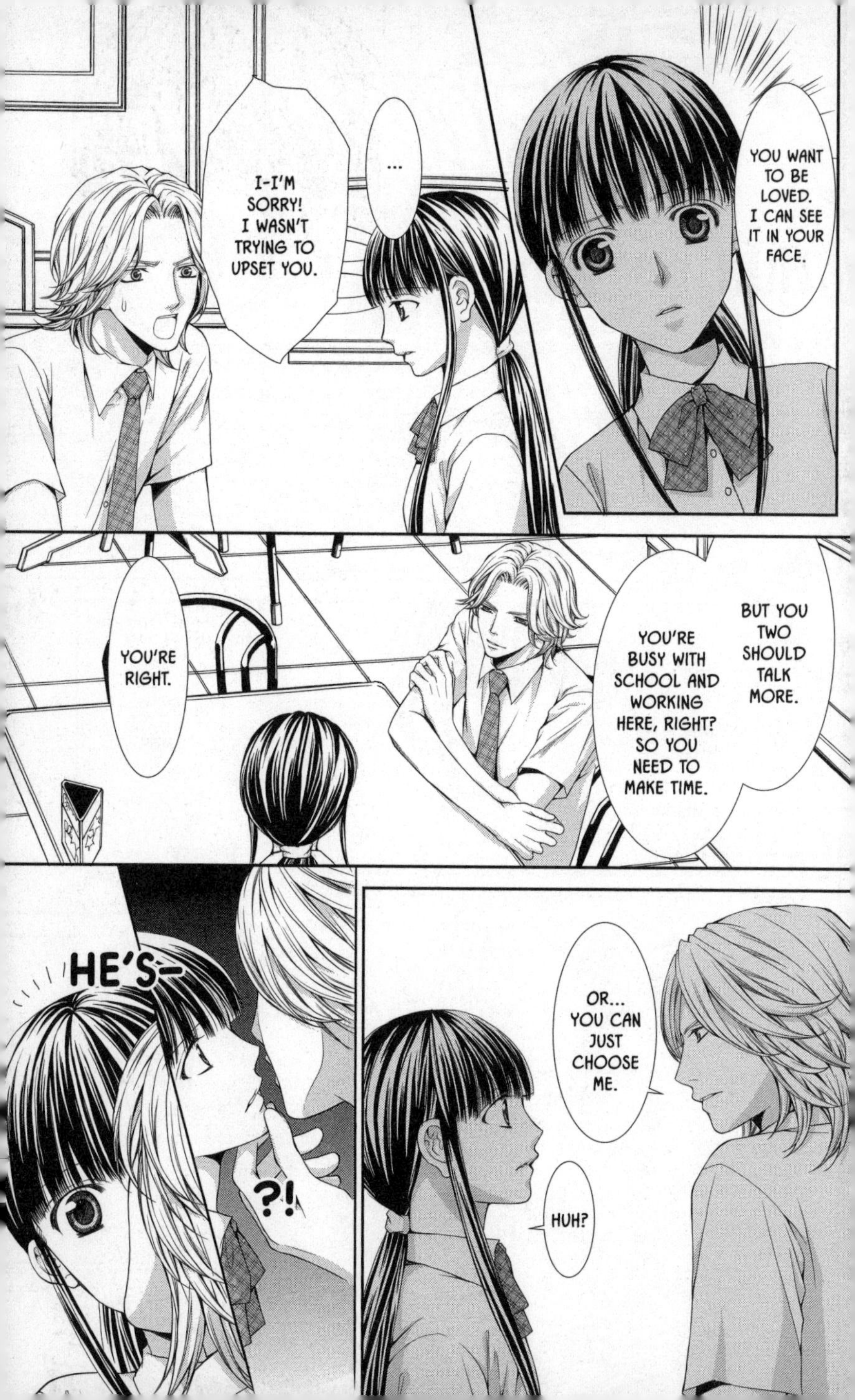
YOU WANT TO BE LOVED. I CAN SEE IT IN YOUR FACE.
...
I-I'M SORRY! I WASN'T TRYING TO UPSET YOU.
BUT YOU TWO SHOULD TALK MORE.
YOU'RE BUSY WITH SCHOOL AND WORKING HERE, RIGHT? SO YOU NEED TO MAKE TIME.
YOU'RE RIGHT.
OR... YOU CAN JUST CHOOSE ME.
HUH?
HE'S—
?!

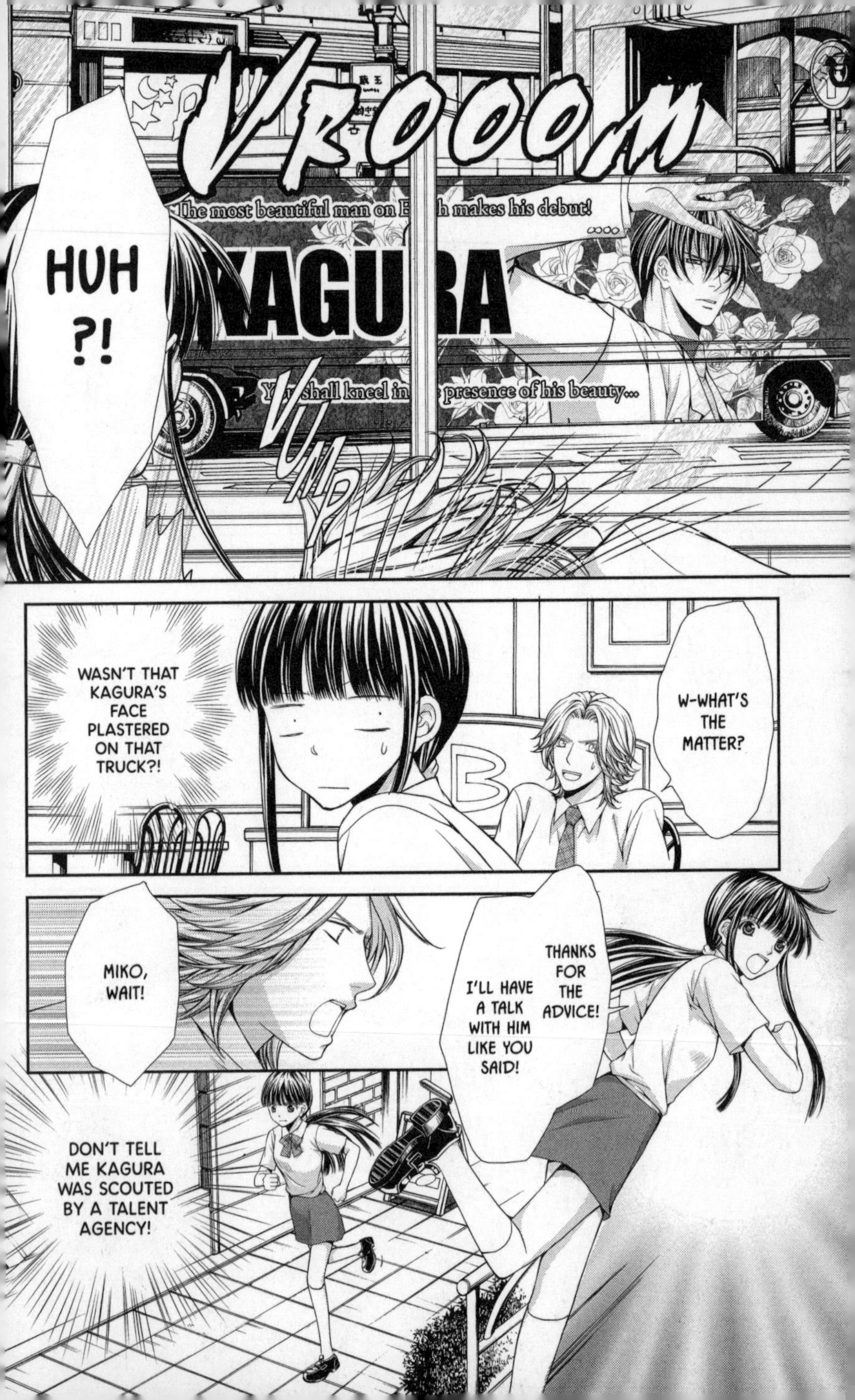

VROOOM
The most beautiful man on E h makes his debut!
KAGURA
Y shall kneel in presence of his beauty...
VUMP
HUH ?!
W-WHAT'S THE MATTER?
WASN'T THAT KAGURA'S FACE PLASTERED ON THAT TRUCK?!
THANKS FOR THE ADVICE!
I'LL HAVE A TALK WITH HIM LIKE YOU SAID!
MIKO, WAIT!
DON'T TELL ME KAGURA WAS SCOUTED BY A TALENT AGENCY!

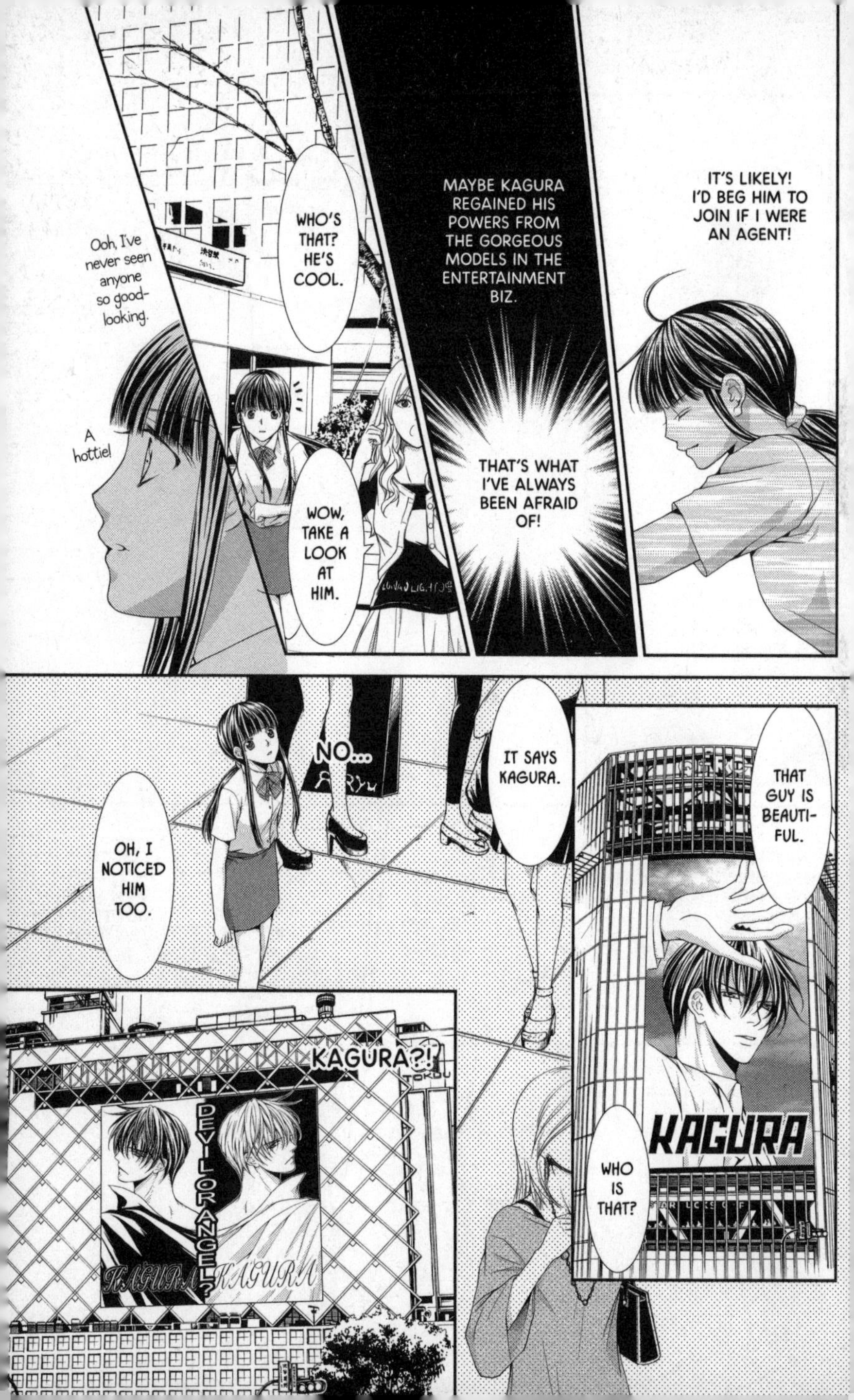
IT'S LIKELY! I'D BEG HIM TO JOIN IF I WERE AN AGENT!
MAYBE KAGURA REGAINED HIS POWERS FROM THE GORGEOUS MODELS IN THE ENTERTAINMENT BIZ.
THAT'S WHAT I'VE ALWAYS BEEN AFRAID OF!
WHO'S THAT? HE'S COOL.
WOW, TAKE A LOOK AT HIM.
Ooh, I've never seen anyone so good-looking.
A hottie!
THAT GUY IS BEAUTIFUL.
KAGURA
WHO IS THAT?
IT SAYS KAGURA.
NO...
OH, I NOTICED HIM TOO.
KAGURA?!
DEVIL OR ANGEL?
KAGURA
KAGURA

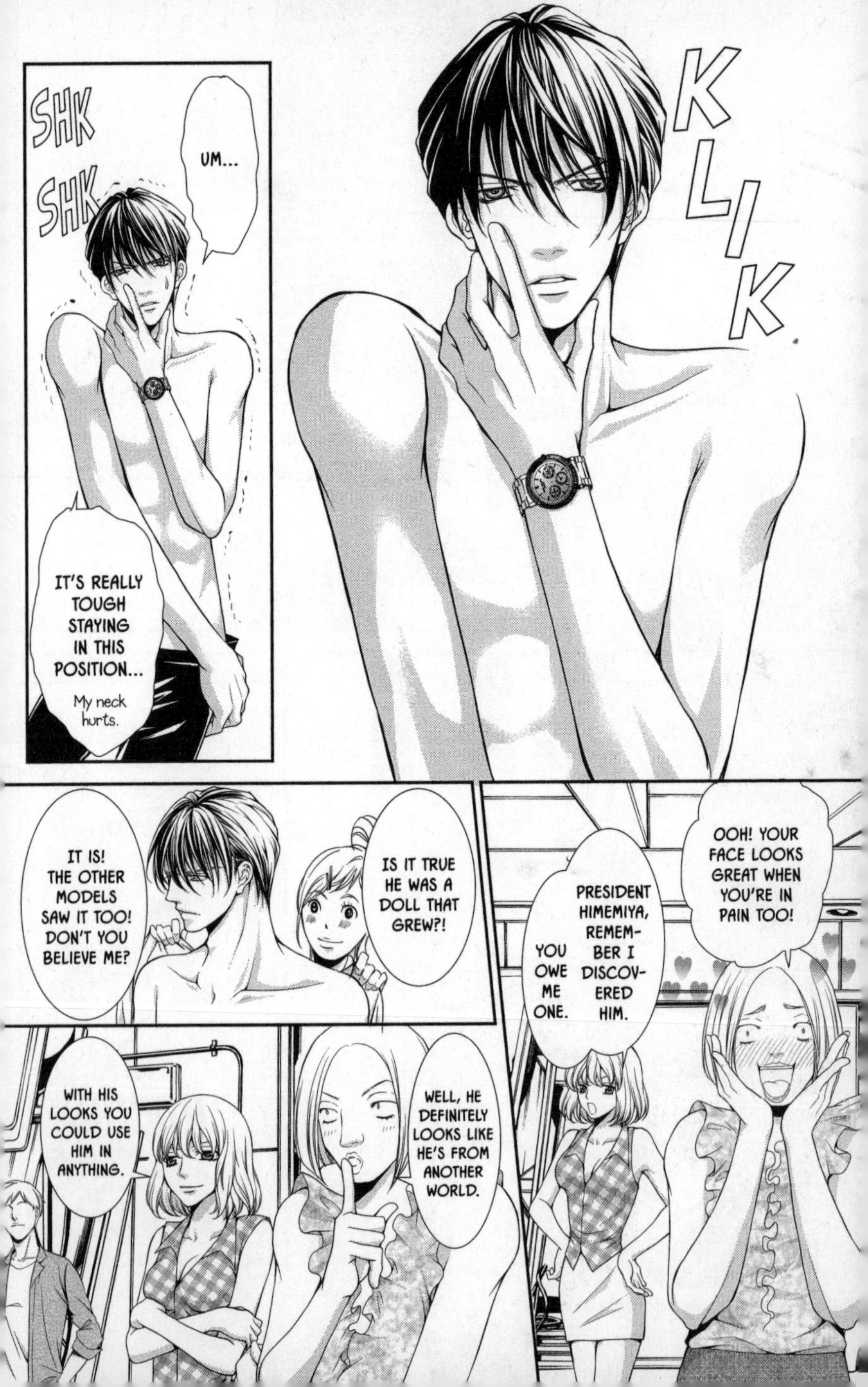
KLIK
SHK SHK
UM...
IT'S REALLY TOUGH STAYING IN THIS POSITION...
My neck hurts.
OOH! YOUR FACE LOOKS GREAT WHEN YOU'RE IN PAIN TOO!
PRESIDENT HIMEMIYA, REMEMBER I DISCOVERED HIM.
YOU OWE ME ONE.
IS IT TRUE HE WAS A DOLL THAT GREW?!
IT IS! THE OTHER MODELS SAW IT TOO! DON'T YOU BELIEVE ME?
WELL, HE DEFINITELY LOOKS LIKE HE'S FROM ANOTHER WORLD.
WITH HIS LOOKS YOU COULD USE HIM IN ANYTHING.

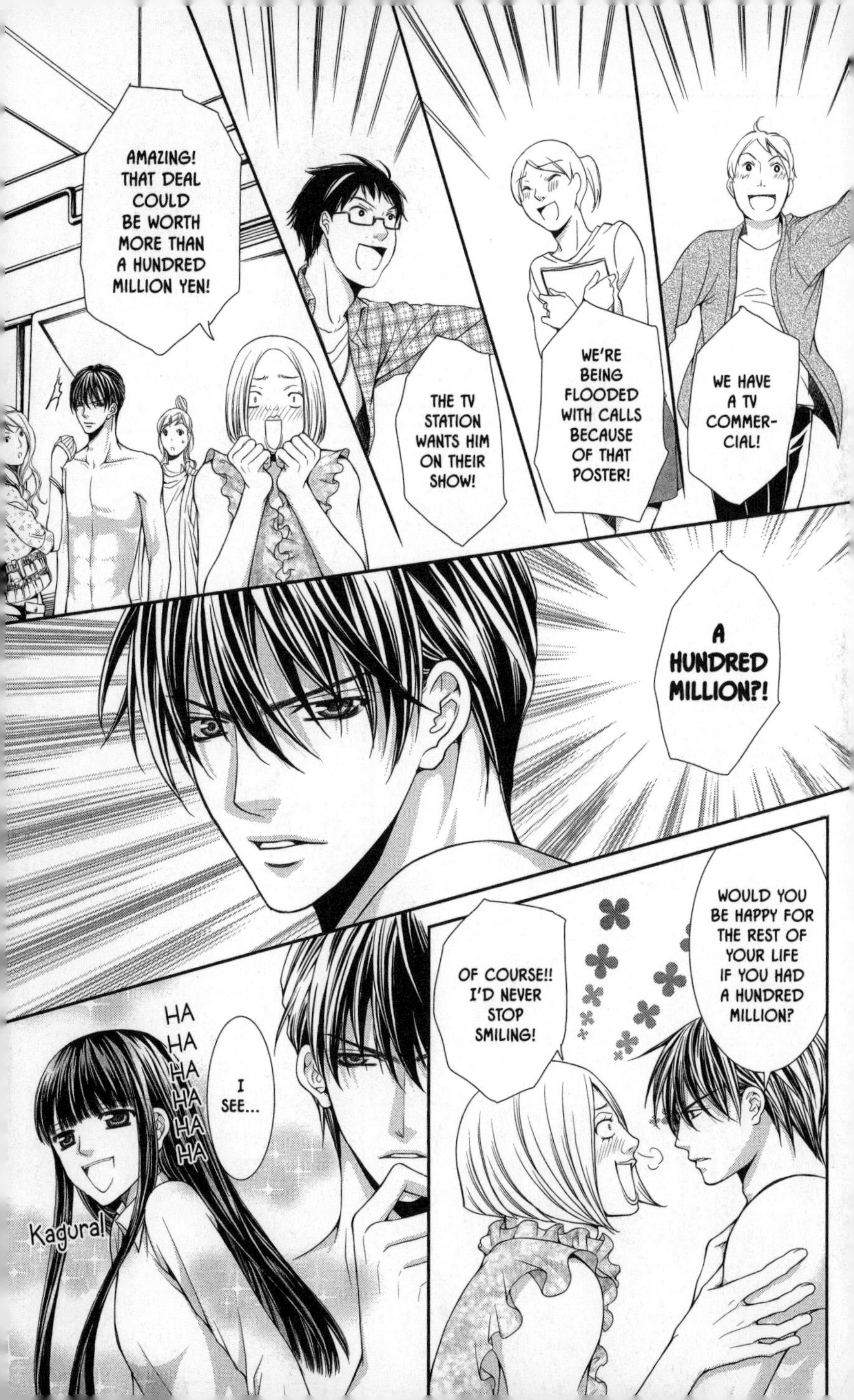
WE HAVE A TV COMMERCIAL!
WE'RE BEING FLOODED WITH CALLS BECAUSE OF THAT POSTER!
THE TV STATION WANTS HIM ON THEIR SHOW!
AMAZING! THAT DEAL COULD BE WORTH MORE THAN A HUNDRED MILLION YEN!
A HUNDRED MILLION?!
WOULD YOU BE HAPPY FOR THE REST OF YOUR LIFE IF YOU HAD A HUNDRED MILLION?
OF COURSE!! I'D NEVER STOP SMILING!
I SEE...
HA HA HA HA HA HA HA
Kagura!

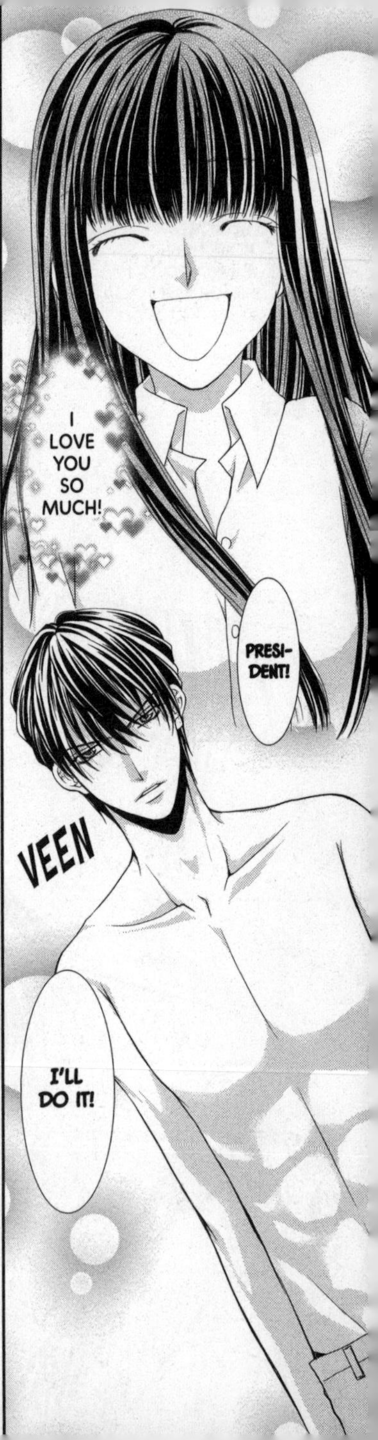
I LOVE YOU SO MUCH!
PRESIDENT!
VEEN
I'LL DO IT!
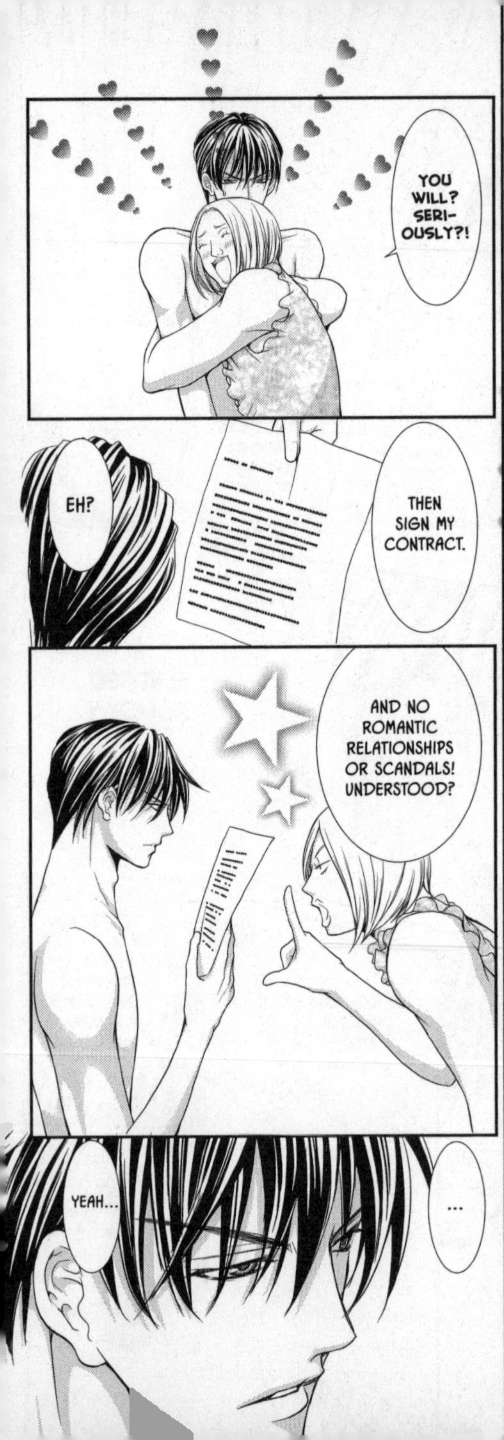
YOU WILL? SERI-OUSLY?!
THEN SIGN MY CONTRACT.
EH?
AND NO ROMANTIC RELATIONSHIPS OR SCANDALS! UNDERSTOOD?
...
YEAH...

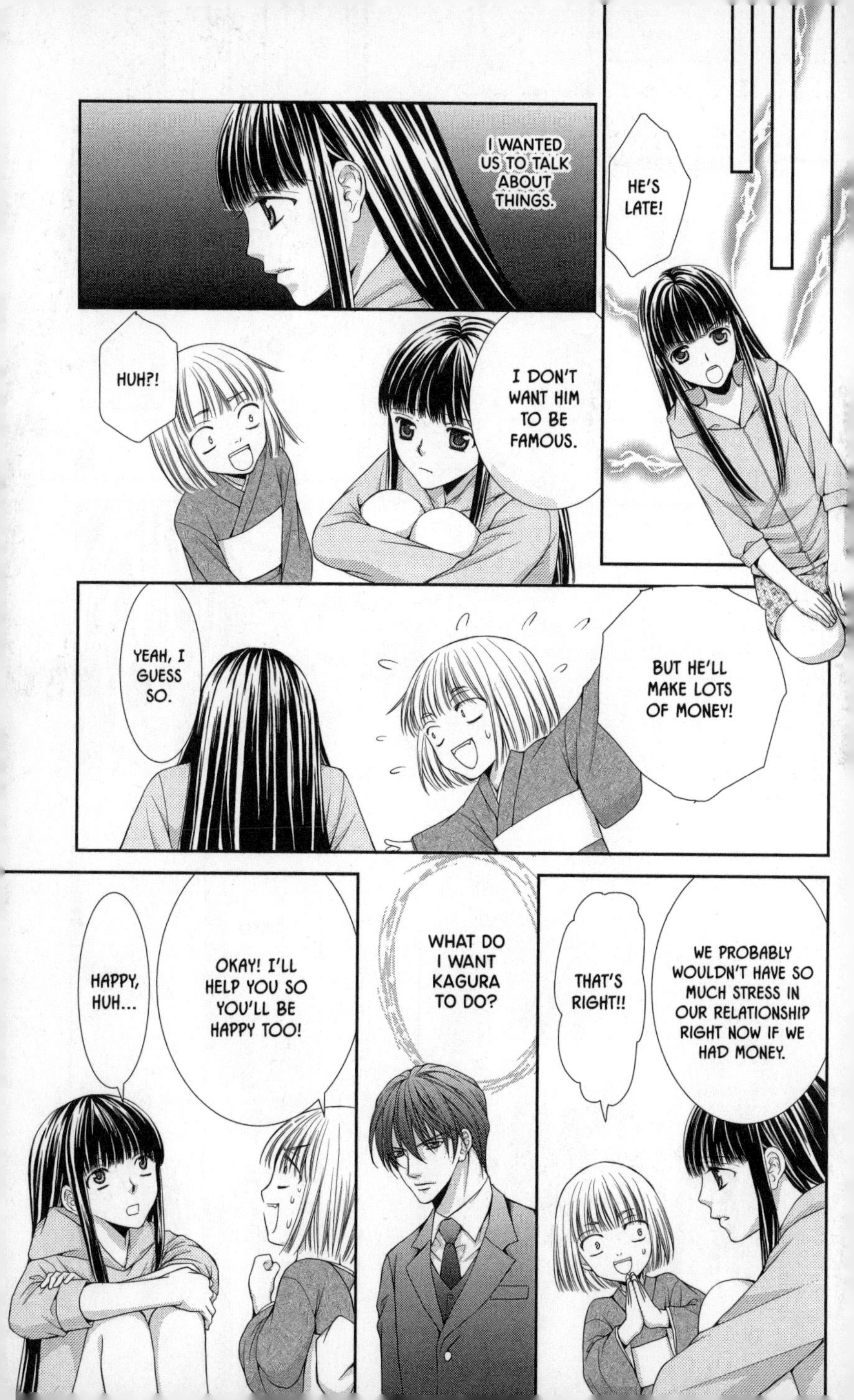
HE'S LATE!
I WANTED US TO TALK ABOUT THINGS.
I DON'T WANT HIM TO BE FAMOUS.
HUH?!
BUT HE'LL MAKE LOTS OF MONEY!
YEAH, I GUESS SO.
WE PROBABLY WOULDN'T HAVE SO MUCH STRESS IN OUR RELATIONSHIP RIGHT NOW IF WE HAD MONEY.
THAT'S RIGHT!!
WHAT DO I WANT KAGURA TO DO?
OKAY! I'LL HELP YOU SO YOU'LL BE HAPPY TOO!
HAPPY, HUH...

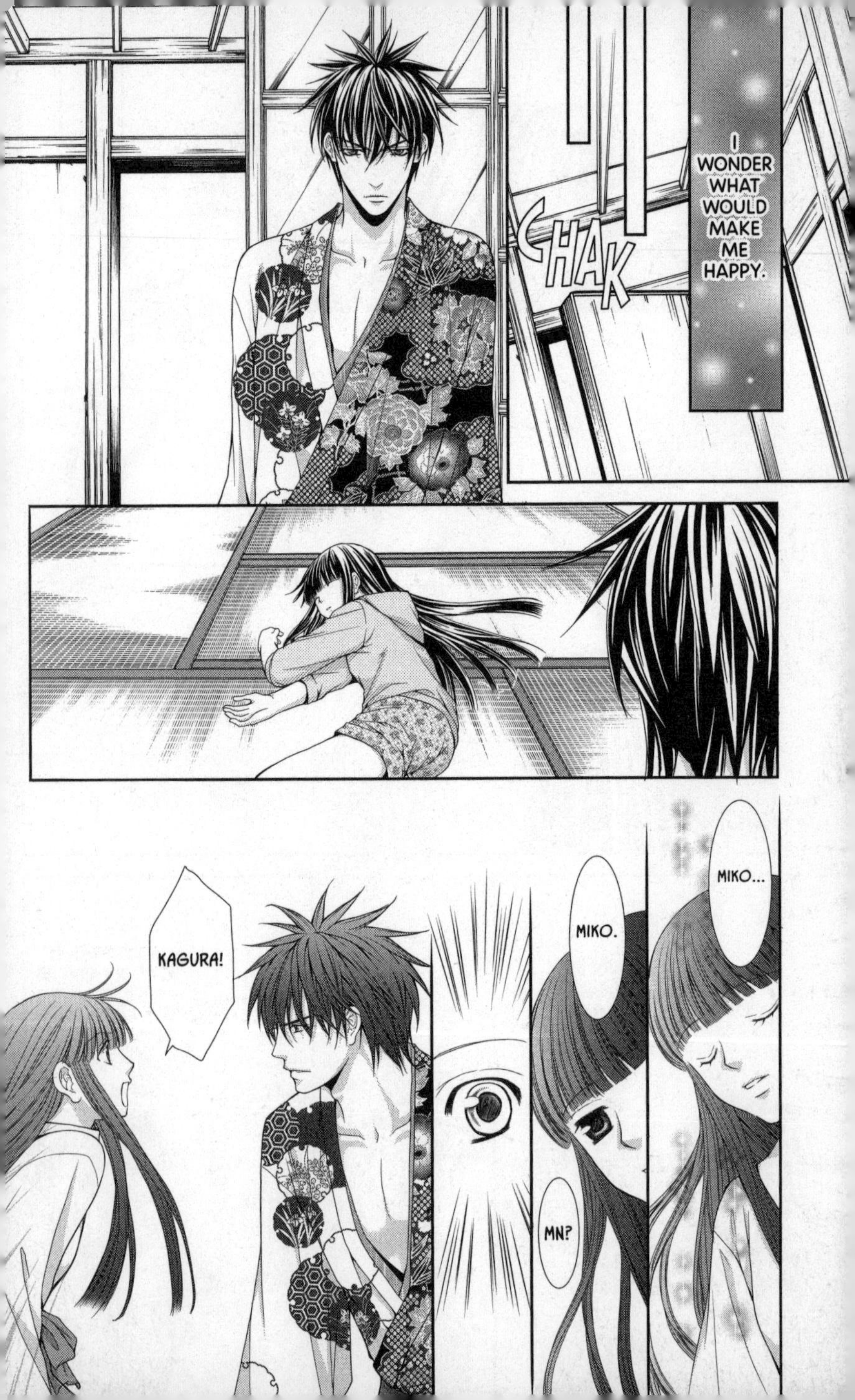
I WONDER WHAT WOULD MAKE ME HAPPY.
CHAK
MIKO...
MIKO.
MN?
KAGURA!

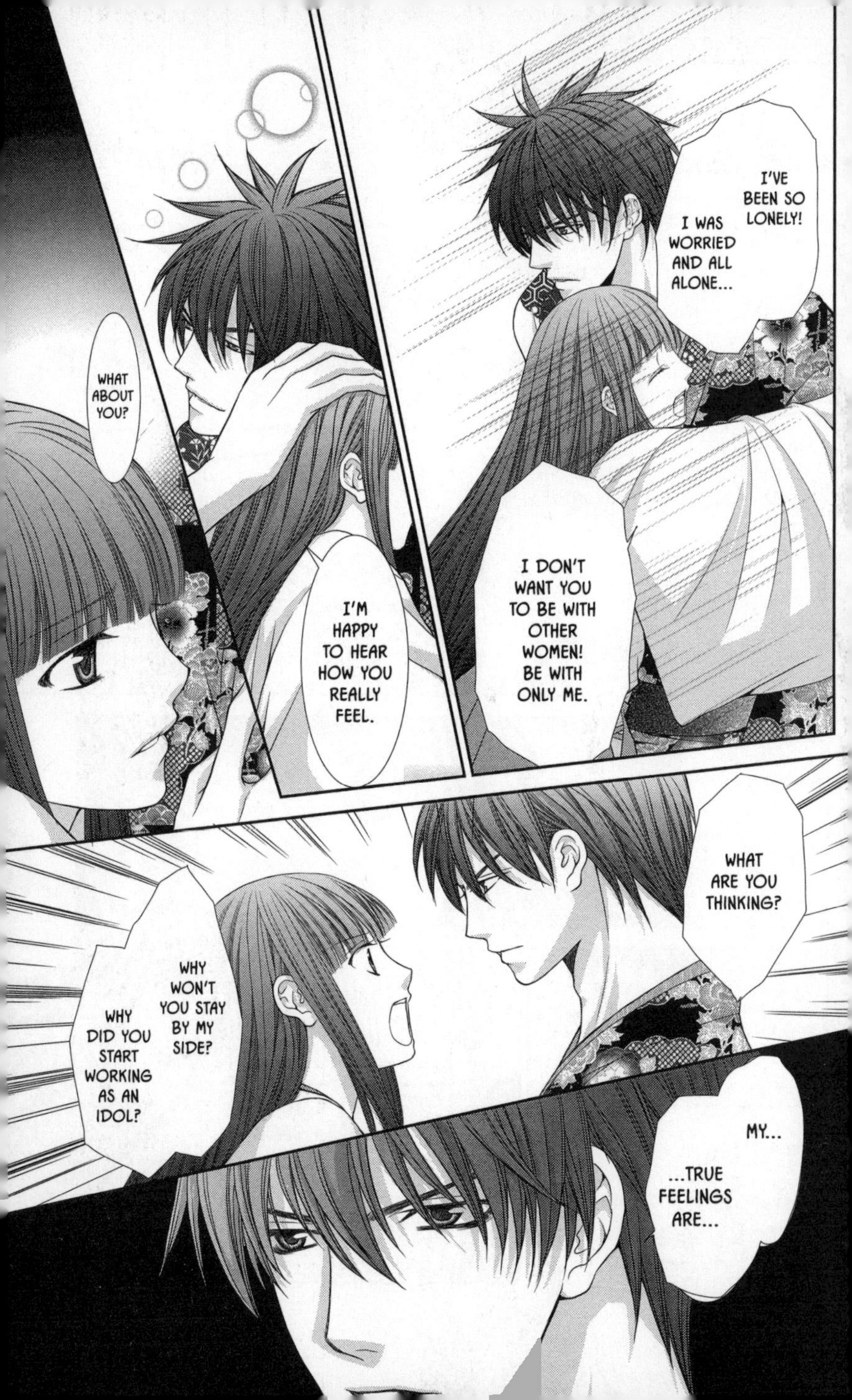
I'VE BEEN SO LONELY!
I WAS WORRIED AND ALL ALONE...
I DON'T WANT YOU TO BE WITH OTHER WOMEN! BE WITH ONLY ME.
I'M HAPPY TO HEAR HOW YOU REALLY FEEL.
WHAT ABOUT YOU?
WHAT ARE YOU THINKING?
WHY WON'T YOU STAY BY MY SIDE?
WHY DID YOU START WORKING AS AN IDOL?
MY...
...TRUE FEELINGS ARE...

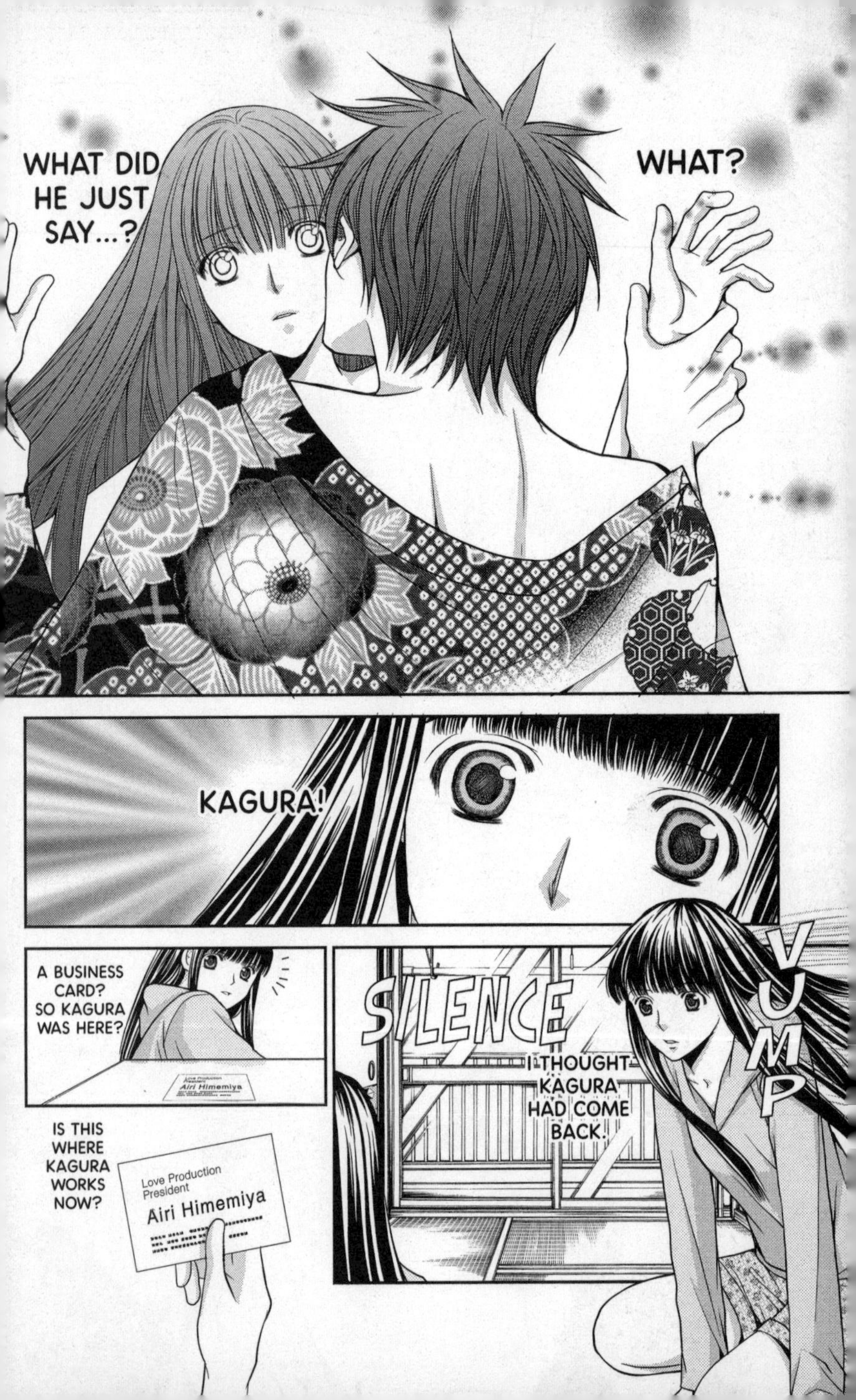
WHAT?
WHAT DID HE JUST SAY...?
KAGURA!
VUMP
SILENCE
I THOUGHT KAGURA HAD COME BACK.
A BUSINESS CARD? SO KAGURA WAS HERE?
Love Production
President
Airi Himemiya
IS THIS WHERE KAGURA WORKS NOW?
Love Production
President
Airi Himemiya

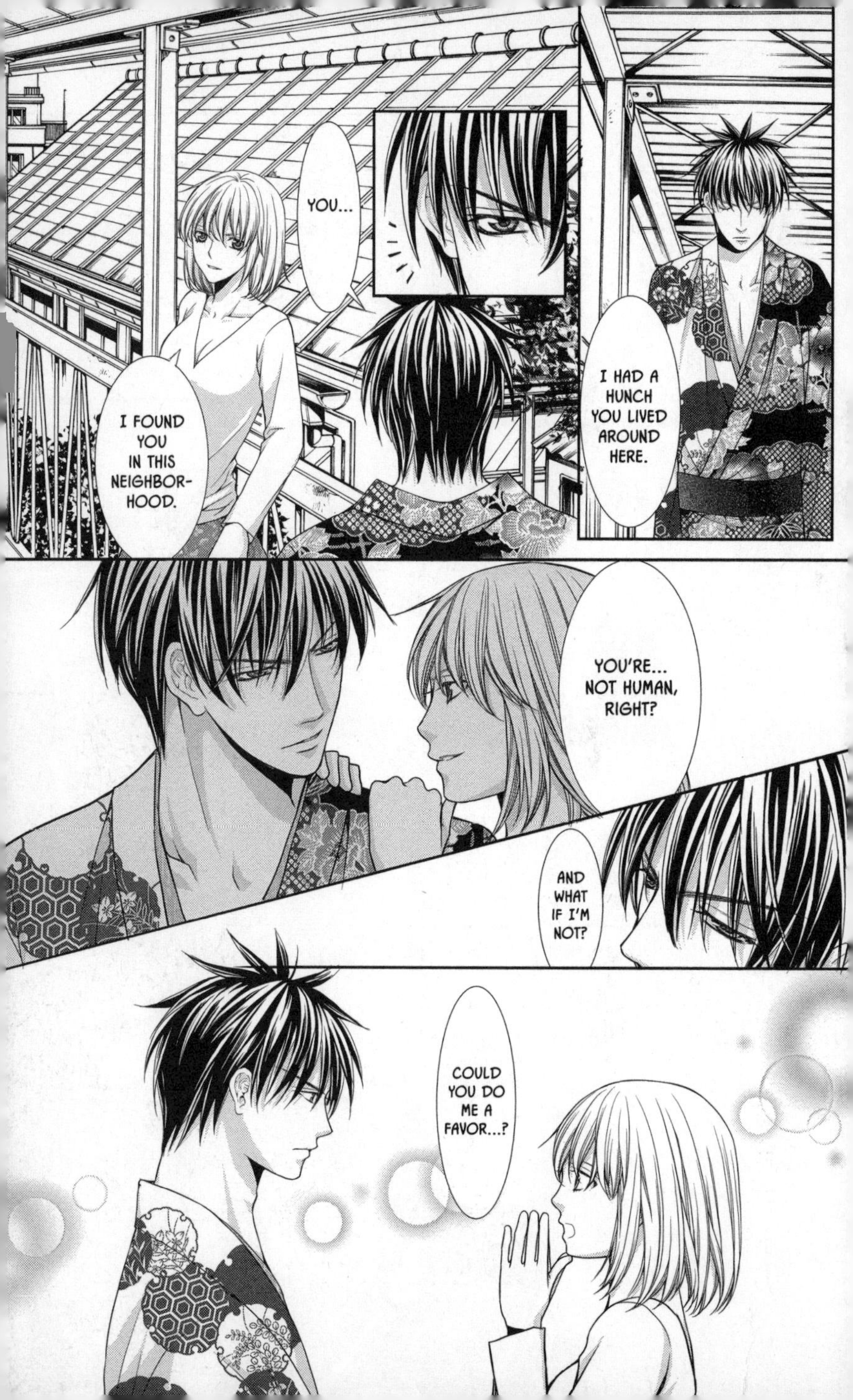
I HAD A HUNCH YOU LIVED AROUND HERE.
YOU...
I FOUND YOU IN THIS NEIGHBOR-HOOD.
YOU'RE... NOT HUMAN, RIGHT?
AND WHAT IF I'M NOT?
COULD YOU DO ME A FAVOR...?

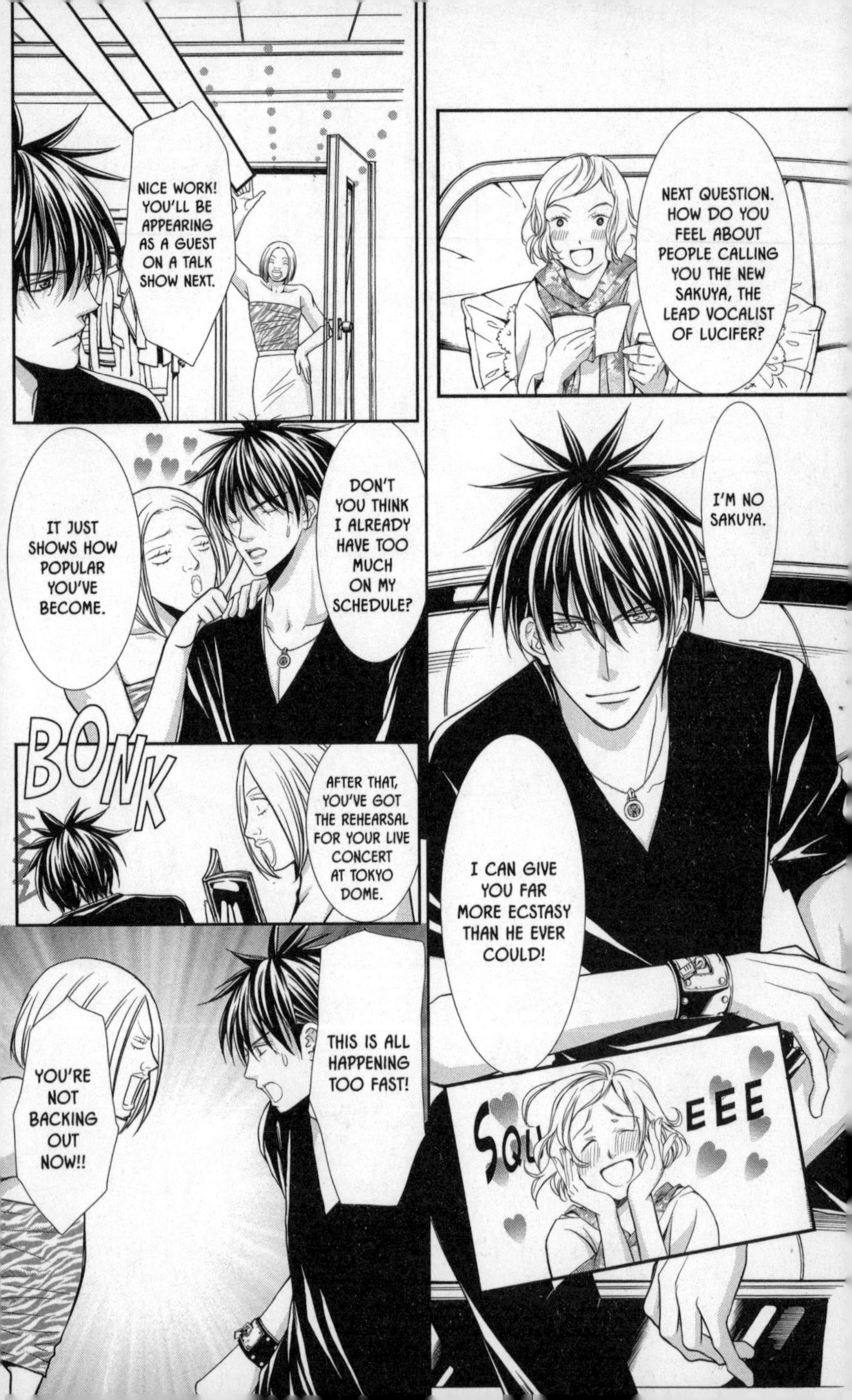
NICE WORK! YOU'LL BE APPEARING AS A GUEST ON A TALK SHOW NEXT.
DON'T YOU THINK I ALREADY HAVE TOO MUCH ON MY SCHEDULE?
IT JUST SHOWS HOW POPULAR YOU'VE BECOME.
BONK
AFTER THAT, YOU'VE GOT THE REHEARSAL FOR YOUR LIVE CONCERT AT TOKYO DOME.
THIS IS ALL HAPPENING TOO FAST!
YOU'RE NOT BACKING OUT NOW!!
NEXT QUESTION. HOW DO YOU FEEL ABOUT PEOPLE CALLING YOU THE NEW SAKUYA, THE LEAD VOCALIST OF LUCIFER?
I'M NO SAKUYA.
I CAN GIVE YOU FAR MORE ECSTASY THAN HE EVER COULD!
SQU EEE

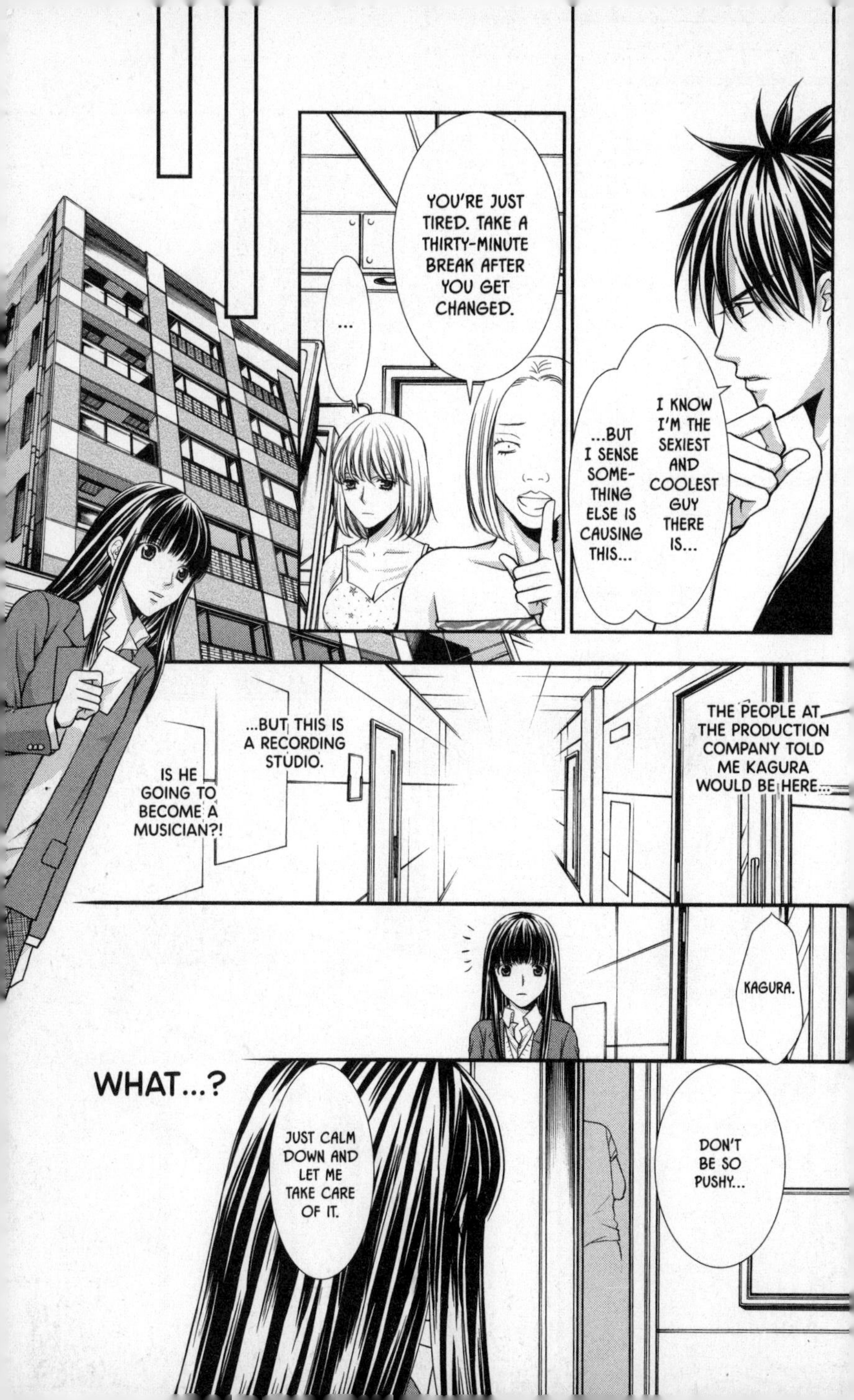
I KNOW I'M THE SEXIEST AND COOLEST GUY THERE IS...
...BUT I SENSE SOME-THING ELSE IS CAUSING THIS...
YOU'RE JUST TIRED. TAKE A THIRTY-MINUTE BREAK AFTER YOU GET CHANGED.
...
THE PEOPLE AT THE PRODUCTION COMPANY TOLD ME KAGURA WOULD BE HERE...
...BUT THIS IS A RECORDING STUDIO.
IS HE GOING TO BECOME A MUSICIAN?!
KAGURA.
DON'T BE SO PUSHY...
JUST CALM DOWN AND LET ME TAKE CARE OF IT.
WHAT...?

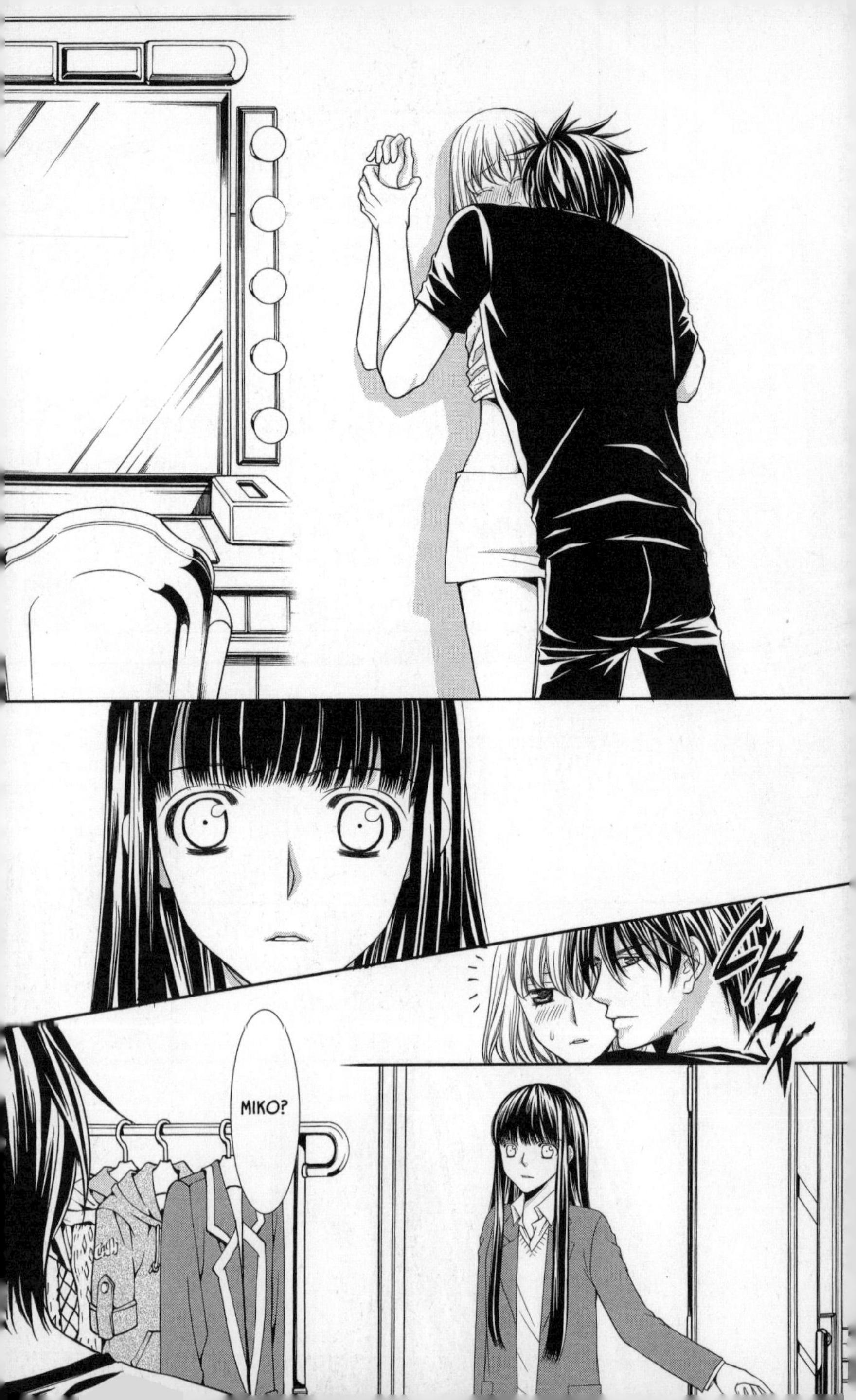
CHAK
MIKO?

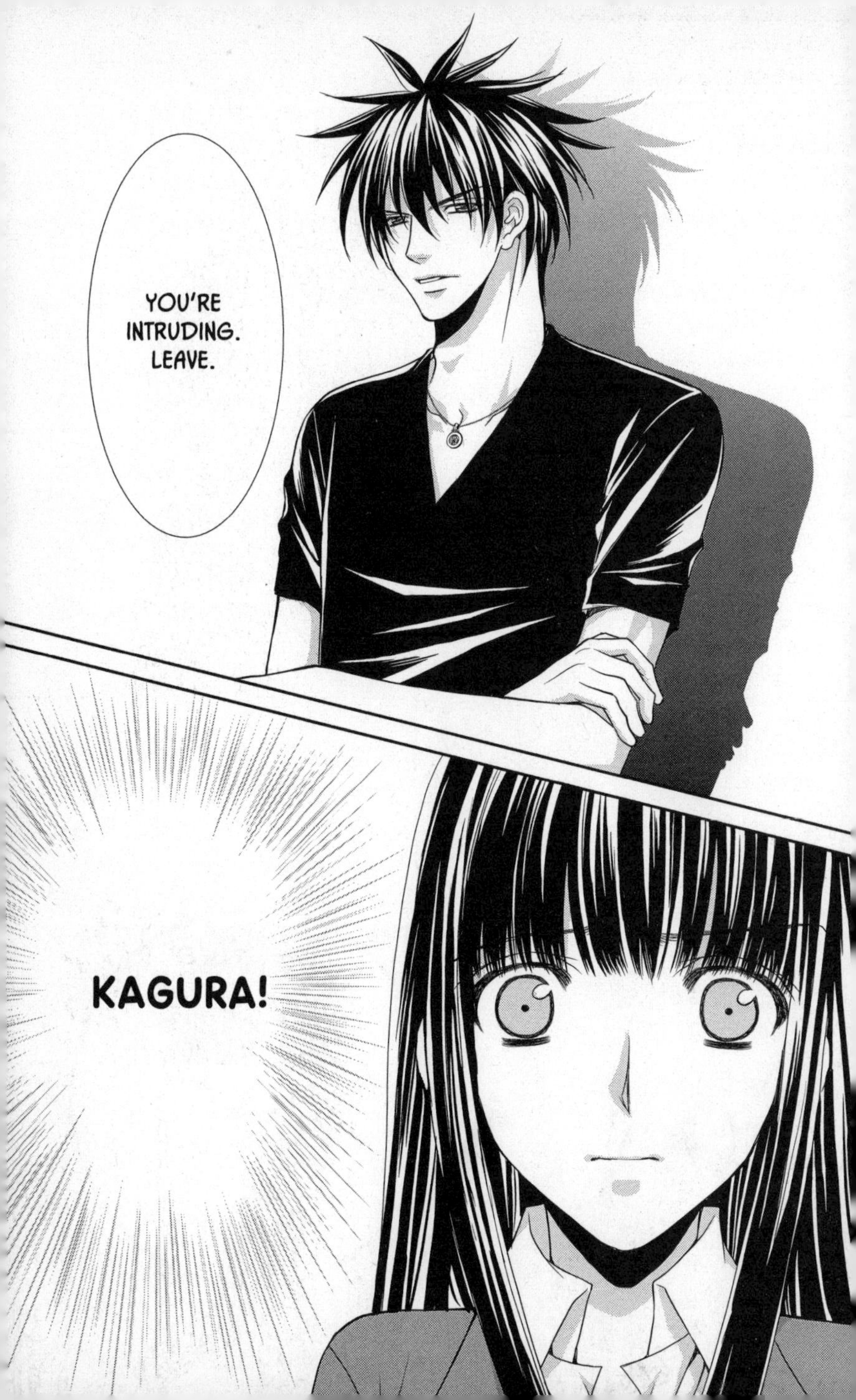
YOU'RE INTRUDING. LEAVE.
KAGURA!

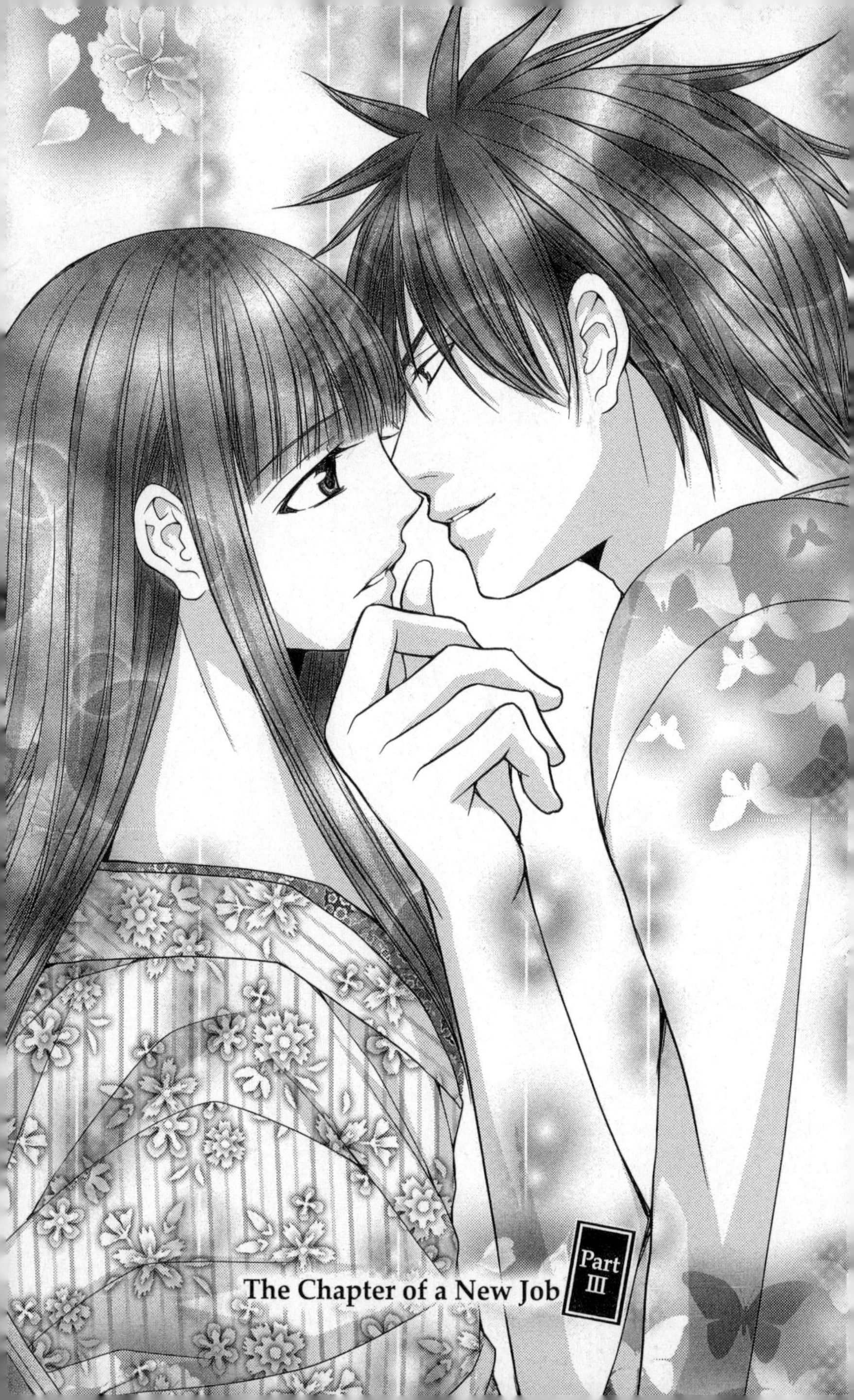
Part III
The Chapter of a New Job

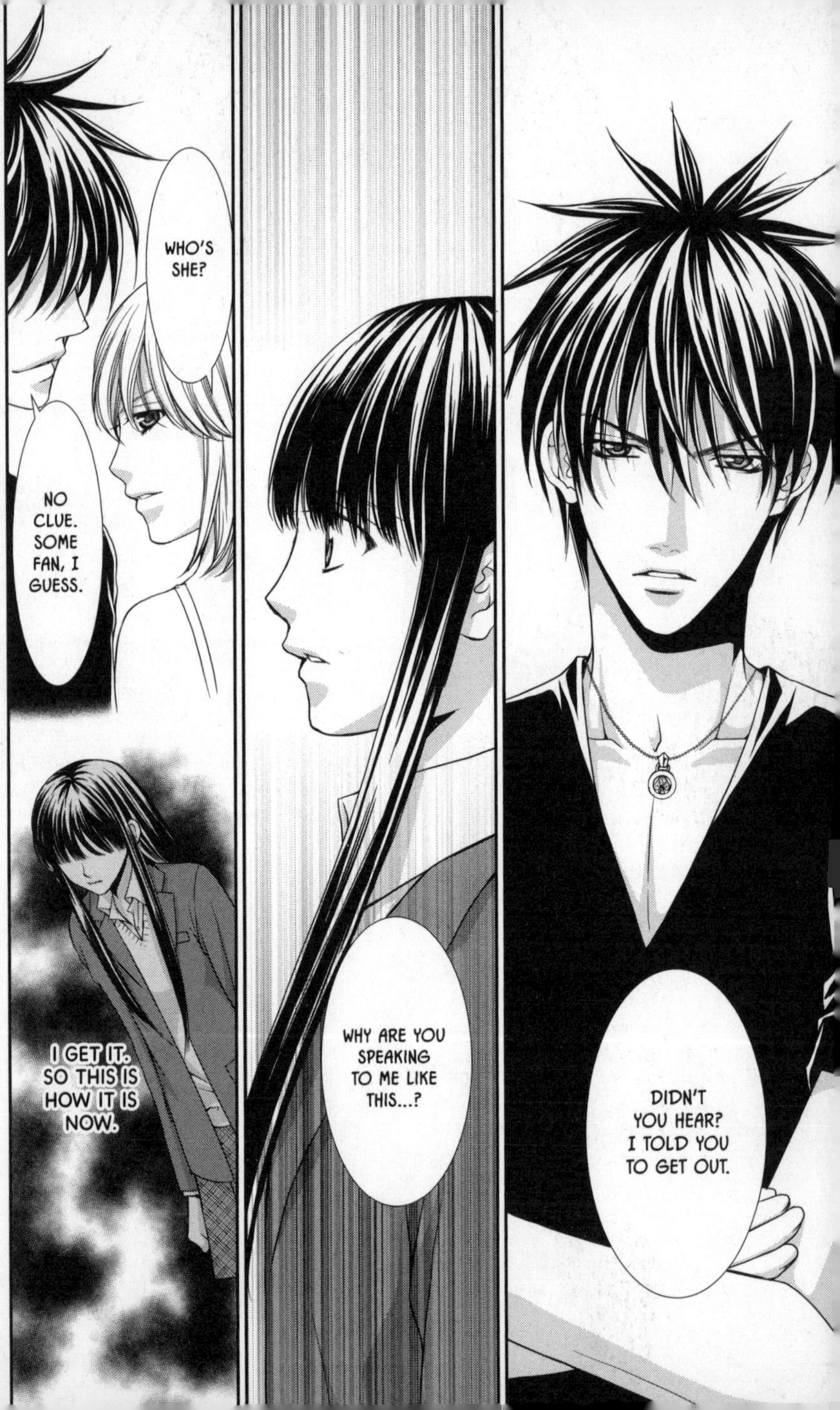
DIDN'T YOU HEAR? I TOLD YOU TO GET OUT.
WHY ARE YOU SPEAKING TO ME LIKE THIS...?
WHO'S SHE?
NO CLUE. SOME FAN, I GUESS.
I GET IT. SO THIS IS HOW IT IS NOW.

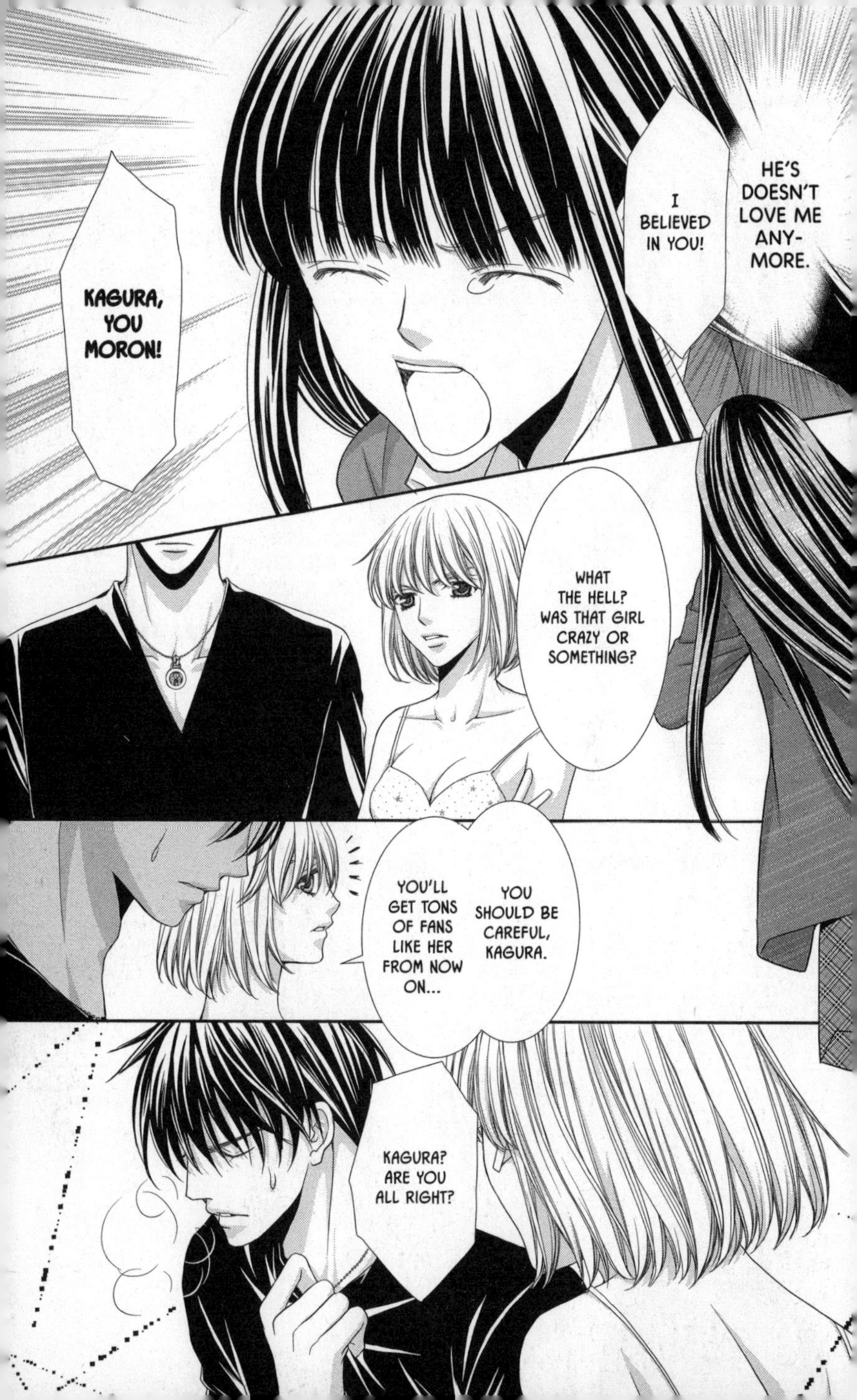
HE'S DOESN'T LOVE ME ANYMORE.
I BELIEVED IN YOU!
KAGURA, YOU MORON!
WHAT THE HELL? WAS THAT GIRL CRAZY OR SOMETHING?
YOU SHOULD BE CAREFUL, KAGURA.
YOU'LL GET TONS OF FANS LIKE HER FROM NOW ON...
KAGURA? ARE YOU ALL RIGHT?

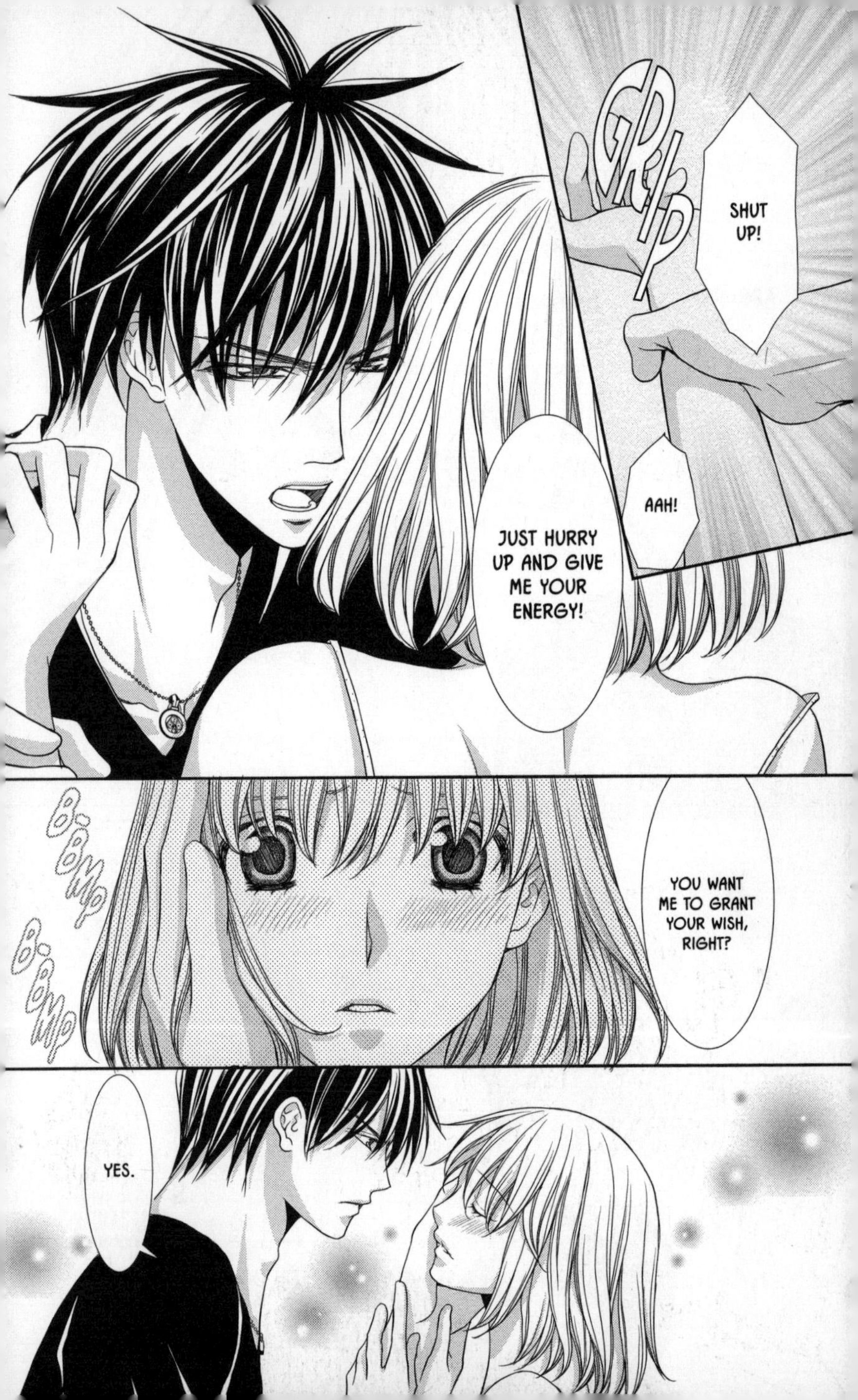
GRIP
SHUT UP!
AAH!
JUST HURRY UP AND GIVE ME YOUR ENERGY!
YOU WANT ME TO GRANT YOUR WISH, RIGHT?
B-BUMP
B-BUMP
YES.

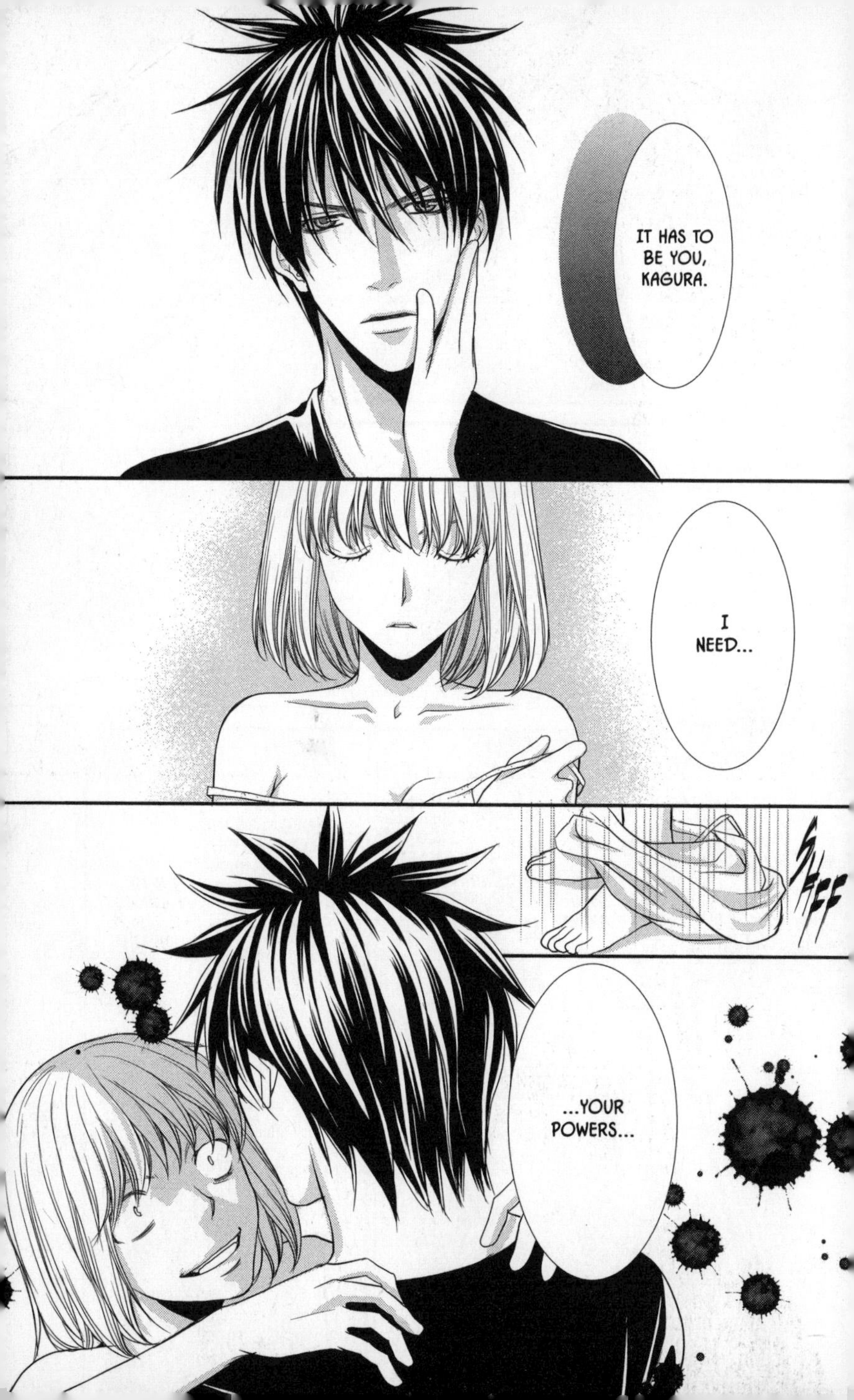
IT HAS TO BE YOU, KAGURA.
I NEED...
SHFF
...YOUR POWERS...

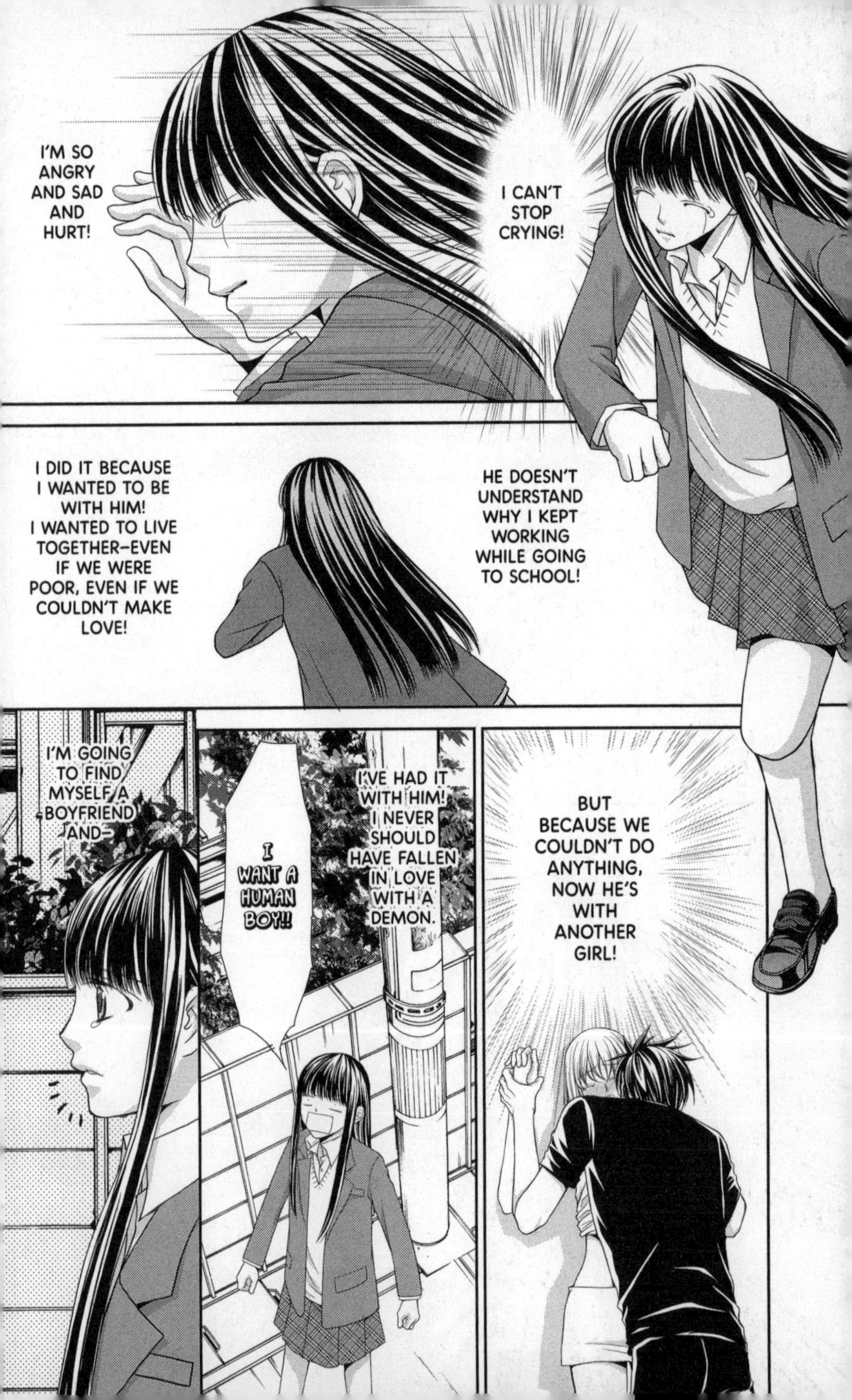
I CAN'T STOP CRYING!
I'M SO ANGRY AND SAD AND HURT!
HE DOESN'T UNDERSTAND WHY I KEPT WORKING WHILE GOING TO SCHOOL!
I DID IT BECAUSE I WANTED TO BE WITH HIM! I WANTED TO LIVE TOGETHER—EVEN IF WE WERE POOR, EVEN IF WE COULDN'T MAKE LOVE!
BUT BECAUSE WE COULDN'T DO ANYTHING, NOW HE'S WITH ANOTHER GIRL!
I'VE HAD IT WITH HIM! I NEVER SHOULD HAVE FALLEN IN LOVE WITH A DEMON.
I WANT A HUMAN BOY!!
I'M GOING TO FIND MYSELF A BOYFRIEND AND—

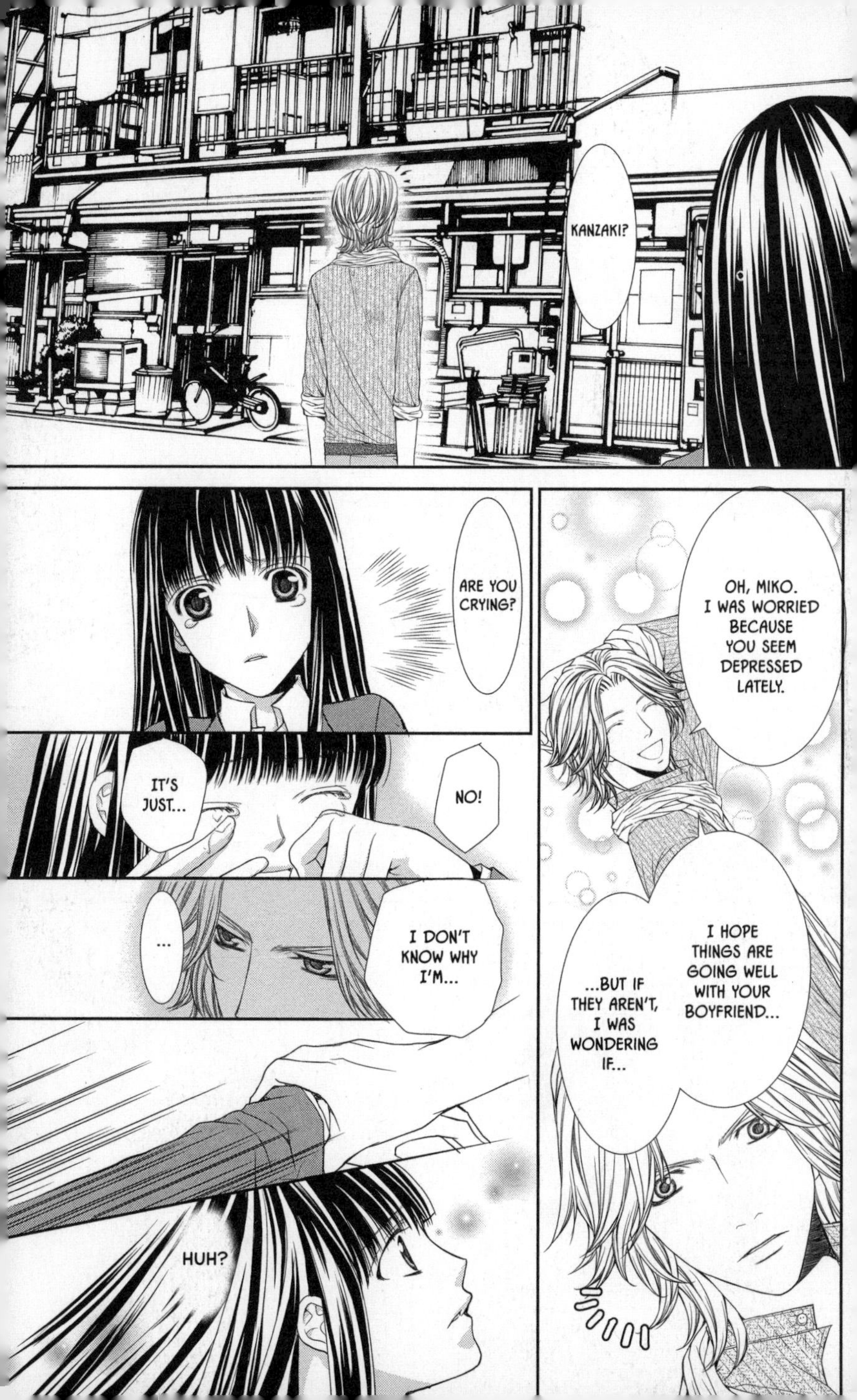
KANZAKI?
OH, MIKO. I WAS WORRIED BECAUSE YOU SEEM DEPRESSED LATELY.
I HOPE THINGS ARE GOING WELL WITH YOUR BOYFRIEND...
...BUT IF THEY AREN'T, I WAS WONDERING IF...
ARE YOU CRYING?
NO!
IT'S JUST...
I DON'T KNOW WHY I'M...
...
HUH?

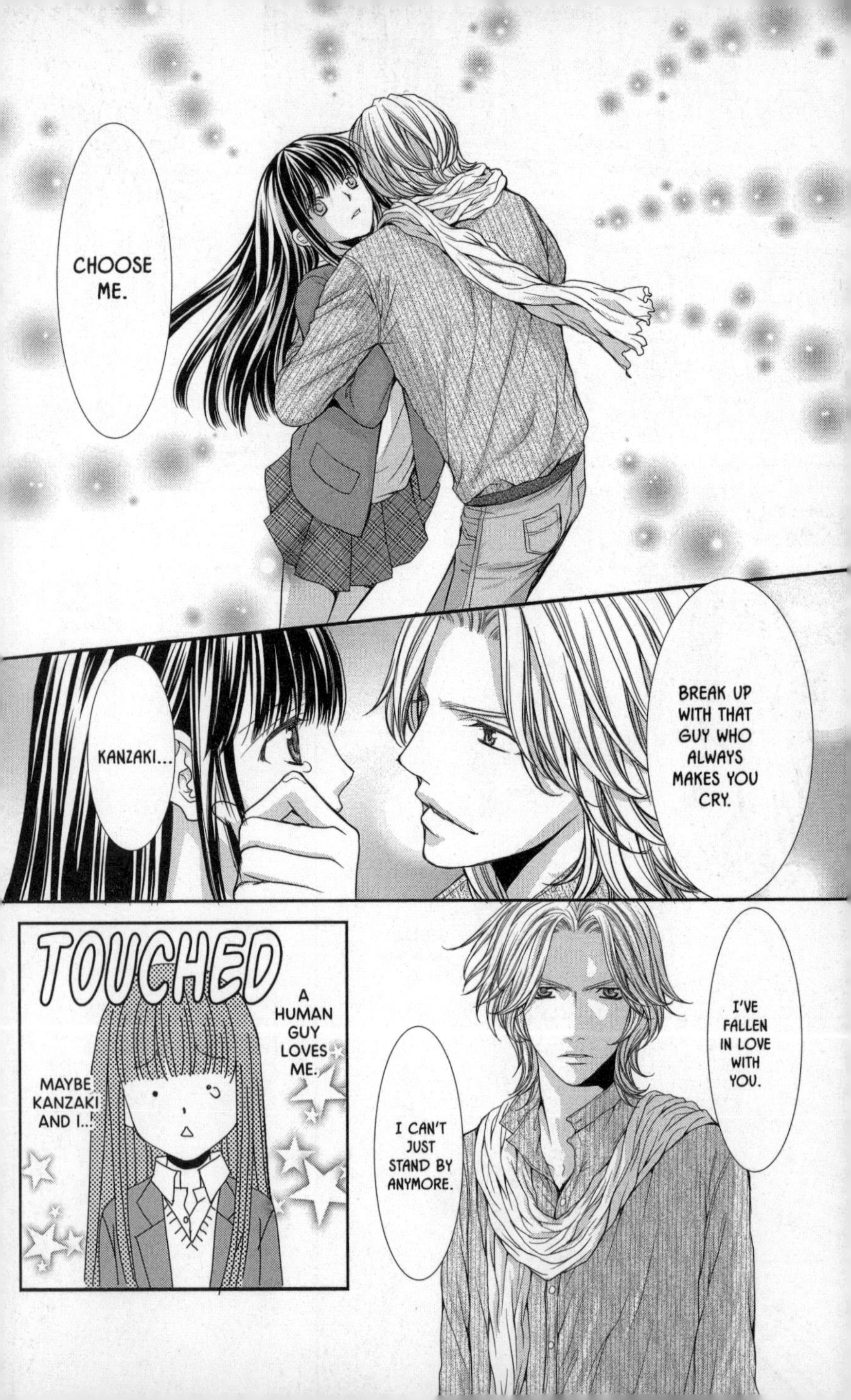
CHOOSE ME.
BREAK UP WITH THAT GUY WHO ALWAYS MAKES YOU CRY.
KANZAKI...
I'VE FALLEN IN LOVE WITH YOU.
I CAN'T JUST STAND BY ANYMORE.
TOUCHED
A HUMAN GUY LOVES ME.
MAYBE KANZAKI AND I..!

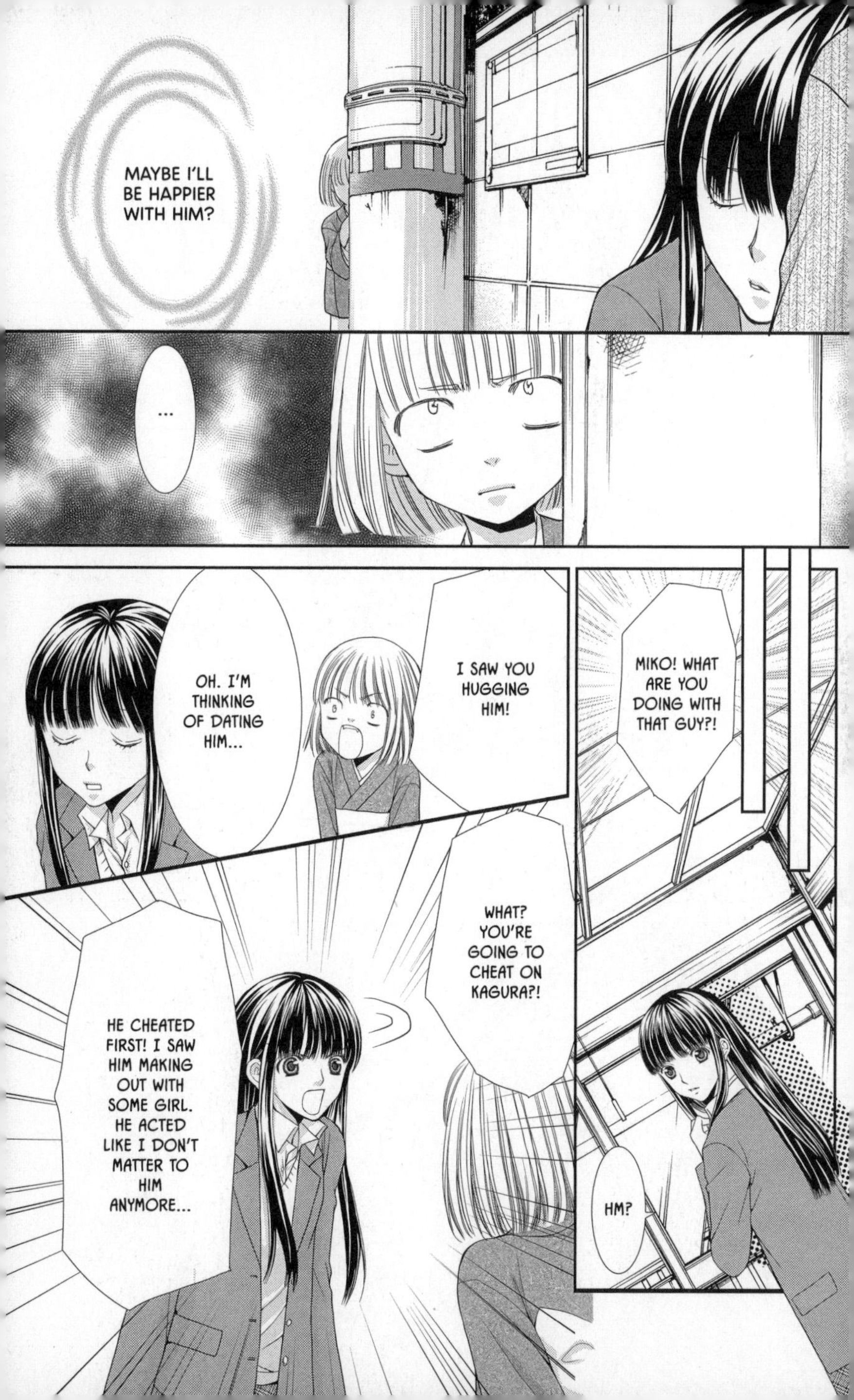
MAYBE I'LL BE HAPPIER WITH HIM?
...
MIKO! WHAT ARE YOU DOING WITH THAT GUY?!
HM?
I SAW YOU HUGGING HIM!
OH. I'M THINKING OF DATING HIM...
WHAT? YOU'RE GOING TO CHEAT ON KAGURA?!
HE CHEATED FIRST! I SAW HIM MAKING OUT WITH SOME GIRL. HE ACTED LIKE I DON'T MATTER TO HIM ANYMORE...

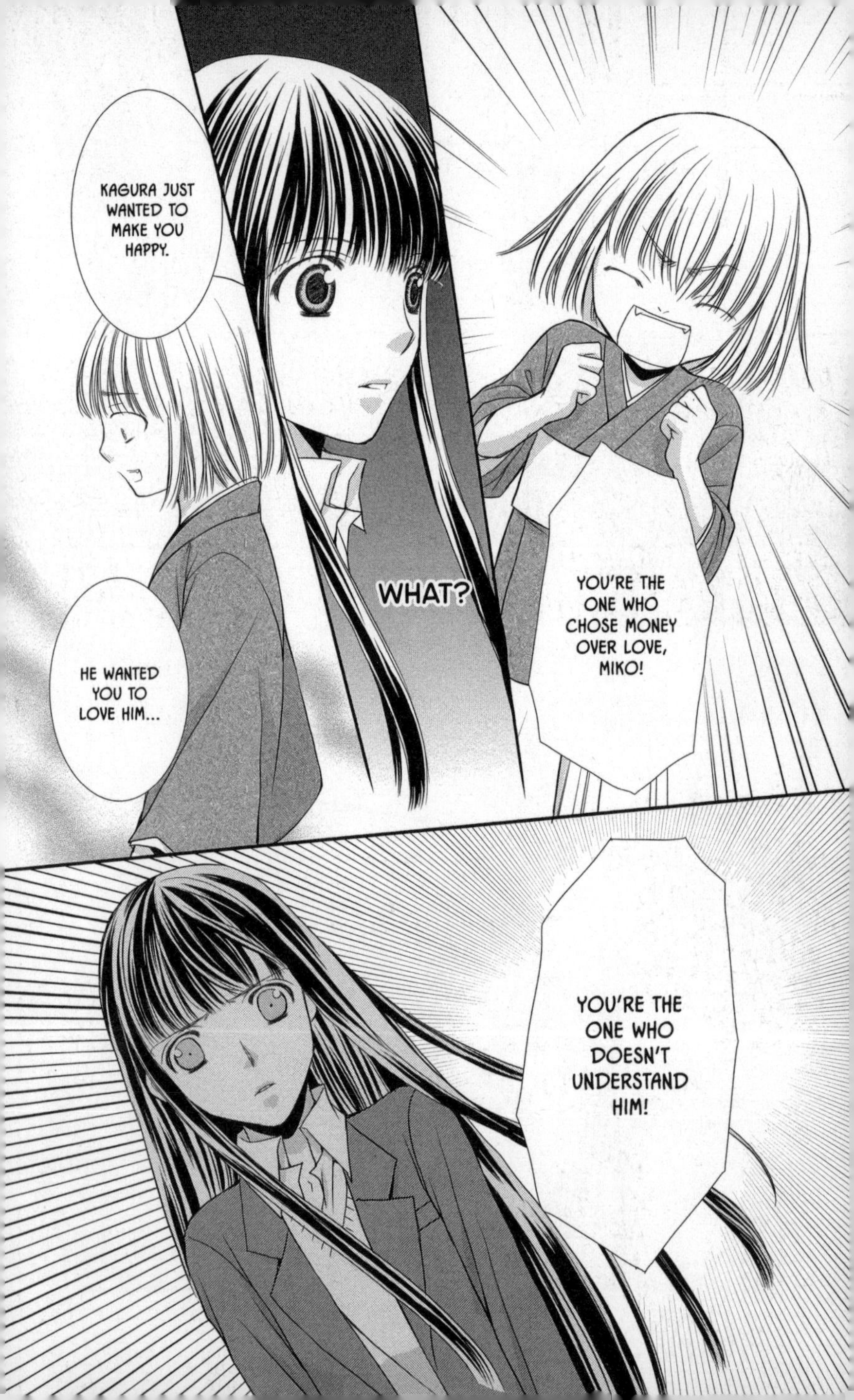
YOU'RE THE ONE WHO CHOSE MONEY OVER LOVE, MIKO!
WHAT?
KAGURA JUST WANTED TO MAKE YOU HAPPY.
HE WANTED YOU TO LOVE HIM...
YOU'RE THE ONE WHO DOESN'T UNDERSTAND HIM!

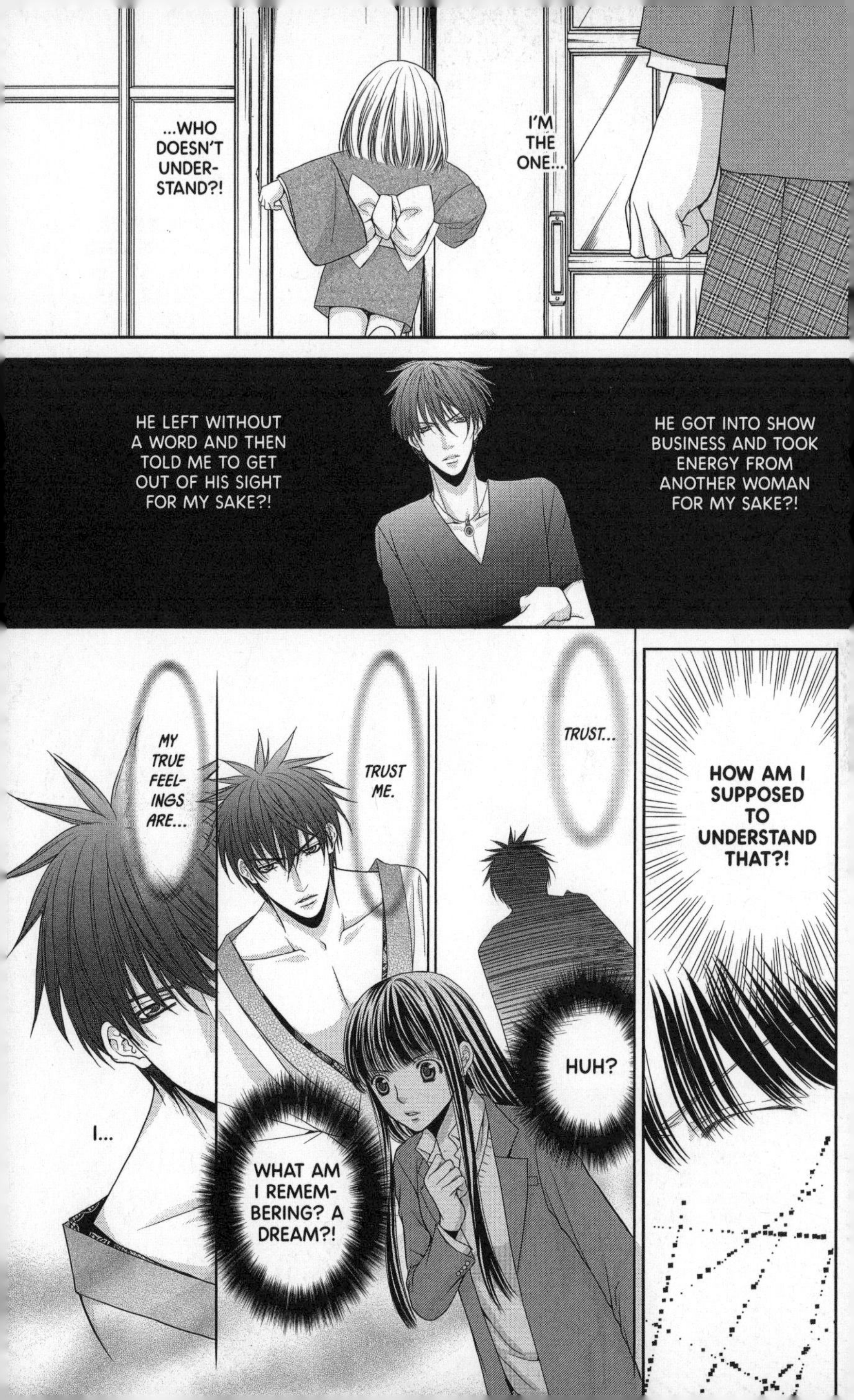
I'M THE ONE...
...WHO DOESN'T UNDERSTAND?!
HE GOT INTO SHOW BUSINESS AND TOOK ENERGY FROM ANOTHER WOMAN FOR MY SAKE?!
HE LEFT WITHOUT A WORD AND THEN TOLD ME TO GET OUT OF HIS SIGHT FOR MY SAKE?!
HOW AM I SUPPOSED TO UNDERSTAND THAT?!
TRUST...
TRUST ME.
MY TRUE FEELINGS ARE...
I...
HUH?
WHAT AM I REMEMBERING? A DREAM?!

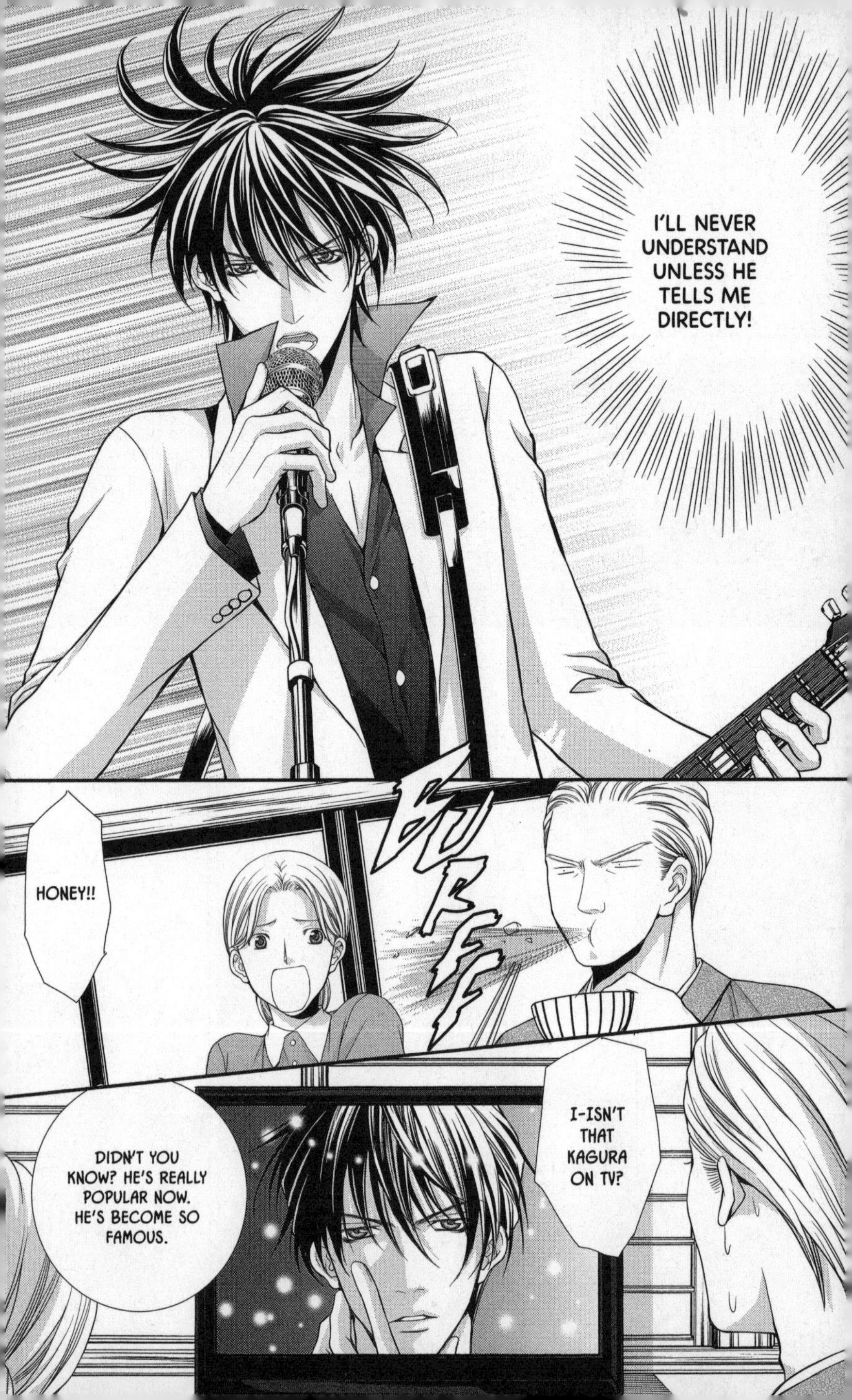
I'LL NEVER UNDERSTAND UNLESS HE TELLS ME DIRECTLY!
HONEY!!
I-ISN'T THAT KAGURA ON TV?
DIDN'T YOU KNOW? HE'S REALLY POPULAR NOW. HE'S BECOME SO FAMOUS.

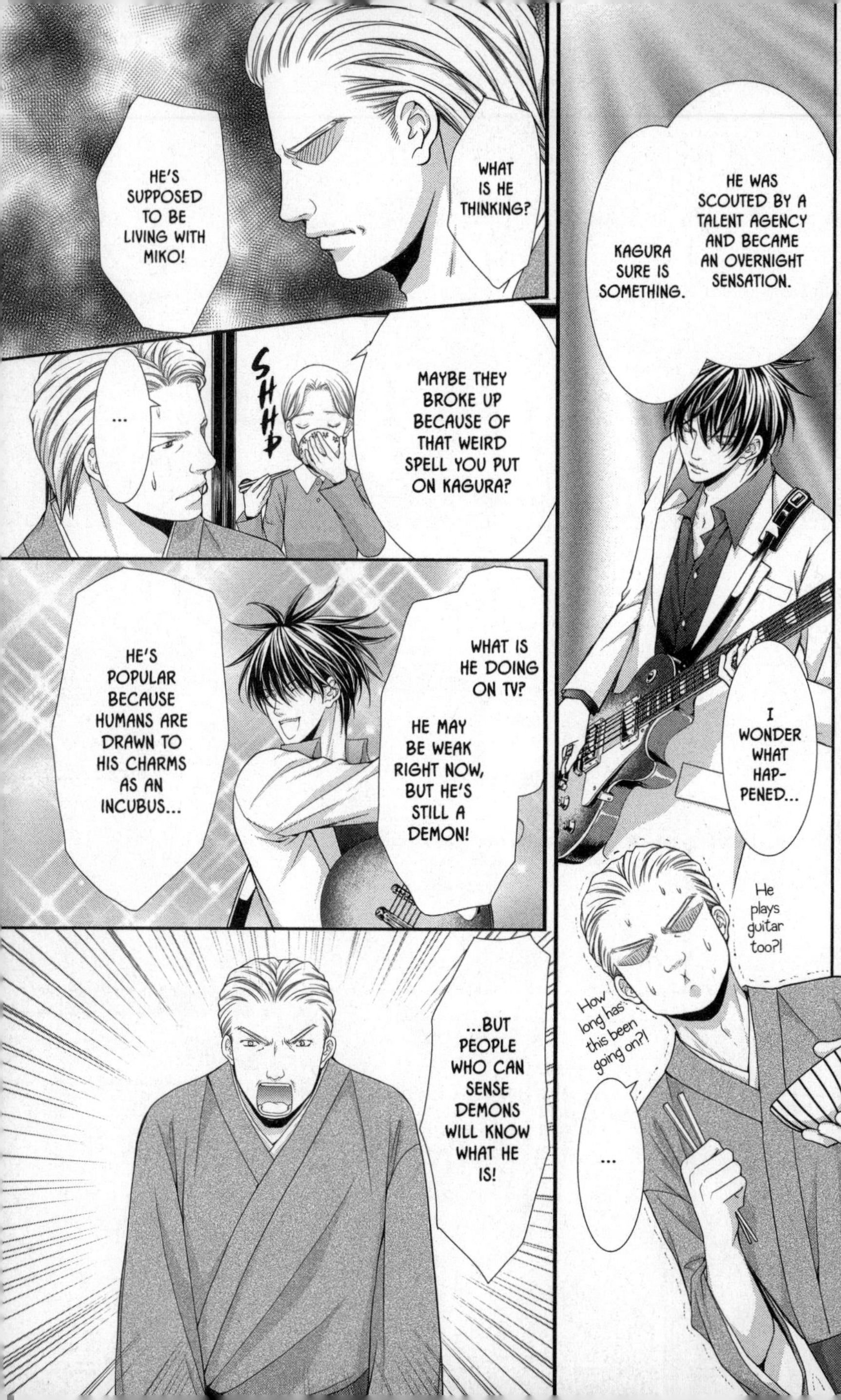
HE WAS SCOUTED BY A TALENT AGENCY AND BECAME AN OVERNIGHT SENSATION.
KAGURA SURE IS SOMETHING.
I WONDER WHAT HAP-PENED...
He plays guitar too?!
How long has this been going on?!
...
WHAT IS HE THINKING?
HE'S SUPPOSED TO BE LIVING WITH MIKO!
MAYBE THEY BROKE UP BECAUSE OF THAT WEIRD SPELL YOU PUT ON KAGURA?
SHHP
...
WHAT IS HE DOING ON TV?
HE MAY BE WEAK RIGHT NOW, BUT HE'S STILL A DEMON!
HE'S POPULAR BECAUSE HUMANS ARE DRAWN TO HIS CHARMS AS AN INCUBUS...
...BUT PEOPLE WHO CAN SENSE DEMONS WILL KNOW WHAT HE IS!

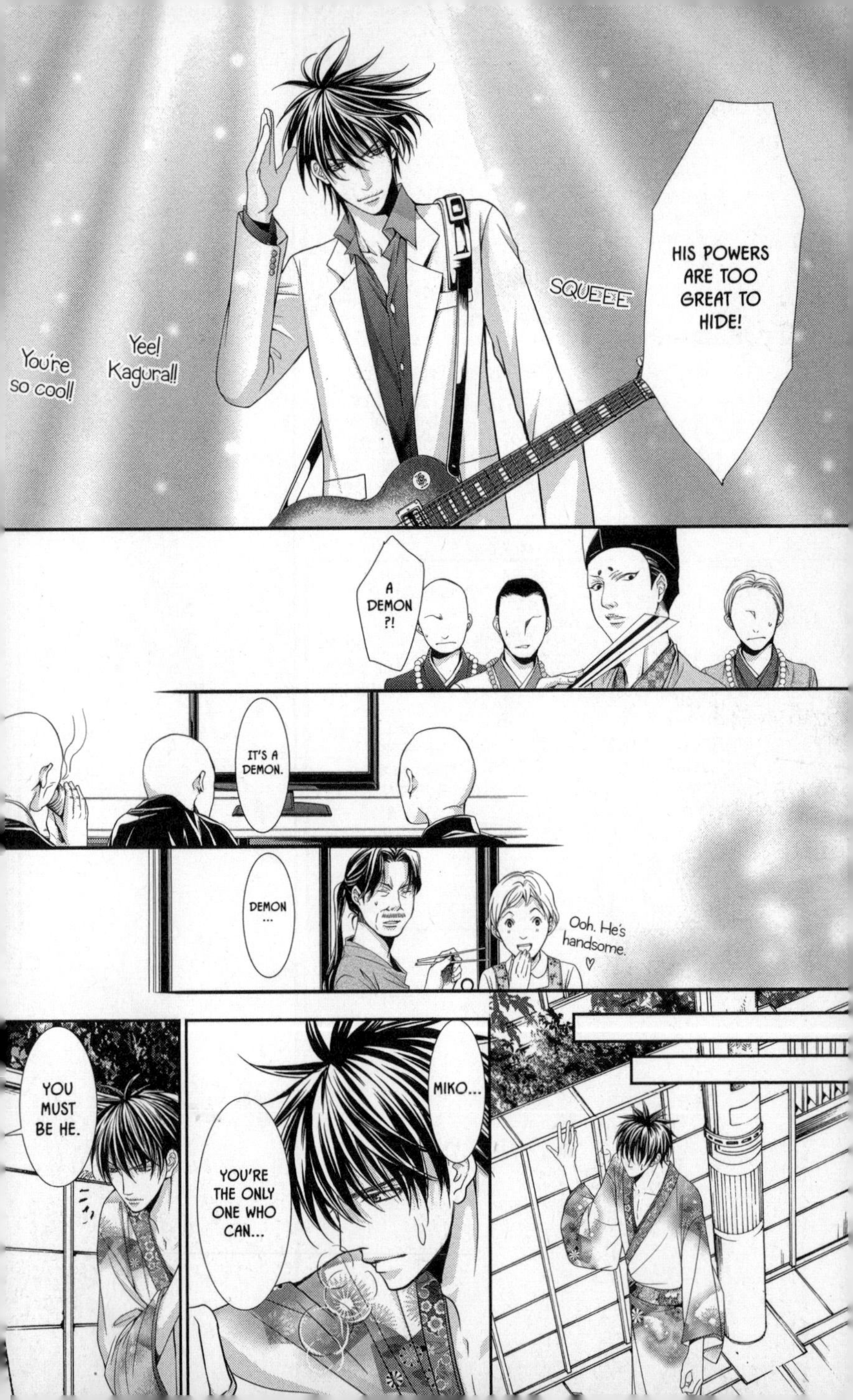
HIS POWERS ARE TOO GREAT TO HIDE!
SQUEEE
Yee! Kagura!!
You're so cool!
A DEMON?!
IT'S A DEMON.
Ooh. He's handsome. ♥
DEMON...
MIKO...
YOU'RE THE ONLY ONE WHO CAN...
YOU MUST BE HE.

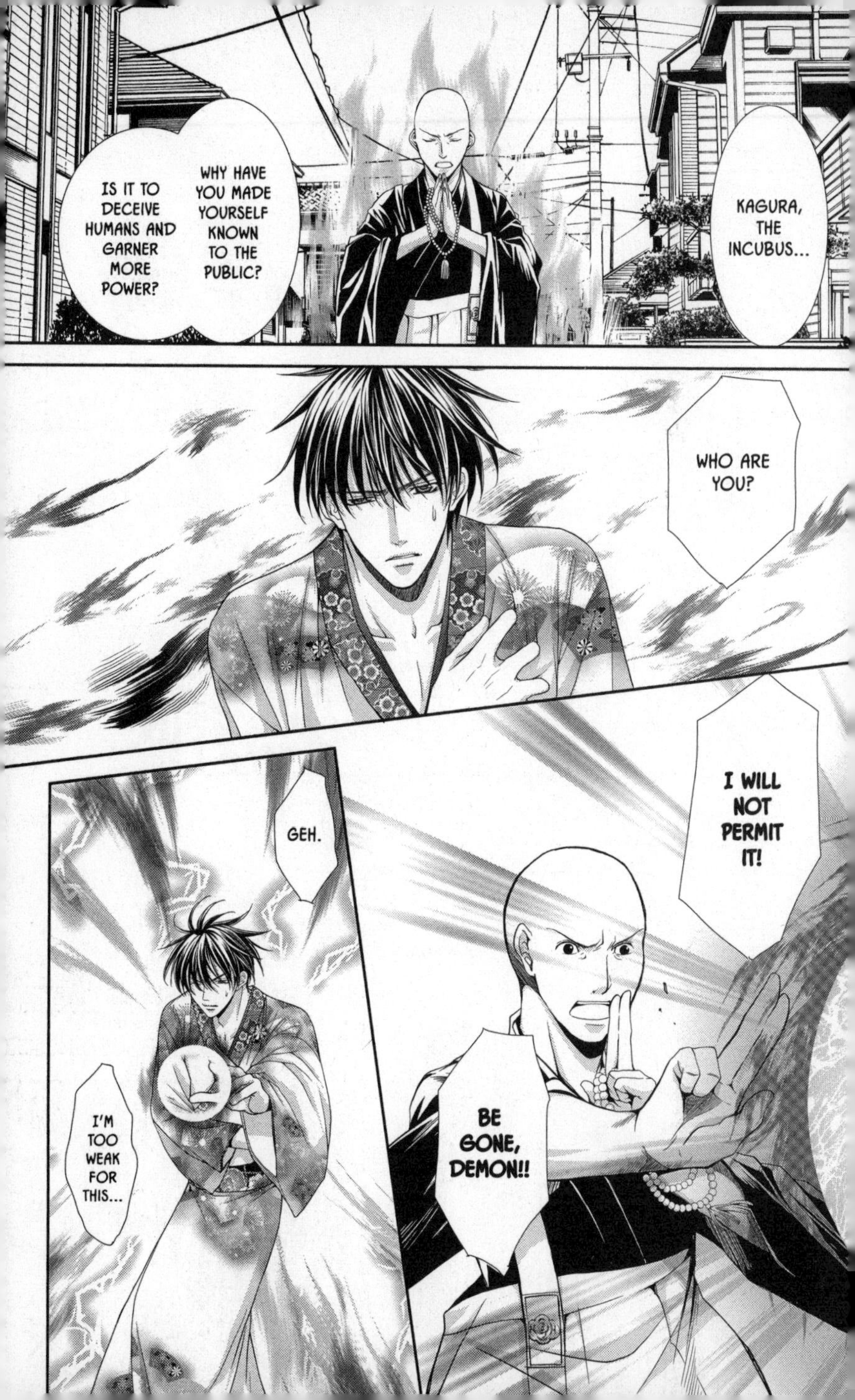
KAGURA, THE INCUBUS...
WHY HAVE YOU MADE YOURSELF KNOWN TO THE PUBLIC?
IS IT TO DECEIVE HUMANS AND GARNER MORE POWER?
WHO ARE YOU?
I WILL NOT PERMIT IT!
GEH.
BE GONE, DEMON!!
I'M TOO WEAK FOR THIS...

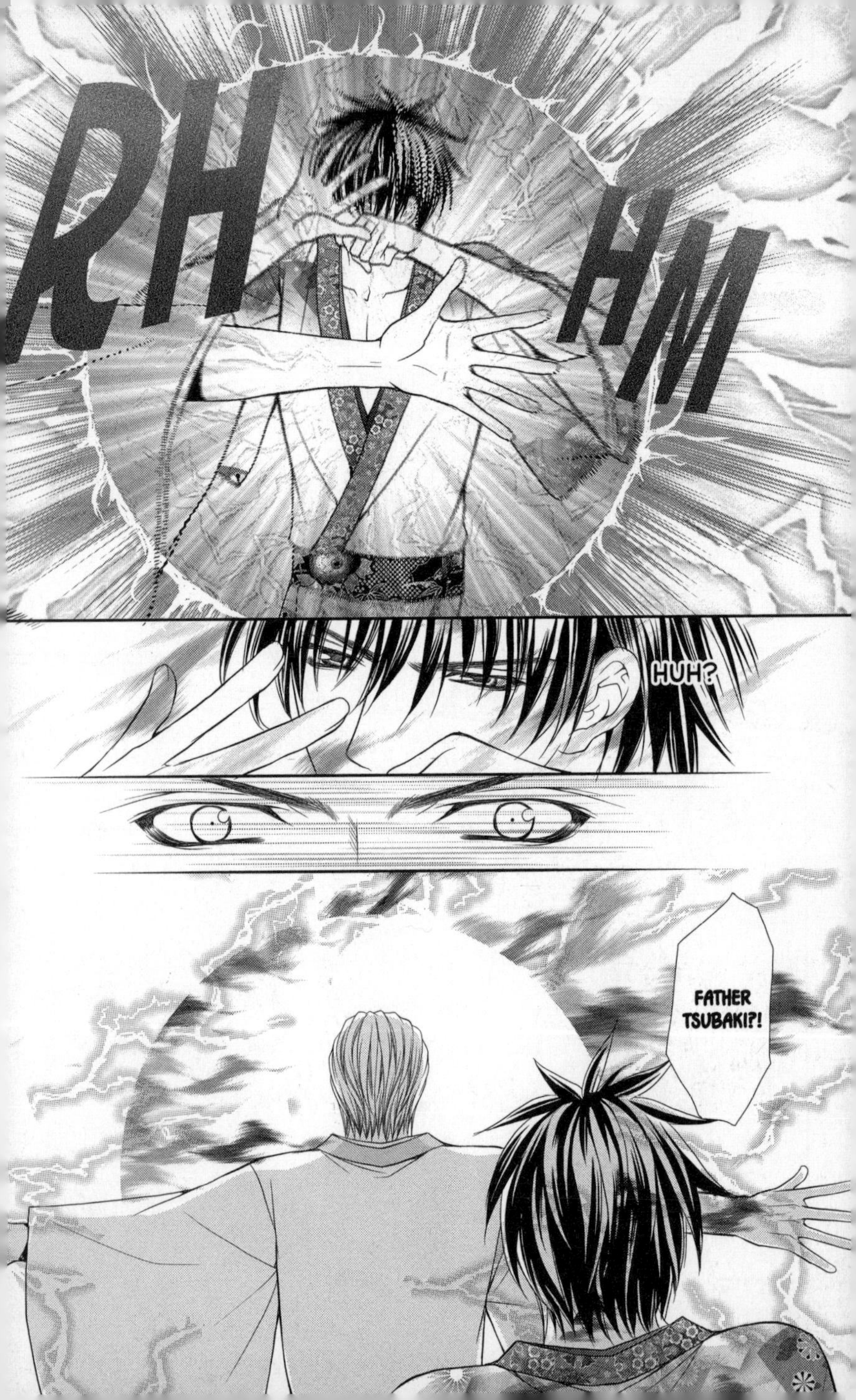
RHHM
HUH?
FATHER TSUBAKI?!

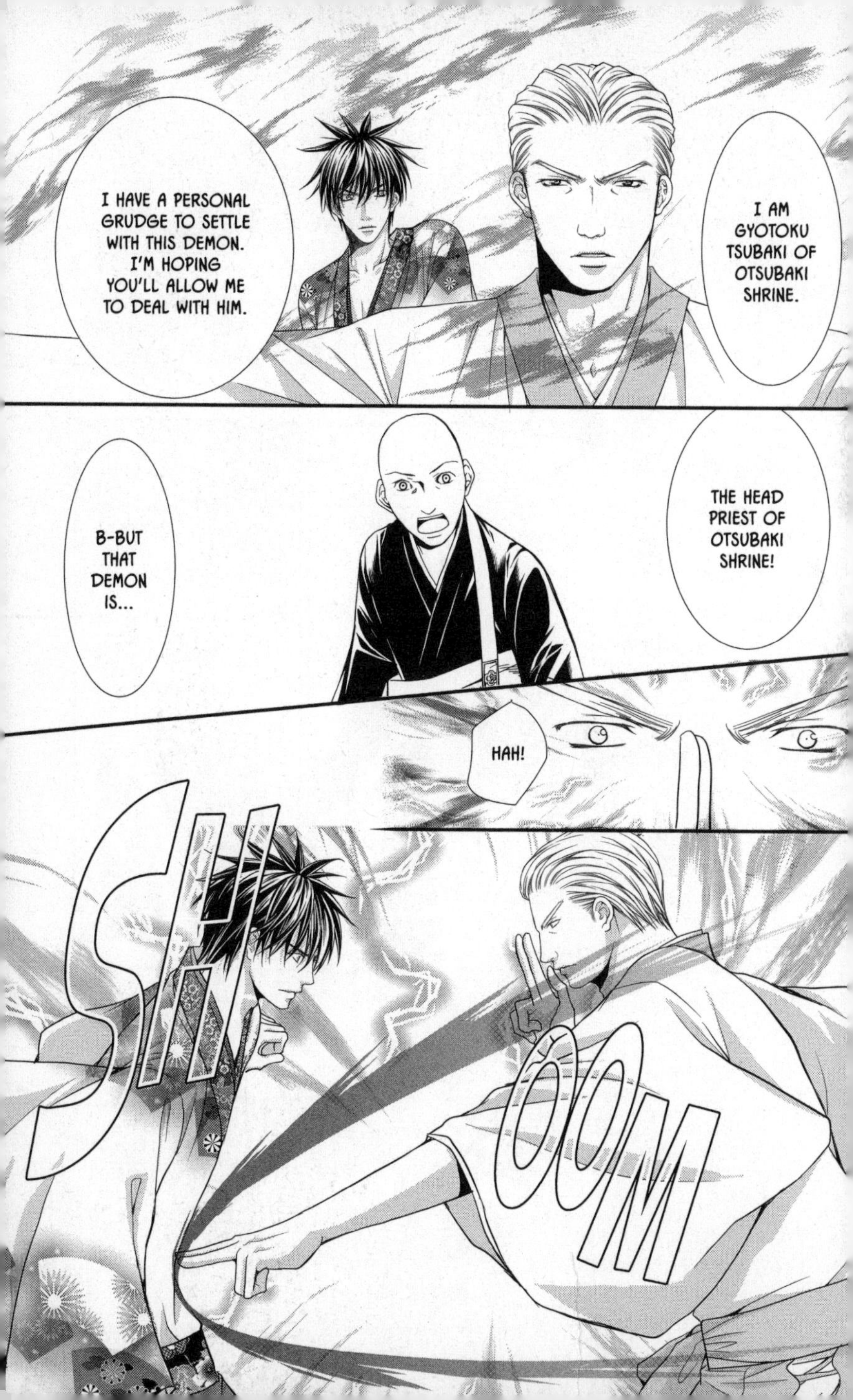
I AM GYOTOKU TSUBAKI OF OTSUBAKI SHRINE.
I HAVE A PERSONAL GRUDGE TO SETTLE WITH THIS DEMON. I'M HOPING YOU'LL ALLOW ME TO DEAL WITH HIM.
THE HEAD PRIEST OF OTSUBAKI SHRINE!
B-BUT THAT DEMON IS...
HAH!
SHH
OOM

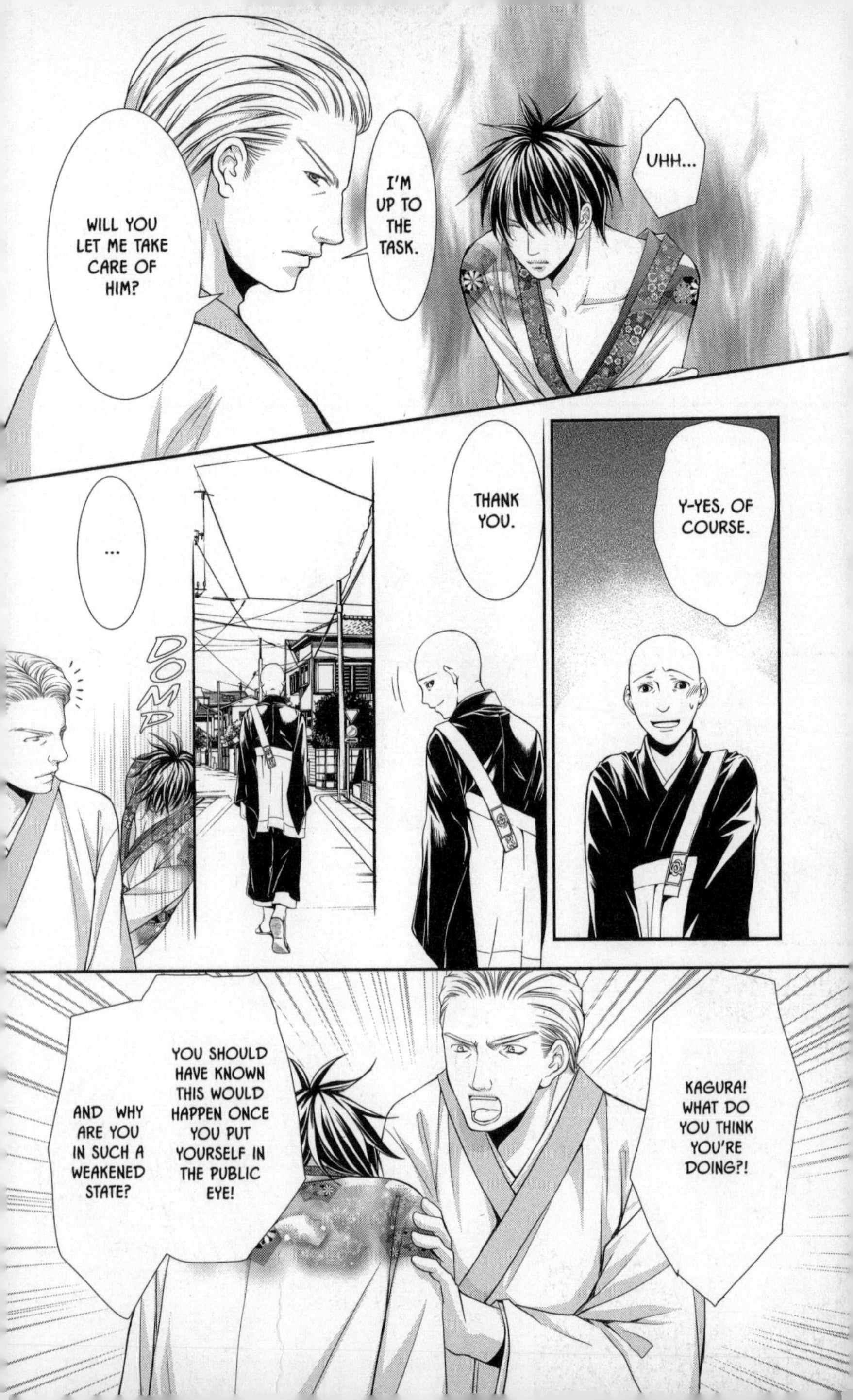
UHH...
I'M UP TO THE TASK.
WILL YOU LET ME TAKE CARE OF HIM?
Y-YES, OF COURSE.
THANK YOU.
...
DOMP
KAGURA! WHAT DO YOU THINK YOU'RE DOING?!
YOU SHOULD HAVE KNOWN THIS WOULD HAPPEN ONCE YOU PUT YOURSELF IN THE PUBLIC EYE!
AND WHY ARE YOU IN SUCH A WEAKENED STATE?

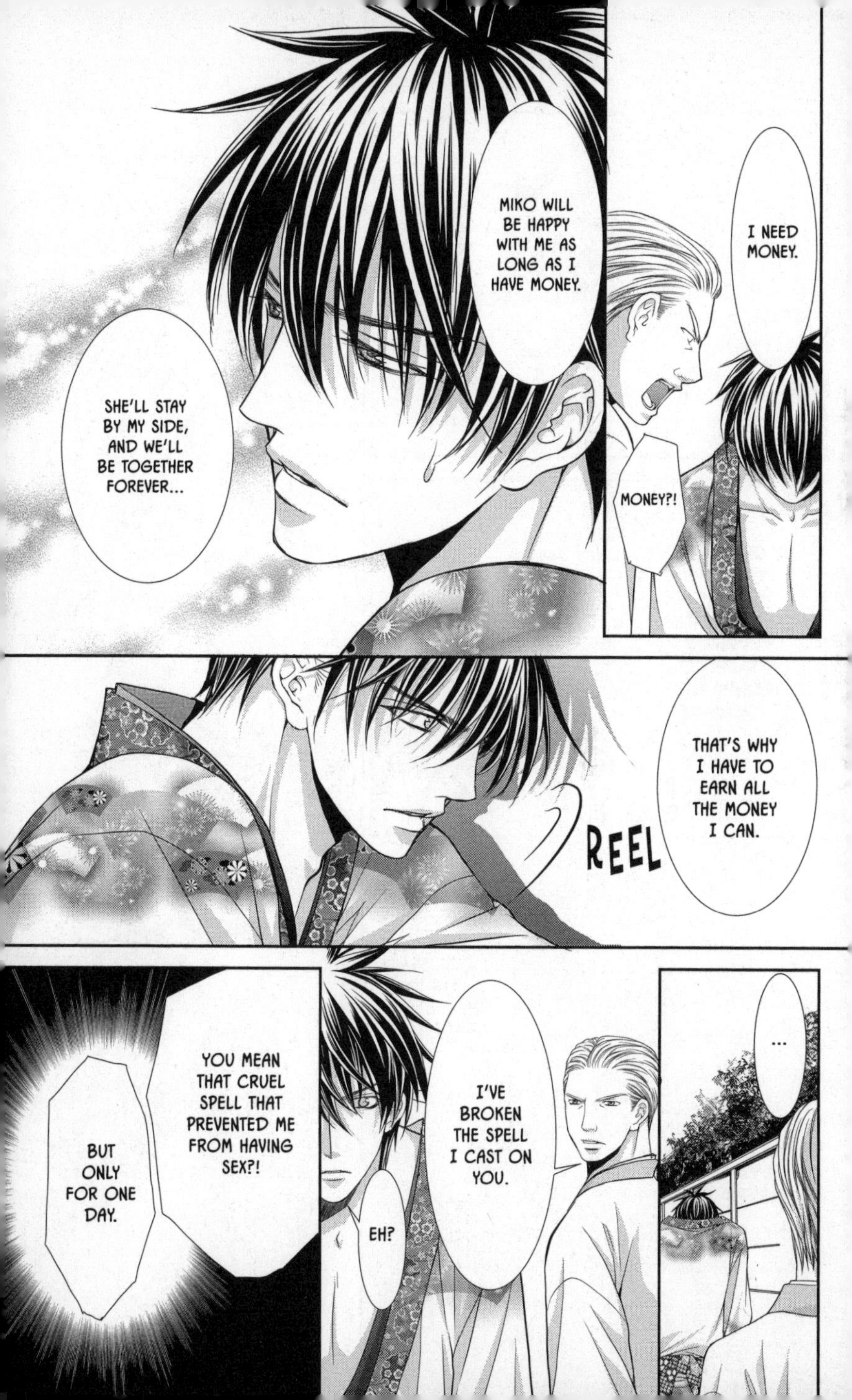
I NEED MONEY.
MONEY?!
MIKO WILL BE HAPPY WITH ME AS LONG AS I HAVE MONEY.
SHE'LL STAY BY MY SIDE, AND WE'LL BE TOGETHER FOREVER...
THAT'S WHY I HAVE TO EARN ALL THE MONEY I CAN.
REEL
...
I'VE BROKEN THE SPELL I CAST ON YOU.
EH?
YOU MEAN THAT CRUEL SPELL THAT PREVENTED ME FROM HAVING SEX?!
BUT ONLY FOR ONE DAY.

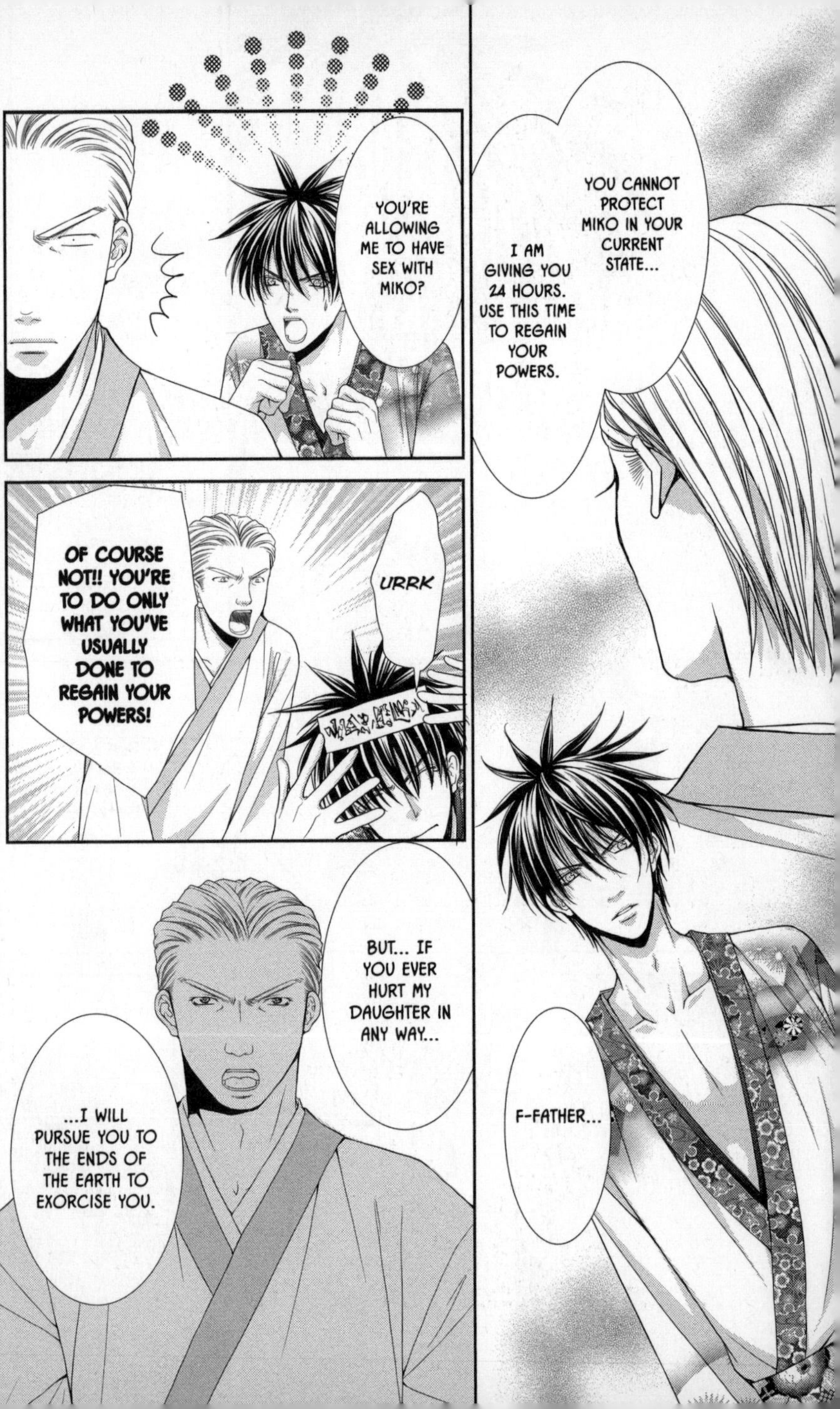
YOU CANNOT PROTECT MIKO IN YOUR CURRENT STATE...
I AM GIVING YOU 24 HOURS. USE THIS TIME TO REGAIN YOUR POWERS.
F-FATHER...
YOU'RE ALLOWING ME TO HAVE SEX WITH MIKO?
URRK
OF COURSE NOT!! YOU'RE TO DO ONLY WHAT YOU'VE USUALLY DONE TO REGAIN YOUR POWERS!
BUT... IF YOU EVER HURT MY DAUGHTER IN ANY WAY...
...I WILL PURSUE YOU TO THE ENDS OF THE EARTH TO EXORCISE YOU.

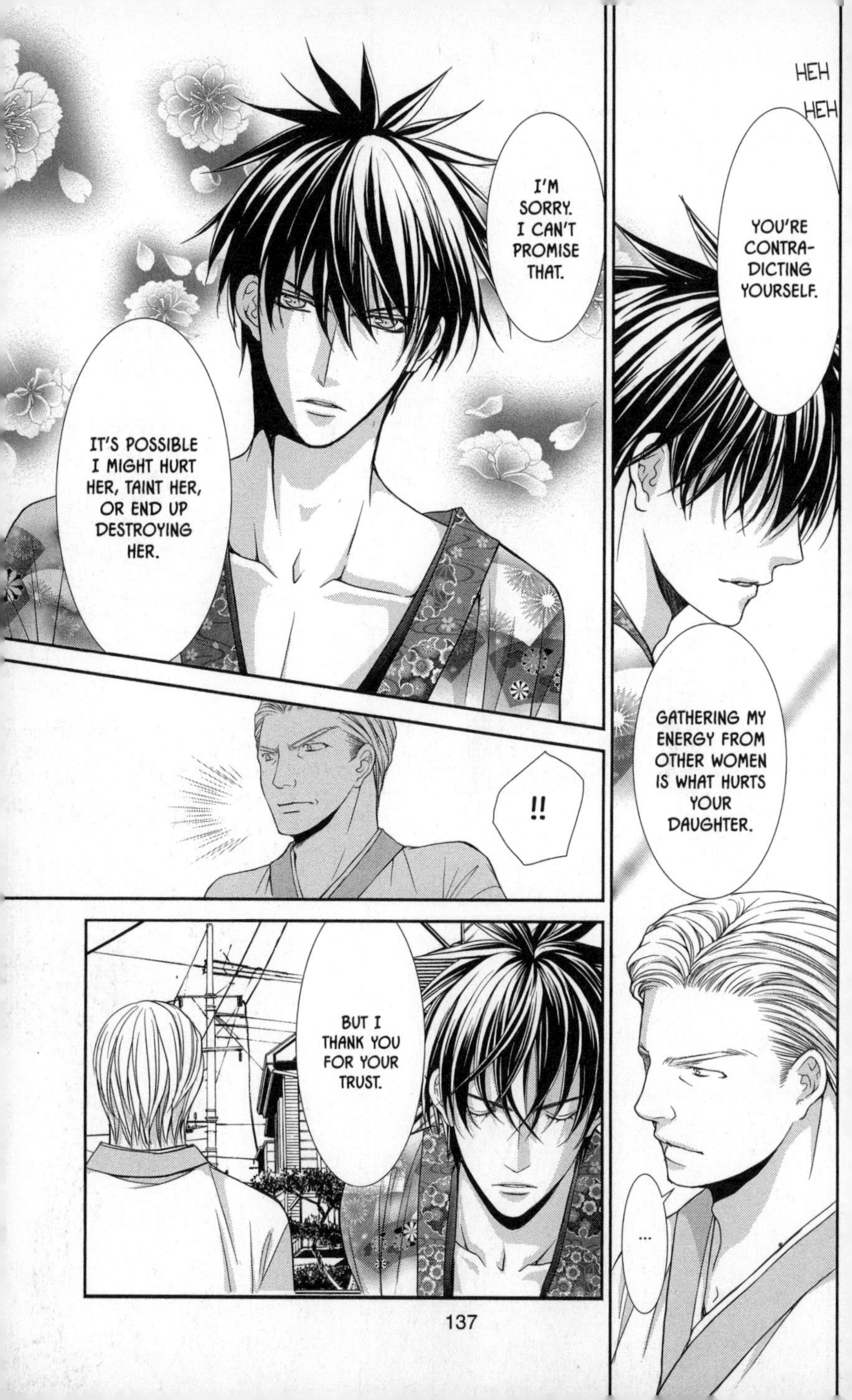
HEH HEH
YOU'RE CONTRA-DICTING YOURSELF.
GATHERING MY ENERGY FROM OTHER WOMEN IS WHAT HURTS YOUR DAUGHTER.
...
I'M SORRY. I CAN'T PROMISE THAT.
IT'S POSSIBLE I MIGHT HURT HER, TAINT HER, OR END UP DESTROYING HER.
!!
BUT I THANK YOU FOR YOUR TRUST.

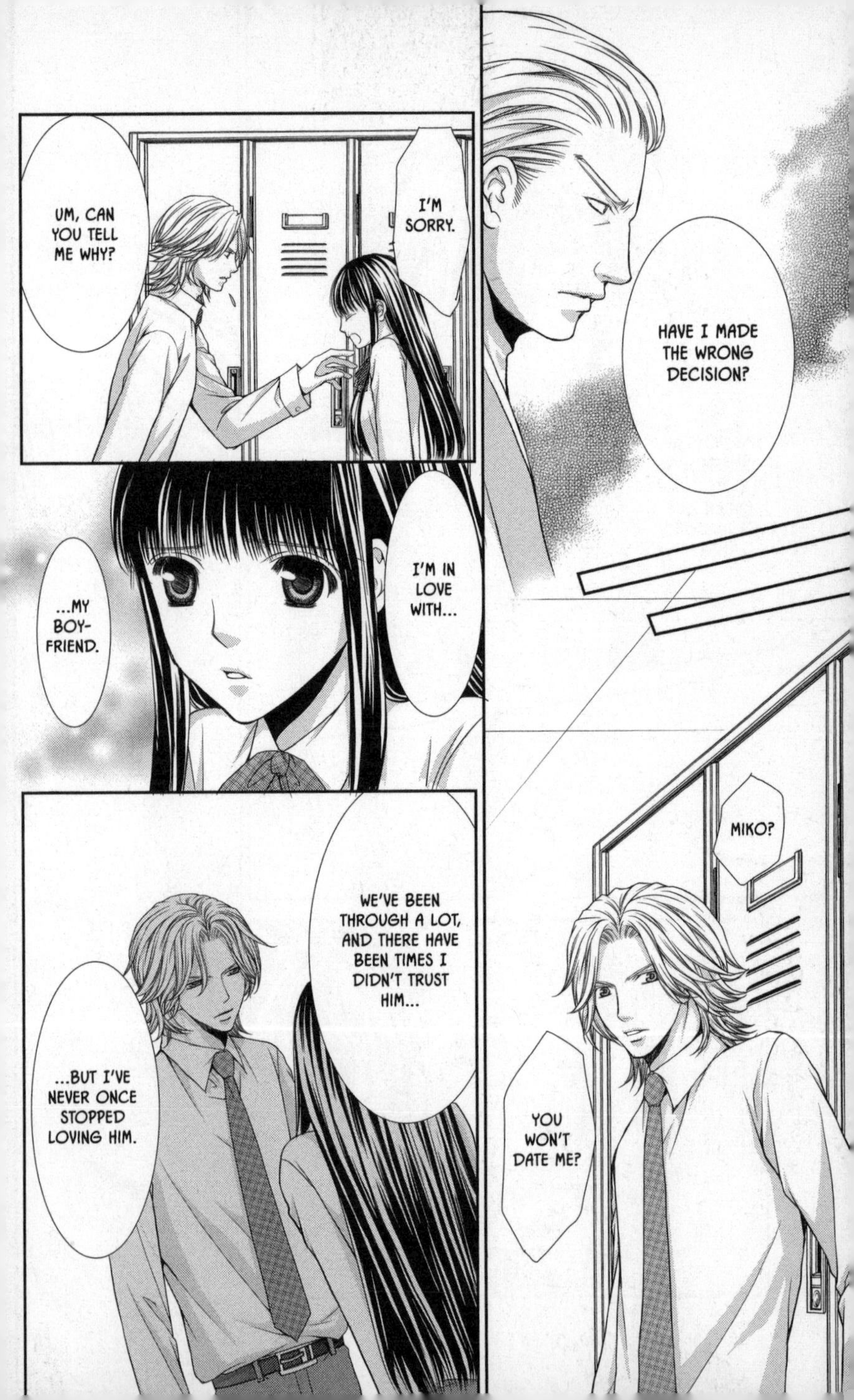
HAVE I MADE THE WRONG DECISION?
MIKO?
YOU WON'T DATE ME?
I'M SORRY.
UM, CAN YOU TELL ME WHY?
I'M IN LOVE WITH...
...MY BOY-FRIEND.
WE'VE BEEN THROUGH A LOT, AND THERE HAVE BEEN TIMES I DIDN'T TRUST HIM...
...BUT I'VE NEVER ONCE STOPPED LOVING HIM.

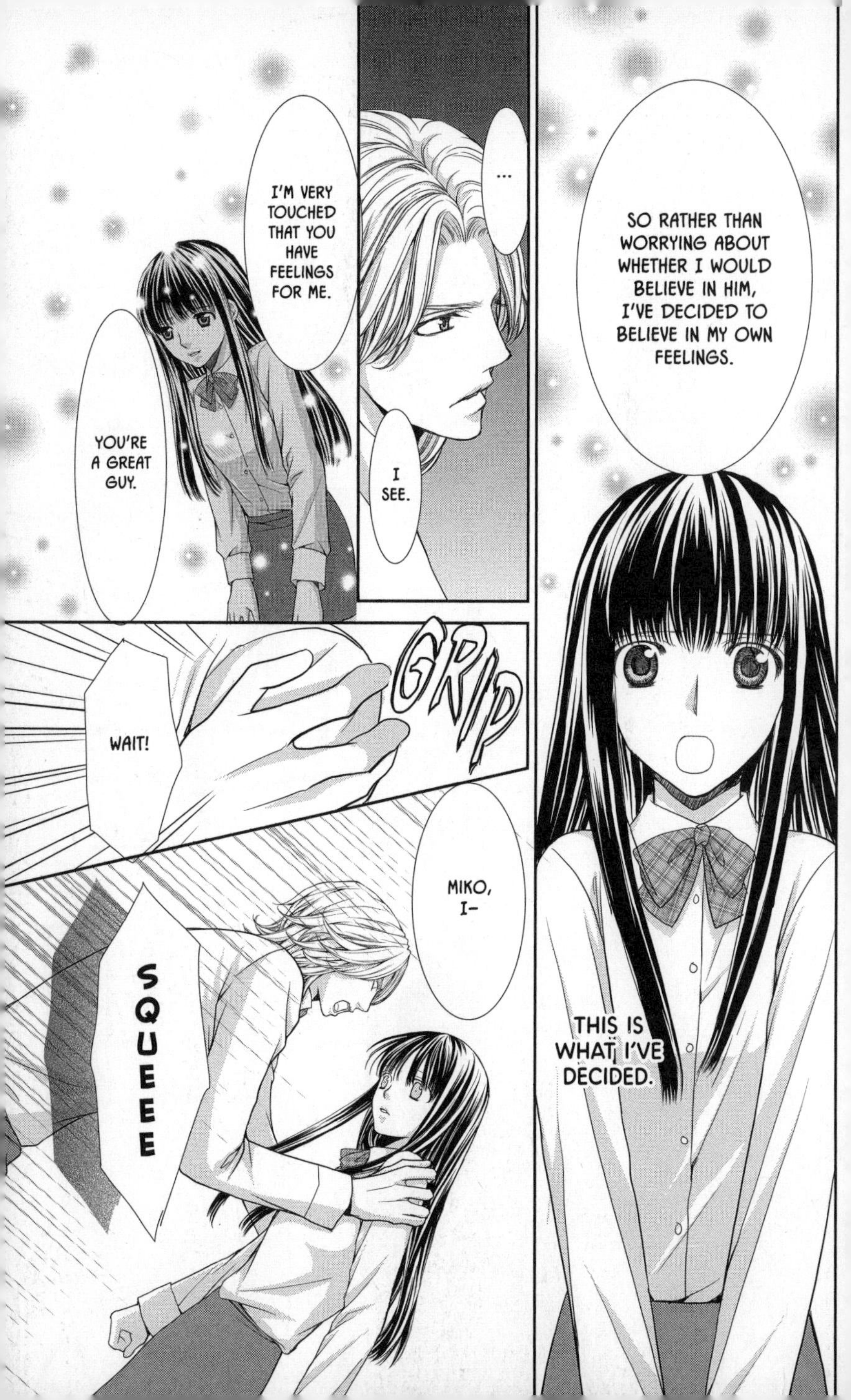

SO RATHER THAN WORRYING ABOUT WHETHER I WOULD BELIEVE IN HIM, I'VE DECIDED TO BELIEVE IN MY OWN FEELINGS.
THIS IS WHAT I'VE DECIDED.
...
I SEE.
I'M VERY TOUCHED THAT YOU HAVE FEELINGS FOR ME.
YOU'RE A GREAT GUY.
GRIP
WAIT!
MIKO, I-
SQUEEE

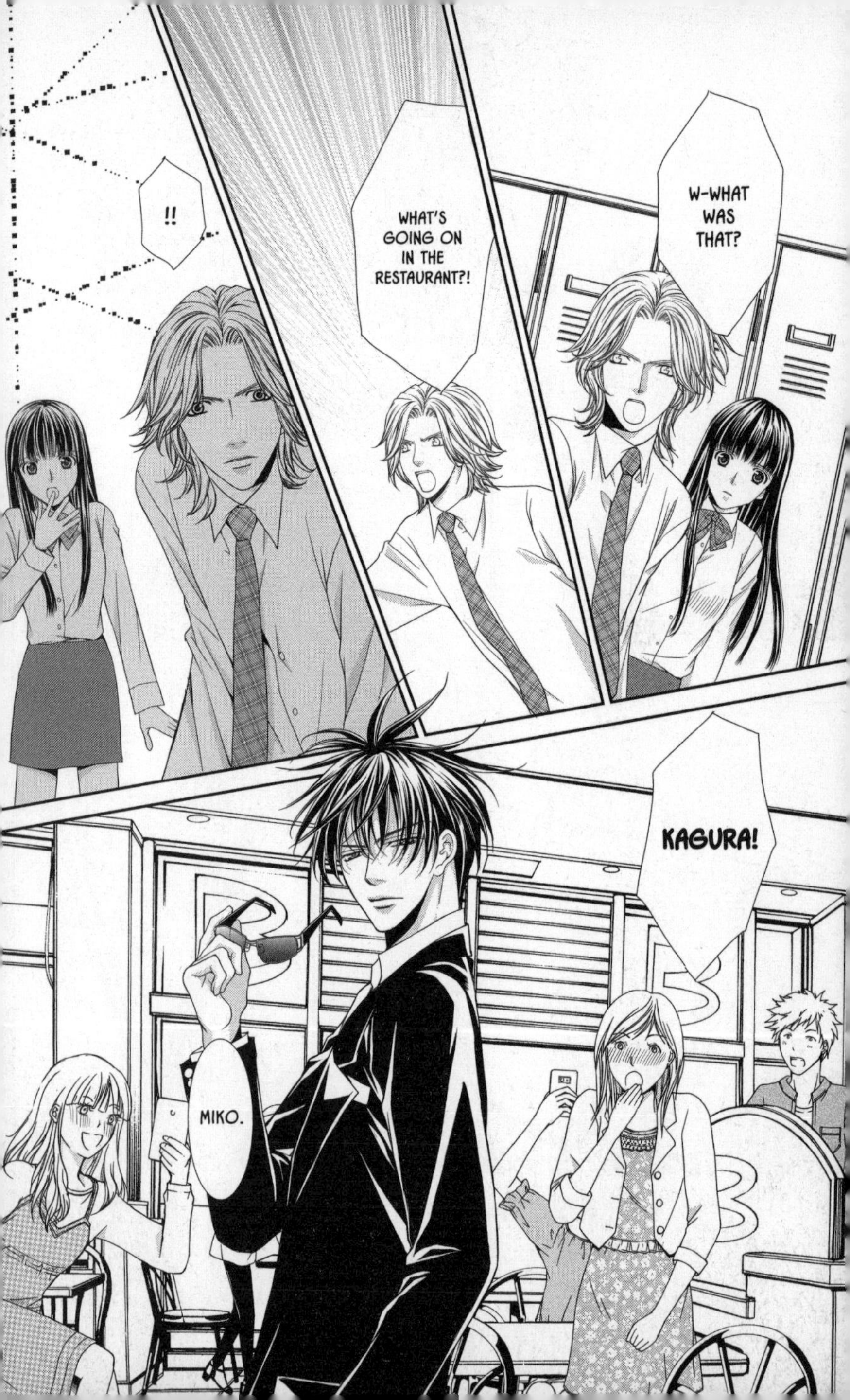
W-WHAT WAS THAT?
WHAT'S GOING ON IN THE RESTAURANT?!
!!
KAGURA!
MIKO.

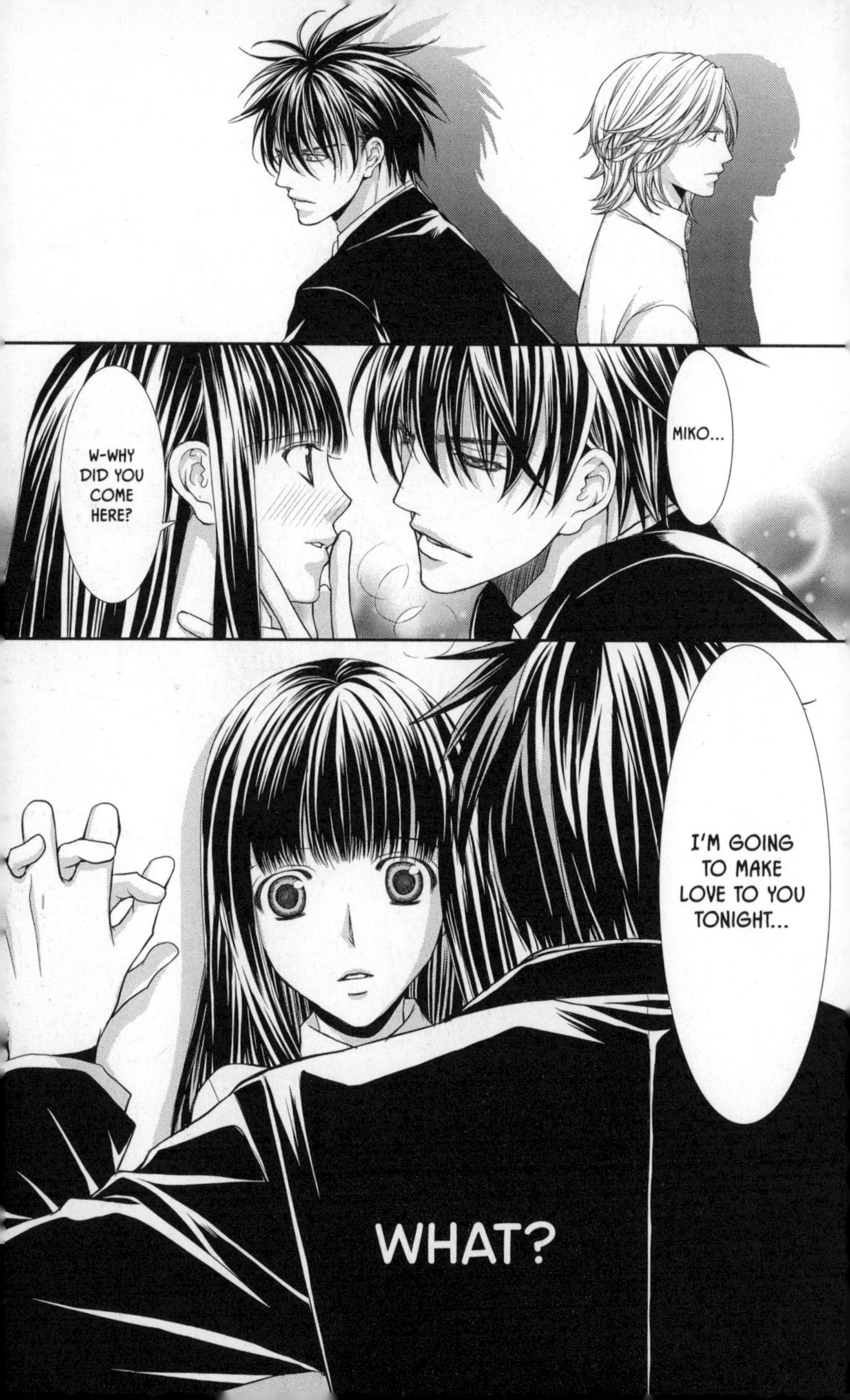

MIKO...
W-WHY DID YOU COME HERE?
I'M GOING TO MAKE LOVE TO YOU TONIGHT...
WHAT?

Something I've always wanted to draw:

Mini Kagura Suffering in the Summer Heat ♡

He didn't have that many scenes in this volume, so I wanted to draw him.
I want more scenes with Mini Kagura!!

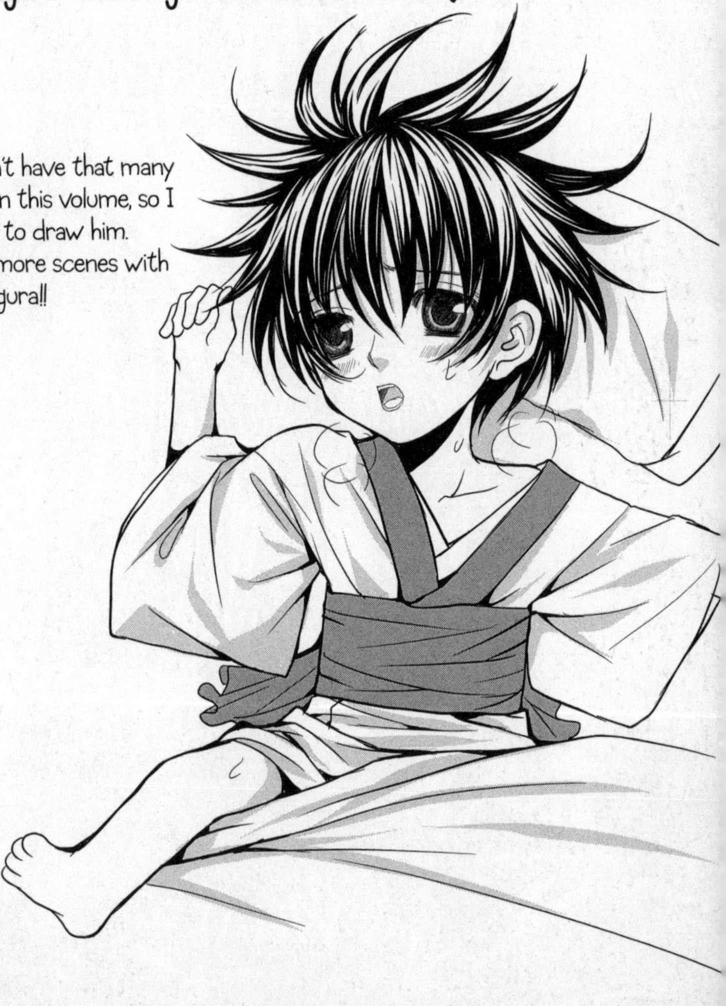

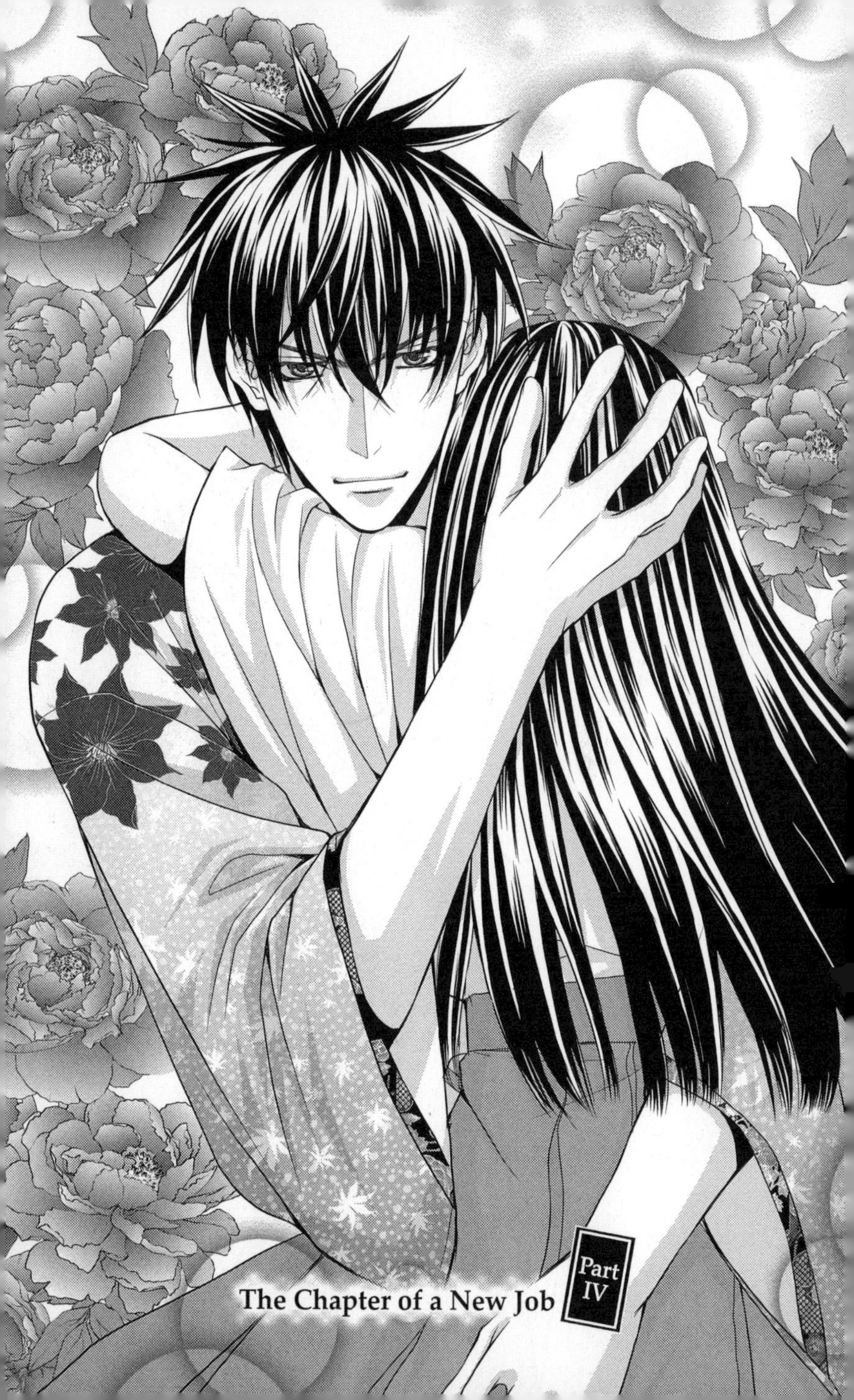
Part IV
The Chapter of a New Job

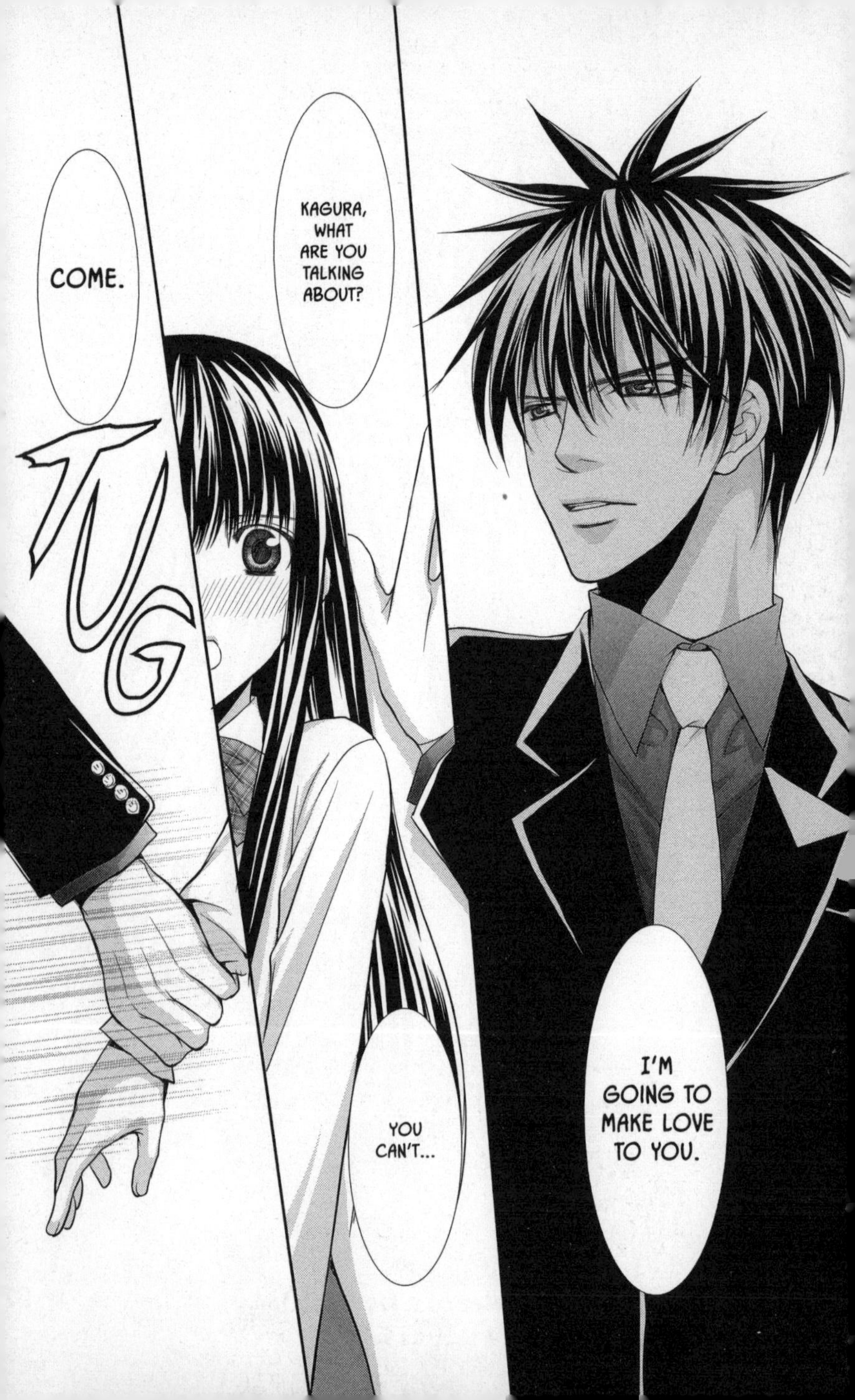
I'M GOING TO MAKE LOVE TO YOU.
KAGURA, WHAT ARE YOU TALKING ABOUT?
YOU CAN'T...
COME.
TUG

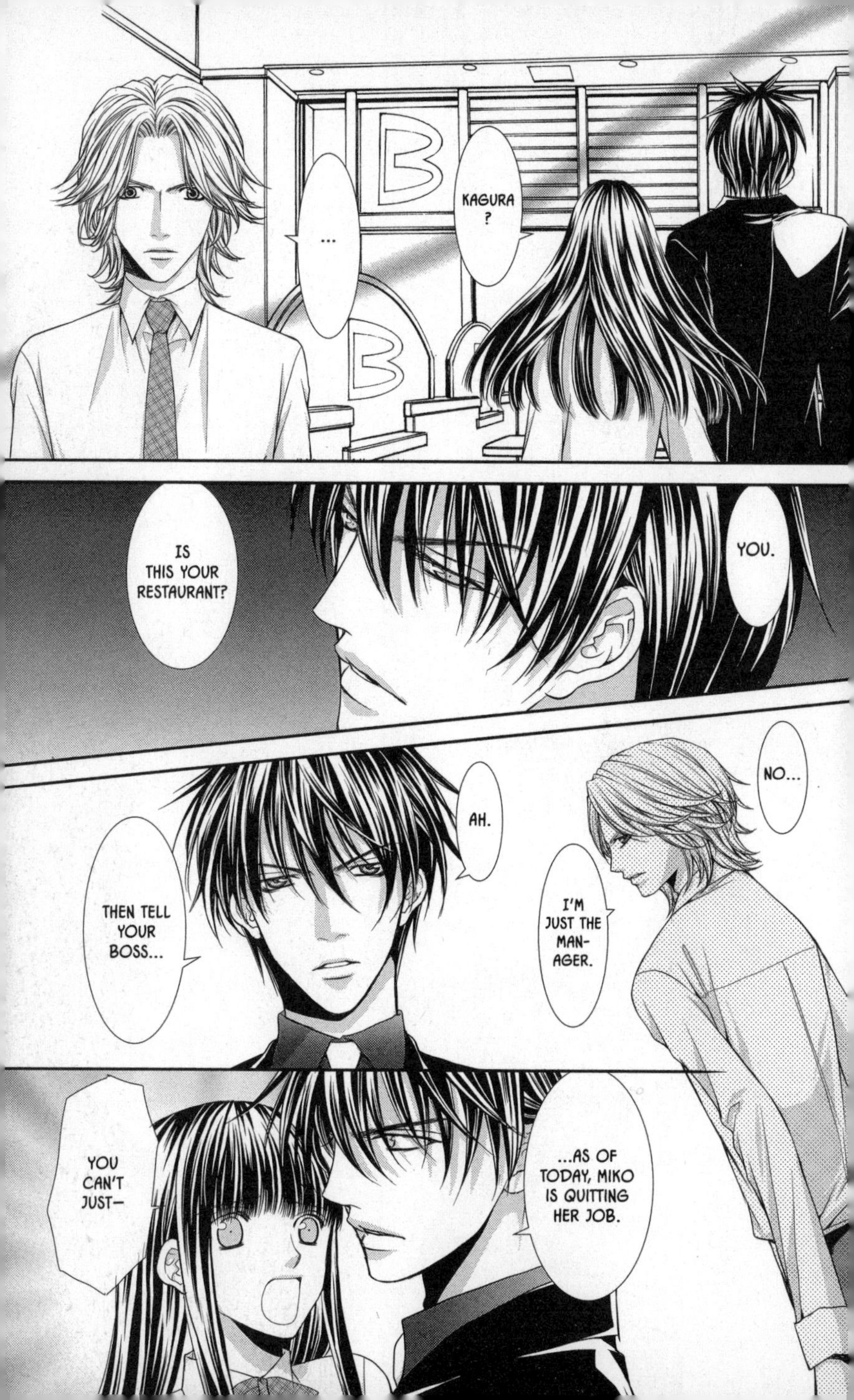
KAGURA ?
...
YOU.
IS THIS YOUR RESTAURANT?
NO...
I'M JUST THE MAN- AGER.
AH.
THEN TELL YOUR BOSS...
...AS OF TODAY, MIKO IS QUITTING HER JOB.
YOU CAN'T JUST—

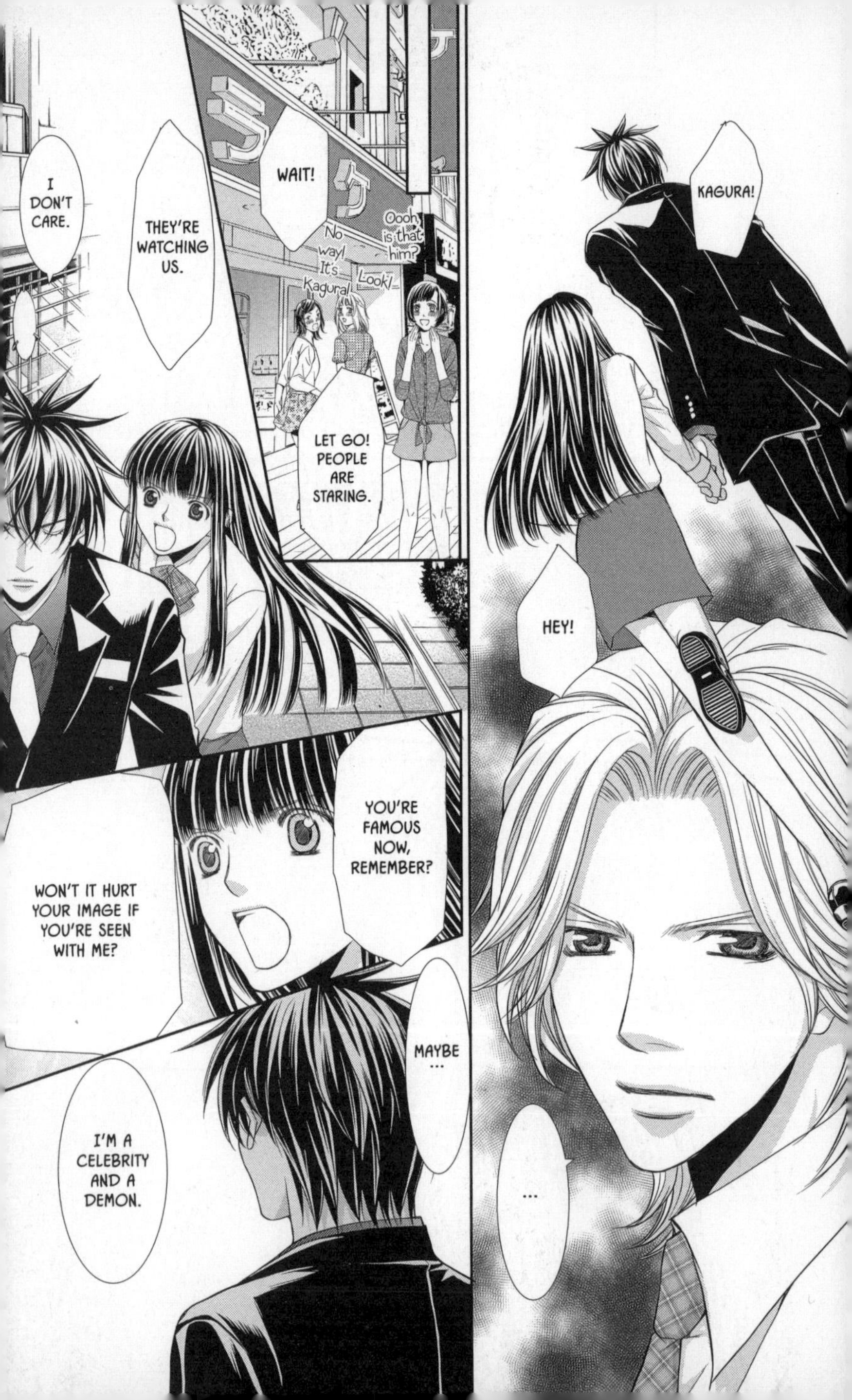
KAGURA!
HEY!
...
WAIT!
Oooh, is that him?
Look!
No way! It's Kagura!
LET GO! PEOPLE ARE STARING.
THEY'RE WATCHING US.
I DON'T CARE.
YOU'RE FAMOUS NOW, REMEMBER?
WON'T IT HURT YOUR IMAGE IF YOU'RE SEEN WITH ME?
MAYBE...
I'M A CELEBRITY AND A DEMON.

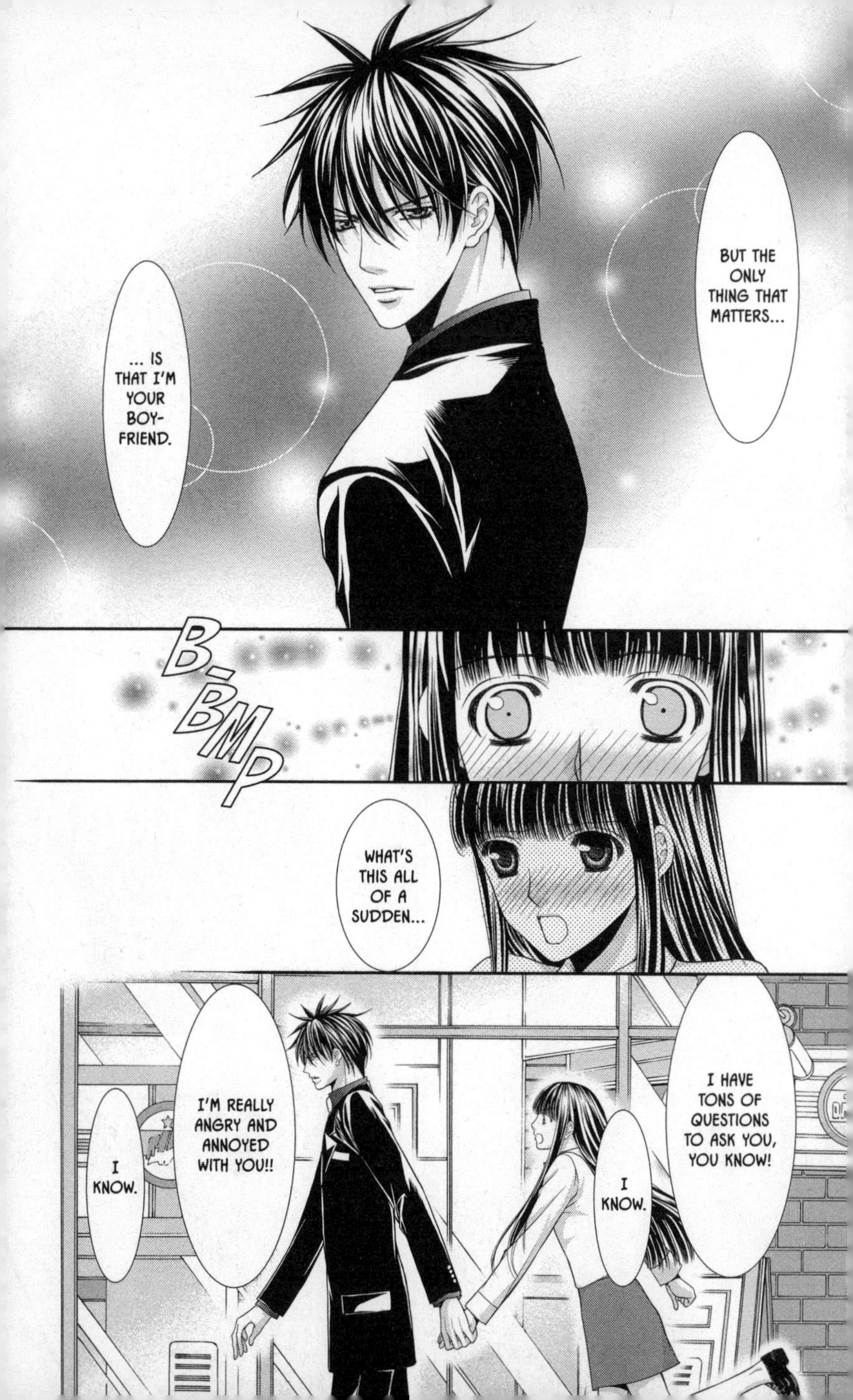
BUT THE ONLY THING THAT MATTERS...
... IS THAT I'M YOUR BOY-FRIEND.
B-BMP
WHAT'S THIS ALL OF A SUDDEN...
I HAVE TONS OF QUESTIONS TO ASK YOU, YOU KNOW!
I KNOW.
I'M REALLY ANGRY AND ANNOYED WITH YOU!!
I KNOW.

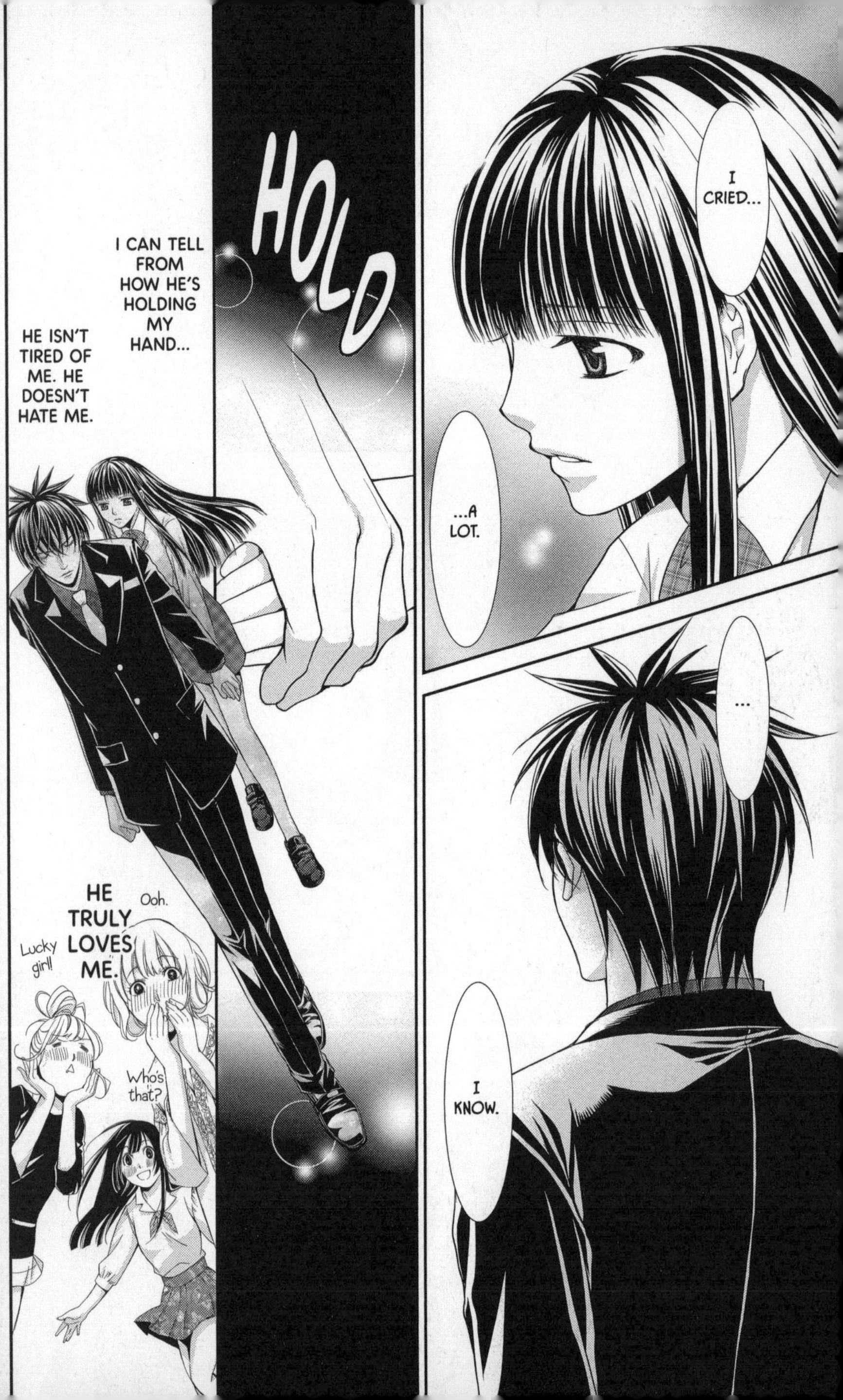
I CRIED...
...A LOT.
...
I KNOW.
HOLD
I CAN TELL FROM HOW HE'S HOLDING MY HAND...
HE ISN'T TIRED OF ME. HE DOESN'T HATE ME.
Ooh.
HE TRULY LOVES ME.
Lucky girl!
Who's that?

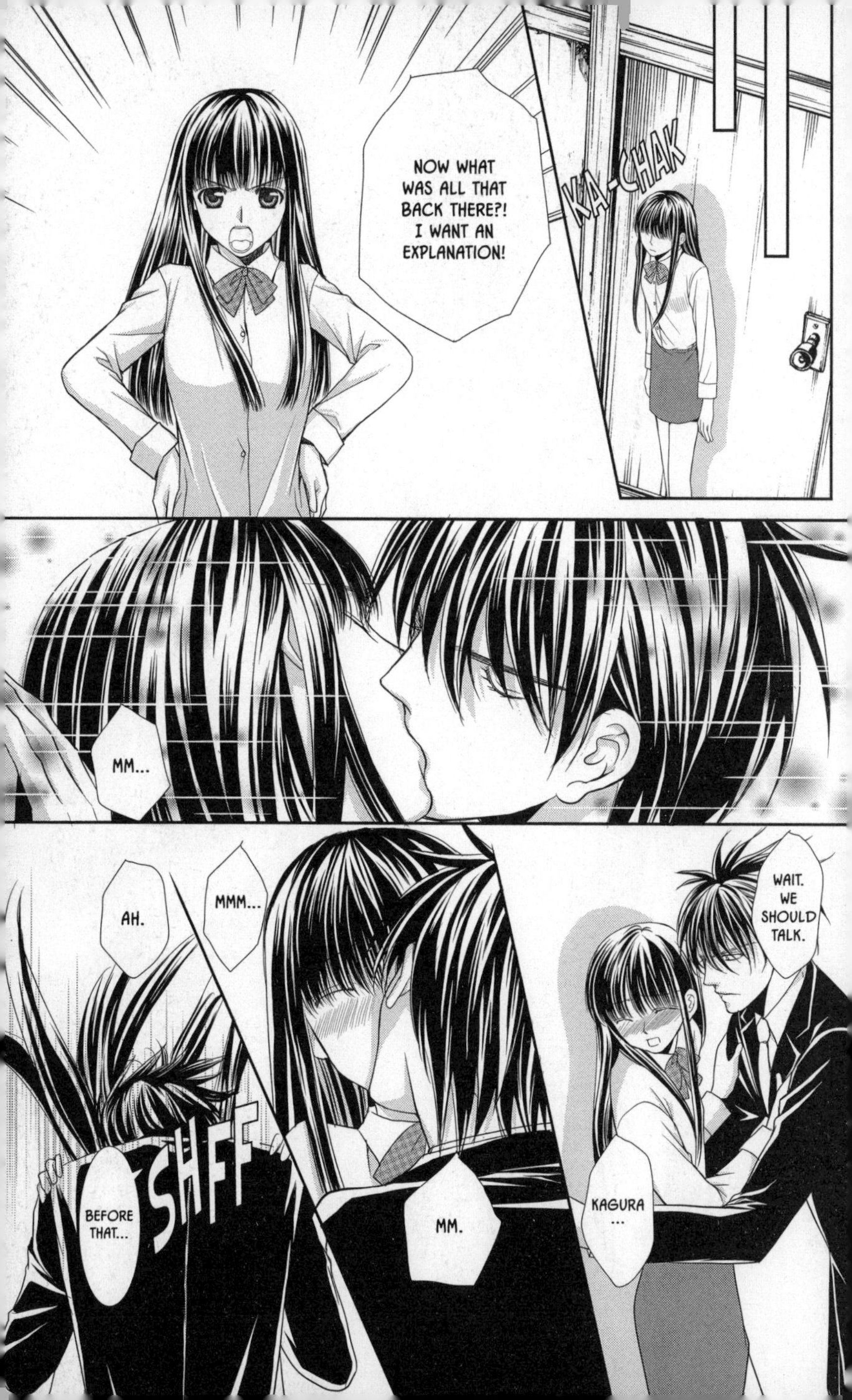
KA-CHAK
NOW WHAT WAS ALL THAT BACK THERE?! I WANT AN EXPLANATION!
MM...
WAIT. WE SHOULD TALK.
KAGURA ...
MMM...
MM.
AH.
SHFF
BEFORE THAT...

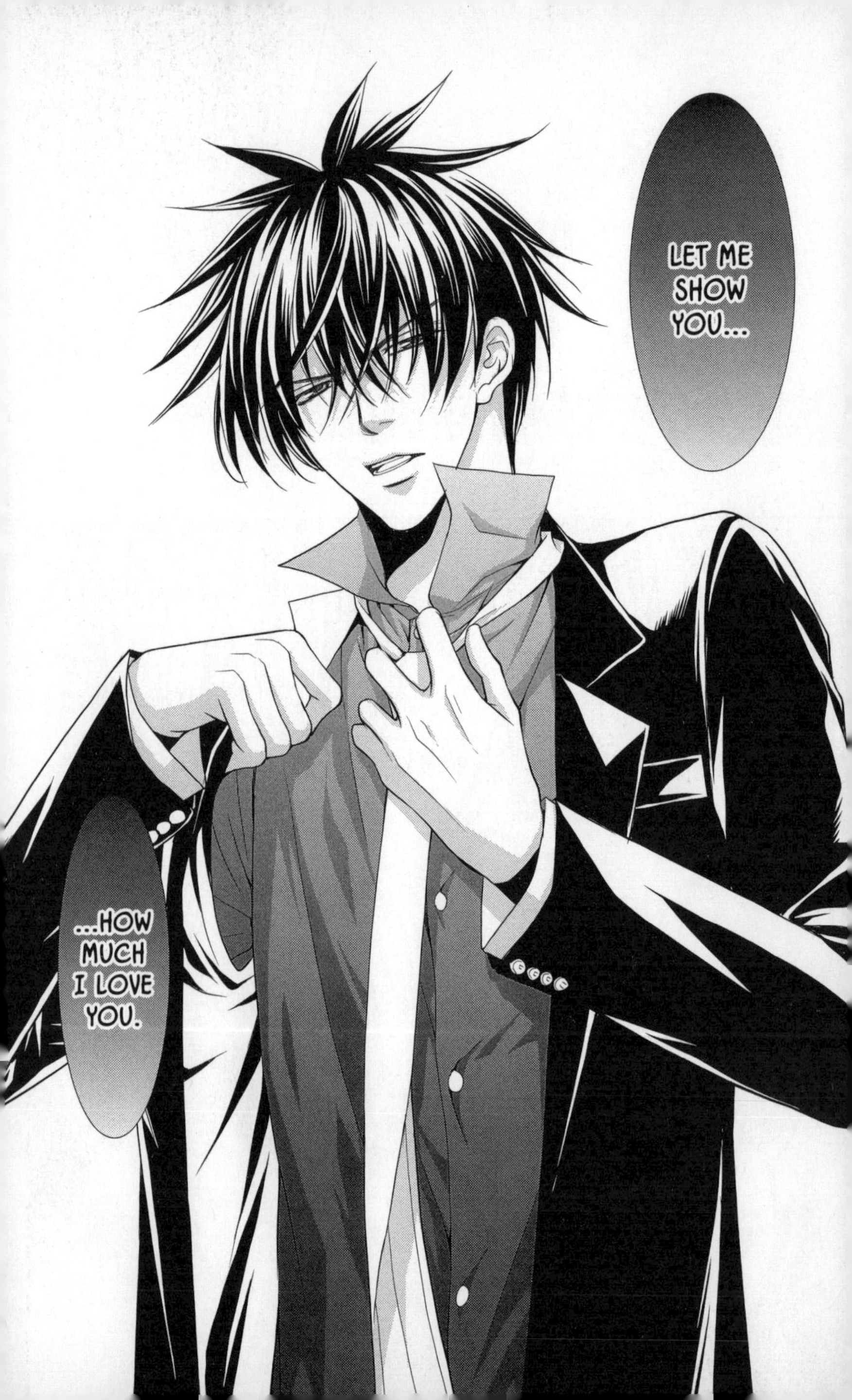
LET ME SHOW YOU...
...HOW MUCH I LOVE YOU.

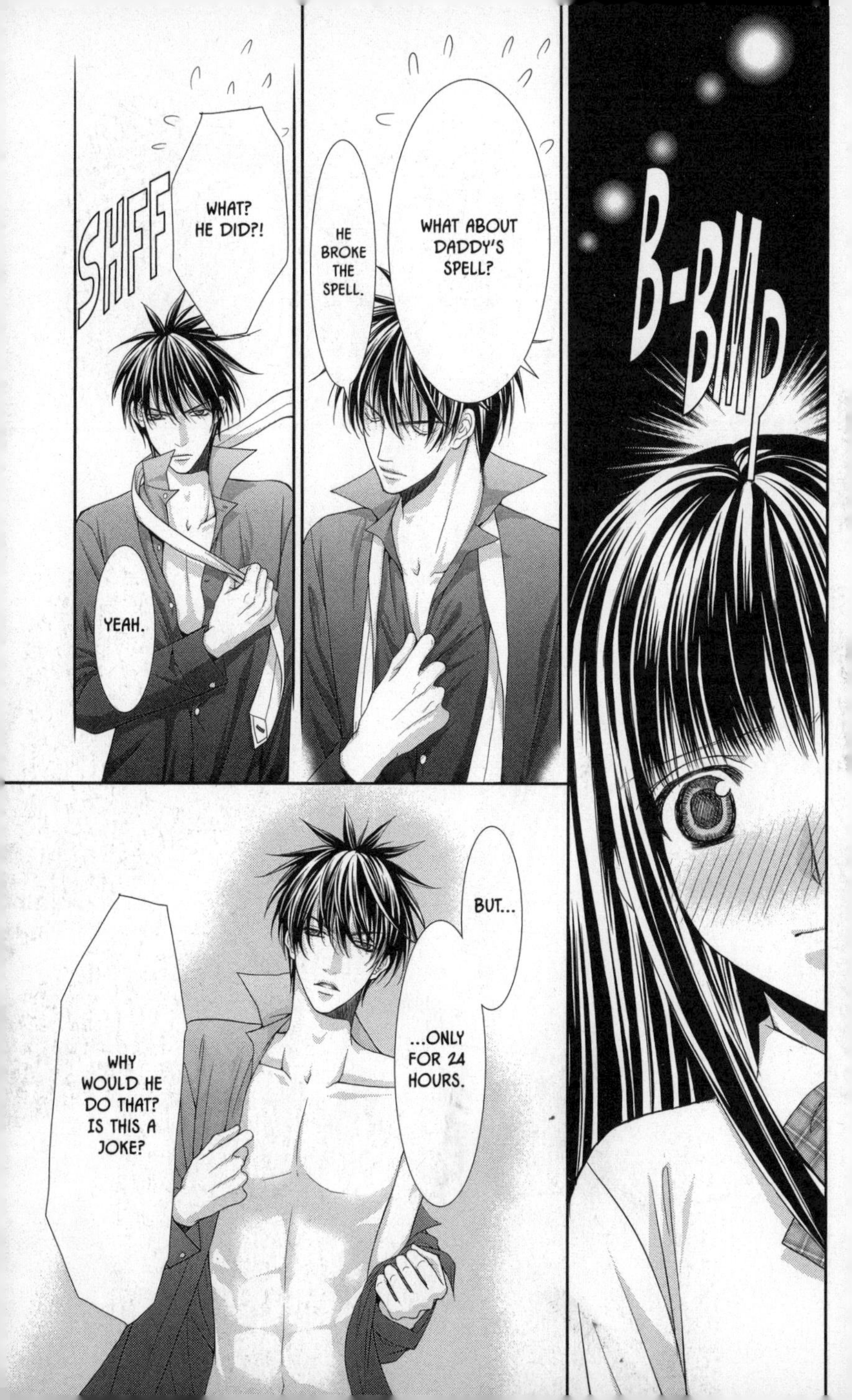
B-BMP
WHAT ABOUT DADDY'S SPELL?
HE BROKE THE SPELL.
WHAT? HE DID?!
SHFF
YEAH.
BUT...
...ONLY FOR 24 HOURS.
WHY WOULD HE DO THAT? IS THIS A JOKE?

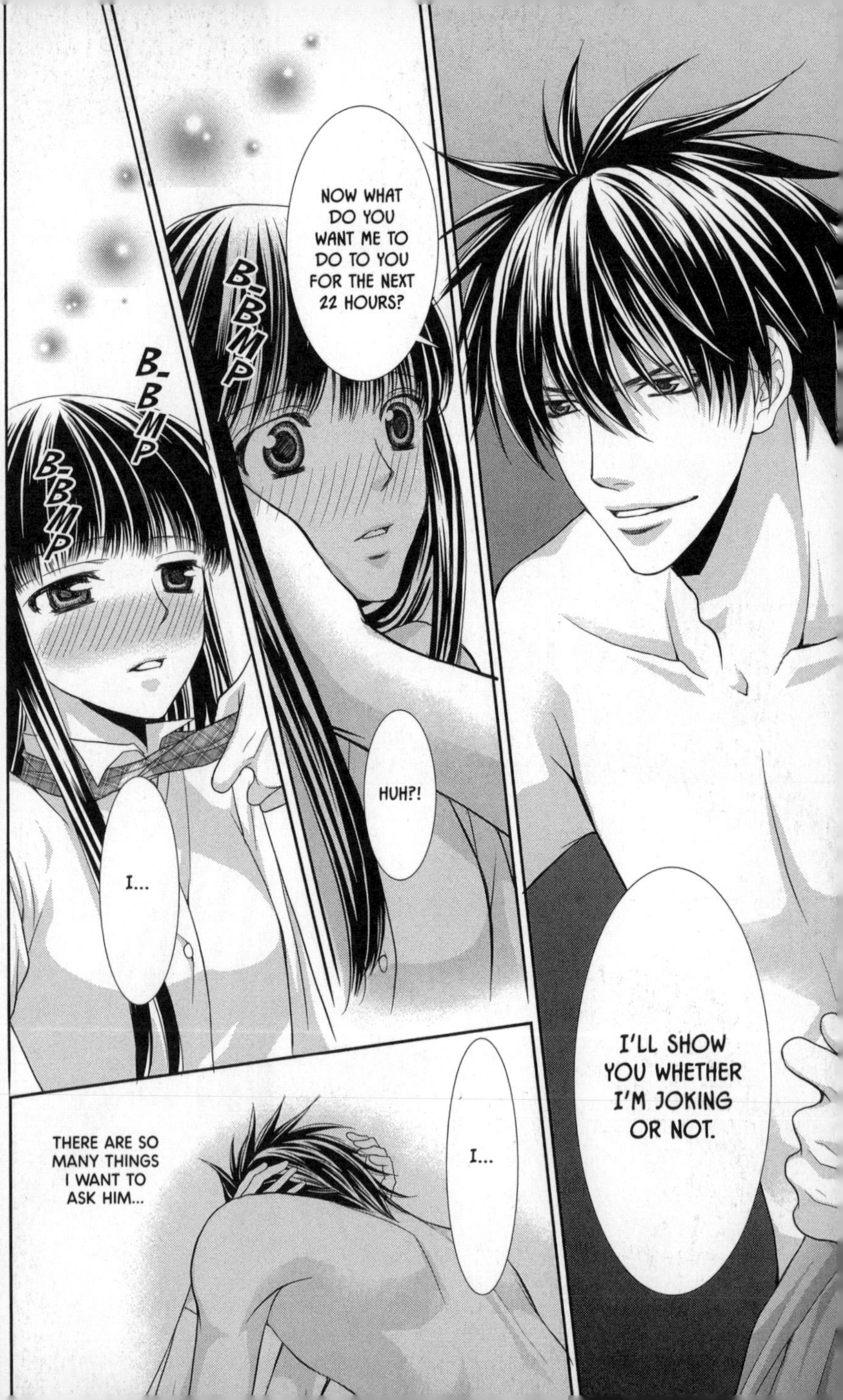
NOW WHAT DO YOU WANT ME TO DO TO YOU FOR THE NEXT 22 HOURS?
I'LL SHOW YOU WHETHER I'M JOKING OR NOT.
B-BMP
HUH?!
B-BMP
B-BMP
I...
I...
THERE ARE SO MANY THINGS I WANT TO ASK HIM...

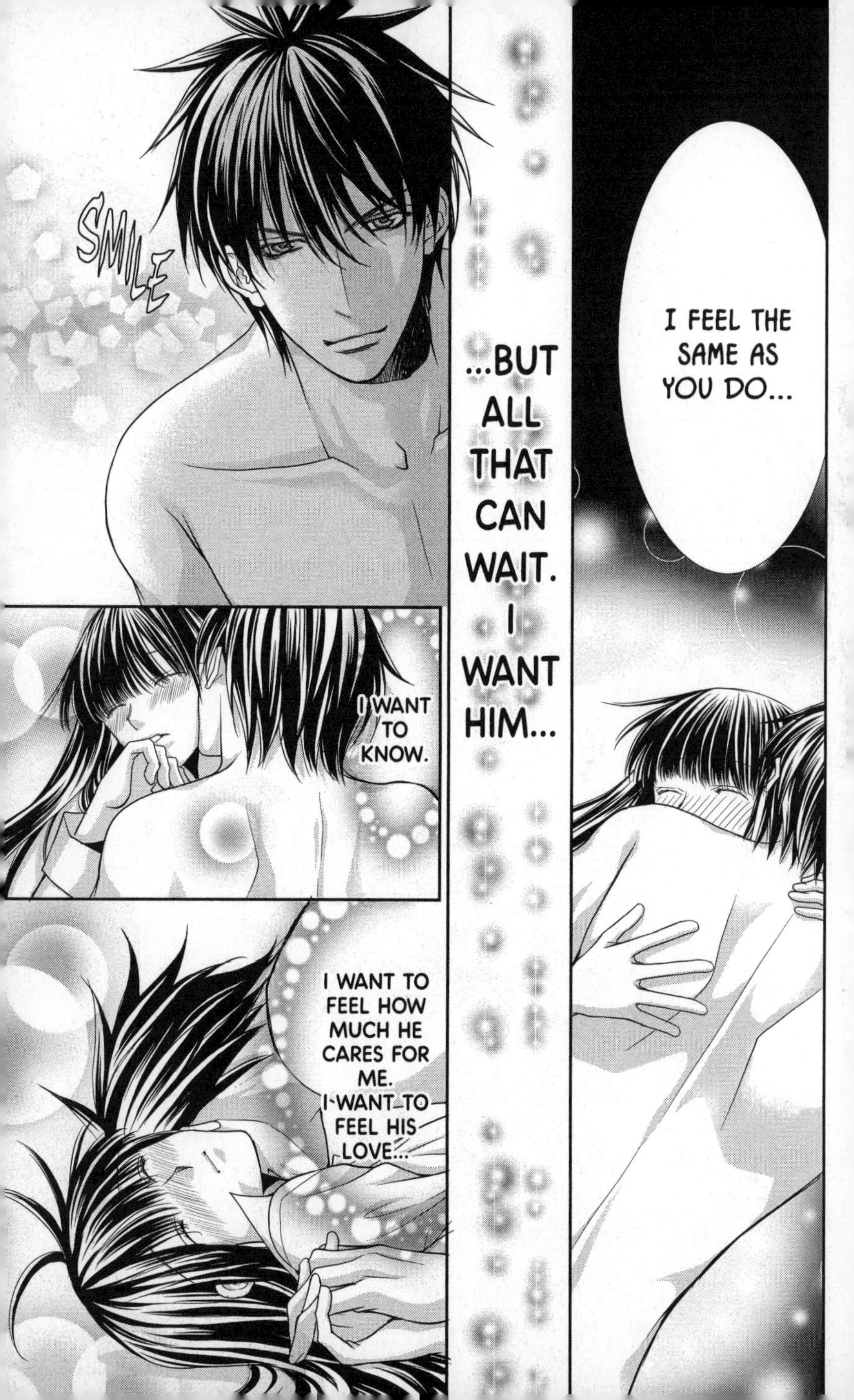
I FEEL THE SAME AS YOU DO...
...BUT ALL THAT CAN WAIT. I WANT HIM...
SMILE
I WANT TO KNOW.
I WANT TO FEEL HOW MUCH HE CARES FOR ME. I WANT TO FEEL HIS LOVE...

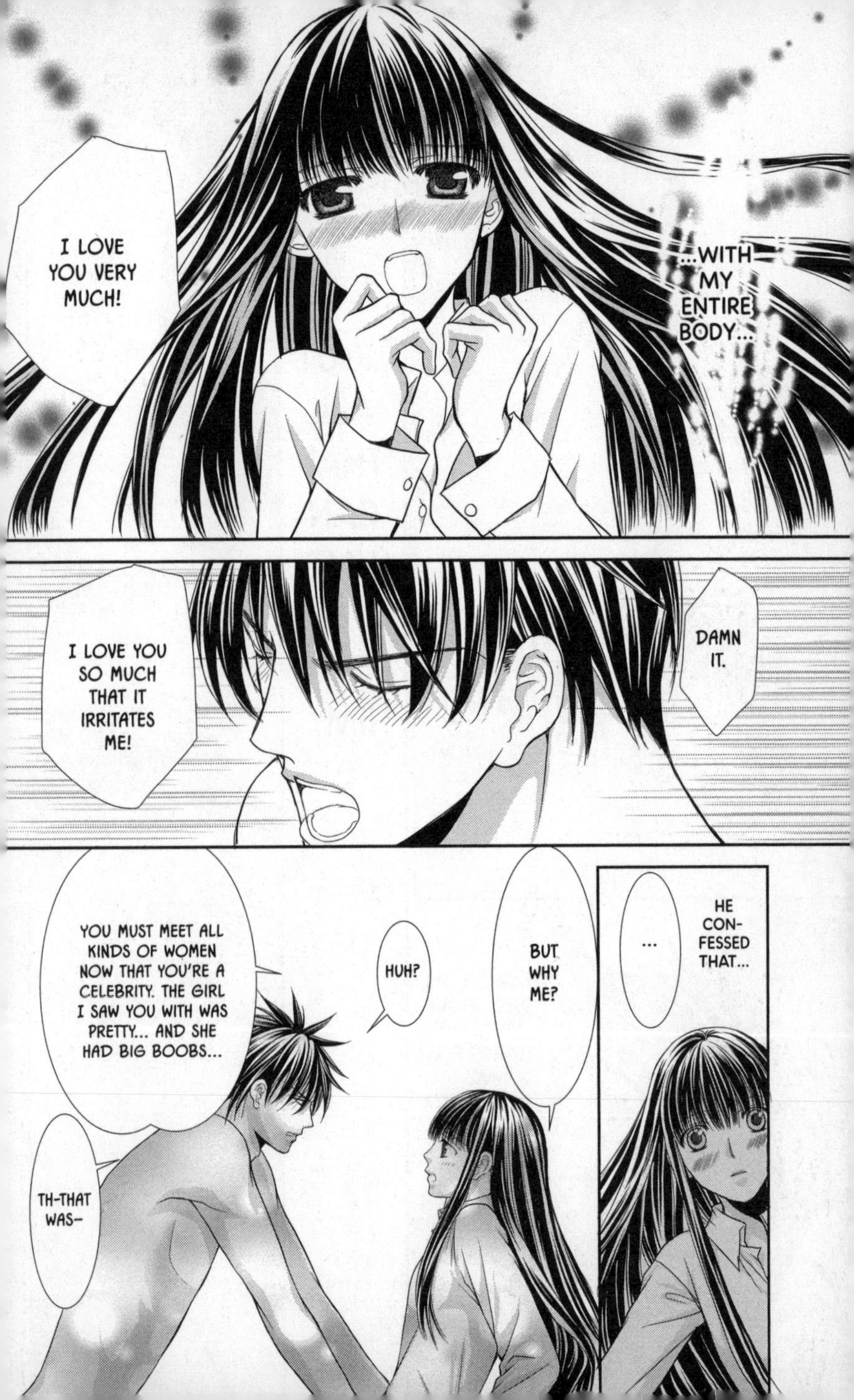
I LOVE YOU VERY MUCH!
...WITH MY ENTIRE BODY...
DAMN IT.
I LOVE YOU SO MUCH THAT IT IRRITATES ME!
HE CON-FESSED THAT...
...
BUT WHY ME?
HUH?
YOU MUST MEET ALL KINDS OF WOMEN NOW THAT YOU'RE A CELEBRITY. THE GIRL I SAW YOU WITH WAS PRETTY... AND SHE HAD BIG BOOBS...
TH-THAT WAS-

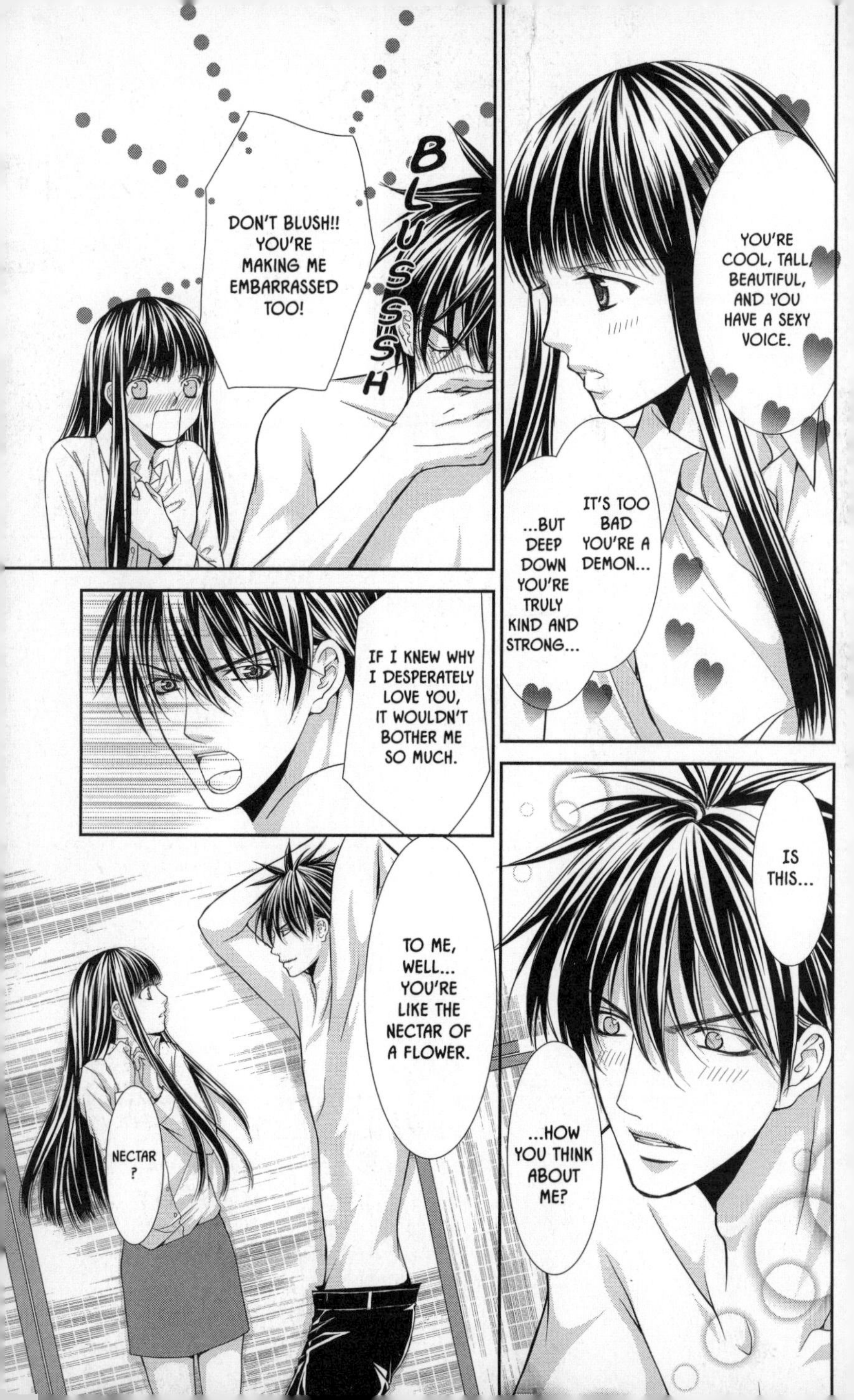
YOU'RE COOL, TALL, BEAUTIFUL, AND YOU HAVE A SEXY VOICE.
IT'S TOO BAD YOU'RE A DEMON...
...BUT DEEP DOWN YOU'RE TRULY KIND AND STRONG...
BLUSSSH
DON'T BLUSH!! YOU'RE MAKING ME EMBARRASSED TOO!
IF I KNEW WHY I DESPERATELY LOVE YOU, IT WOULDN'T BOTHER ME SO MUCH.
IS THIS...
...HOW YOU THINK ABOUT ME?
TO ME, WELL... YOU'RE LIKE THE NECTAR OF A FLOWER.
NECTAR?

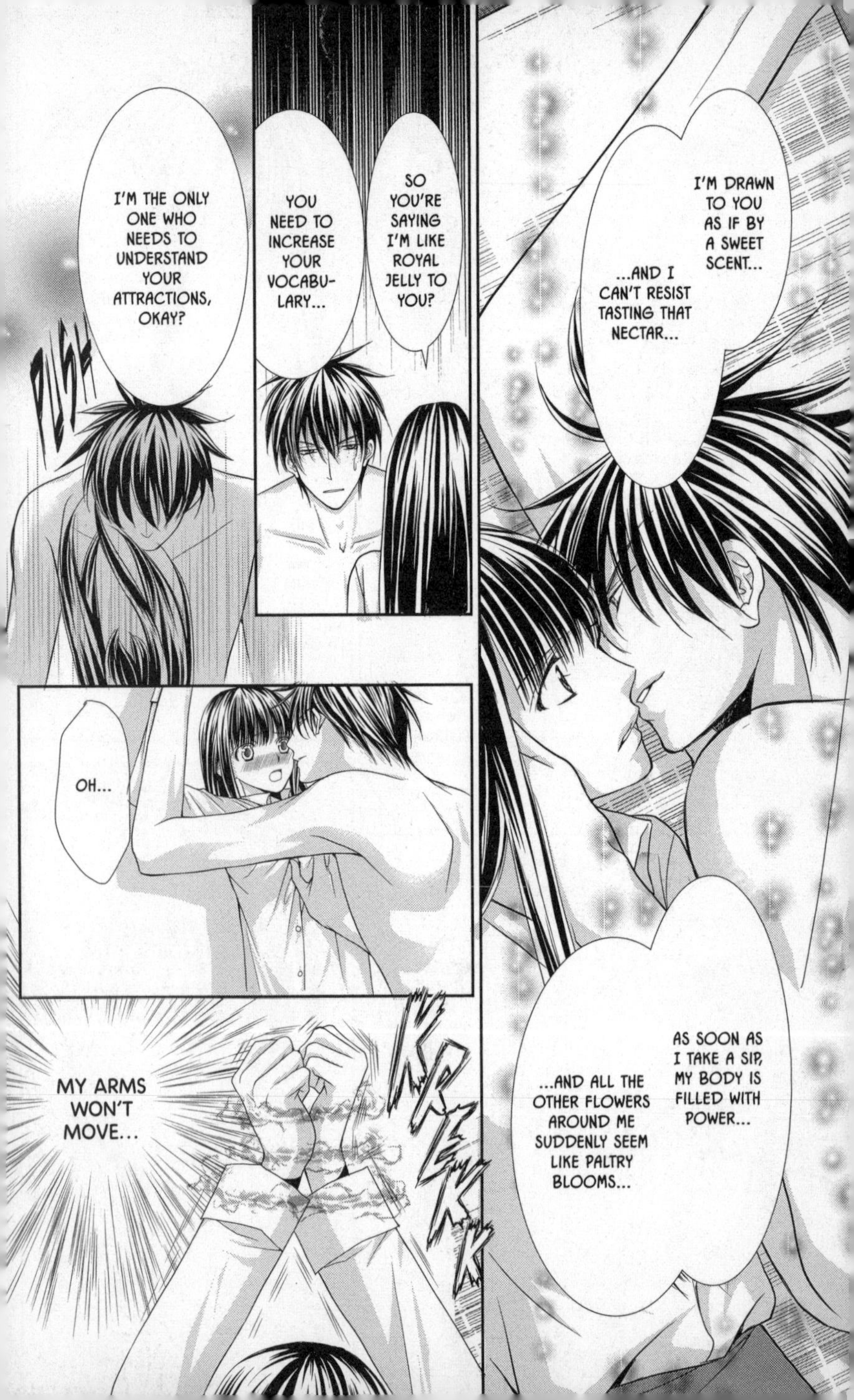
I'M DRAWN TO YOU AS IF BY A SWEET SCENT...
...AND I CAN'T RESIST TASTING THAT NECTAR...
AS SOON AS I TAKE A SIP, MY BODY IS FILLED WITH POWER...
...AND ALL THE OTHER FLOWERS AROUND ME SUDDENLY SEEM LIKE PALTRY BLOOMS...
SO YOU'RE SAYING I'M LIKE ROYAL JELLY TO YOU?
YOU NEED TO INCREASE YOUR VOCABU-LARY...
PUSH
I'M THE ONLY ONE WHO NEEDS TO UNDERSTAND YOUR ATTRACTIONS, OKAY?
OH...
MY ARMS WON'T MOVE...

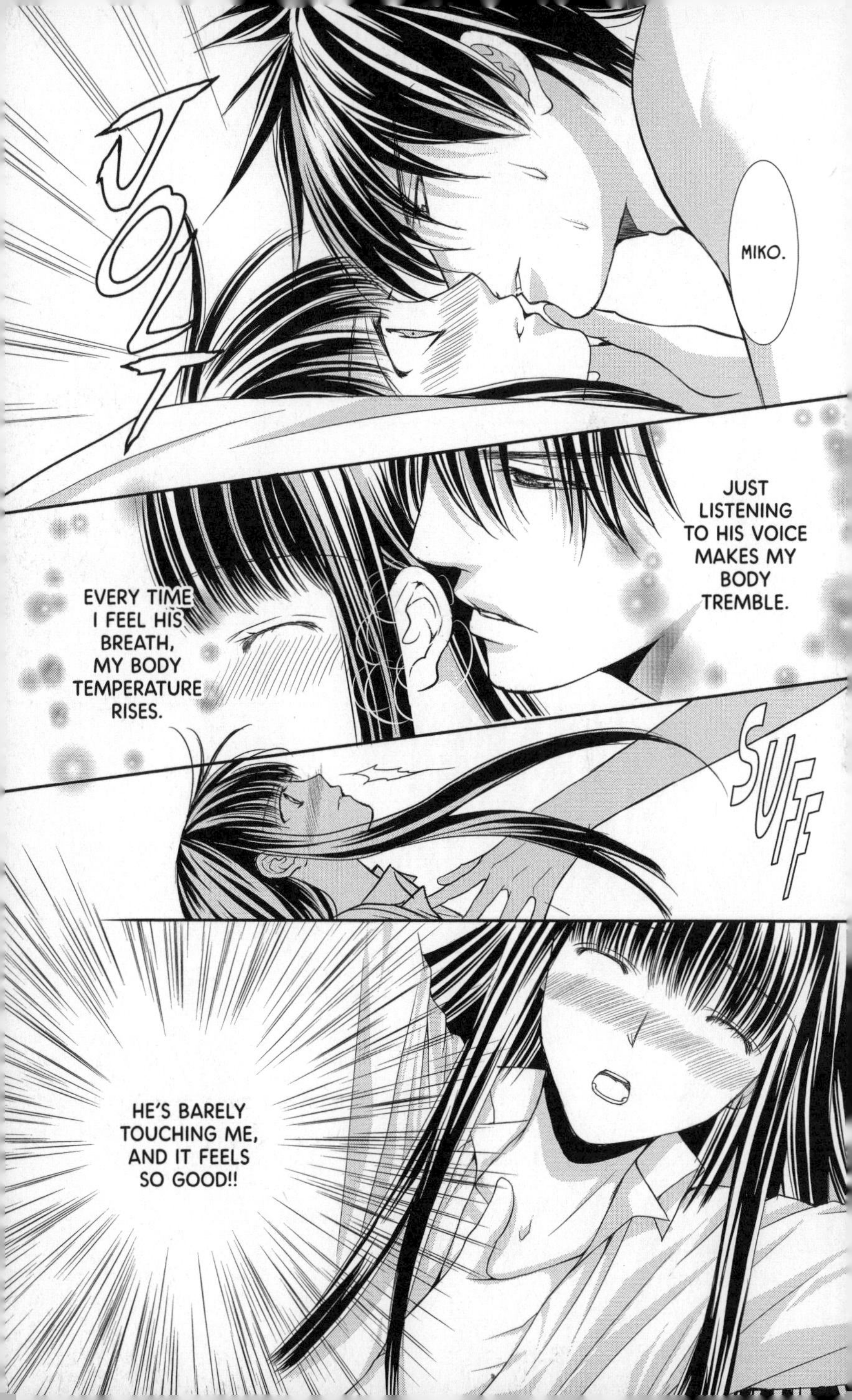
MIKO.
JOLT
JUST LISTENING TO HIS VOICE MAKES MY BODY TREMBLE.
EVERY TIME I FEEL HIS BREATH, MY BODY TEMPERATURE RISES.
SUFF
HE'S BARELY TOUCHING ME, AND IT FEELS SO GOOD!!

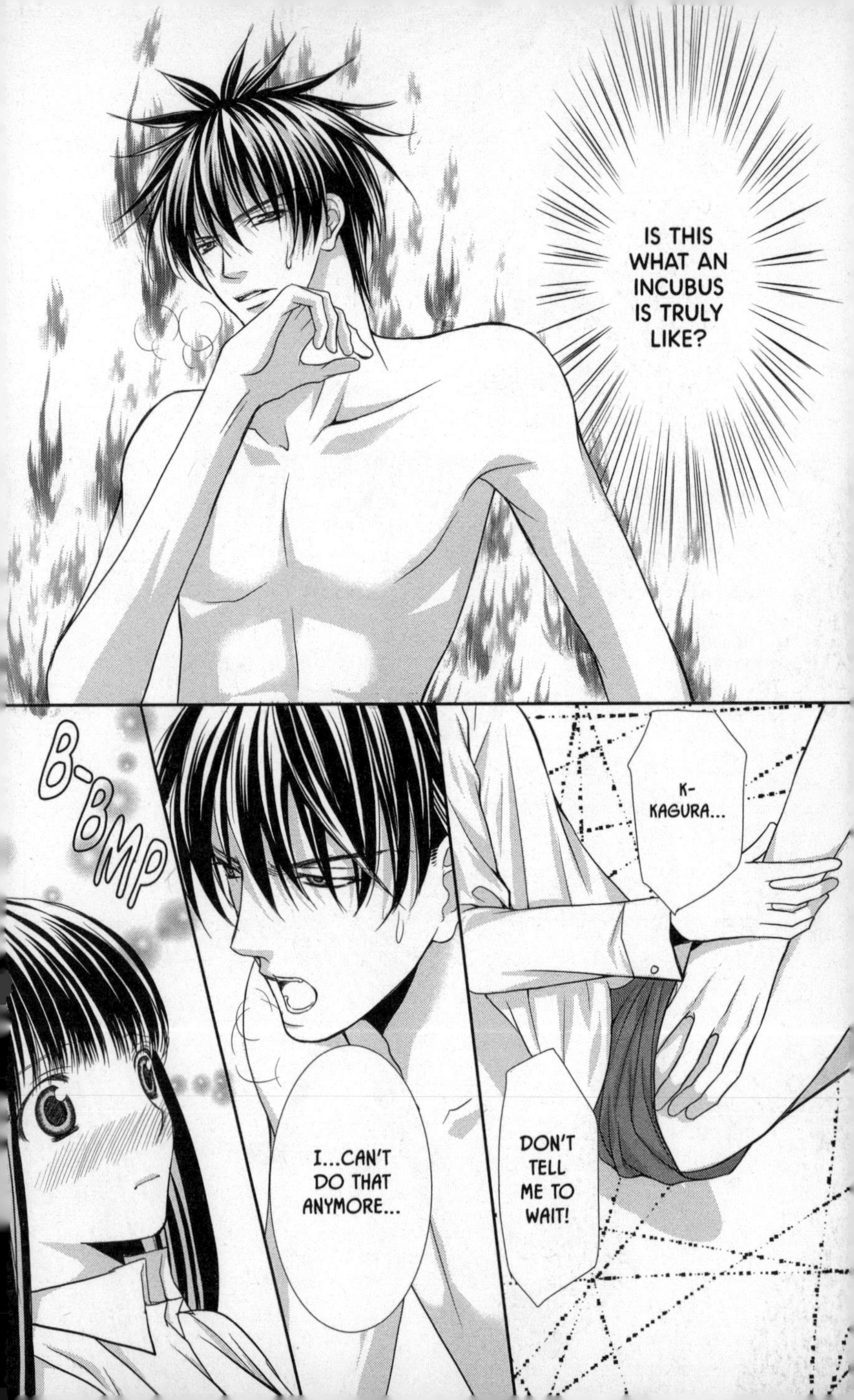
IS THIS WHAT AN INCUBUS IS TRULY LIKE?
K- KAGURA...
DON'T TELL ME TO WAIT!
I...CAN'T DO THAT ANYMORE...
B-BMP

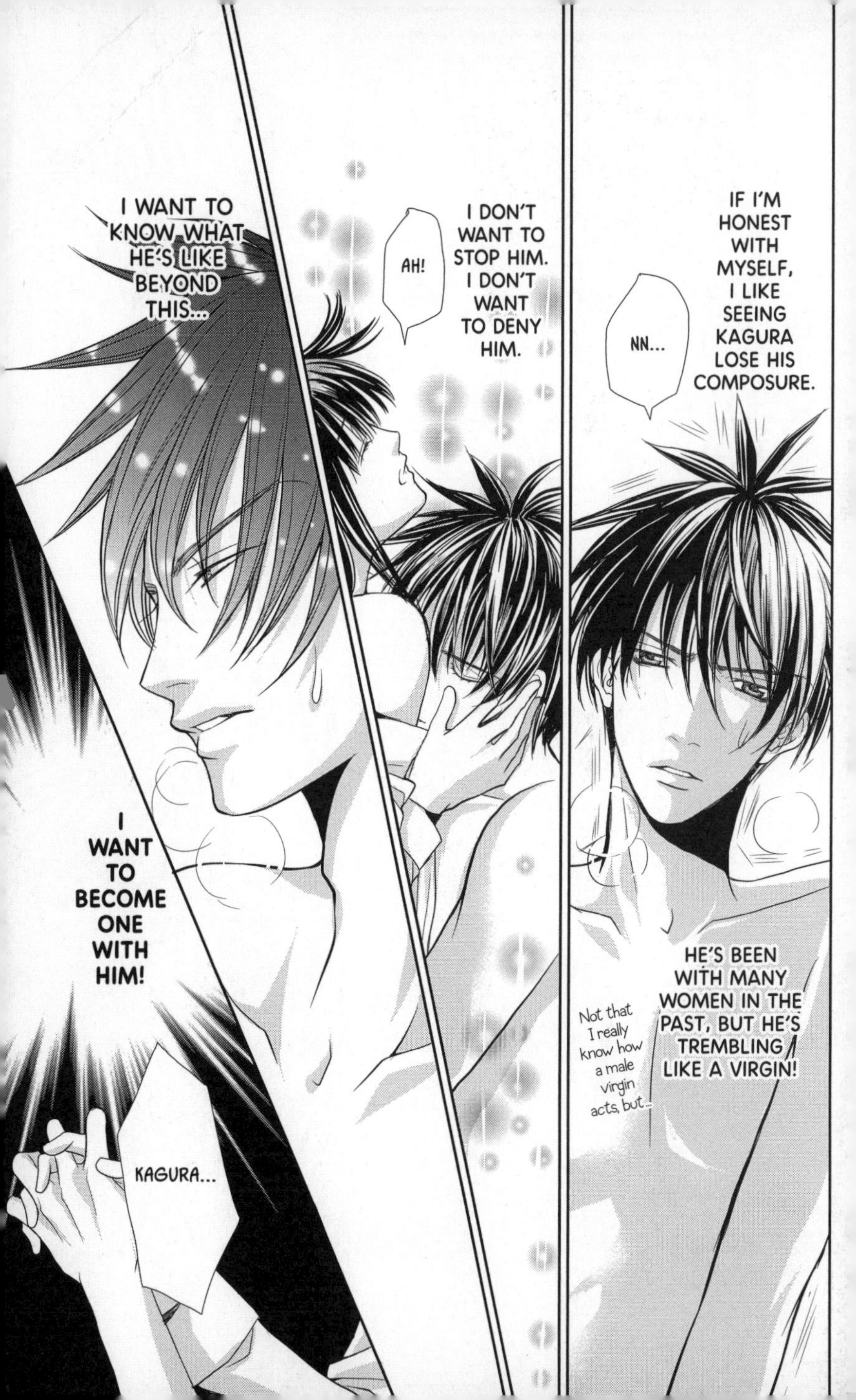
IF I'M HONEST WITH MYSELF, I LIKE SEEING KAGURA LOSE HIS COMPOSURE.
NN...
HE'S BEEN WITH MANY WOMEN IN THE PAST, BUT HE'S TREMBLING LIKE A VIRGIN!
Not that I really know how a male virgin acts, but...
I DON'T WANT TO STOP HIM. I DON'T WANT TO DENY HIM.
AH!
I WANT TO KNOW WHAT HE'S LIKE BEYOND THIS...
I WANT TO BECOME ONE WITH HIM!
KAGURA...

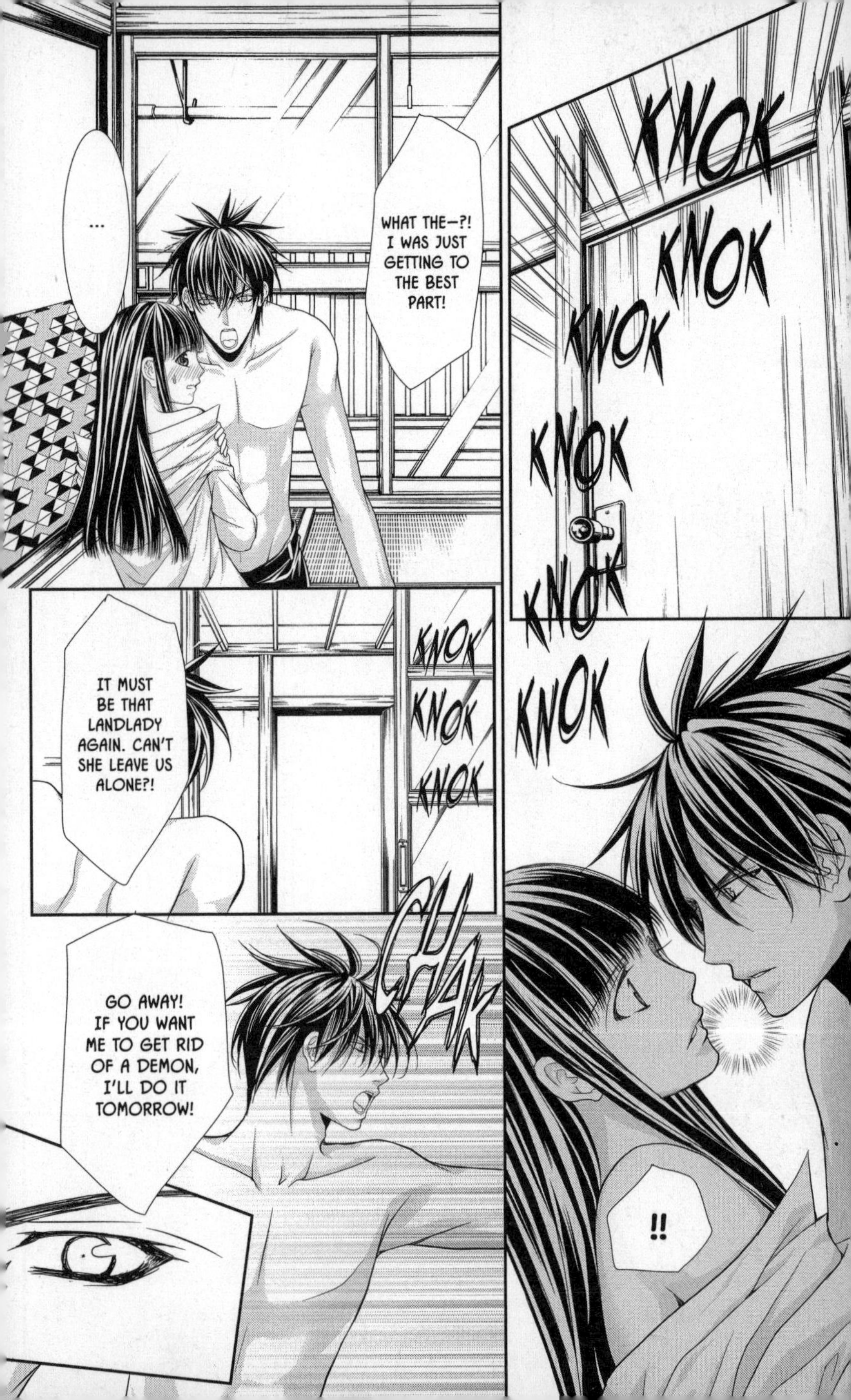
KNOK KNOK KNOK KNOK KNOK KNOK
!!
...
WHAT THE—?! I WAS JUST GETTING TO THE BEST PART!
KNOK KNOK KNOK
IT MUST BE THAT LANDLADY AGAIN. CAN'T SHE LEAVE US ALONE?!
CHAK
GO AWAY! IF YOU WANT ME TO GET RID OF A DEMON, I'LL DO IT TOMORROW!

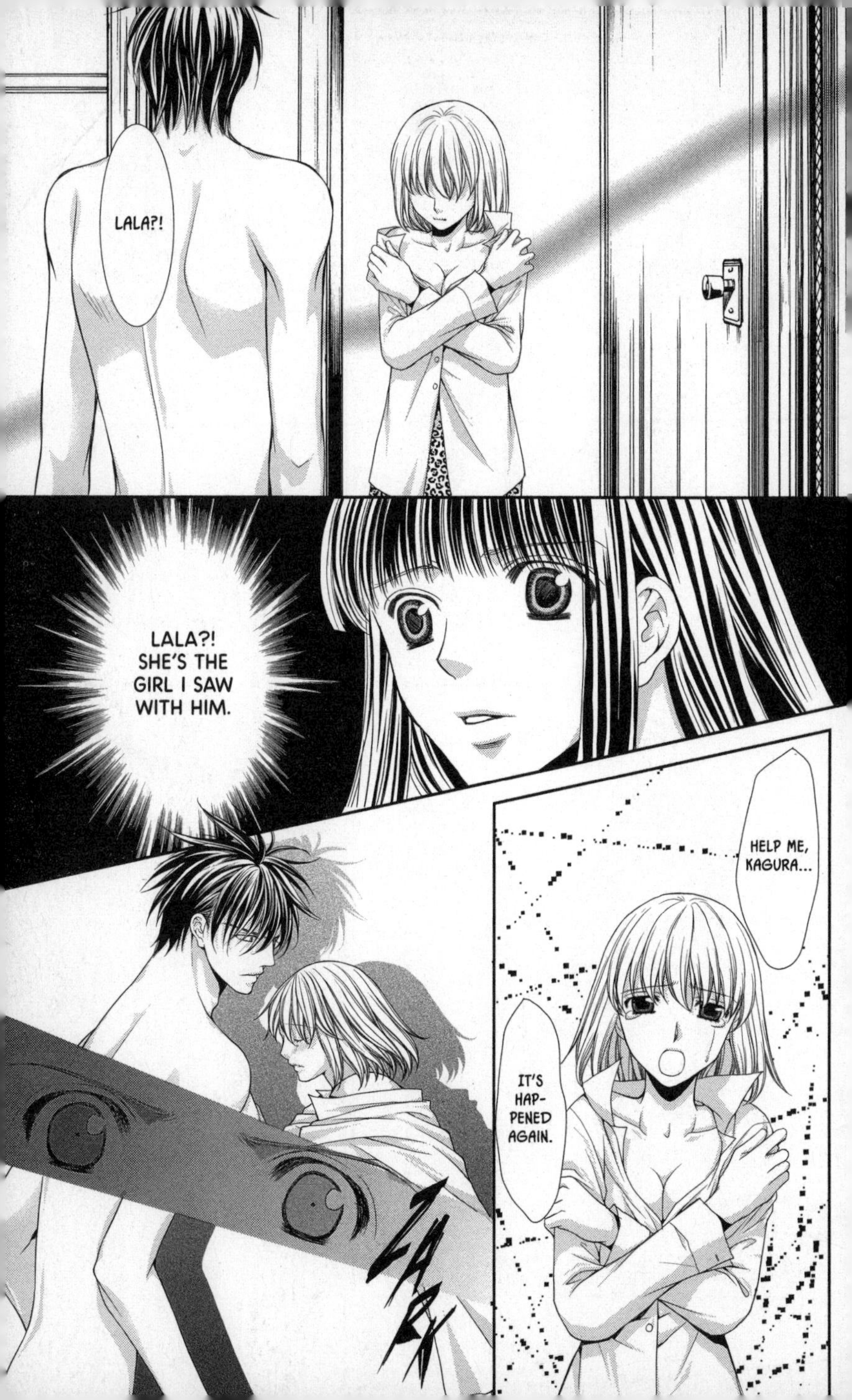
LALA?!
LALA?! SHE'S THE GIRL I SAW WITH HIM.
HELP ME, KAGURA...
IT'S HAP-PENED AGAIN.
ZAK

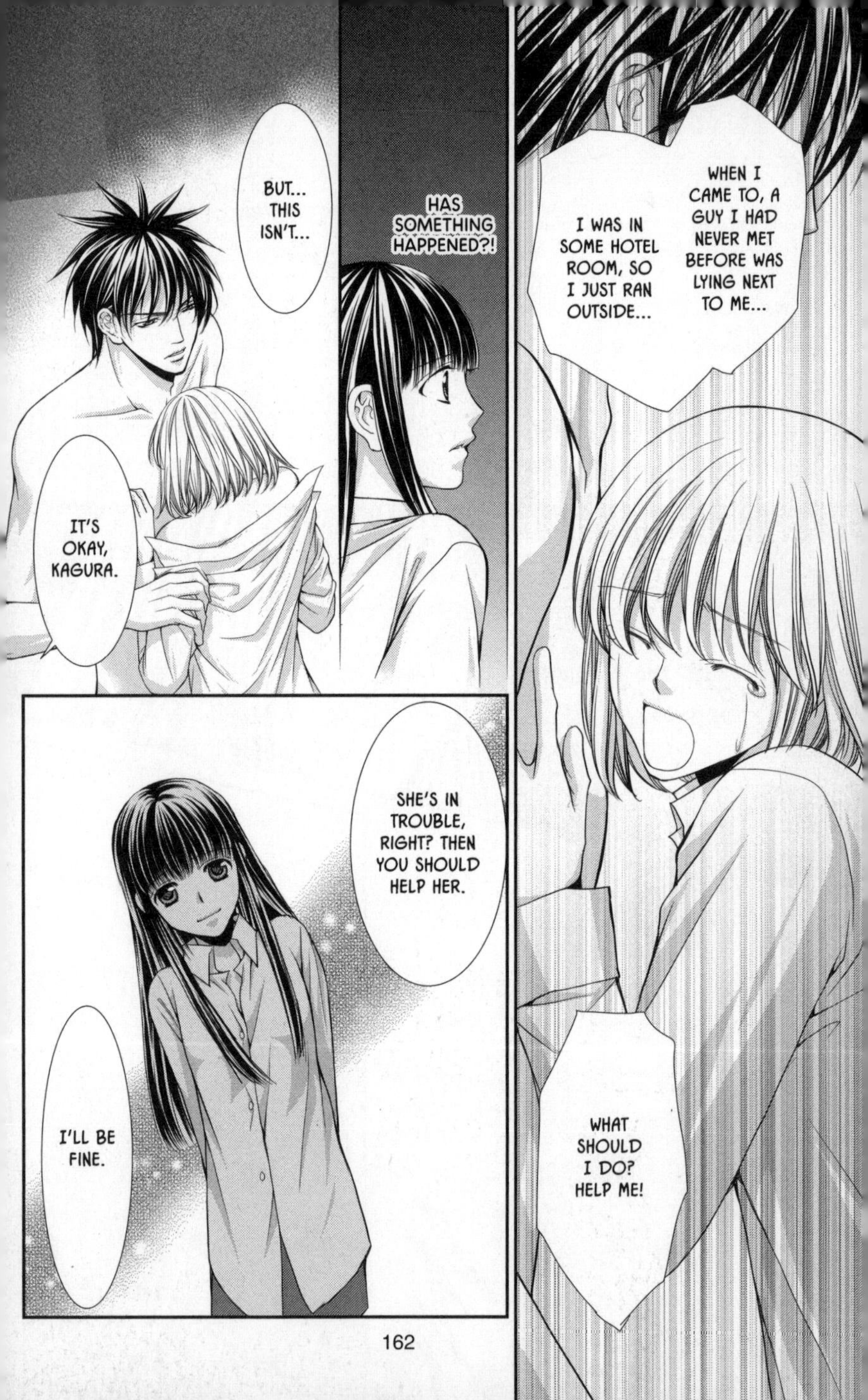
WHEN I CAME TO, A GUY I HAD NEVER MET BEFORE WAS LYING NEXT TO ME...
I WAS IN SOME HOTEL ROOM, SO I JUST RAN OUTSIDE...
WHAT SHOULD I DO? HELP ME!
HAS SOMETHING HAPPENED?!
BUT... THIS ISN'T...
IT'S OKAY, KAGURA.
SHE'S IN TROUBLE, RIGHT? THEN YOU SHOULD HELP HER.
I'LL BE FINE.

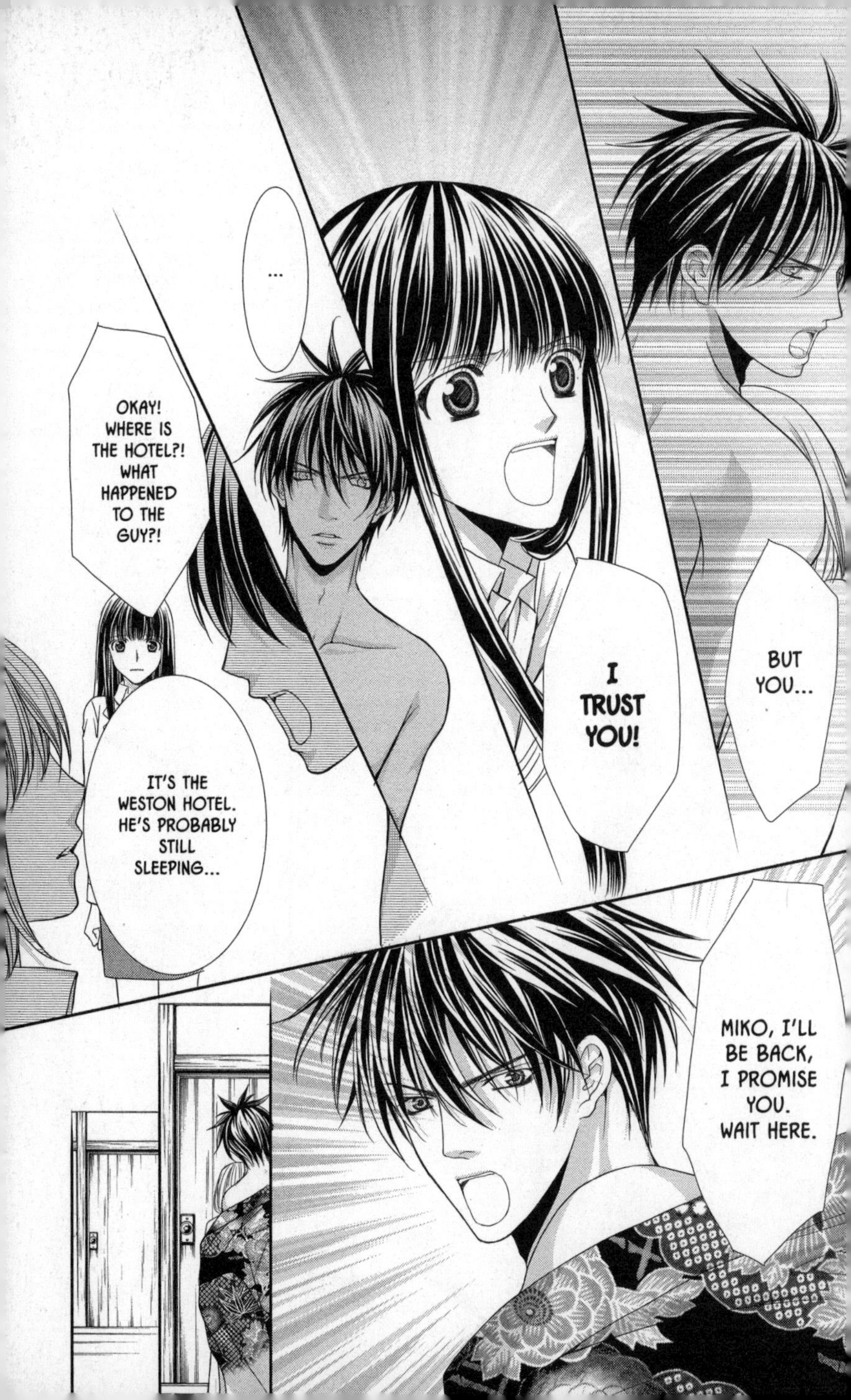
BUT YOU...
I TRUST YOU!
...
OKAY! WHERE IS THE HOTEL?! WHAT HAPPENED TO THE GUY?!
IT'S THE WESTON HOTEL. HE'S PROBABLY STILL SLEEPING...
MIKO, I'LL BE BACK, I PROMISE YOU. WAIT HERE.

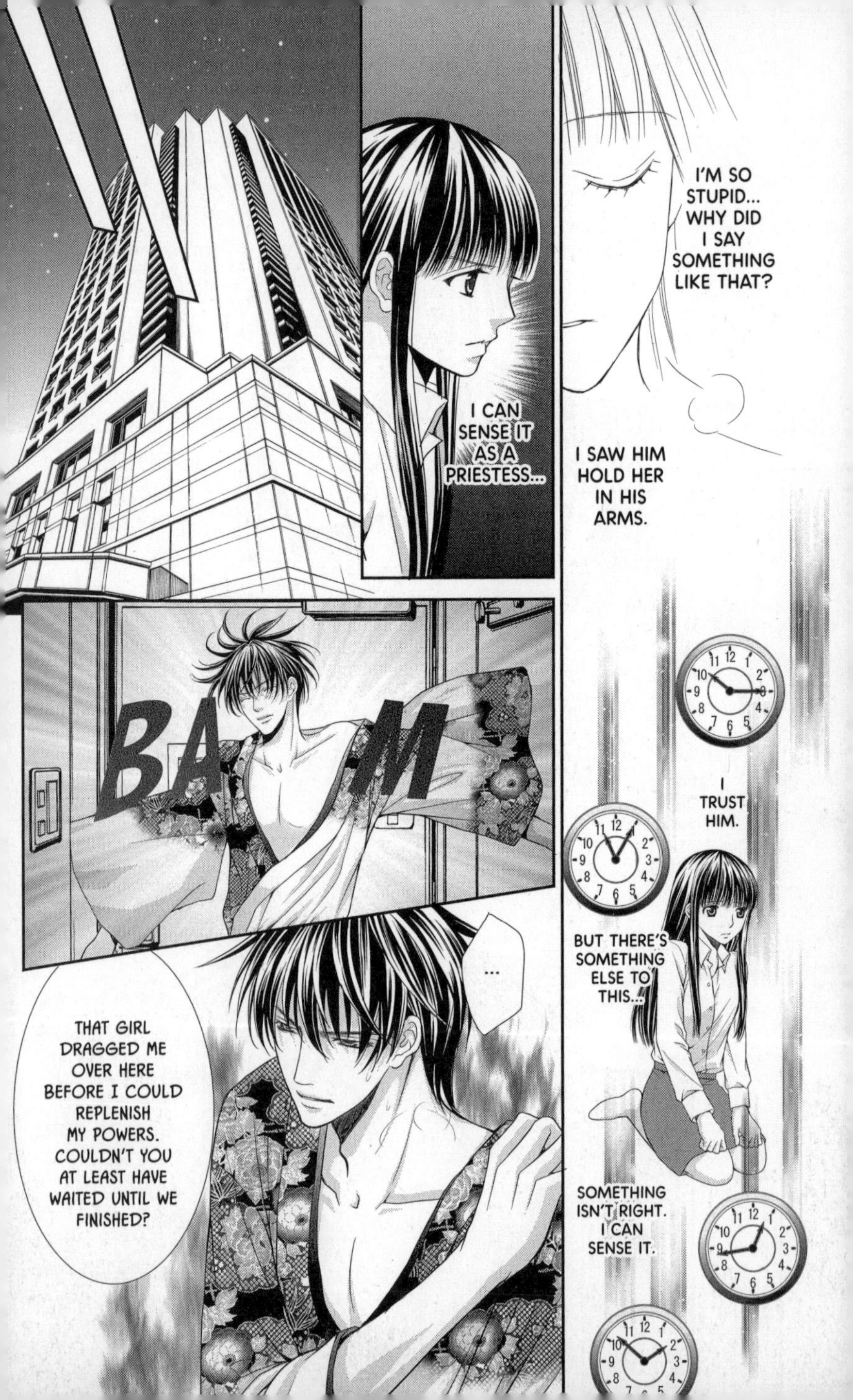
I'M SO STUPID... WHY DID I SAY SOMETHING LIKE THAT?
I SAW HIM HOLD HER IN HIS ARMS.
I TRUST HIM.
BUT THERE'S SOMETHING ELSE TO THIS...
SOMETHING ISN'T RIGHT. I CAN SENSE IT.
I CAN SENSE IT AS A PRIESTESS...
BAM
...
THAT GIRL DRAGGED ME OVER HERE BEFORE I COULD REPLENISH MY POWERS. COULDN'T YOU AT LEAST HAVE WAITED UNTIL WE FINISHED?

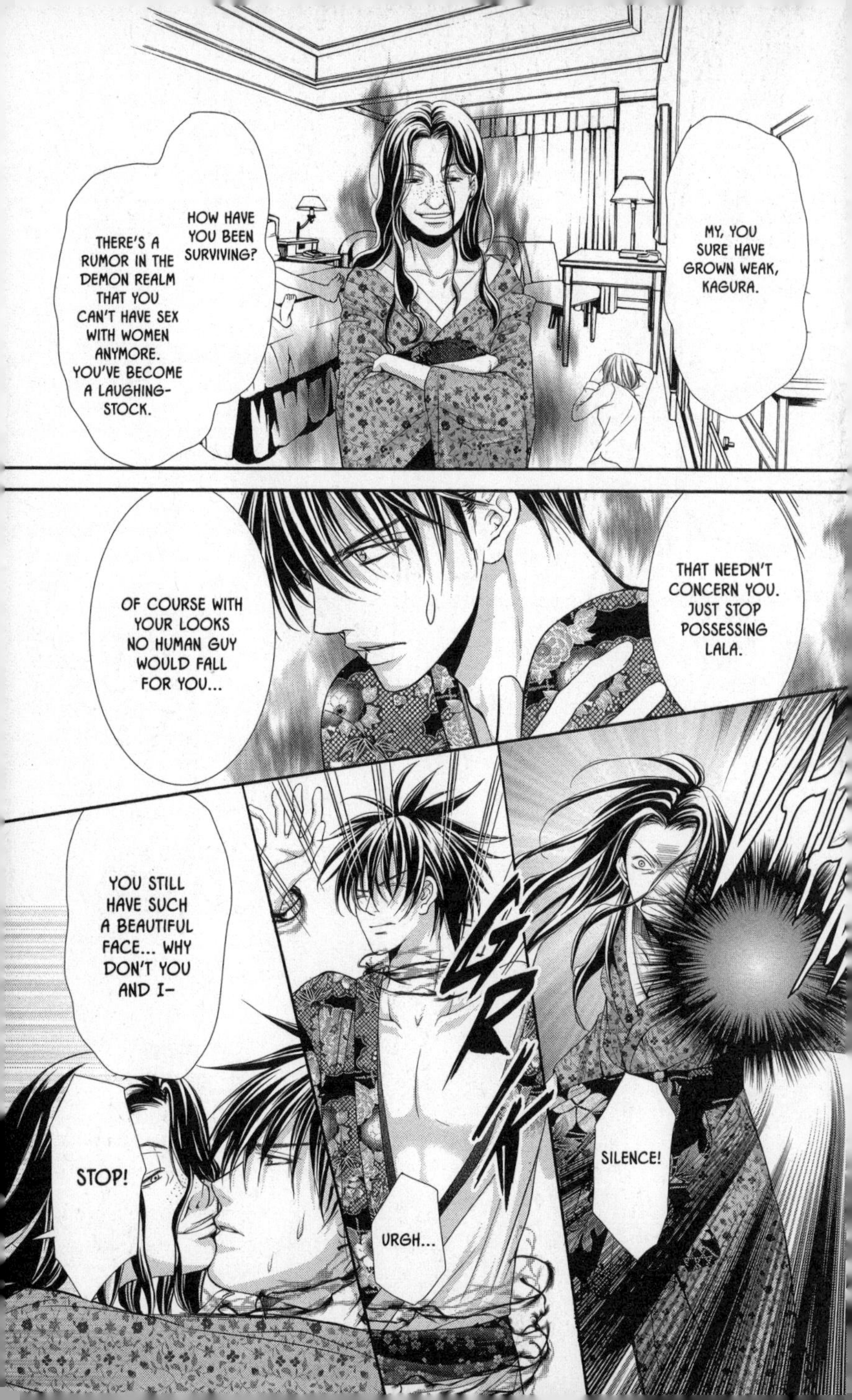
MY, YOU SURE HAVE GROWN WEAK, KAGURA.
HOW HAVE YOU BEEN SURVIVING?
THERE'S A RUMOR IN THE DEMON REALM THAT YOU CAN'T HAVE SEX WITH WOMEN ANYMORE. YOU'VE BECOME A LAUGHING-STOCK.
THAT NEEDN'T CONCERN YOU. JUST STOP POSSESSING LALA.
OF COURSE WITH YOUR LOOKS NO HUMAN GUY WOULD FALL FOR YOU...
SILENCE!
URGH...
YOU STILL HAVE SUCH A BEAUTIFUL FACE... WHY DON'T YOU AND I-
STOP!

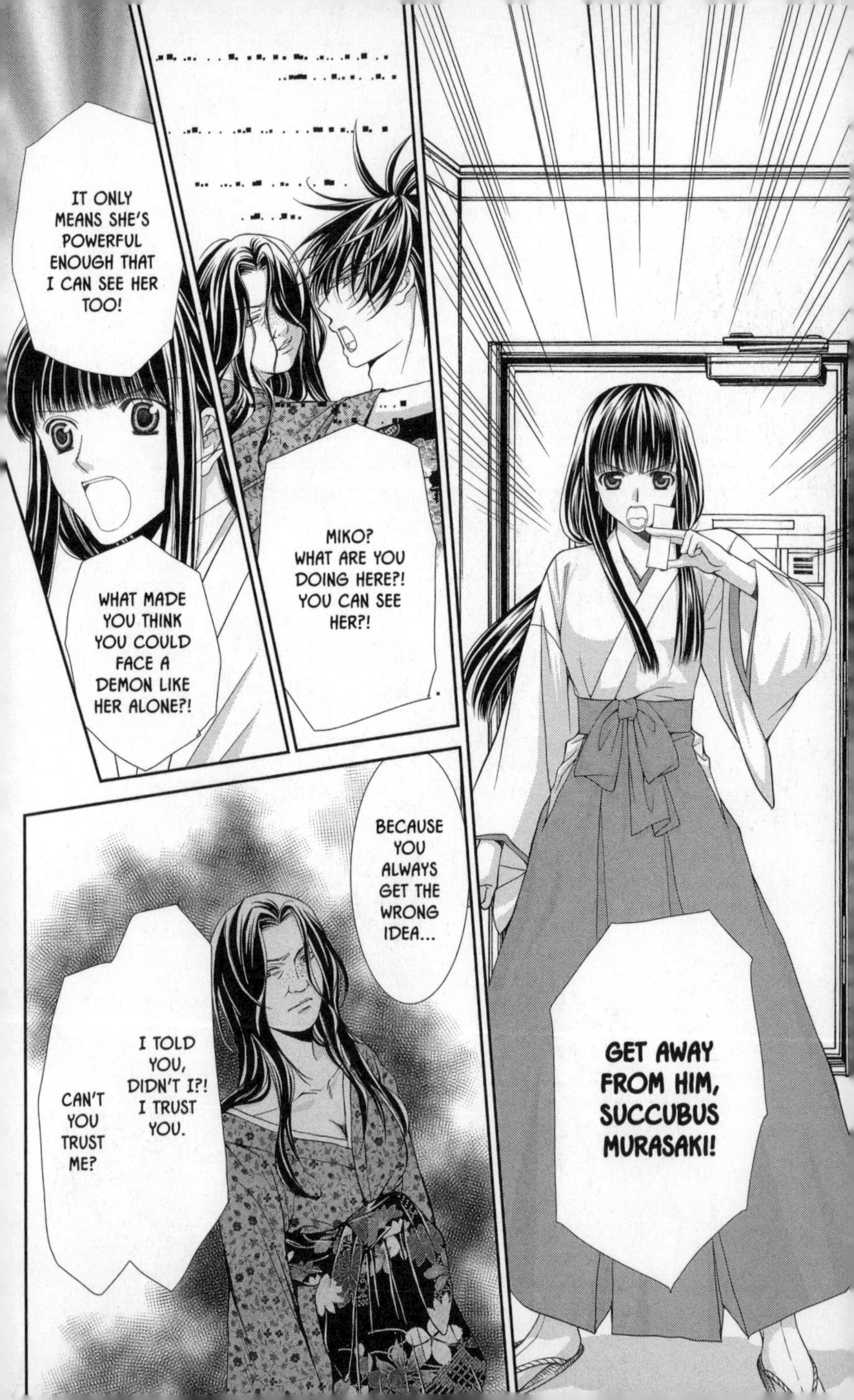
GET AWAY FROM HIM, SUCCUBUS MURASAKI!
MIKO? WHAT ARE YOU DOING HERE?! YOU CAN SEE HER?!
IT ONLY MEANS SHE'S POWERFUL ENOUGH THAT I CAN SEE HER TOO!
WHAT MADE YOU THINK YOU COULD FACE A DEMON LIKE HER ALONE?!
BECAUSE YOU ALWAYS GET THE WRONG IDEA...
I TOLD YOU, DIDN'T I?! I TRUST YOU.
CAN'T YOU TRUST ME?

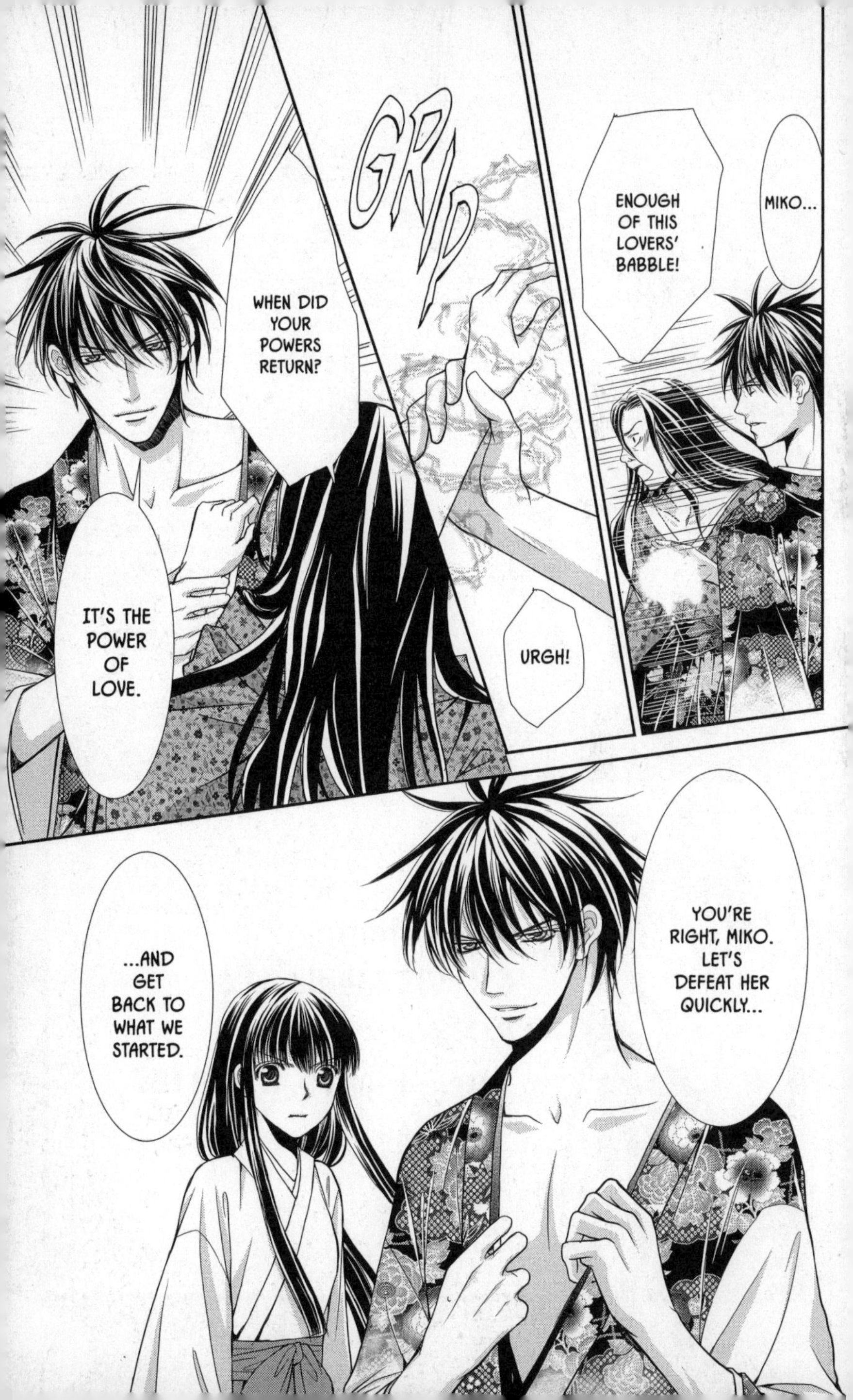
MIKO...
ENOUGH OF THIS LOVERS' BABBLE!
GRIP
URGH!
WHEN DID YOUR POWERS RETURN?
IT'S THE POWER OF LOVE.
YOU'RE RIGHT, MIKO. LET'S DEFEAT HER QUICKLY...
...AND GET BACK TO WHAT WE STARTED.

SEND YOUR FAN MAIL TO THIS ADDRESS: ♥

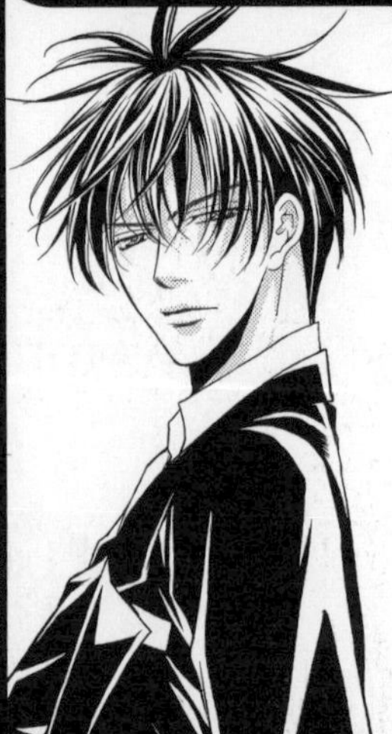

Mayu Shinjo
C/O VIZ Media, LLC
P.O. Box 77010
San Francisco, CA 94107

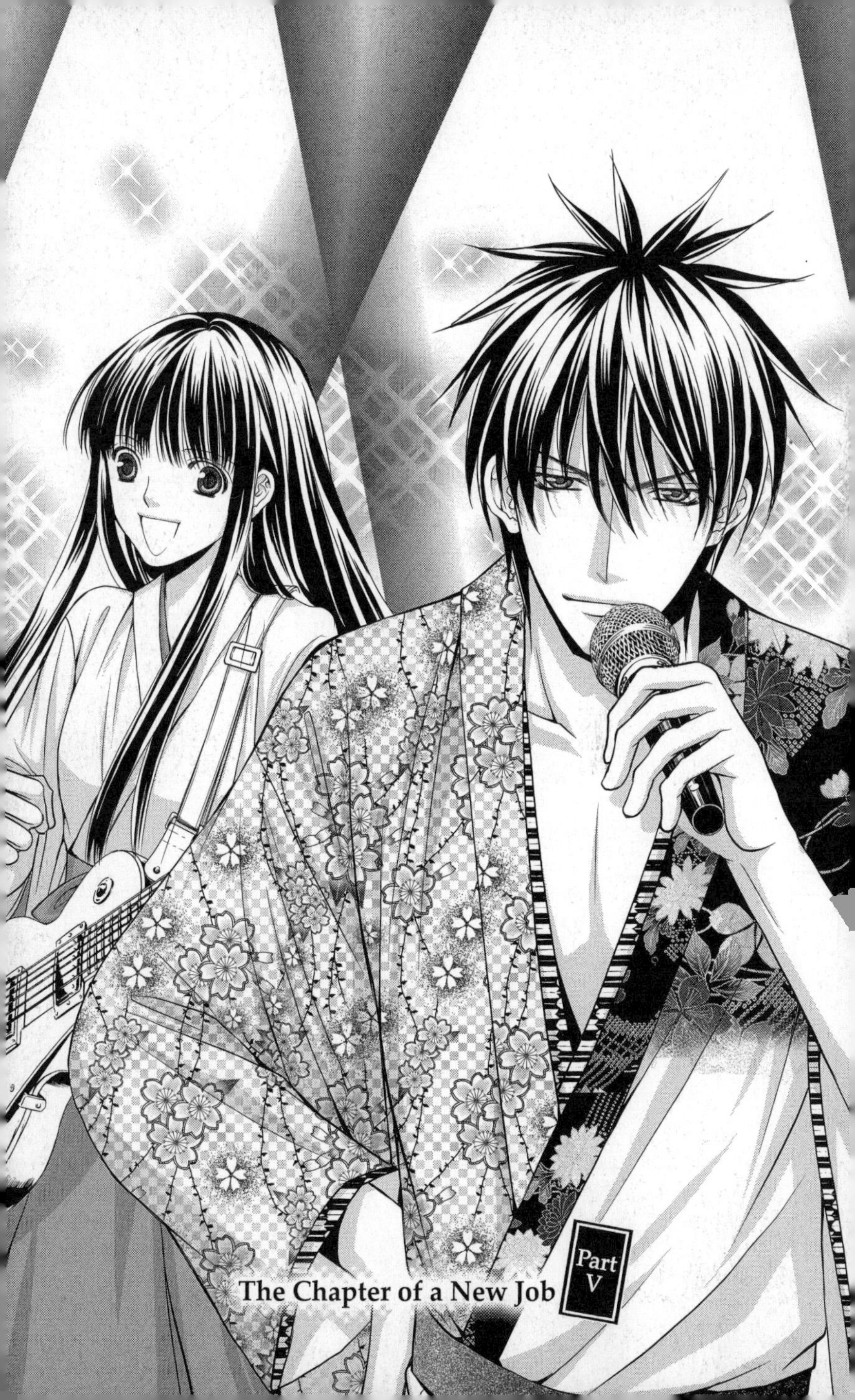
Part V
The Chapter of a New Job

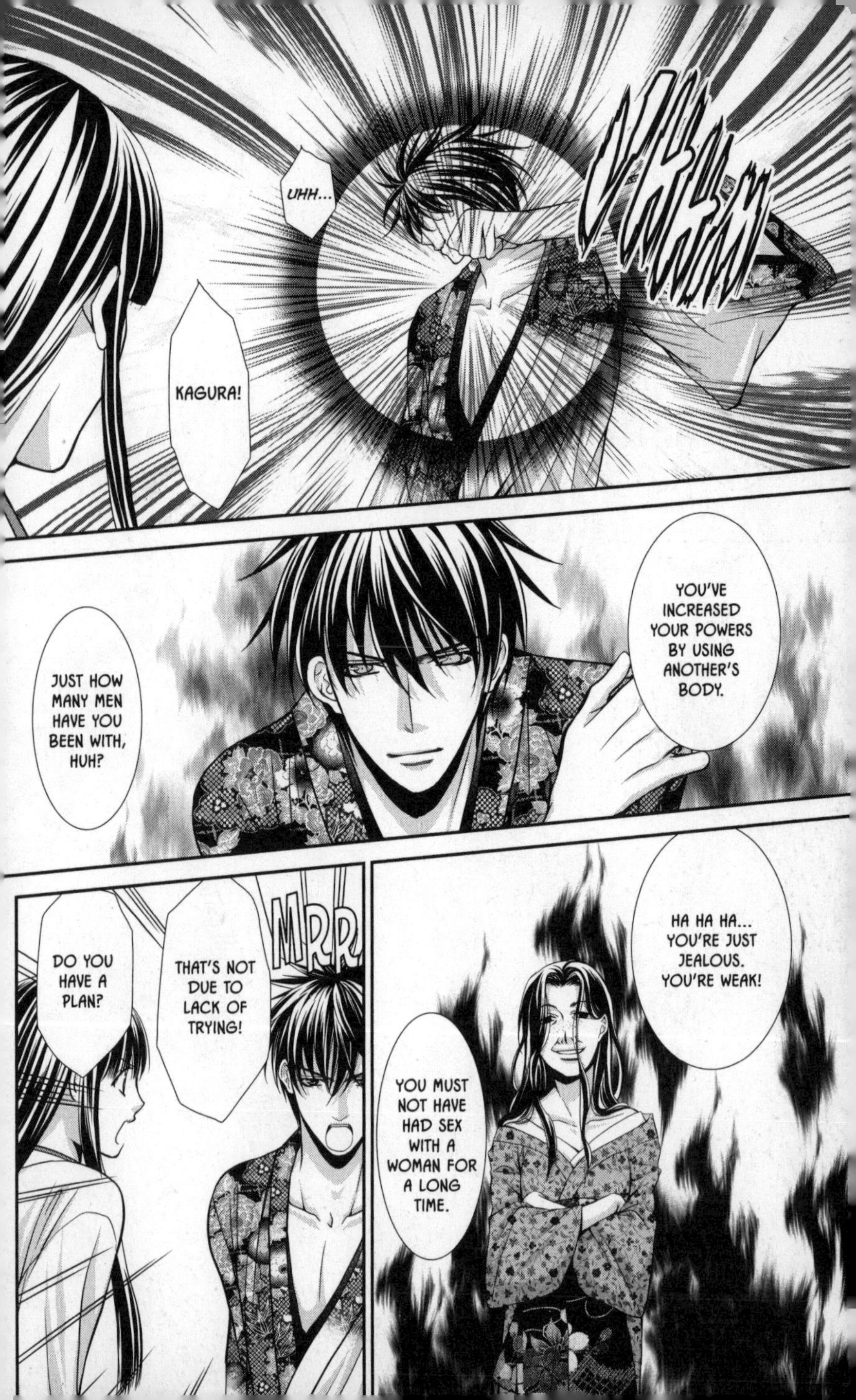
UHH...
KAGURA!
YOU'VE INCREASED YOUR POWERS BY USING ANOTHER'S BODY.
JUST HOW MANY MEN HAVE YOU BEEN WITH, HUH?
HA HA HA... YOU'RE JUST JEALOUS. YOU'RE WEAK!
YOU MUST NOT HAVE HAD SEX WITH A WOMAN FOR A LONG TIME.
MRR
THAT'S NOT DUE TO LACK OF TRYING!
DO YOU HAVE A PLAN?

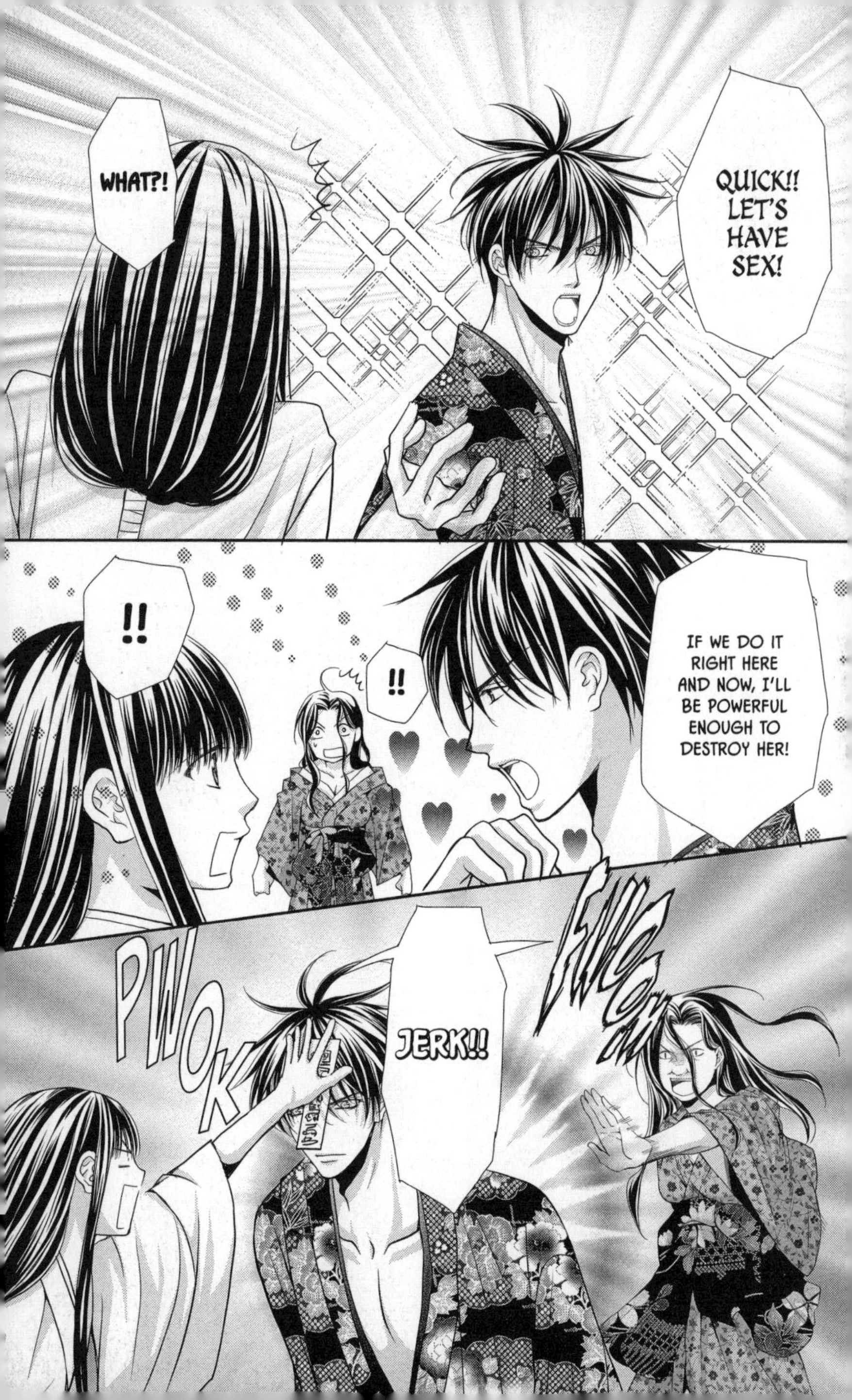
QUICK!! LET'S HAVE SEX!
WHAT?!
IF WE DO IT RIGHT HERE AND NOW, I'LL BE POWERFUL ENOUGH TO DESTROY HER!
!!
!!
JERK!!
PWOK

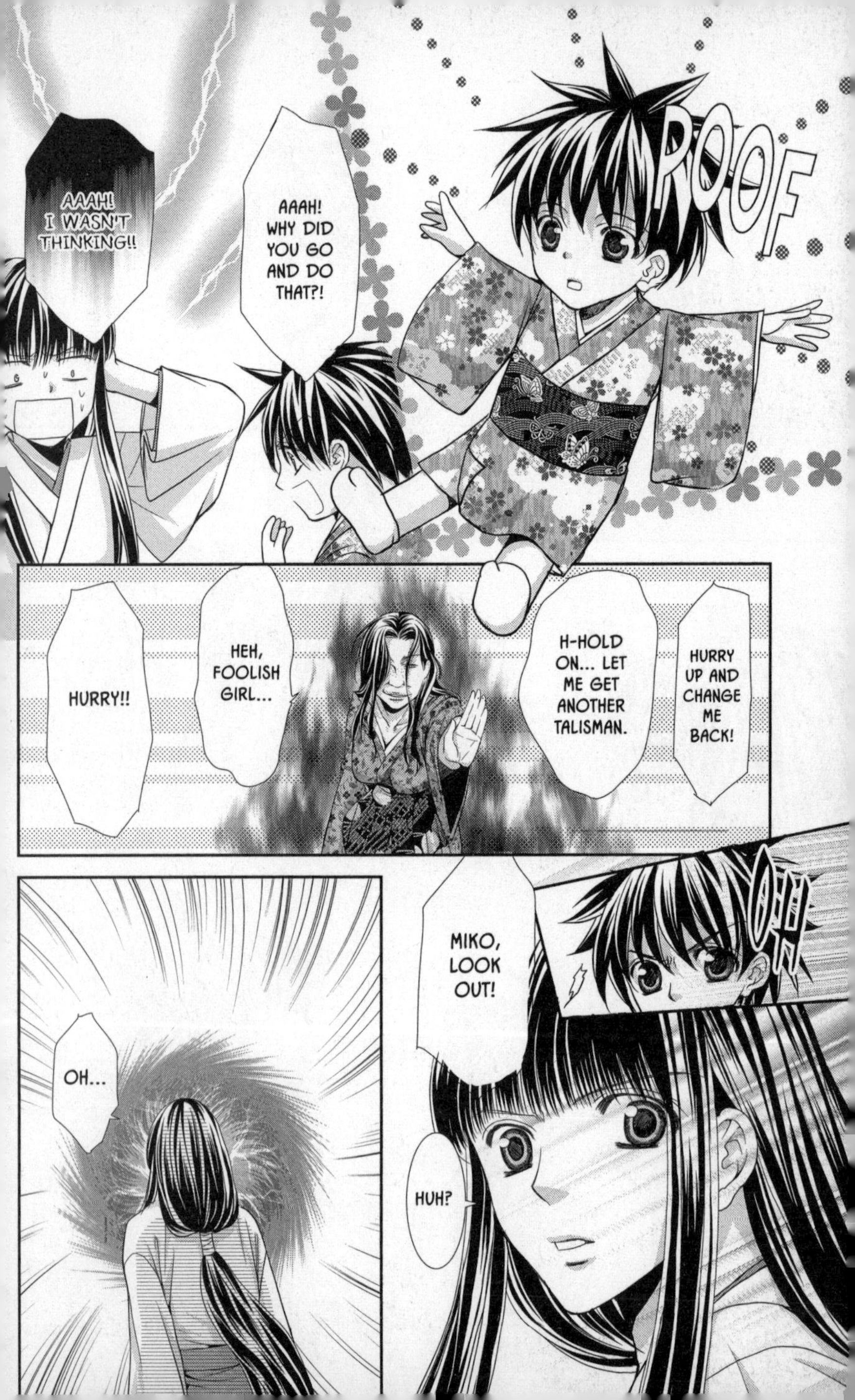
POOF
AAAH! WHY DID YOU GO AND DO THAT?!
AAAH! I WASN'T THINKING!!
HURRY UP AND CHANGE ME BACK!
H-HOLD ON... LET ME GET ANOTHER TALISMAN.
HEH, FOOLISH GIRL...
HURRY!!
MIKO, LOOK OUT!
HUH?
OH...

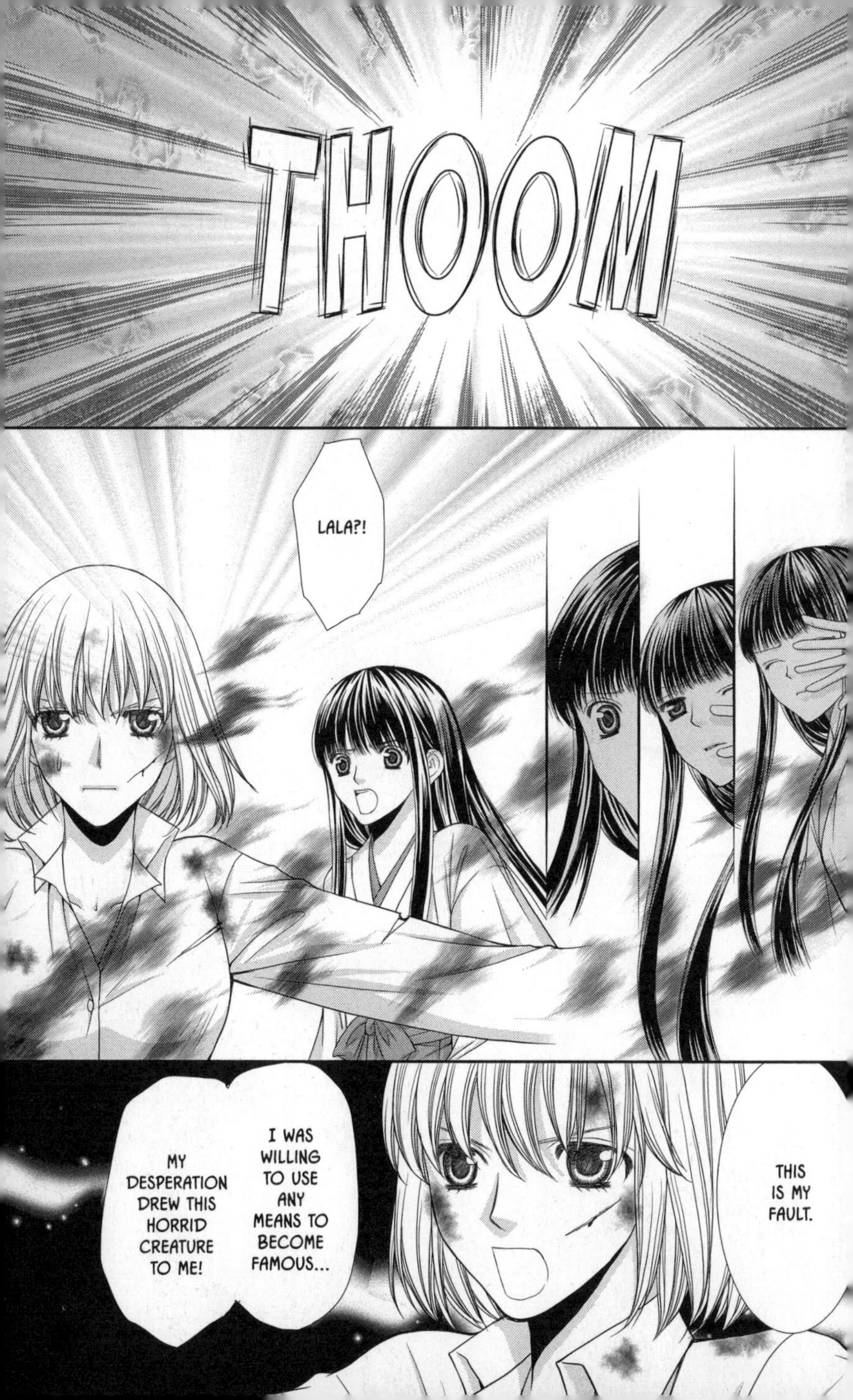
THOOM
LALA?!
THIS IS MY FAULT.
I WAS WILLING TO USE ANY MEANS TO BECOME FAMOUS...
MY DESPERATION DREW THIS HORRID CREATURE TO ME!

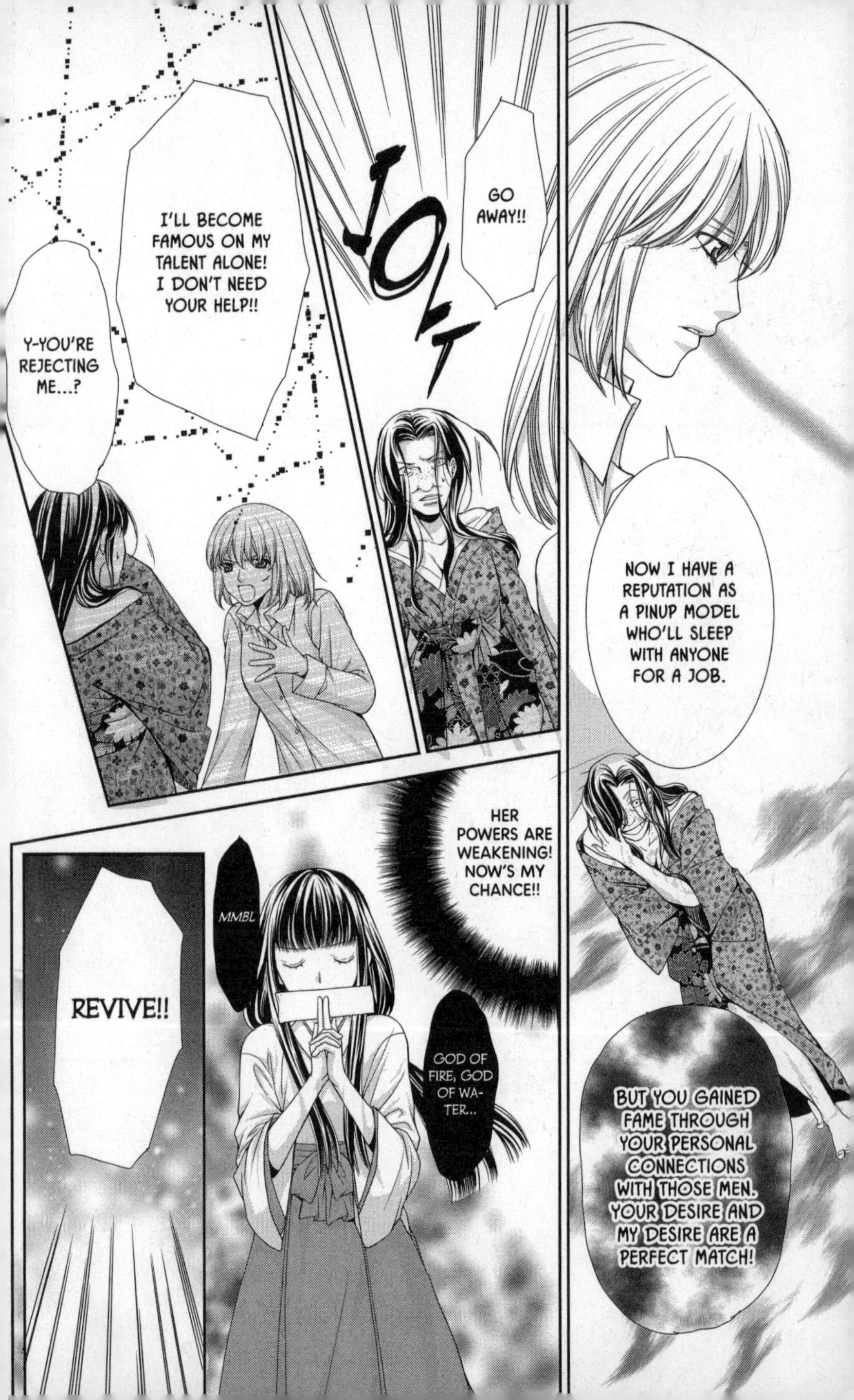
NOW I HAVE A REPUTATION AS A PINUP MODEL WHO'LL SLEEP WITH ANYONE FOR A JOB.
BUT YOU GAINED FAME THROUGH YOUR PERSONAL CONNECTIONS WITH THOSE MEN. YOUR DESIRE AND MY DESIRE ARE A PERFECT MATCH!
GO AWAY!!
JOLT
I'LL BECOME FAMOUS ON MY TALENT ALONE! I DON'T NEED YOUR HELP!!
Y-YOU'RE REJECTING ME...?
HER POWERS ARE WEAKENING! NOW'S MY CHANCE!!
MMBL
GOD OF FIRE, GOD OF WA-TER...
REVIVE!!

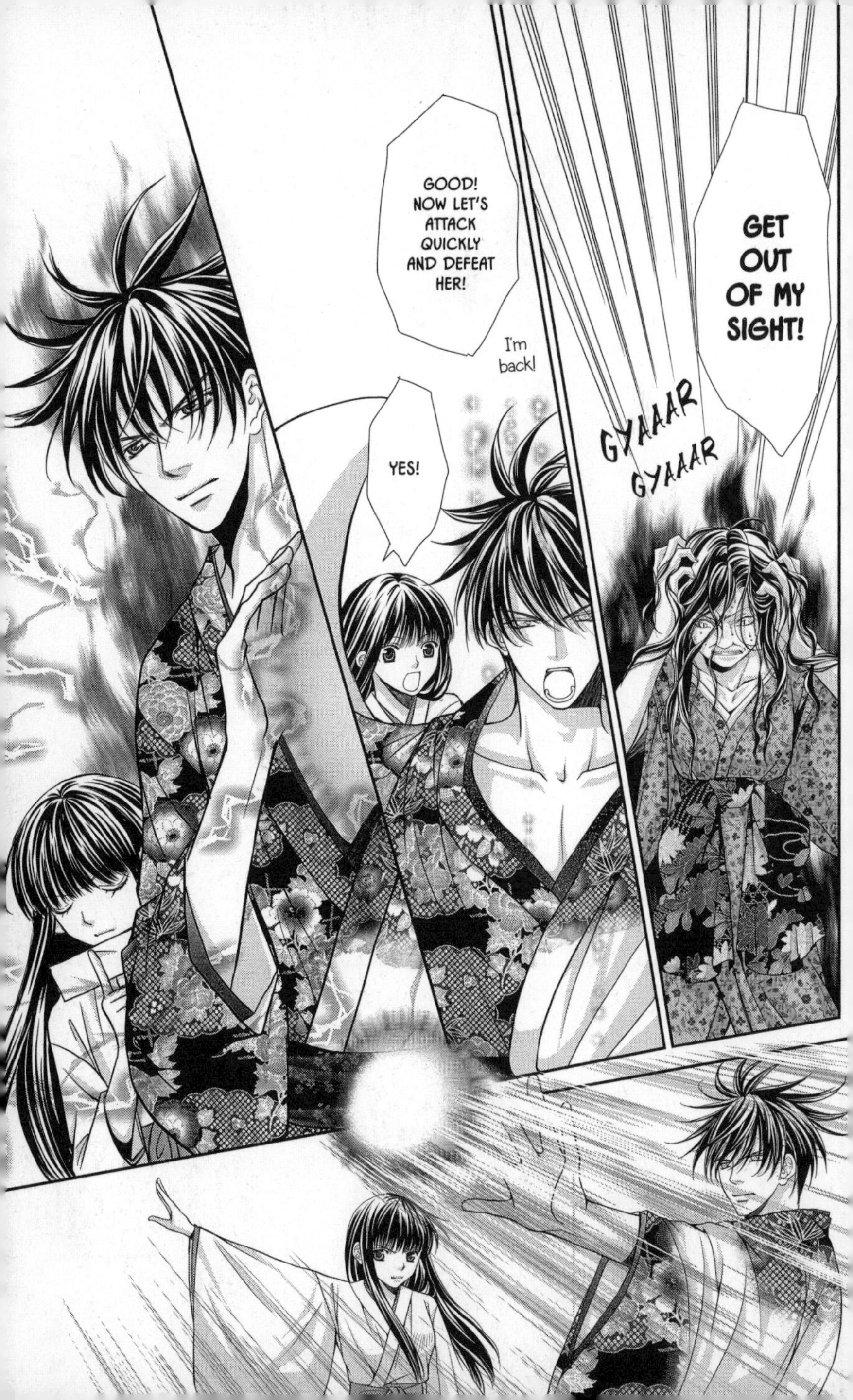
GET OUT OF MY SIGHT!
GYAAAR
GYAAAR
GOOD! NOW LET'S ATTACK QUICKLY AND DEFEAT HER!
I'm back!
YES!

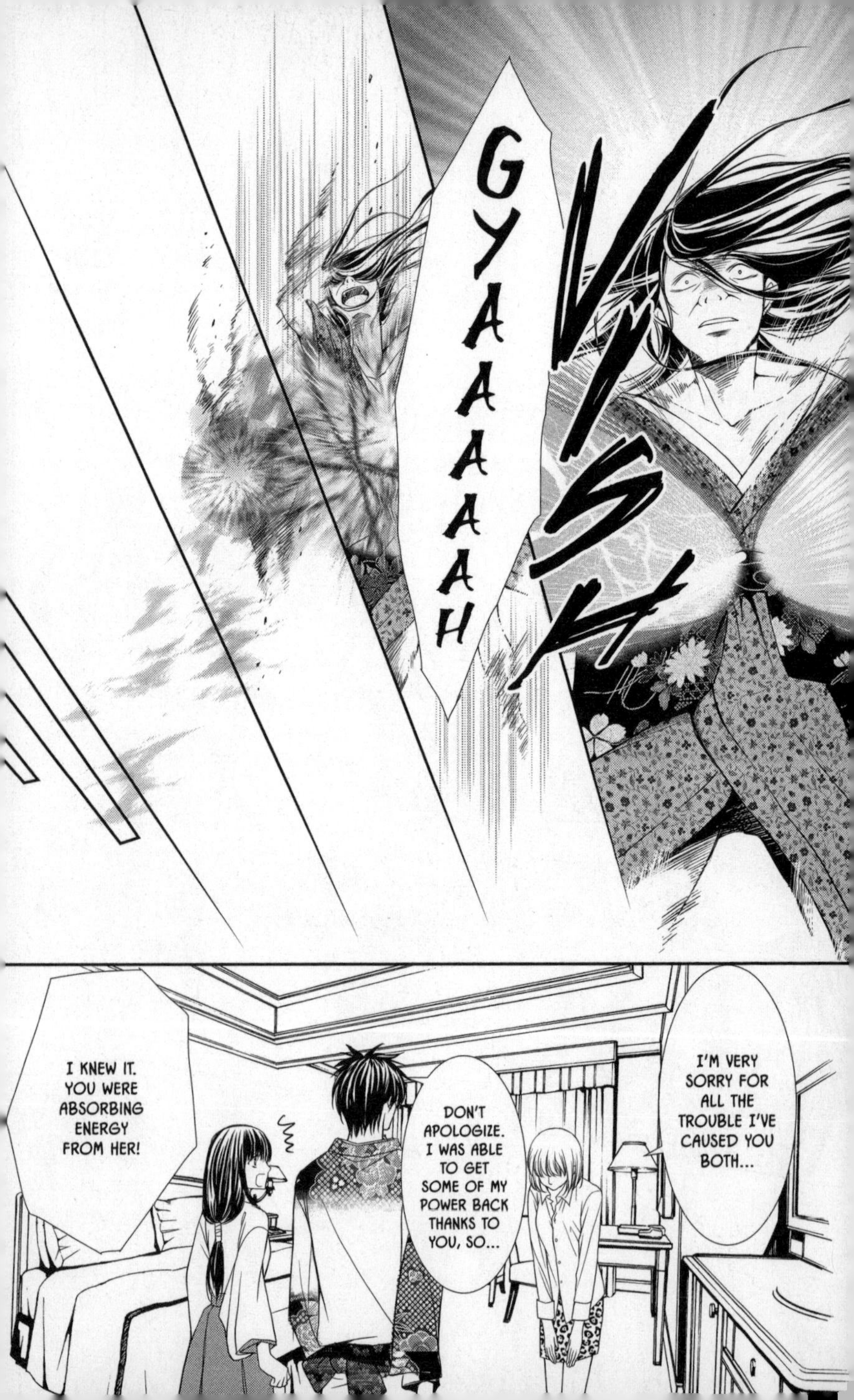
GYAAAAAH
I'M VERY SORRY FOR ALL THE TROUBLE I'VE CAUSED YOU BOTH...
DON'T APOLOGIZE. I WAS ABLE TO GET SOME OF MY POWER BACK THANKS TO YOU, SO...
I KNEW IT. YOU WERE ABSORBING ENERGY FROM HER!

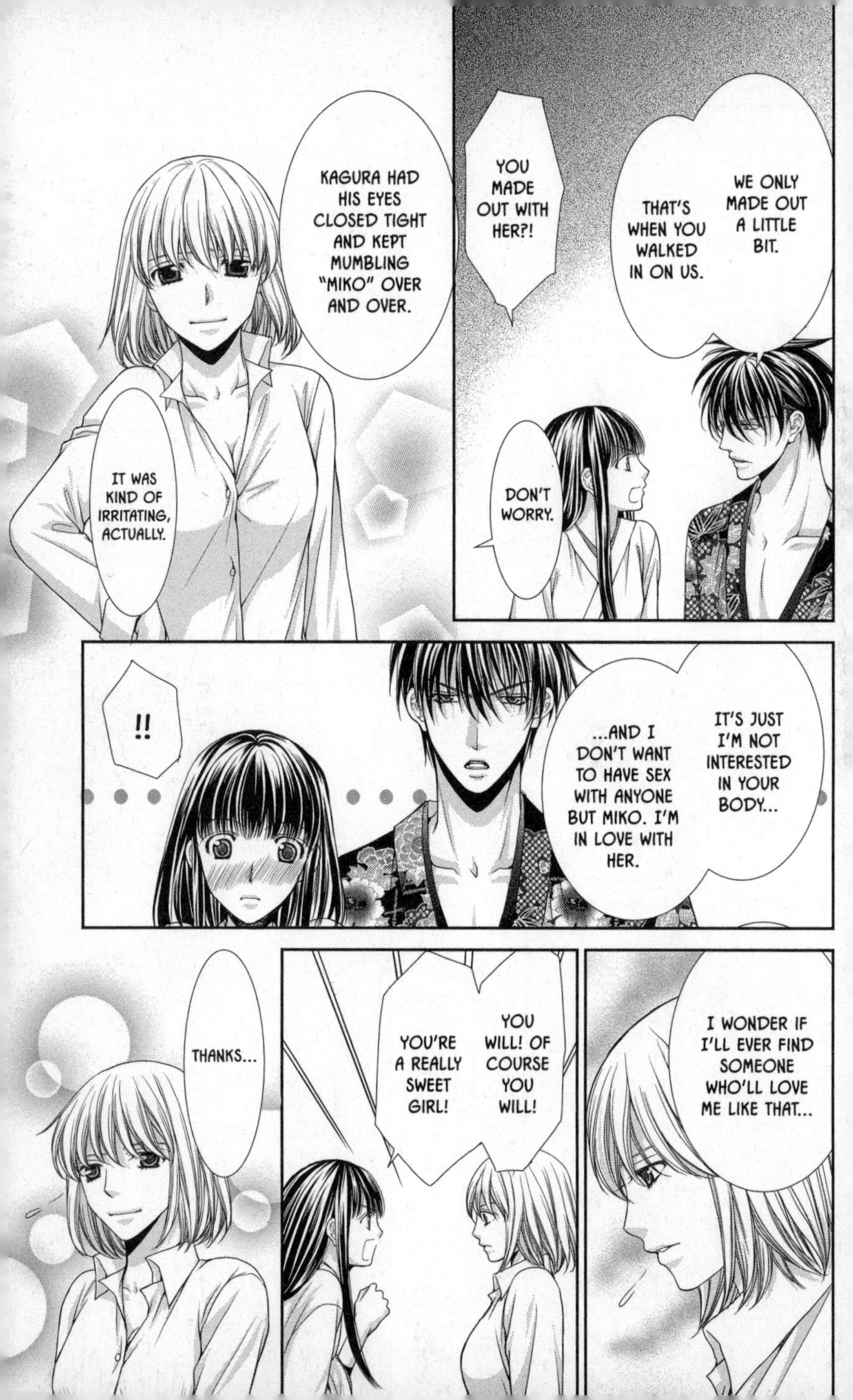
WE ONLY MADE OUT A LITTLE BIT.
THAT'S WHEN YOU WALKED IN ON US.
YOU MADE OUT WITH HER?!
DON'T WORRY.
KAGURA HAD HIS EYES CLOSED TIGHT AND KEPT MUMBLING "MIKO" OVER AND OVER.
IT WAS KIND OF IRRITATING, ACTUALLY.
IT'S JUST I'M NOT INTERESTED IN YOUR BODY...
...AND I DON'T WANT TO HAVE SEX WITH ANYONE BUT MIKO. I'M IN LOVE WITH HER.
!!
I WONDER IF I'LL EVER FIND SOMEONE WHO'LL LOVE ME LIKE THAT...
YOU WILL! OF COURSE YOU WILL!
YOU'RE A REALLY SWEET GIRL!
THANKS...

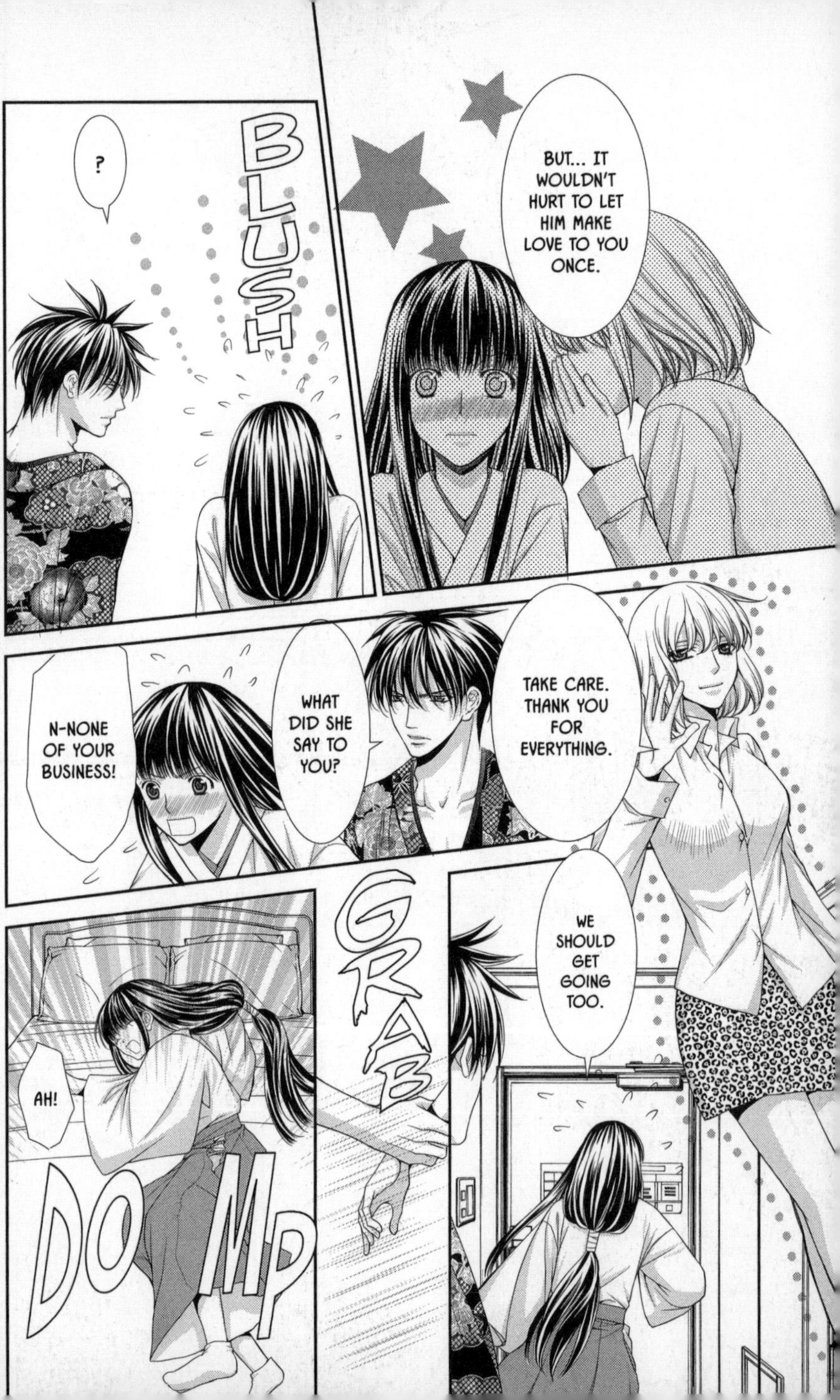
BUT... IT WOULDN'T HURT TO LET HIM MAKE LOVE TO YOU ONCE.
BLUSH
?
TAKE CARE. THANK YOU FOR EVERYTHING.
WHAT DID SHE SAY TO YOU?
N-NONE OF YOUR BUSINESS!
WE SHOULD GET GOING TOO.
GRAB
AH!
DOMP

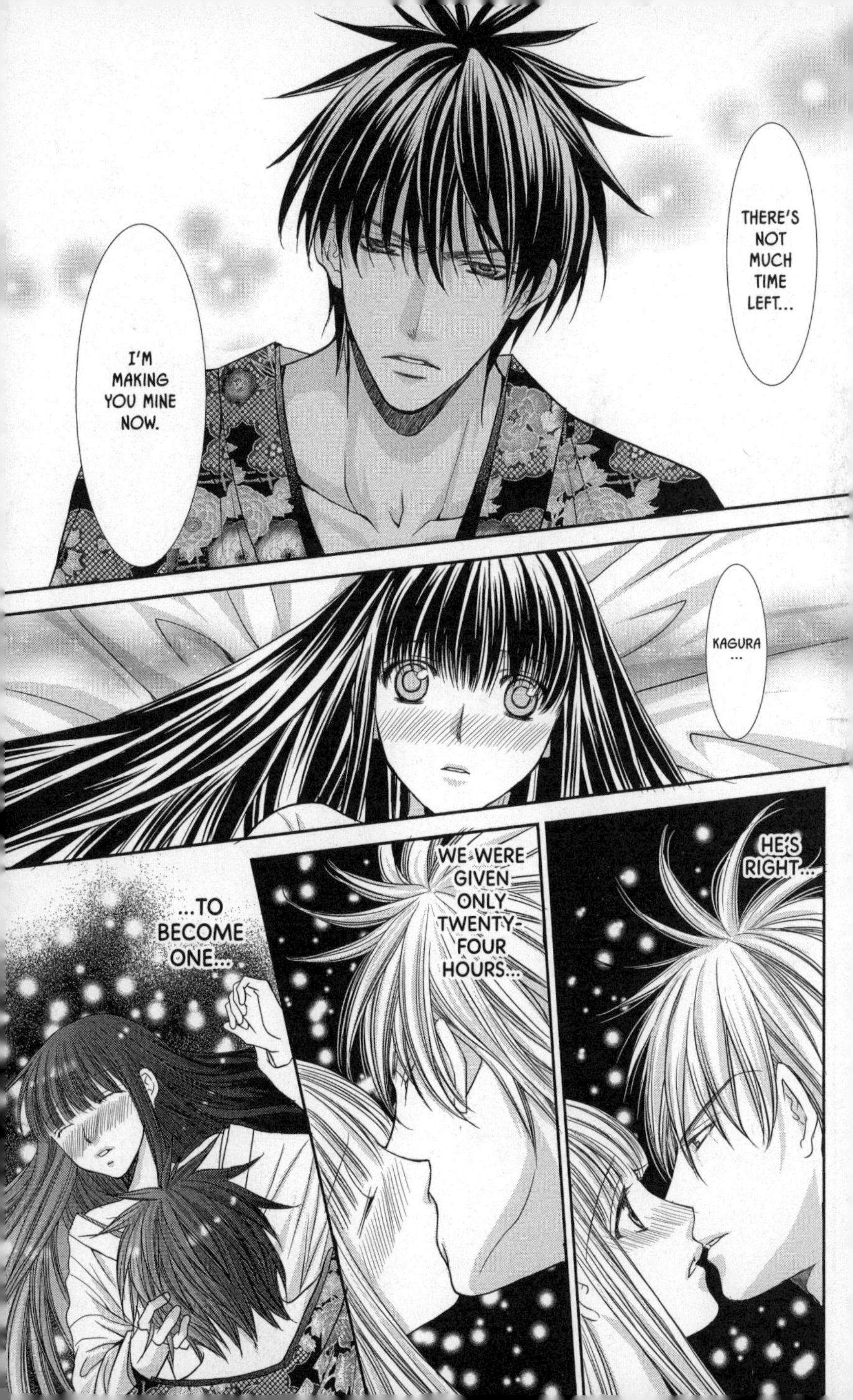
THERE'S NOT MUCH TIME LEFT...
I'M MAKING YOU MINE NOW.
KAGURA ...
HE'S RIGHT...
WE WERE GIVEN ONLY TWENTY-FOUR HOURS...
...TO BECOME ONE...

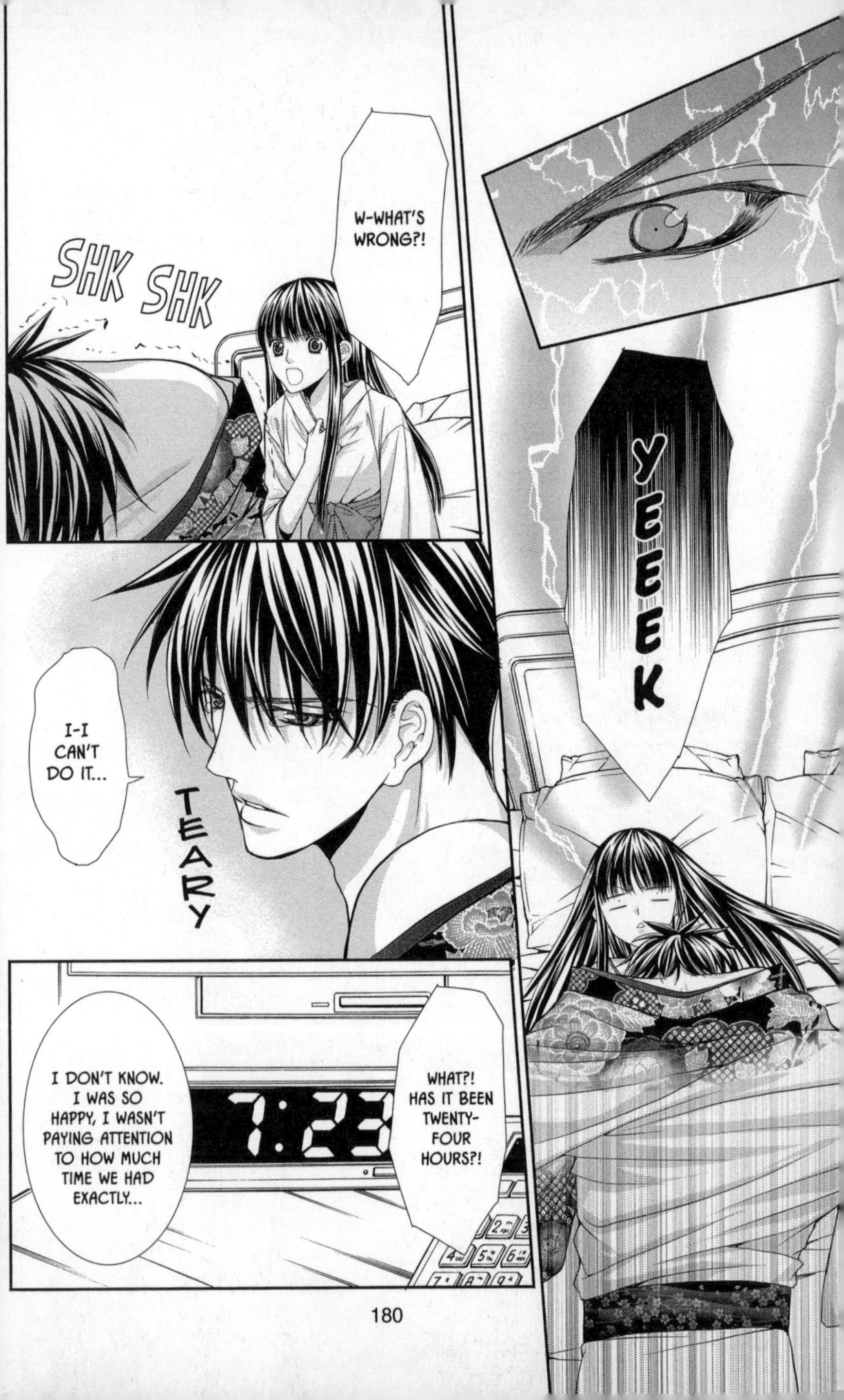
YEEEK
W-WHAT'S WRONG?!
SHK SHK
I-I CAN'T DO IT...
TEARY
WHAT?! HAS IT BEEN TWENTY-FOUR HOURS?!
7:23
I DON'T KNOW. I WAS SO HAPPY, I WASN'T PAYING ATTENTION TO HOW MUCH TIME WE HAD EXACTLY...

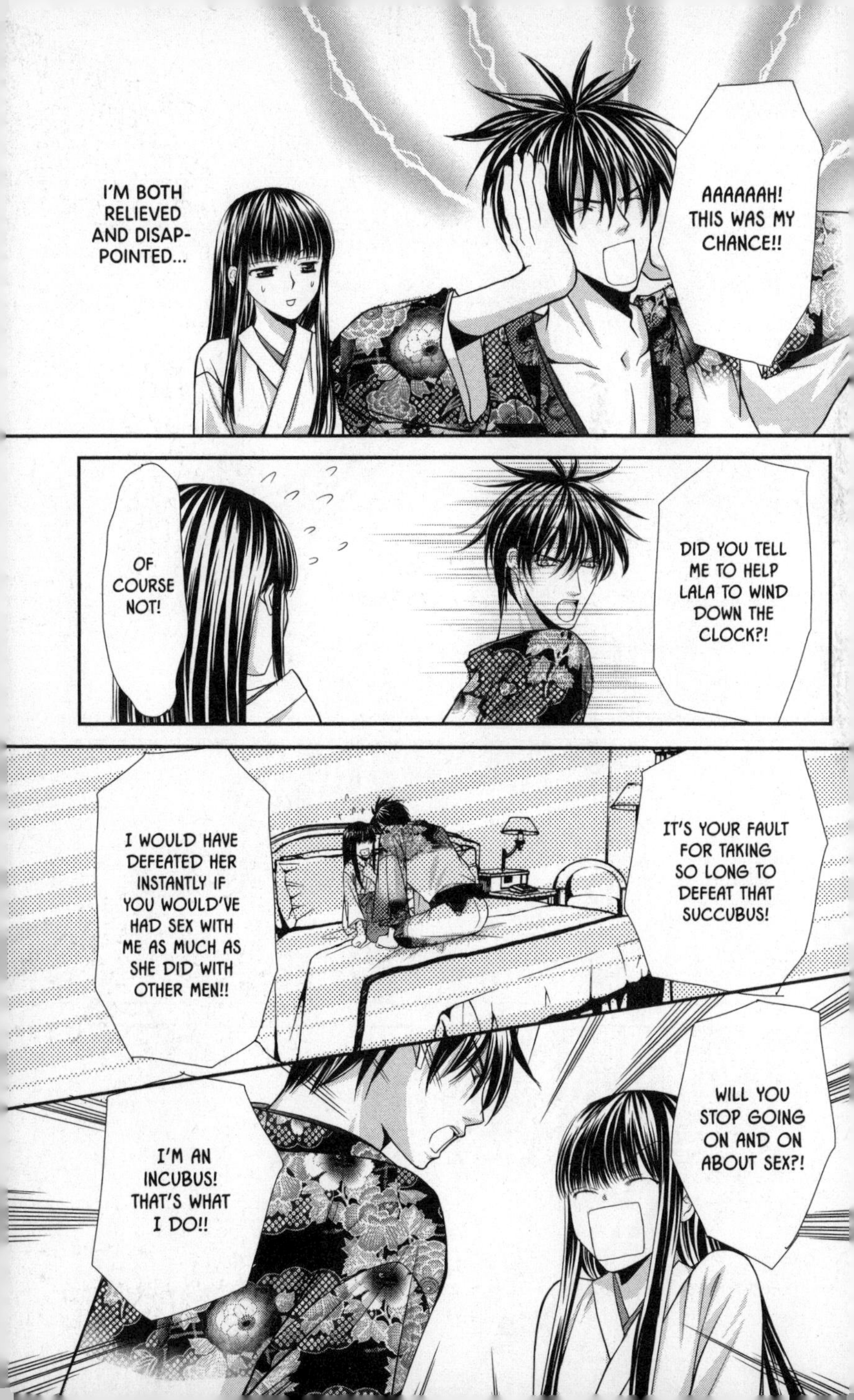
AAAAAAH! THIS WAS MY CHANCE!!
I'M BOTH RELIEVED AND DISAP-POINTED...
DID YOU TELL ME TO HELP LALA TO WIND DOWN THE CLOCK?!
OF COURSE NOT!
IT'S YOUR FAULT FOR TAKING SO LONG TO DEFEAT THAT SUCCUBUS!
I WOULD HAVE DEFEATED HER INSTANTLY IF YOU WOULD'VE HAD SEX WITH ME AS MUCH AS SHE DID WITH OTHER MEN!!
WILL YOU STOP GOING ON AND ON ABOUT SEX?!
I'M AN INCUBUS! THAT'S WHAT I DO!!

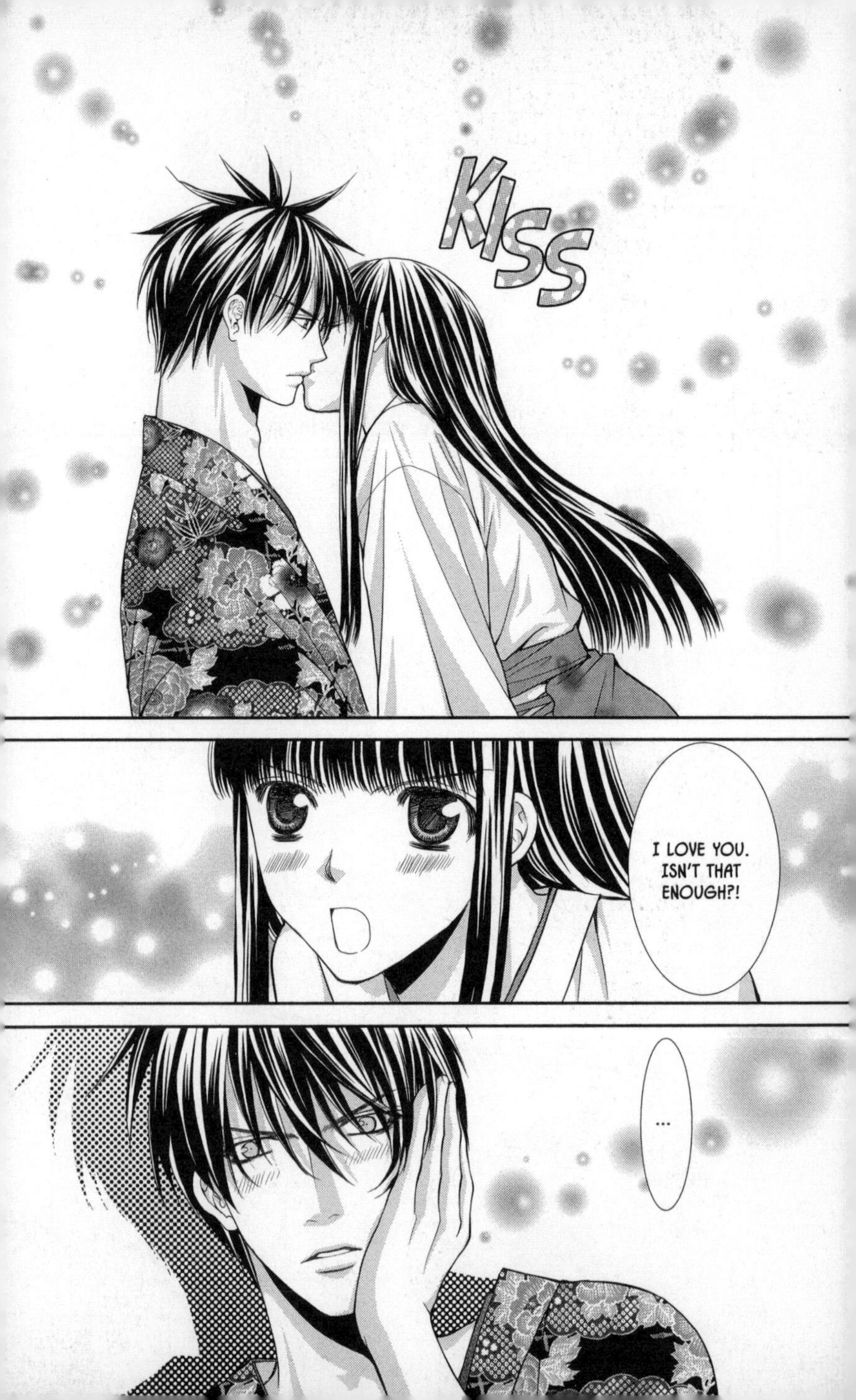
KISS
I LOVE YOU. ISN'T THAT ENOUGH?!
...

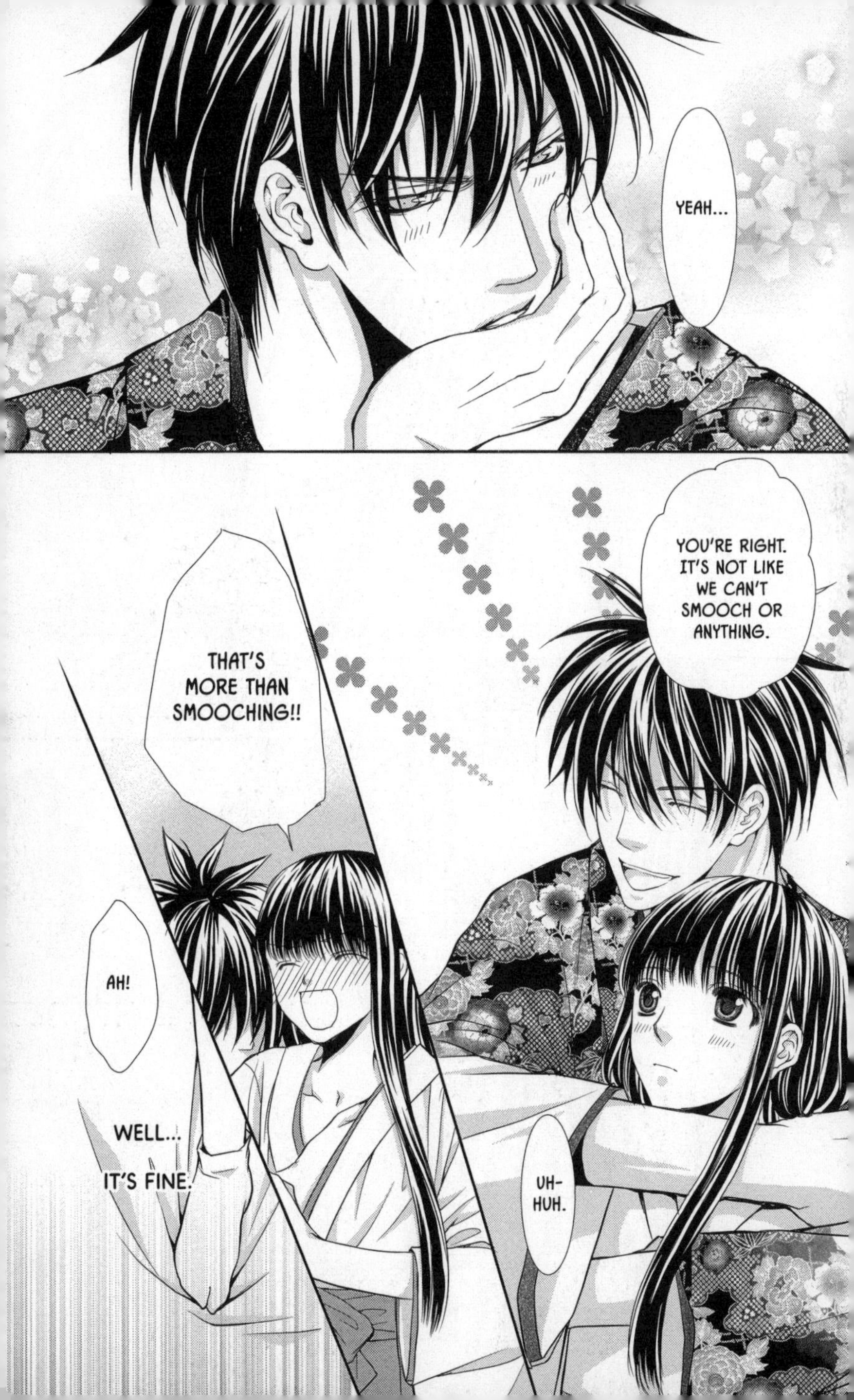
YEAH...
YOU'RE RIGHT. IT'S NOT LIKE WE CAN'T SMOOCH OR ANYTHING.
UH-HUH.
THAT'S MORE THAN SMOOCHING!!
AH!
WELL...
IT'S FINE.

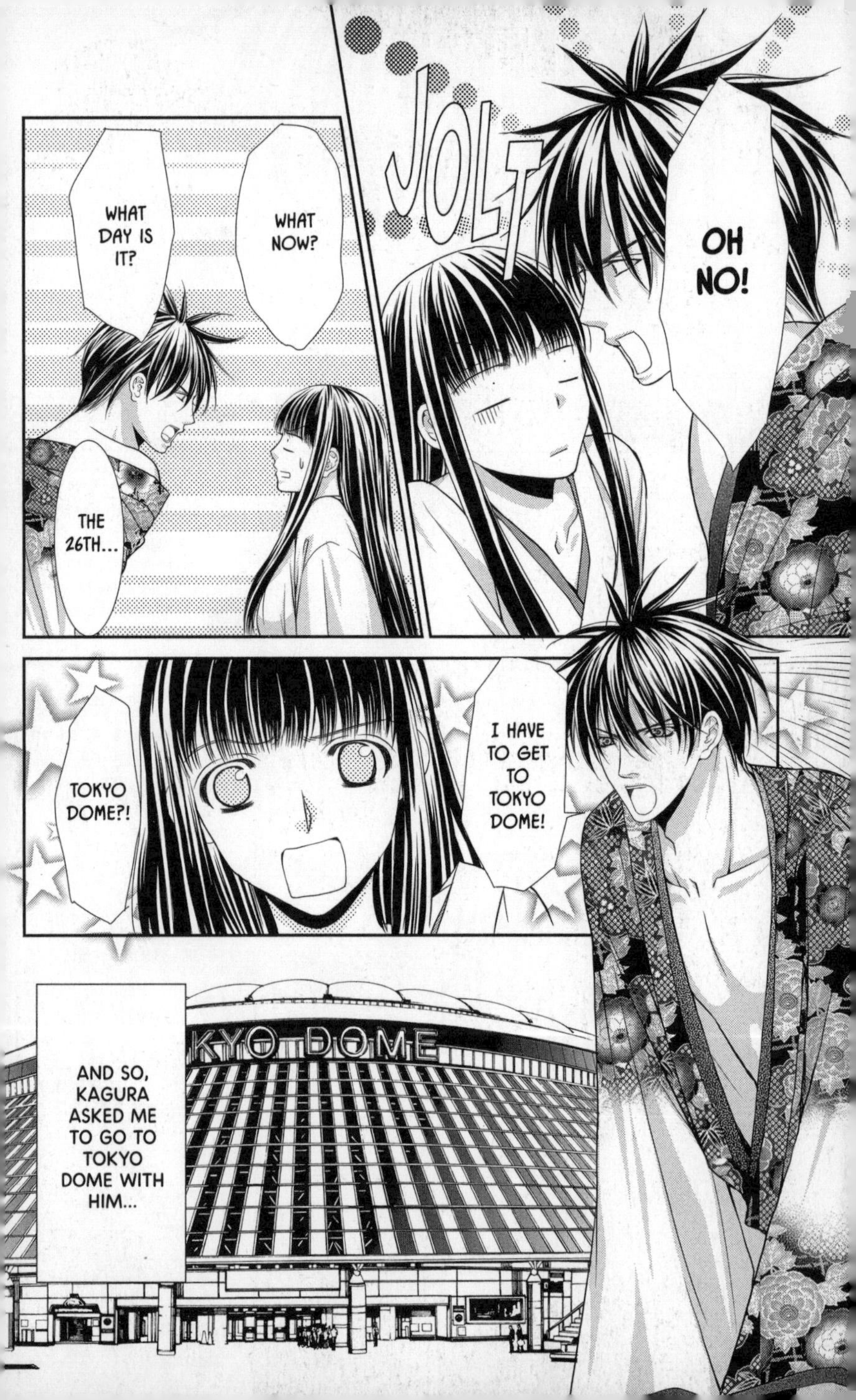
WHAT NOW?
WHAT DAY IS IT?
THE 26TH...
JOLT
OH NO!
I HAVE TO GET TO TOKYO DOME!
TOKYO DOME?!
AND SO, KAGURA ASKED ME TO GO TO TOKYO DOME WITH HIM...
KYO DOME

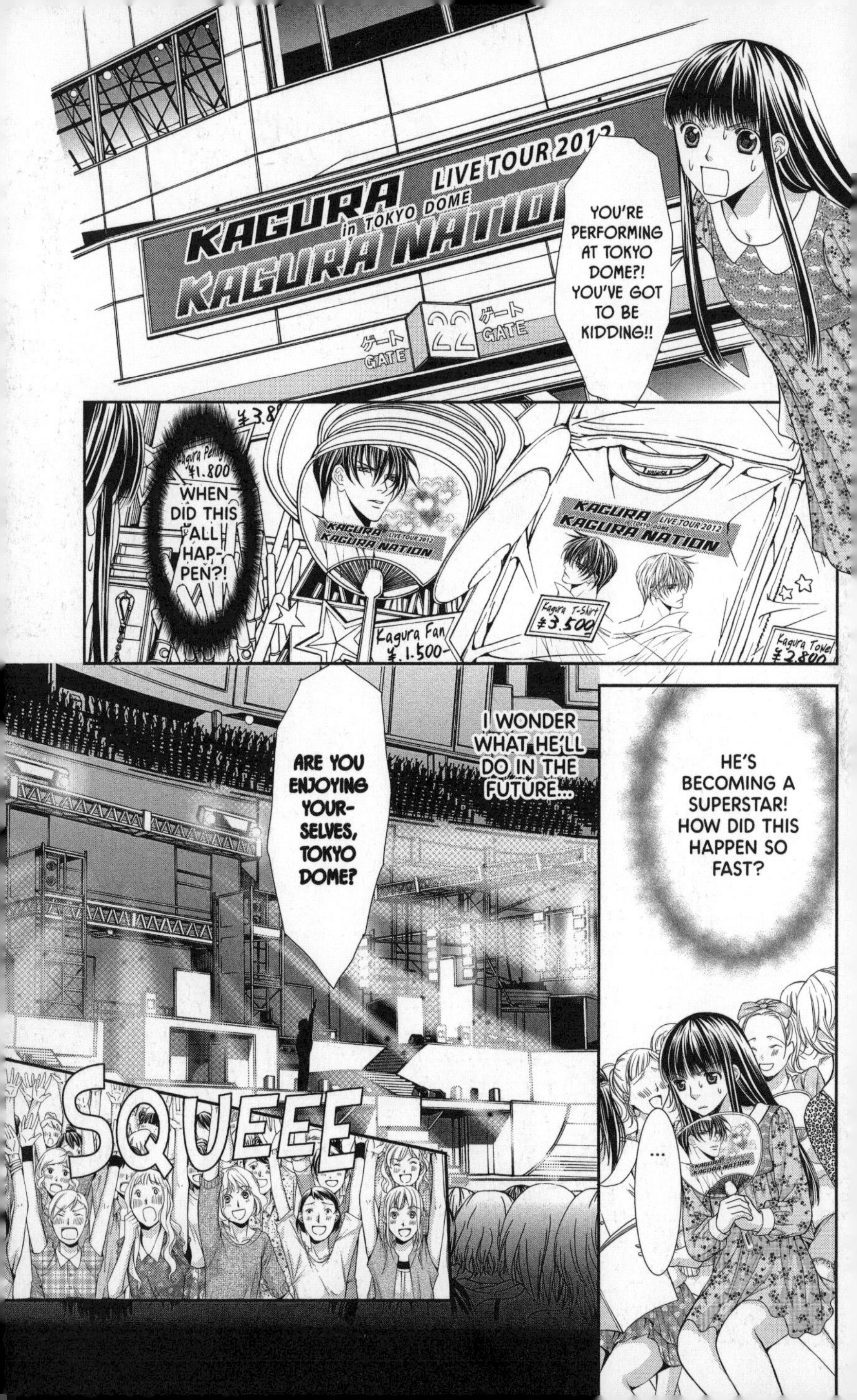
KAGURA LIVE TOUR 2012
in TOKYO DOME
KAGURA NATION
ゲート GATE 22 ゲート GATE
YOU'RE PERFORMING AT TOKYO DOME?! YOU'VE GOT TO BE KIDDING!!
KAGURA LIVE TOUR 2012 KAGURA NATION
Kagura Towel ¥2,800
Kagura T-Shirt ¥3,500
Kagura Fan ¥1,500-
¥1,800
WHEN DID THIS ALL HAP-PEN?!
HE'S BECOMING A SUPERSTAR! HOW DID THIS HAPPEN SO FAST?
...
I WONDER WHAT HE'LL DO IN THE FUTURE...
ARE YOU ENJOYING YOUR-SELVES, TOKYO DOME?
SQUEEE

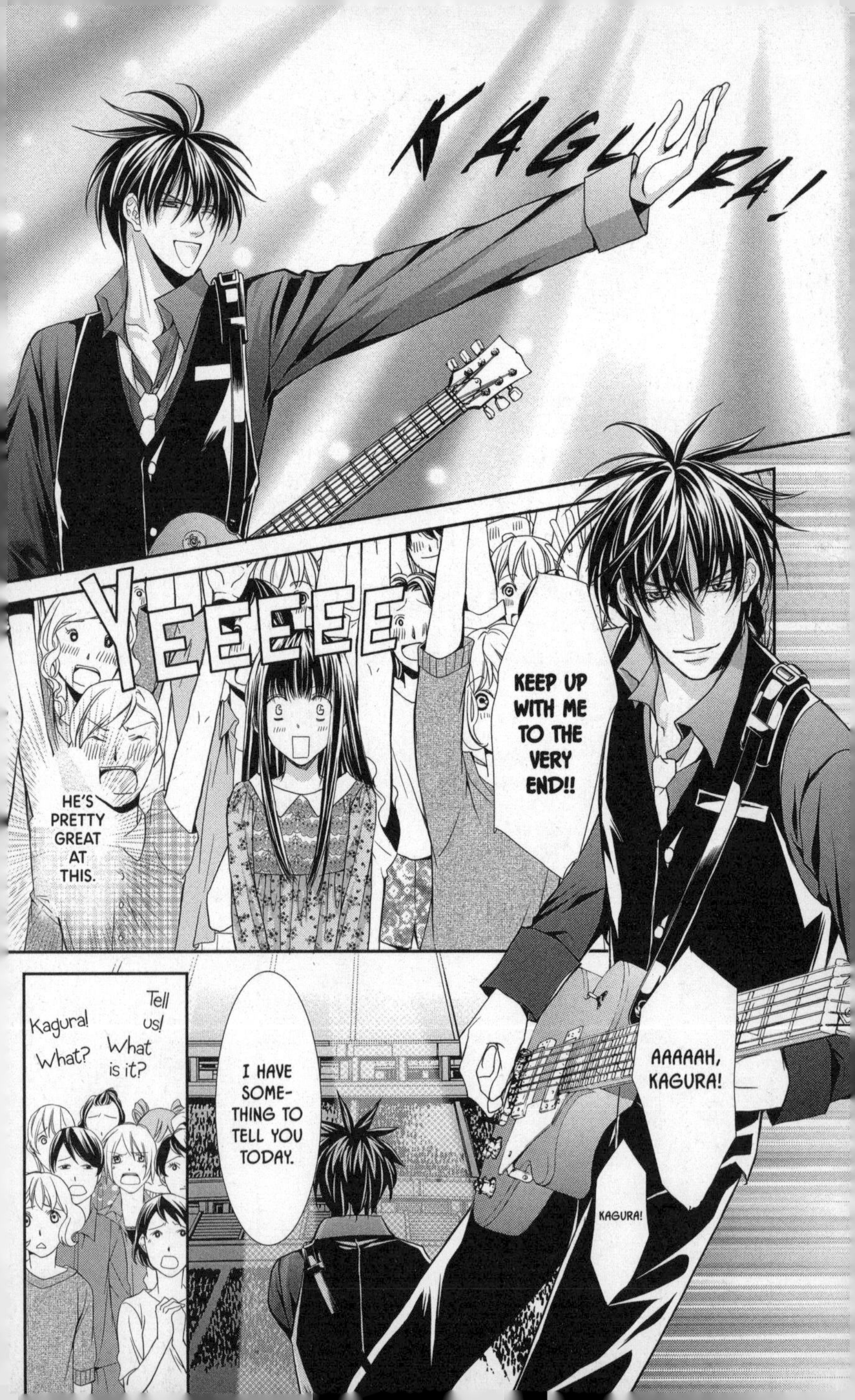
KAGURA!
KEEP UP WITH ME TO THE VERY END!!
YEEEEE
HE'S PRETTY GREAT AT THIS.
AAAAAH, KAGURA!
KAGURA!
I HAVE SOME-THING TO TELL YOU TODAY.
Tell us!
Kagura!
What is it?
What?

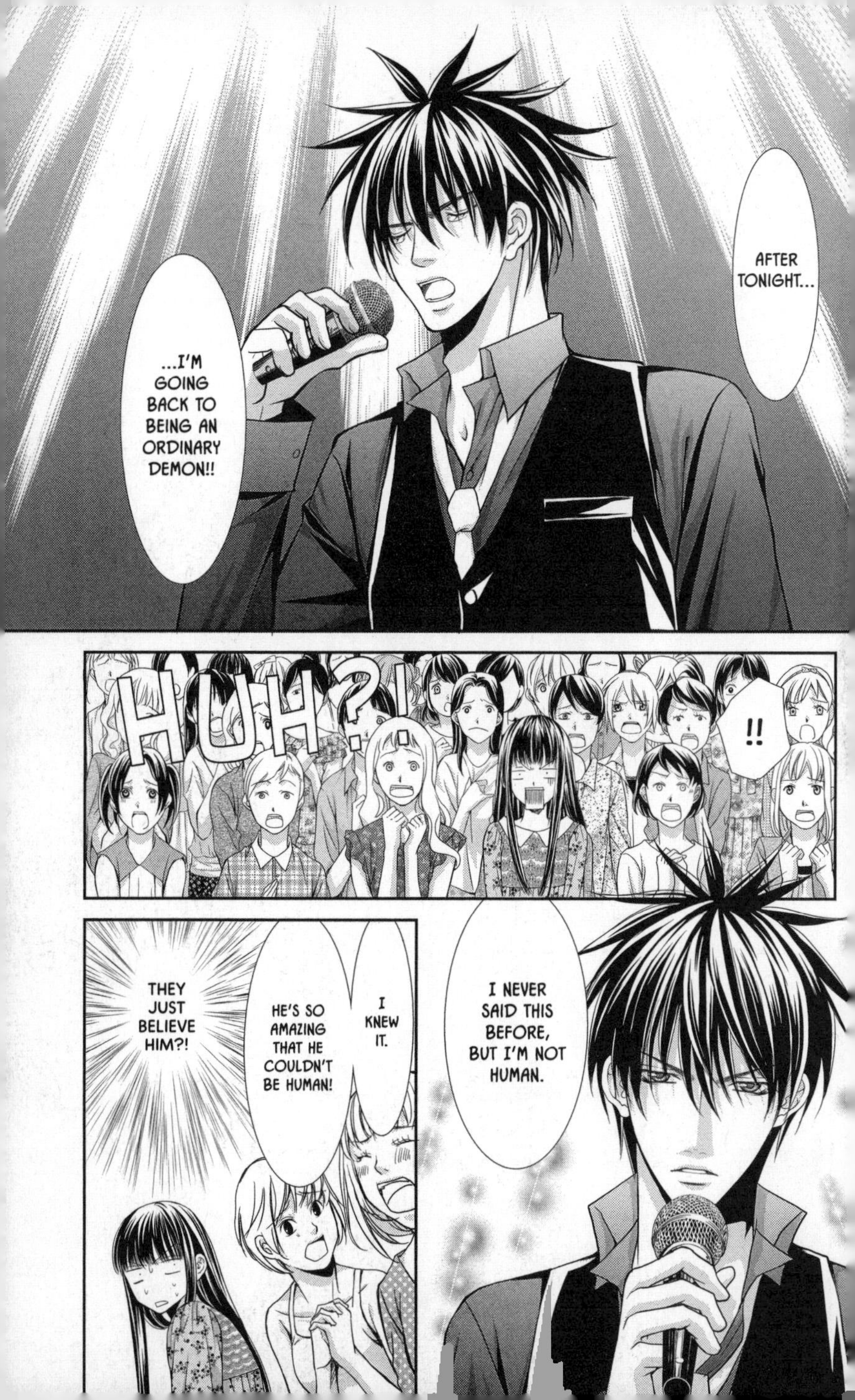
AFTER TONIGHT...
...I'M GOING BACK TO BEING AN ORDINARY DEMON!!
!!
HUH?!
I NEVER SAID THIS BEFORE, BUT I'M NOT HUMAN.
I KNEW IT.
HE'S SO AMAZING THAT HE COULDN'T BE HUMAN!
THEY JUST BELIEVE HIM?!

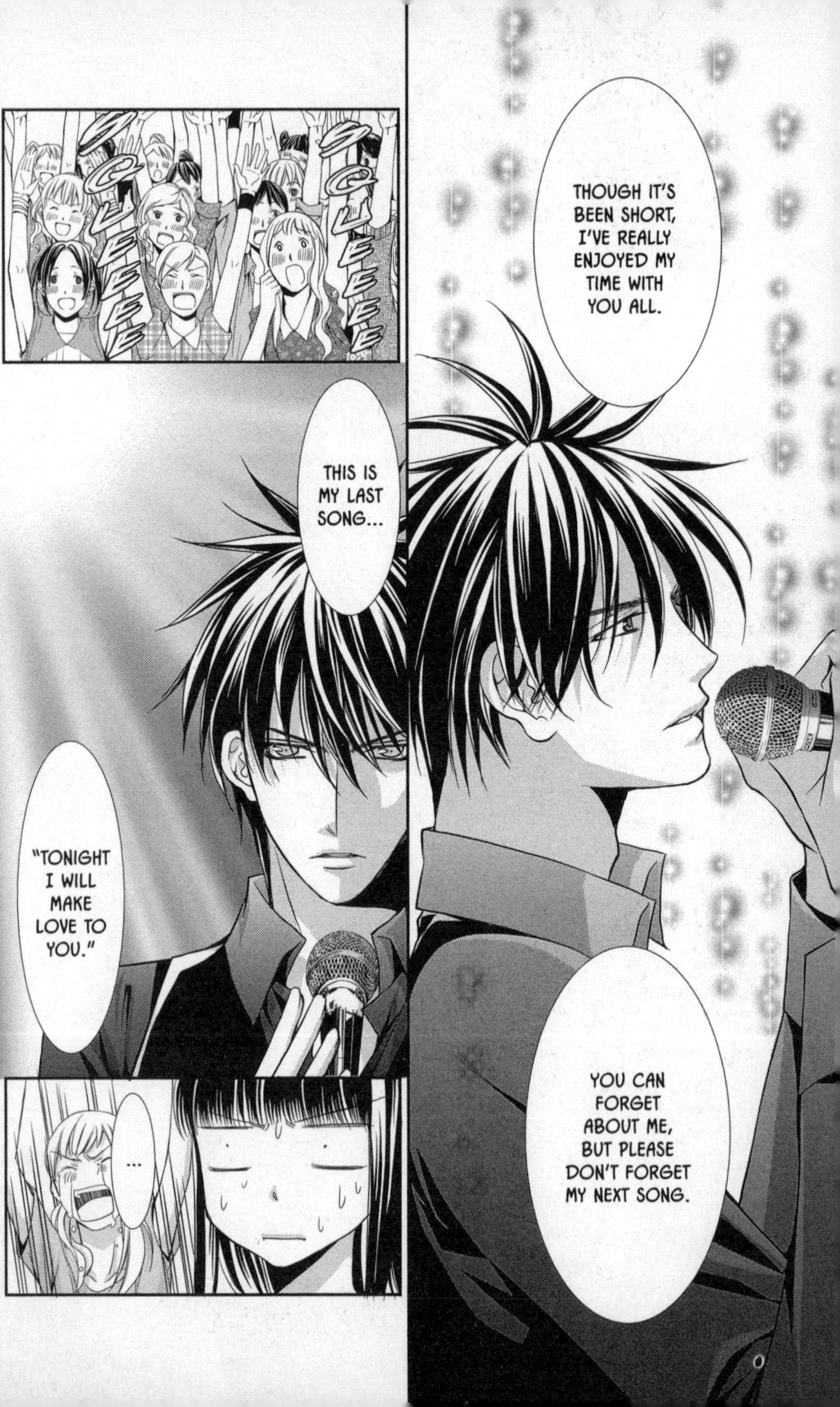
THOUGH IT'S BEEN SHORT, I'VE REALLY ENJOYED MY TIME WITH YOU ALL.
YOU CAN FORGET ABOUT ME, BUT PLEASE DON'T FORGET MY NEXT SONG.
THIS IS MY LAST SONG...
"TONIGHT I WILL MAKE LOVE TO YOU."
...

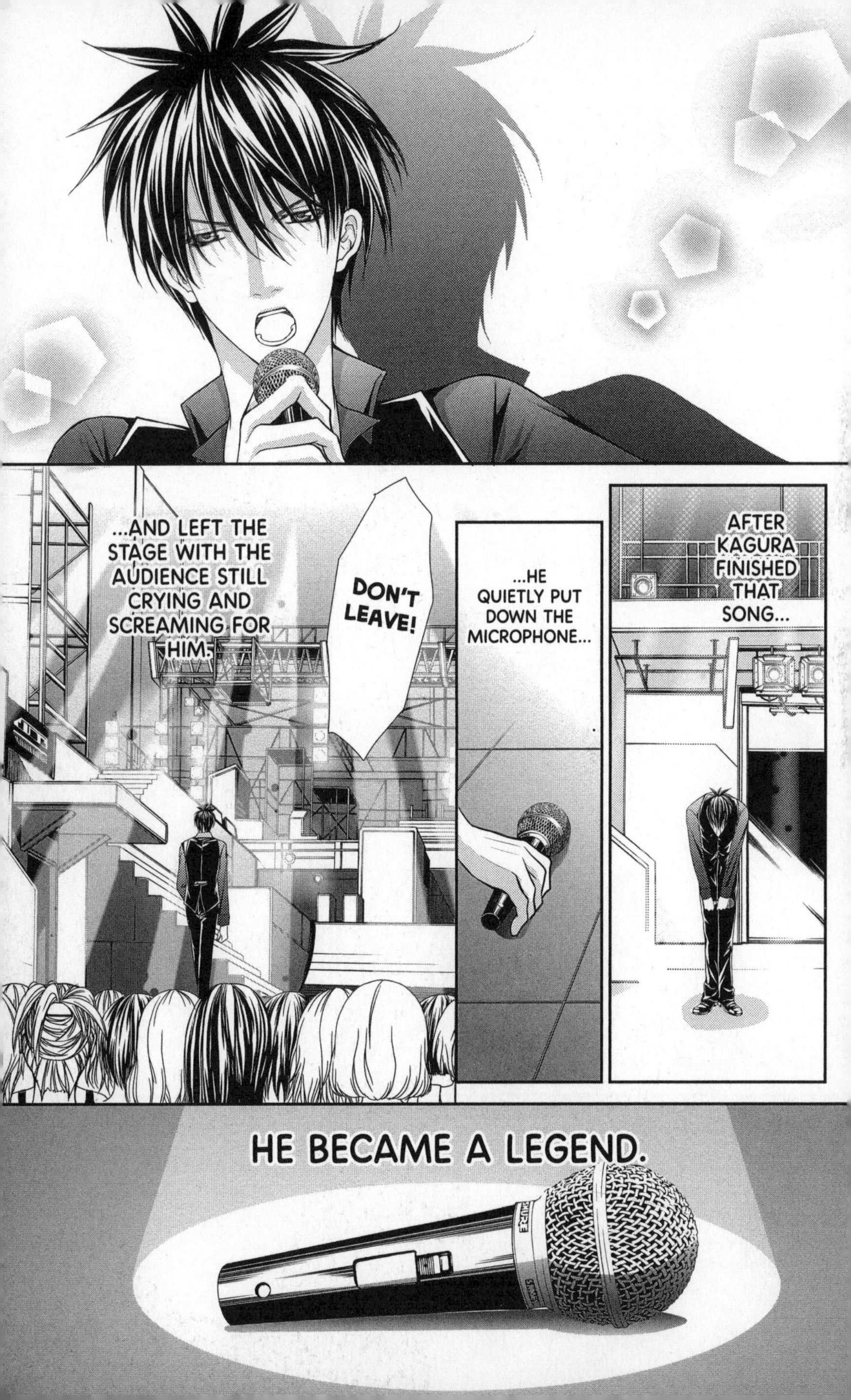
AFTER KAGURA FINISHED THAT SONG...
...HE QUIETLY PUT DOWN THE MICROPHONE...
DON'T LEAVE!
...AND LEFT THE STAGE WITH THE AUDIENCE STILL CRYING AND SCREAMING FOR HIM.
HE BECAME A LEGEND.

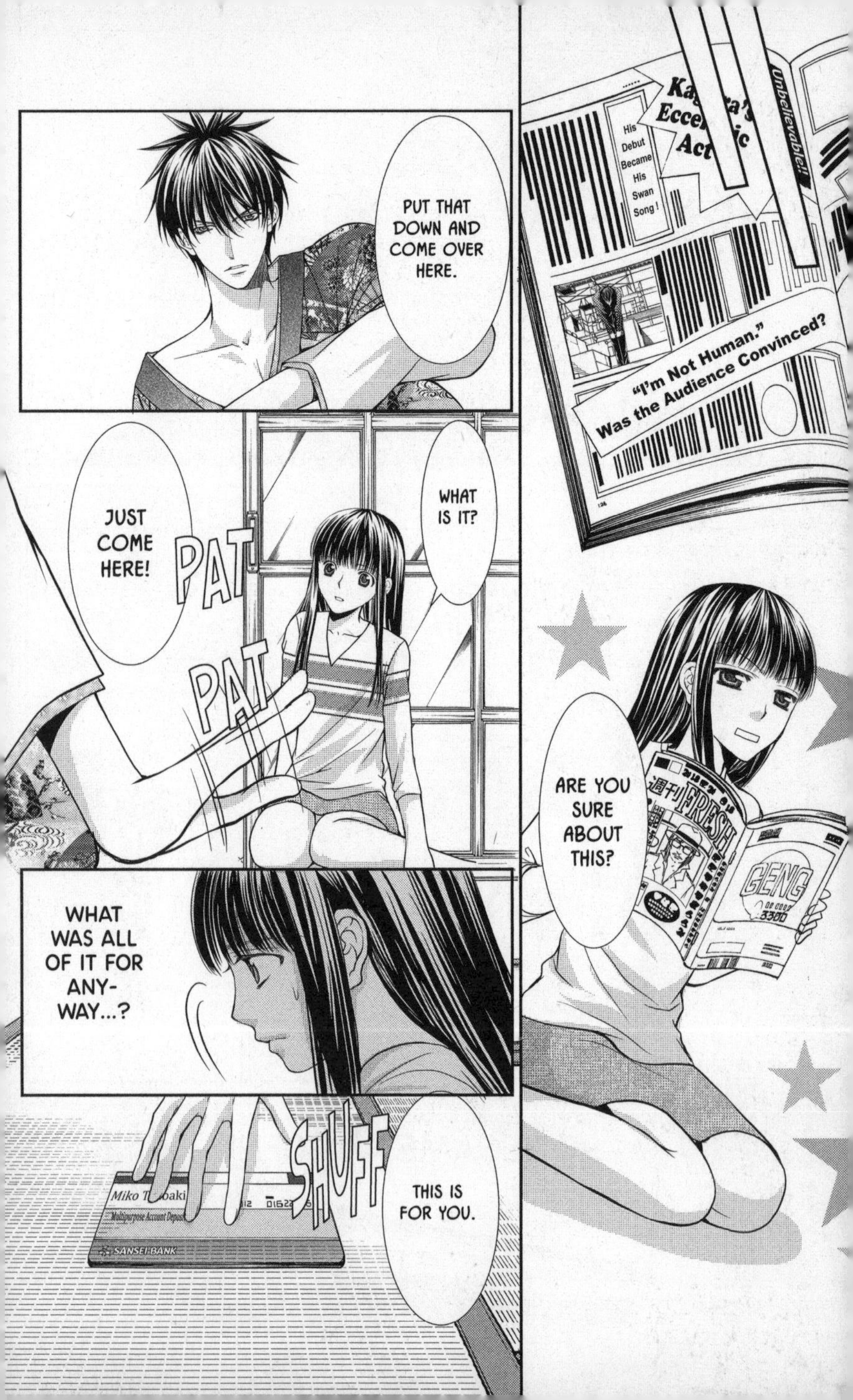
Unbelievable!!
His Debut Became His Swan Song!
"I'm Not Human." Was the Audience Convinced?
ARE YOU SURE ABOUT THIS?
FRESH
GENG
PUT THAT DOWN AND COME OVER HERE.
WHAT IS IT?
JUST COME HERE!
PAT
PAT
WHAT WAS ALL OF IT FOR ANY-WAY...?
SHUFF
THIS IS FOR YOU.
SANSEI BANK

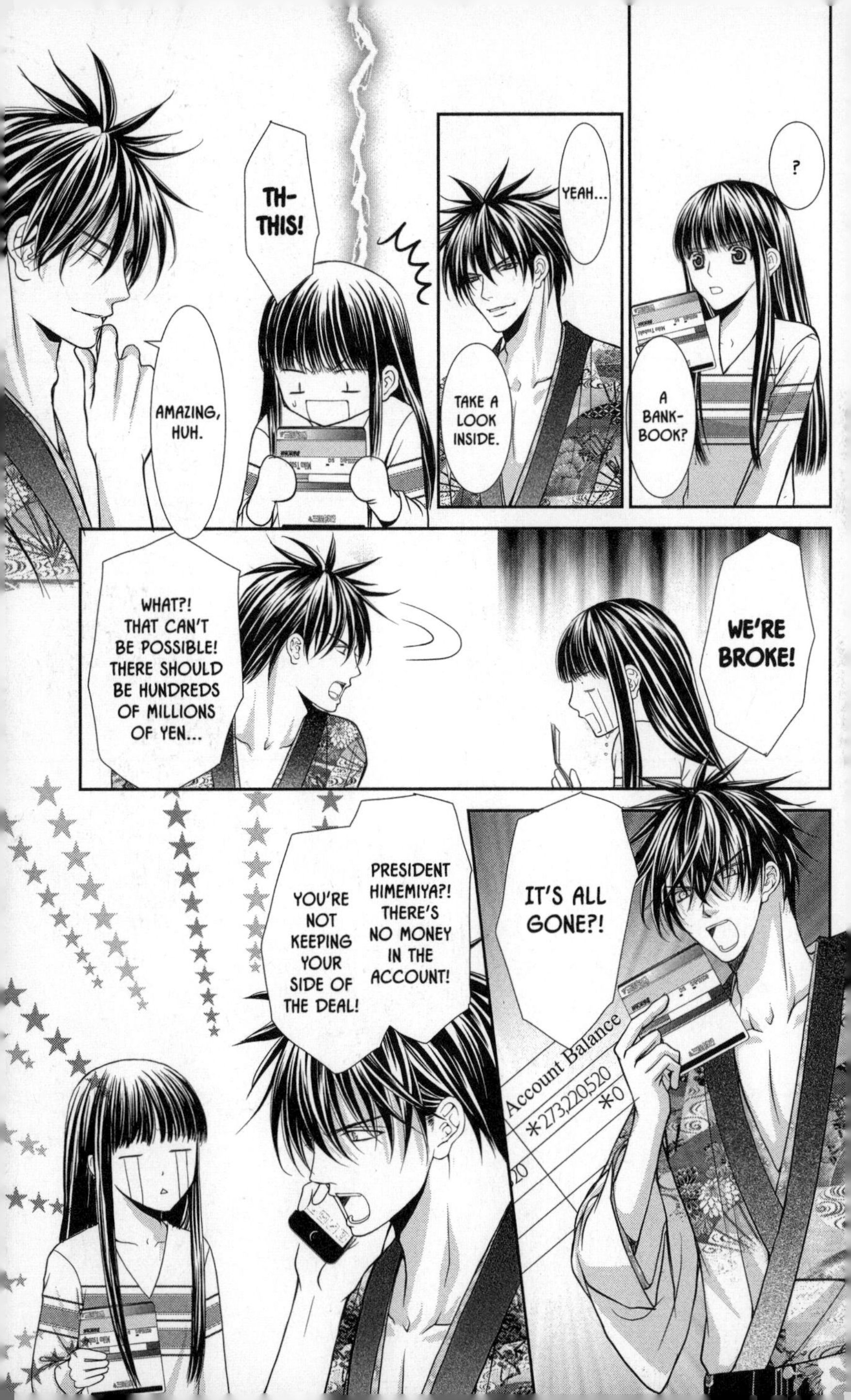
?
A BANK-BOOK?
YEAH...
TAKE A LOOK INSIDE.
TH-THIS!
AMAZING, HUH.
WE'RE BROKE!
WHAT?! THAT CAN'T BE POSSIBLE! THERE SHOULD BE HUNDREDS OF MILLIONS OF YEN...
IT'S ALL GONE?!
Account Balance
*273,220,520
*0
PRESIDENT HIMEMIYA?! THERE'S NO MONEY IN THE ACCOUNT!
YOU'RE NOT KEEPING YOUR SIDE OF THE DEAL!

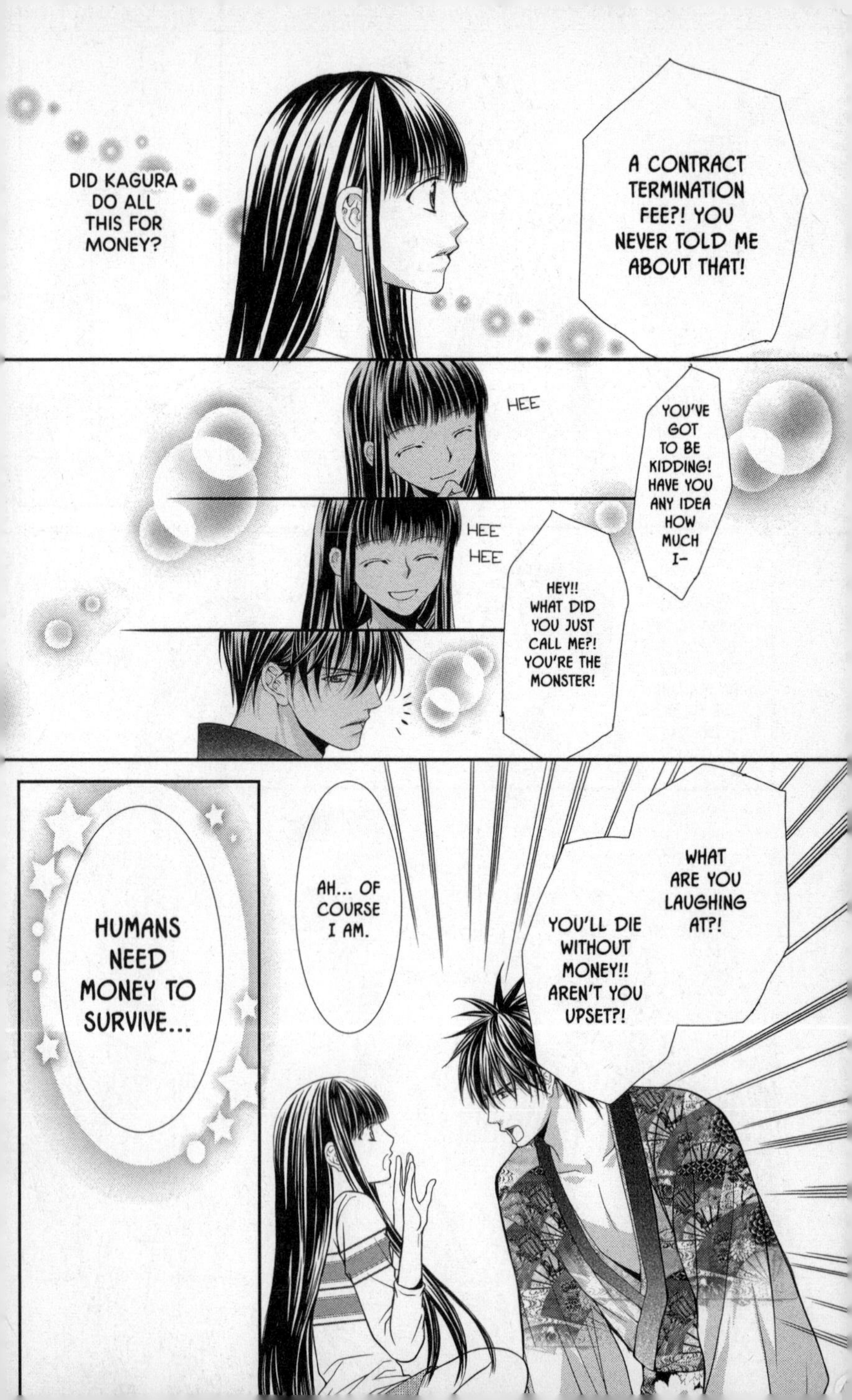
A CONTRACT TERMINATION FEE?! YOU NEVER TOLD ME ABOUT THAT!
DID KAGURA DO ALL THIS FOR MONEY?
YOU'VE GOT TO BE KIDDING! HAVE YOU ANY IDEA HOW MUCH I–
HEE
HEE HEE
HEY!! WHAT DID YOU JUST CALL ME?! YOU'RE THE MONSTER!
WHAT ARE YOU LAUGHING AT?!
YOU'LL DIE WITHOUT MONEY!! AREN'T YOU UPSET?!
AH... OF COURSE I AM.
HUMANS NEED MONEY TO SURVIVE...

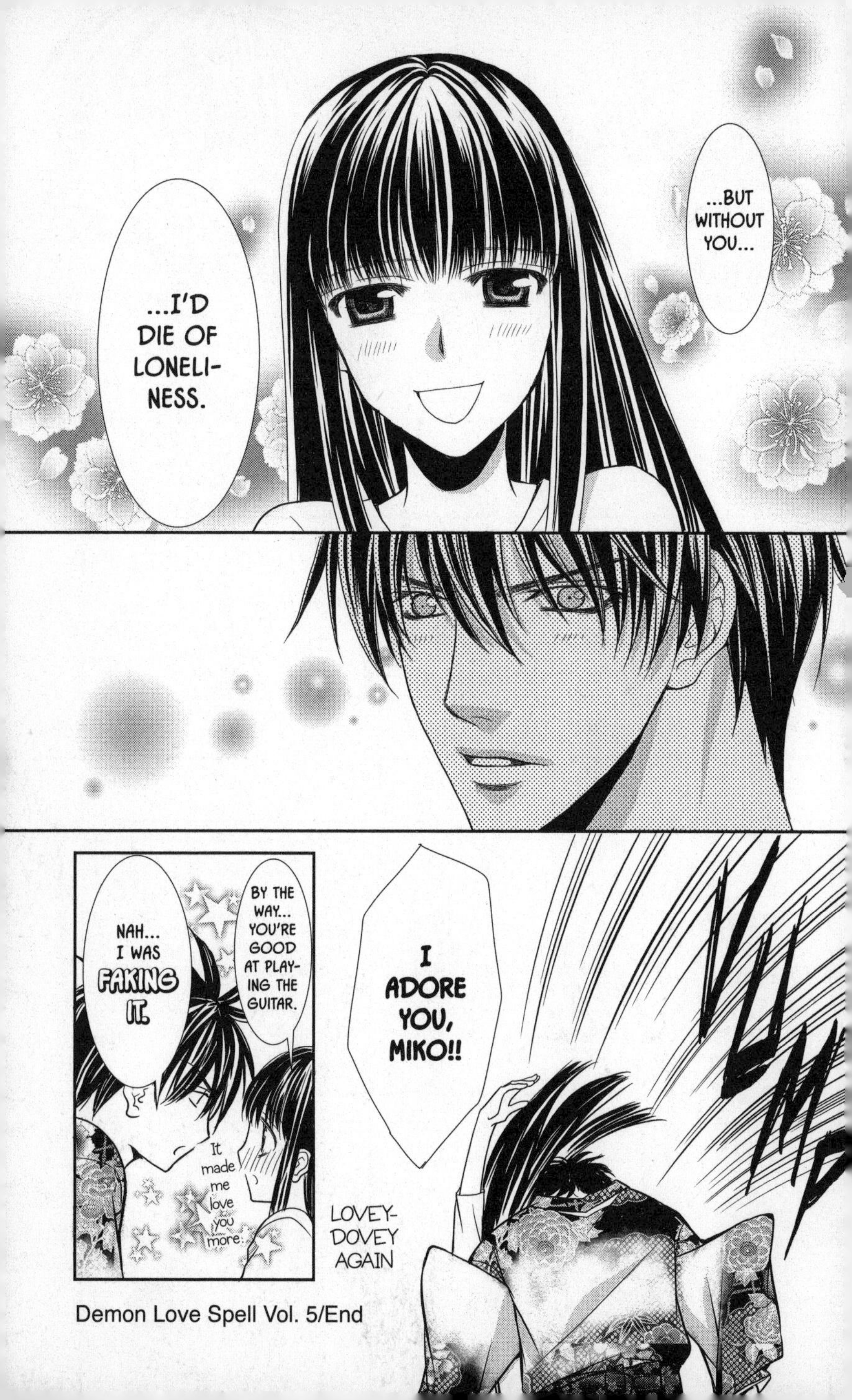
...BUT WITHOUT YOU...
...I'D DIE OF LONELI-NESS.
I ADORE YOU, MIKO!!
LOVEY-DOVEY AGAIN
BY THE WAY... YOU'RE GOOD AT PLAY-ING THE GUITAR.
NAH... I WAS FAKING IT.
It made me love you more.

Demon Love Spell Vol. 5/End

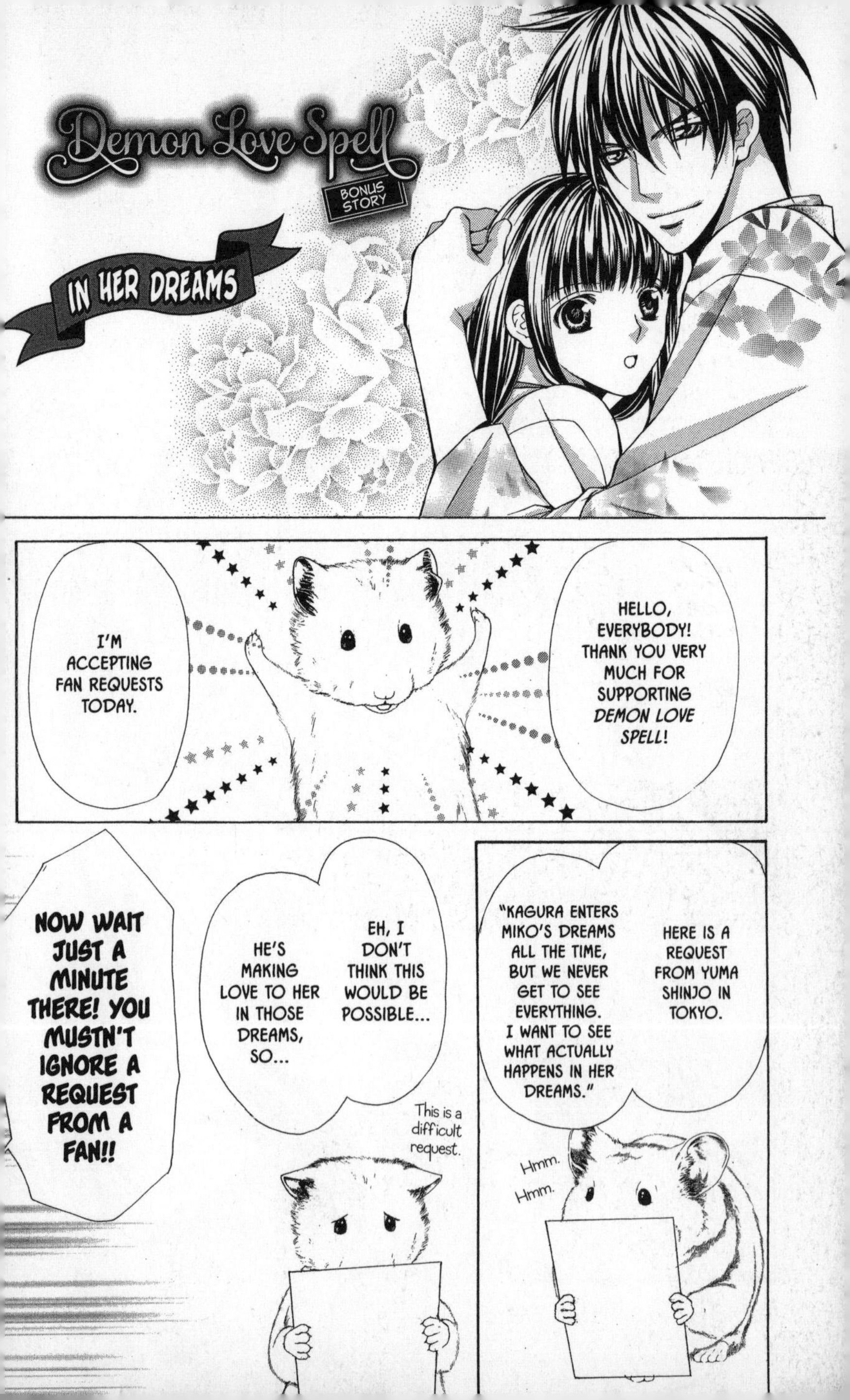
Demon Love Spell
BONUS STORY
IN HER DREAMS
HELLO, EVERYBODY! THANK YOU VERY MUCH FOR SUPPORTING *DEMON LOVE SPELL*!
I'M ACCEPTING FAN REQUESTS TODAY.
HERE IS A REQUEST FROM YUMA SHINJO IN TOKYO.
"KAGURA ENTERS MIKO'S DREAMS ALL THE TIME, BUT WE NEVER GET TO SEE EVERYTHING. I WANT TO SEE WHAT ACTUALLY HAPPENS IN HER DREAMS."
Hmm.
Hmm.
EH, I DON'T THINK THIS WOULD BE POSSIBLE...
HE'S MAKING LOVE TO HER IN THOSE DREAMS, SO...
This is a difficult request.
NOW WAIT JUST A MINUTE THERE! YOU MUSTN'T IGNORE A REQUEST FROM A FAN!!

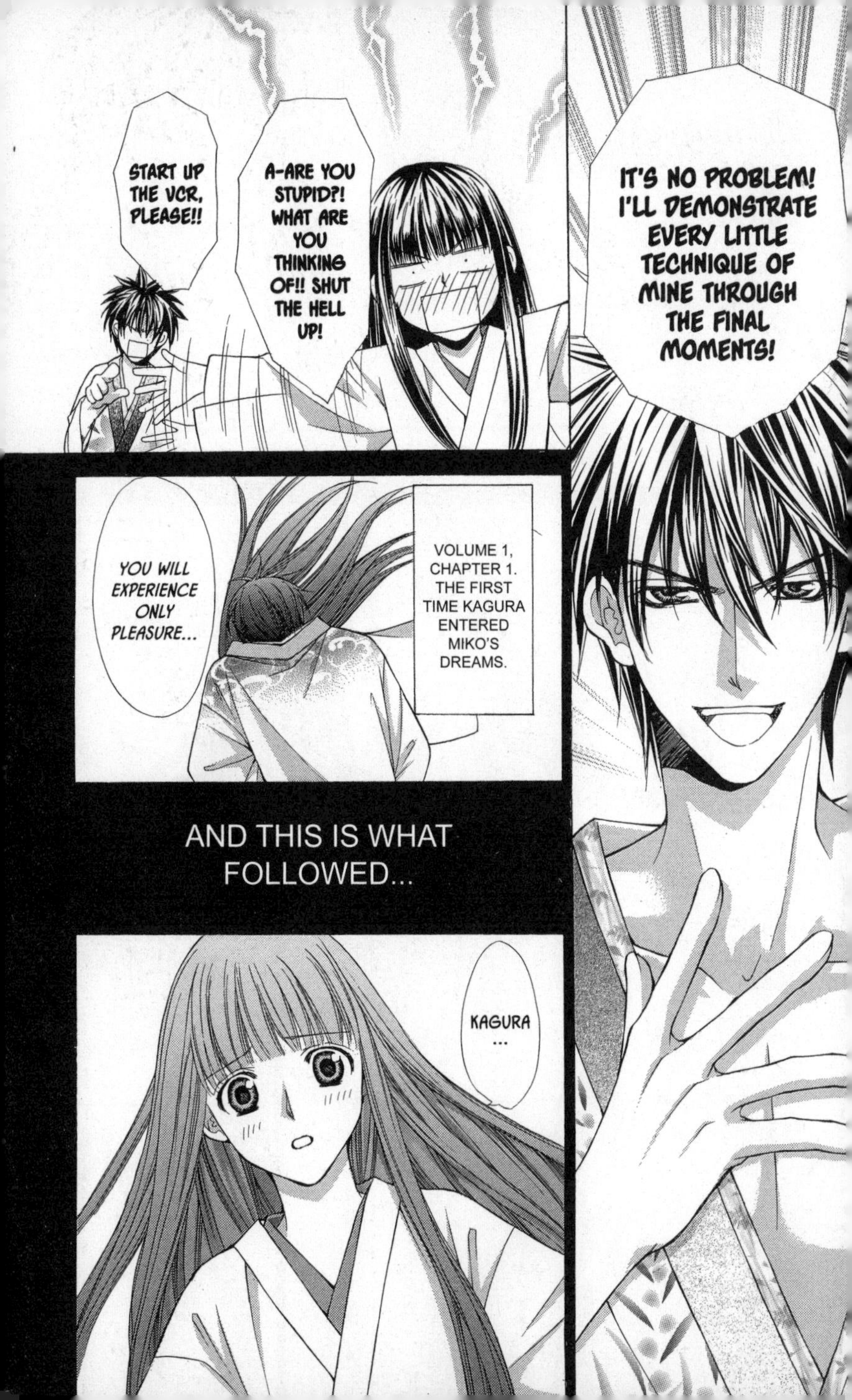
IT'S NO PROBLEM! I'LL DEMONSTRATE EVERY LITTLE TECHNIQUE OF MINE THROUGH THE FINAL MOMENTS!
A-ARE YOU STUPID?! WHAT ARE YOU THINKING OF!! SHUT THE HELL UP!
START UP THE VCR, PLEASE!!
VOLUME 1, CHAPTER 1. THE FIRST TIME KAGURA ENTERED MIKO'S DREAMS.
YOU WILL EXPERIENCE ONLY PLEASURE...
AND THIS IS WHAT FOLLOWED...
KAGURA ...

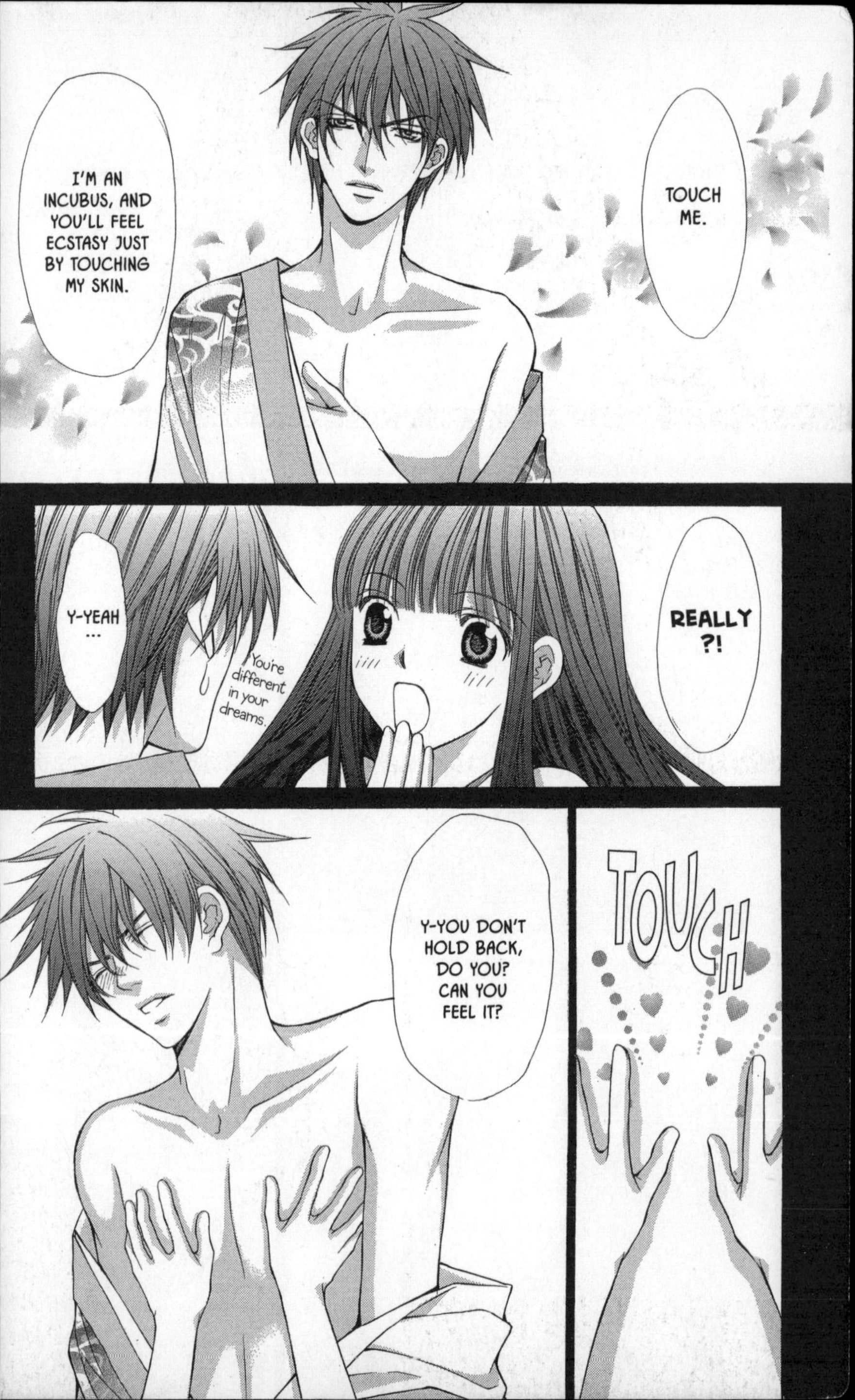
TOUCH ME.
I'M AN INCUBUS, AND YOU'LL FEEL ECSTASY JUST BY TOUCHING MY SKIN.
REALLY ?!
You're different in your dreams.
Y-YEAH ...
TOUCH
Y-YOU DON'T HOLD BACK, DO YOU? CAN YOU FEEL IT?

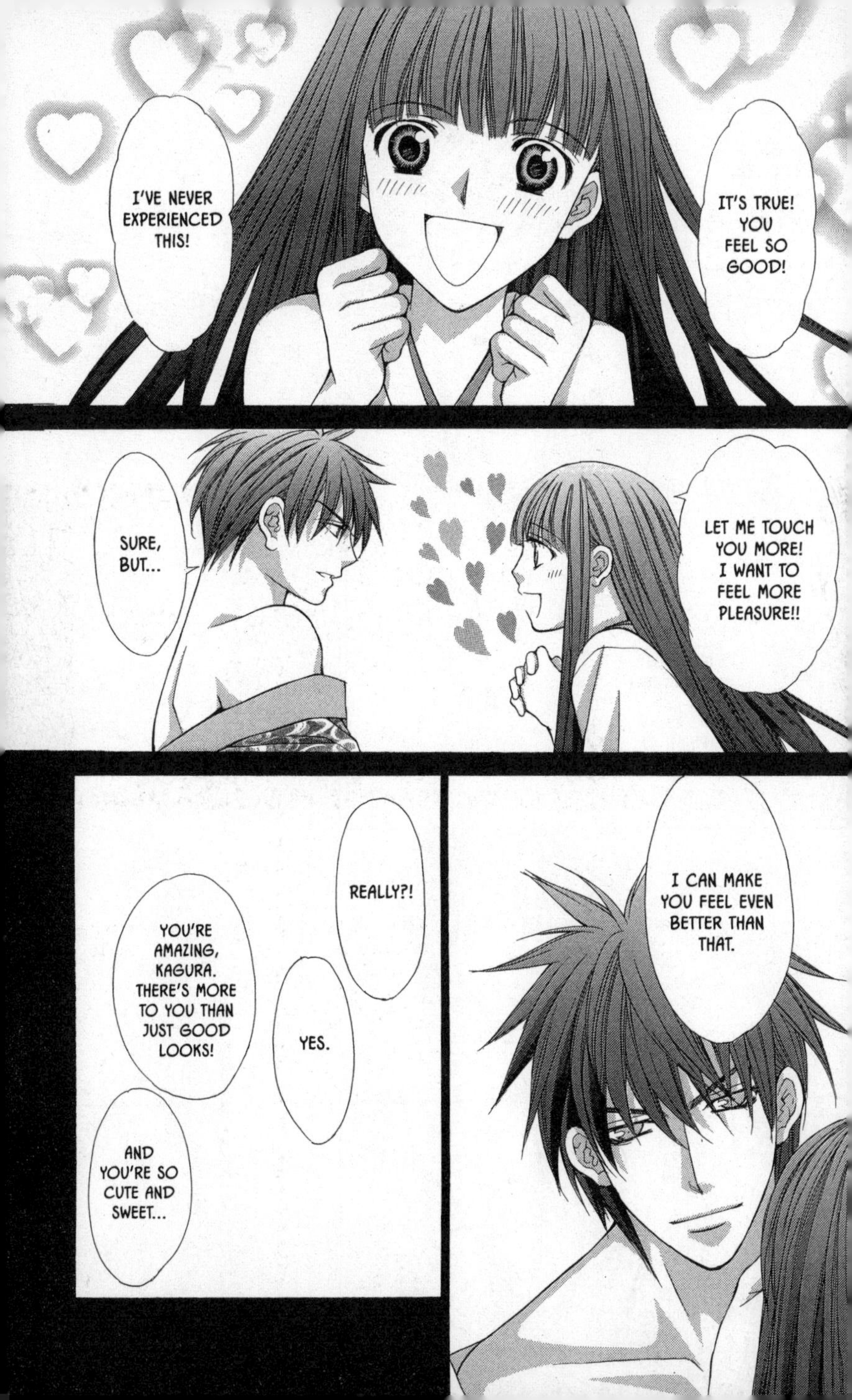
IT'S TRUE! YOU FEEL SO GOOD!
I'VE NEVER EXPERIENCED THIS!
LET ME TOUCH YOU MORE! I WANT TO FEEL MORE PLEASURE!!
SURE, BUT...
I CAN MAKE YOU FEEL EVEN BETTER THAN THAT.
REALLY?!
YES.
YOU'RE AMAZING, KAGURA. THERE'S MORE TO YOU THAN JUST GOOD LOOKS!
AND YOU'RE SO CUTE AND SWEET...

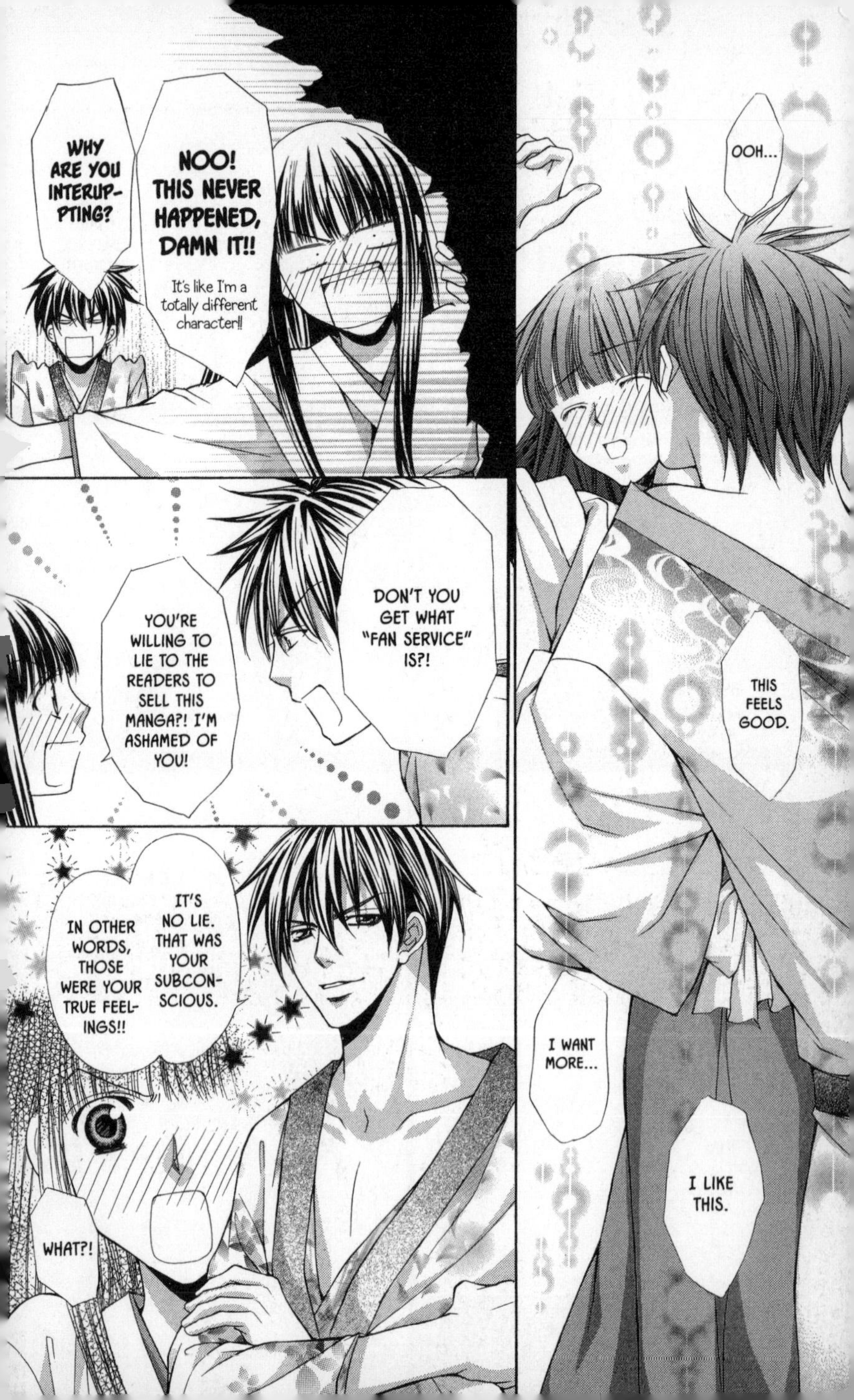
OOH...
THIS FEELS GOOD.
I WANT MORE...
I LIKE THIS.
NOO! THIS NEVER HAPPENED, DAMN IT!!
It's like I'm a totally different character!!
WHY ARE YOU INTERUP-PTING?
DON'T YOU GET WHAT "FAN SERVICE" IS?!
YOU'RE WILLING TO LIE TO THE READERS TO SELL THIS MANGA?! I'M ASHAMED OF YOU!
IT'S NO LIE. THAT WAS YOUR SUBCON-SCIOUS.
IN OTHER WORDS, THOSE WERE YOUR TRUE FEEL-INGS!!
WHAT?!

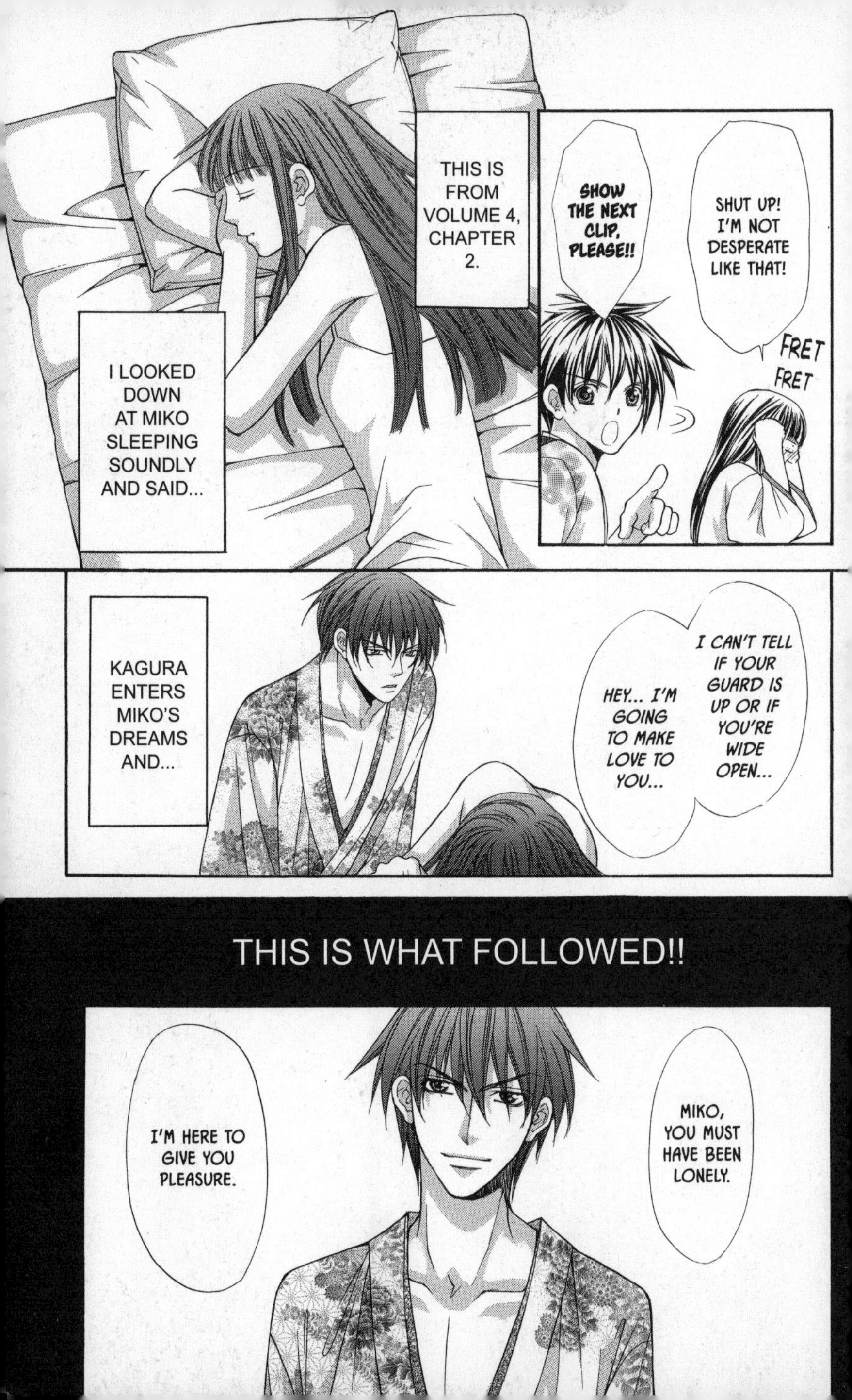
SHUT UP! I'M NOT DESPERATE LIKE THAT!
SHOW THE NEXT CLIP, PLEASE!!
FRET FRET
THIS IS FROM VOLUME 4, CHAPTER 2.
I LOOKED DOWN AT MIKO SLEEPING SOUNDLY AND SAID...
I CAN'T TELL IF YOUR GUARD IS UP OR IF YOU'RE WIDE OPEN...
HEY... I'M GOING TO MAKE LOVE TO YOU...
KAGURA ENTERS MIKO'S DREAMS AND...
THIS IS WHAT FOLLOWED!!
MIKO, YOU MUST HAVE BEEN LONELY.
I'M HERE TO GIVE YOU PLEASURE.

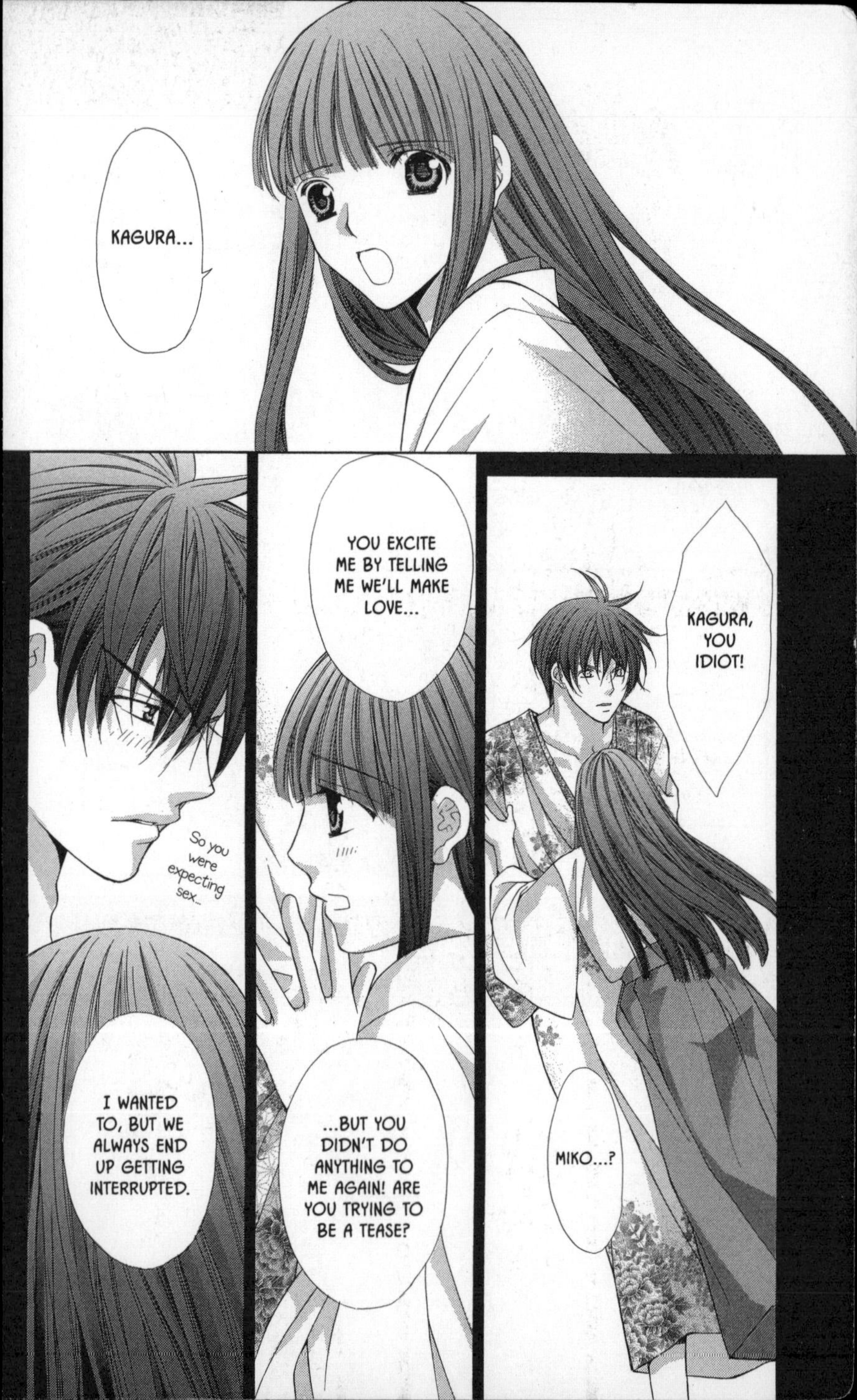
KAGURA...
KAGURA, YOU IDIOT!
MIKO...?
YOU EXCITE ME BY TELLING ME WE'LL MAKE LOVE...
...BUT YOU DIDN'T DO ANYTHING TO ME AGAIN! ARE YOU TRYING TO BE A TEASE?
So you were expecting sex...
I WANTED TO, BUT WE ALWAYS END UP GETTING INTERRUPTED.

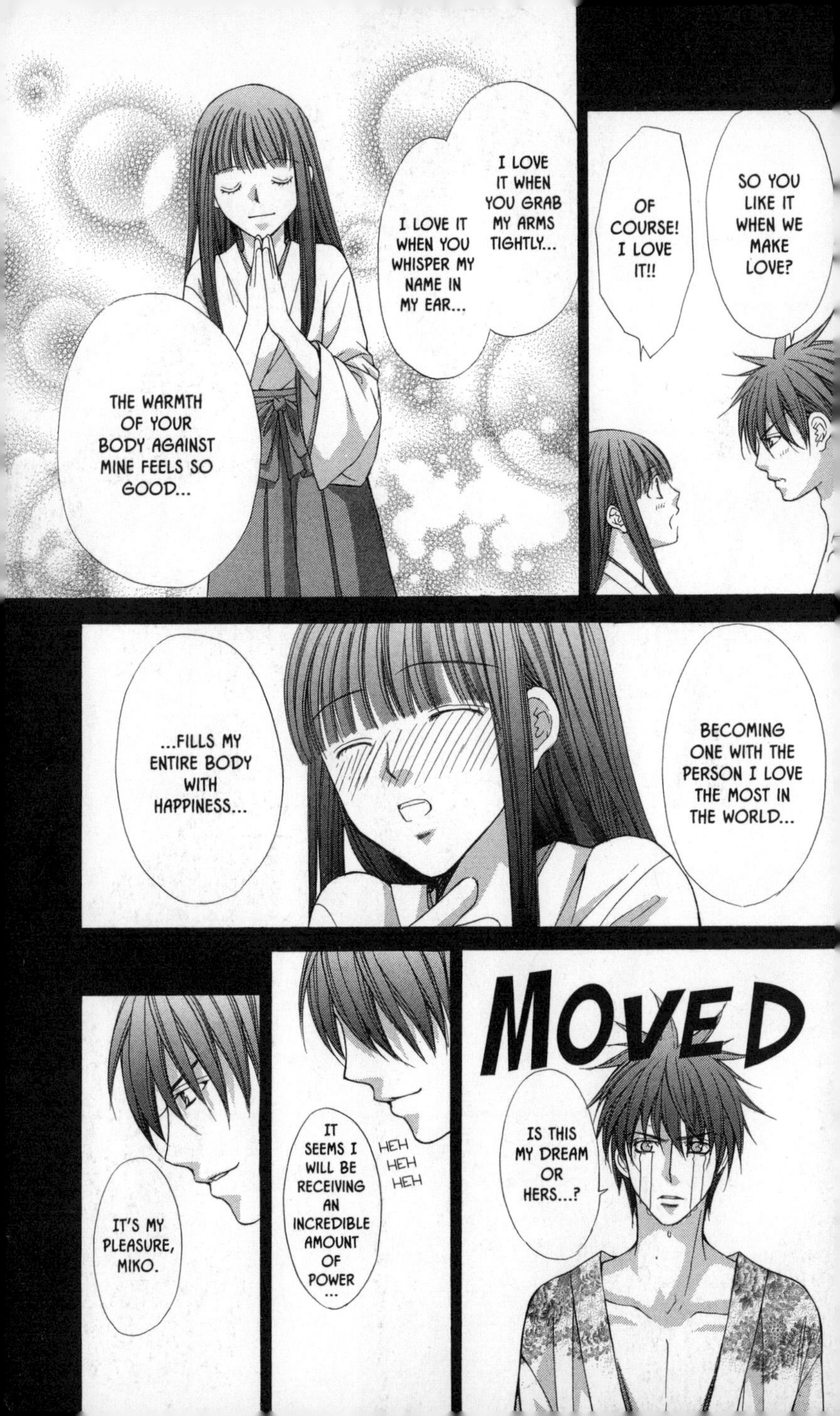
SO YOU LIKE IT WHEN WE MAKE LOVE?
OF COURSE! I LOVE IT!!
I LOVE IT WHEN YOU GRAB MY ARMS TIGHTLY...
I LOVE IT WHEN YOU WHISPER MY NAME IN MY EAR...
THE WARMTH OF YOUR BODY AGAINST MINE FEELS SO GOOD...
BECOMING ONE WITH THE PERSON I LOVE THE MOST IN THE WORLD...
...FILLS MY ENTIRE BODY WITH HAPPINESS...
MOVED
IS THIS MY DREAM OR HERS...?
IT SEEMS I WILL BE RECEIVING AN INCREDIBLE AMOUNT OF POWER...
HEH HEH HEH
IT'S MY PLEASURE, MIKO.

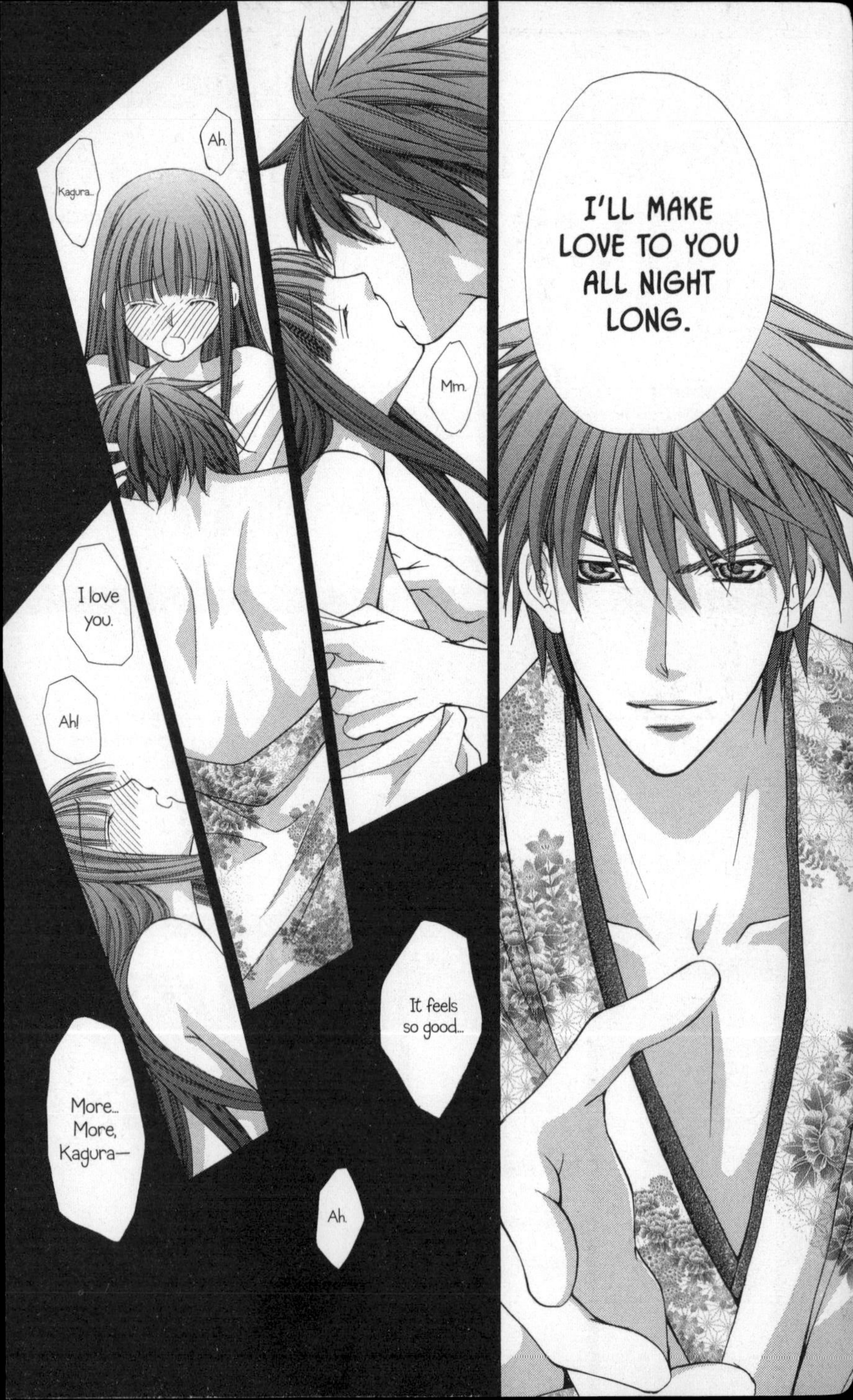
I'LL MAKE LOVE TO YOU ALL NIGHT LONG.
Ah.
Kagura...
Mm.
I love you.
Ah!
It feels so good...
More... More, Kagura—
Ah.

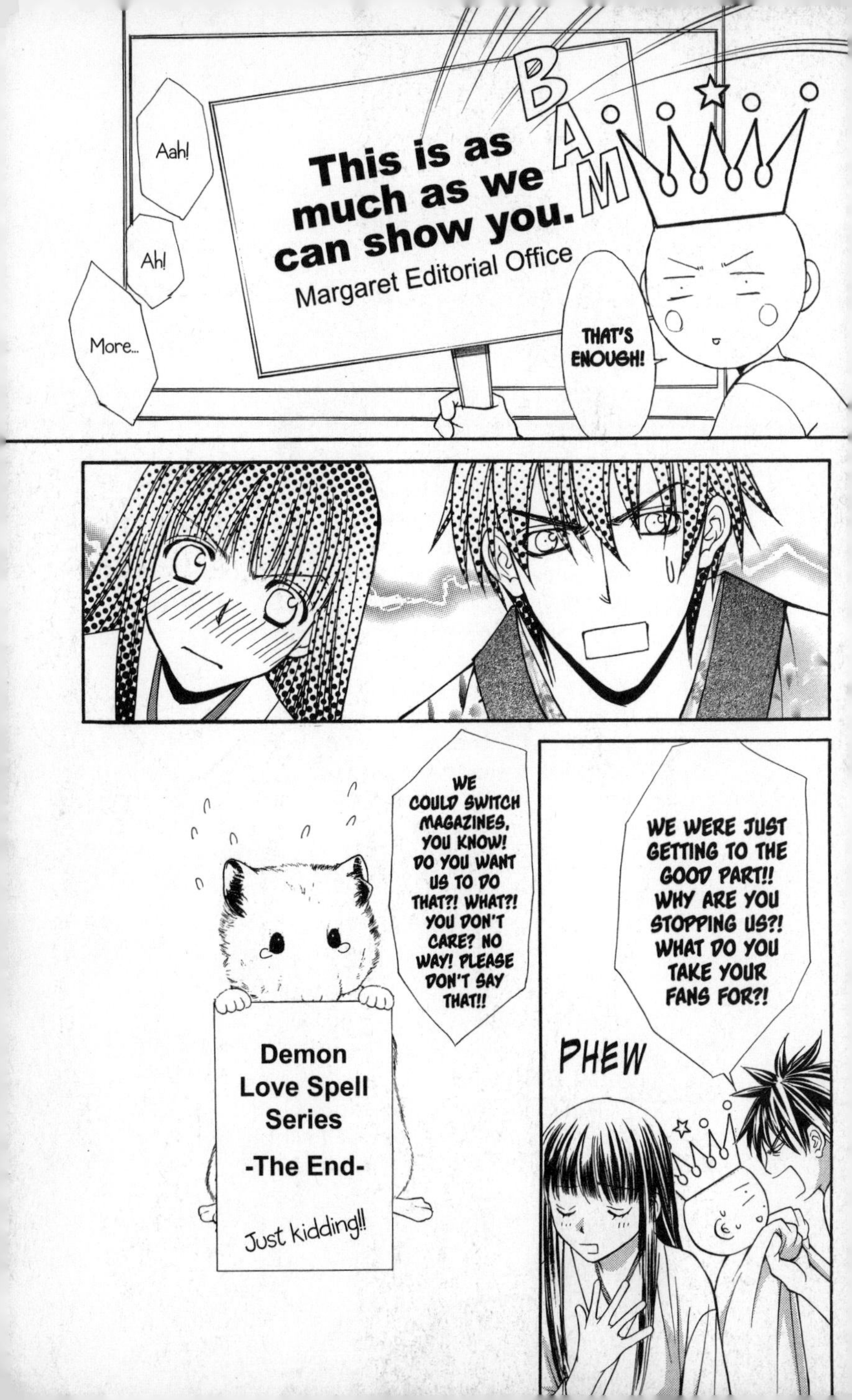
BAM
THAT'S ENOUGH!
This is as much as we can show you.
Margaret Editorial Office
Aah!
Ah!
More...
WE WERE JUST GETTING TO THE GOOD PART!! WHY ARE YOU STOPPING US?! WHAT DO YOU TAKE YOUR FANS FOR?!
PHEW
WE COULD SWITCH MAGAZINES, YOU KNOW! DO YOU WANT US TO DO THAT?! WHAT?! YOU DON'T CARE? NO WAY! PLEASE DON'T SAY THAT!!
Demon Love Spell Series
-The End-
Just kidding!!

I never thought this series would last
five volumes. Every time I finish a story
arc I think, "Maybe this will be the end?"
But I have been given the opportunity
to continue the series. And currently,
much to my surprise, I am in the midst
of writing volume 6. This turned out to
be a series I've been able to have a long
relationship with, and that is thanks to
the readers who've supported this series.
Thank you very much!

—Mayu Shinjo

MAYU SHINJO was born on January 26.
She is a prolific writer of shojo manga,
including the series *Sensual Phrase*
and *Ai Ore!* Her hobbies are cars,
shopping and taking baths. Shinjo
likes The Prodigy, Nirvana, U2 and
Masaharu Fukuyama.

Demon Love Spell

Vol. 5
Shojo Beat Edition

STORY AND ART BY *Mayu Shinjo*

Translation
Tetsuichiro Miyaki

Touch-up Art & Lettering
Inori Fukuda Trant

Design
Fawn Lau

Editor
Nancy Thistlethwaite

AYAKASHI KOI EMAKI © 2008 by Mayu Shinjo
All rights reserved.
First published in Japan in 2008 by SHUEISHA Inc., Tokyo.
English translation rights arranged by SHUEISHA Inc.

The stories, characters and incidents mentioned in
this publication are entirely fictional.

Printed in the U.S.A.

Published by VIZ Media, LLC
P.O. Box 77010
San Francisco, CA 94107

10 9 8 7 6 5 4 3 2 1
First printing, December 2013

www.viz.com

PARENTAL ADVISORY
DEMON LOVE SPELL is rated T+ for Older
Teen and is recommended for ages 16 and up.
This volume contains sexual themes.
ratings.viz.com

www.shojobeat.com

You may be reading the wrong way!

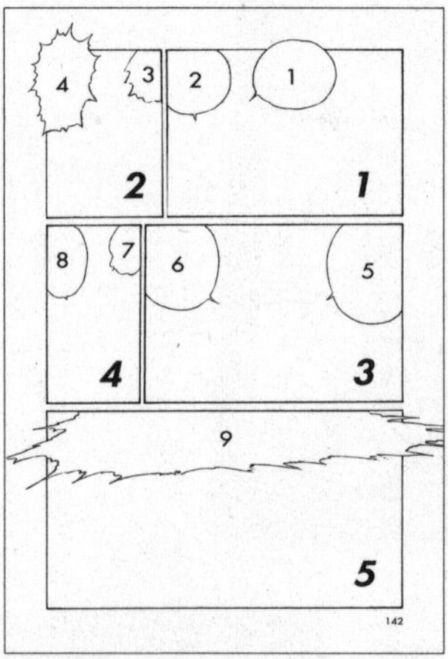

IT'S TRUE: In keeping with the original Japanese comic format, this book reads from right to left—so action, sound effects, and word balloons are completely reversed. This preserves the orientation of the original artwork—plus, it's fun! Check out the diagram shown here to get the hang of things, and then turn to the other side of the book to get started!

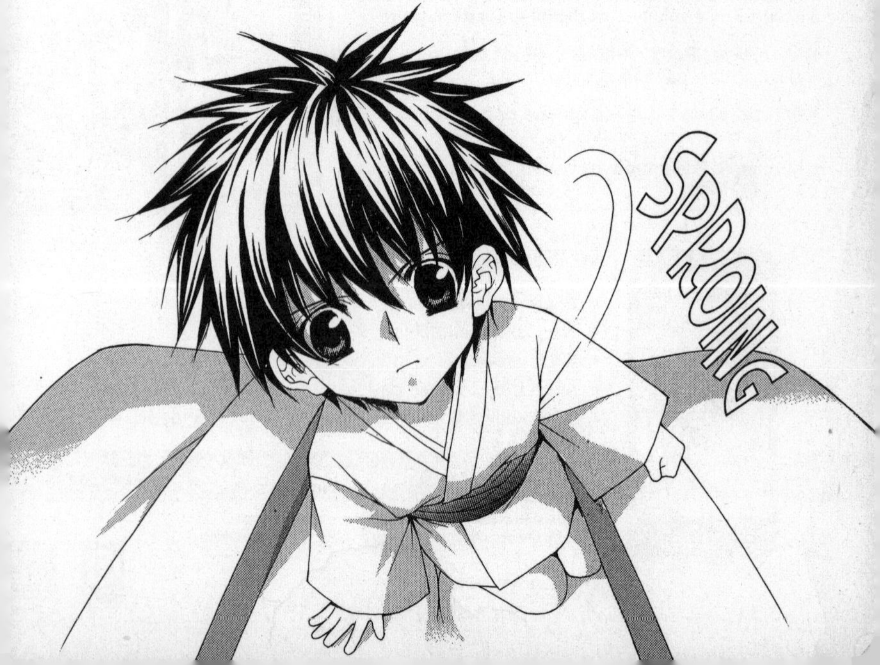
SPROING